word study lessons

Phonics, Spelling, and Vocabulary

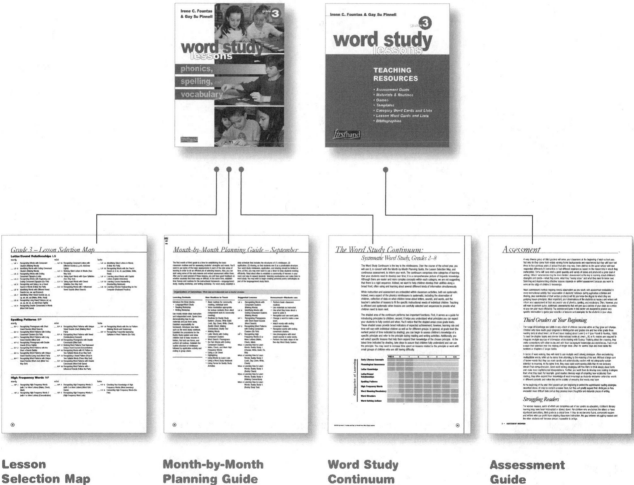

Lesson Selection Map
(page 32)

Month-by-Month Planning Guide
(page 36)

Word Study Continuum
(page 45)

Assessment Guide
(first tab in the *Teaching Resources* binder)

Your Essential Teaching Tools

FirstHand
An imprint of Heinemann
A division of Reed Elsevier Inc.
361 Hanover Street
Portsmouth, NH 03801–3912
www.firsthand.heinemann.com

Offices and agents throughout the world

0-325-00616-4

Library of Congress Cataloging-in-Publication Data
Irene C. Fountas
    Word study lessons : phonics, spelling, and vocabulary / by Irene C. Fountas and Gay Su Pinnell.
        p. cm.
    Includes bibliographical references.
    Contents: [1] Grade K — [2] Grade 1 — [3] Grade 2.
    ISBN 0-325-00616-4
    1. Word recognition. 2. Reading—Phonetic method. 3. English language—Orthography and spelling—Study and teaching
        (Elementary) 5. Third grade (Education) I. Pinnell, Gay Su. II. Title.

    LB1573.6 .F68 2004
    372.61—dc22

Printed in the United States of America on acid-free paper

08 07 06 05 04 ML 1 2 3 4 5 6

Word Study Lessons
Phonics, Spelling, and Vocabulary

Contents

WS · Word Structure

WSA · Word-Solving Actions

Word Study: Why and How

Welcome to *Word Study Lessons 3: Phonics, Spelling, and Vocabulary*, a collection of one hundred minilessons. These brief minilessons (so called to emphasize their targeted focus in both content and delivery) enable you to help children attend to and learn about how words work. The lessons in this book are appropriate for most third graders, particularly if they have had a systematic word study program in kindergarten and grades one and two. If your third graders are very inexperienced and unsophisticated in their knowledge of words, give close attention to summary lessons early in the year and consult the companion volume, *Phonics Lessons 2: Letters, Words and How They Work*. These lessons take into account what children already know and help them acquire the knowledge and concepts they need to learn next. You may connect the lessons to word solving in reading and writing across the language and literacy curriculum or use them as prototypes for other word study minilessons that you design yourself. Most important, each lesson is organized around a language principle—an essential understanding about language and how it works—thus enabling you to plan and teach efficiently and systematically.

Why Teach Word Study?

The true purpose and promise of word study is to expand and refine children's reading and writing powers. In the complex processes of reading and writing, letters, sounds, and words are the keys to help children grasp and use language as a tool. Most children acquire this tool and learn how to use it at school under the guidance of a skilled teacher who provides a wide range of learning opportunities. While this volume focuses on phonics, spelling, and vocabulary, it is important to remember that *word study is not a complete reading program, nor is it even the most important component of a reading program*. The lessons here enhance but do not take the place of experiences with real texts. As described here, word study takes only about ten or fifteen minutes of explicit teaching each day, with students spending an additional fifteen to twenty minutes a day applying, sharing, and evaluating what they have learned and linking their understandings to reading and writing.

What's the Best Way to Teach Children How Words Work?

Phonics is typically seen as an important instructional area for children who are just learning to read and write. By becoming aware of the sounds and their relationship to letters, young children can solve simple words in reading and writing and they can also use this information to check on the accuracy of their reading. Most third graders are well beyond this "cracking the code" stage. They know simple and even more complex letter/sound relationships and also have a core of known words that allows them to read and write fluently at appropriate levels. They are, however, still learning about word structure as they explore more complex words that present challenges to decoding and spelling. In fact, they will continue learning how words "work" throughout elementary school.

Phonics, spelling, and word structure are best taught as part of a wide range of engaging literacy experiences accompanied by rigorous teaching. As teachers work alongside readers and writers, they demonstrate effective behaviors, draw attention to important information, and prompt children to use their knowledge. The great majority of time in the classroom is devoted to reading and writing continuous text. Children learn to solve words "on the run" while reading for meaning and writing to communicate. The curriculum is content rich and includes a range of instructional approaches, from demonstrating and explicit teaching to supporting children's independent work.

In the arguments about what constitutes effective instruction, two issues often arise:

► Should instruction be explicit, focused directly on language elements, or implicit, that is, embedded in the processes of reading and writing?

► Should we teach children directly or allow them to discover or generalize essential concepts for themselves?

Extreme positions are dangerous. Leaving everything to discovery will almost surely mean that many children will not attend to or acquire the understanding they need. Yet assuming that children learn only through direct teaching may lead us to neglect the power of the learning brain, that is, the excitement that makes learning real and the continuing curiosity and desire to learn that are the result.

We must remember that children learn more than we teach them. With a foundation of good instruction, one that involves showing children how to learn new words while reading and writing, children will develop systems for expanding their spelling, reading, and vocabulary skills.

Lessons must also contain an element of inquiry. In these minilessons, the principle is stated in simple language appropriate for use in the classroom, but the children are also encouraged to categorize words, notice features of letters and words, and search for examples. In any lesson, you decide whether to state the principle first and then generate examples that will make it clear, always leaving room for children to notice more about letters, sounds, and words, or to show some clear examples first and invite children to make connections and generalizations. The combination of discovery and direct teaching makes learning efficient; teaching prompts discovery.

Direct Teaching		**Discovery**	
⟶		⟶	
Principle	**Examples**	**Examples**	**Principle**

The Word Study Continuum

The linguistic foundation for the lessons presented in this book is the Word Study Continuum, which summarizes a comprehensive body of knowledge about written language in nine major areas:

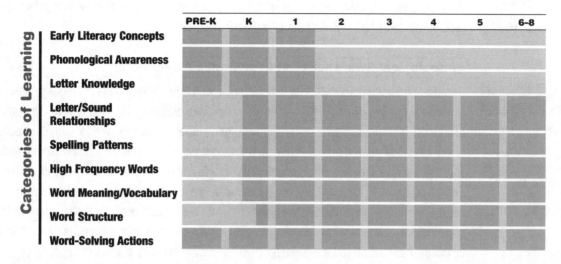

The Continuum gives us as teachers an extensive and organized understanding of the body of knowledge that forms the foundation for expert word solving. As indicated above, most third graders will have fully developed the understandings they need in the first three areas: Early Literacy Concepts, Phonological Awareness, and Letter Knowledge. That is not to say that they will not revisit these areas as needed (for example, examining letters closely as they learn to write in cursive handwriting, develop their own writing styles, or explore sounds as they read and write poetry). But specific lessons for the entire class in those areas will probably not be needed. The lessons in this book begin with Letter/Sound Relationships.

Each category showcases multiple principles, easier to harder, that your students will develop over time, but a rigid sequence of learning items is not implied. Children develop their abilities along a broad front, often using and learning about several different kinds of information simultaneously.

The Word Study Continuum is based on a body of research on the nature of language and on language and literacy learning. At the heart of literacy is a process in which children use their knowledge of oral language and connect it to print (Clay 1991). The semantic (meaning), syntactic (language structure and patterns), and phonological (sound) systems of language all refer to the language we speak. These systems are the foundation for the acquisition of literacy. Students continue to expand oral language skills throughout elementary school; at the same time, they learn about the features and processes of print.

Word recognition and word solving must become rapid and automatic so that children's attention is freed to think about the more complex meaning of the texts they are reading (Armbruster, Lehr, & Osborn 2001; Pressley 1998). As they continue to study words, older students learn the more complex relationships between meaning, the rules of grammar, and word structure.

Let's look at the nine Categories of Learning in more detail.

Nine Categories of Learning

Early Literacy Concepts

Early literacy concepts are basic understandings about how print works—for example, that you read left to right and match one spoken word with one word in print—and that there are capital and lower case letters. We do not include lessons in this category, but if you have a small group of children who are still learning about print, you will want to work with them in small groups. Some good techniques are interactive writing (creating a piece of writing together with children sharing the task), shared reading (reading an enlarged text together and examining words within it), building words using magnetic letters, and sorting words.

Phonological Awareness (and Phonemic Awareness)

Because most third graders have a satisfactory knowledge of the sounds of language, lessons are not included in this category. Work in small groups with children who need to give more attention to sounds. Third graders will use their knowledge of syllables as they work with multisyllable words, and they will still be developing understanding of complex letter patterns representing sounds in words. They will be expanding their knowledge of the sounds of language as they explore poetry; they will learn new words and new uses of words that are already in their vocabularies, including figurative language. They will enjoy word play that draws attention to combinations of sounds. You may want to give special and meaningful attention to the sounds of language, especially if you are teaching children whose first language is not English.

Letter Knowledge

Third graders who have low letter knowledge will need a great deal of extra help in order to process print. We have not included lessons on letters here, but your assessment will quickly reveal students who are having a great deal of difficulty. You may want to refer to *Phonics Lessons K* or *Phonics Lessons 1* (Pinnell and Fountas) for supporting material. When you use the Buddy Study System, give these students very simple words to study. Using magnetic letters, Look, Say, Cover, Write, Check, and other exercises will help them develop systems for noticing visual features of letters and words.

Letter/Sound Relationships

While third graders will probably have good knowledge of predictable sound-to-letter relationships as well as some less regular ones, they will still be learning large letter patterns (clusters, endings, onsets, and rimes) and irregular patterns that can be connected to sounds. The lessons in this category will help them work with larger units of written language, which, in turn, will help them become more efficient as readers and writers. You will also notice lessons on cursive handwriting and keyboarding for the computer.

Spelling Patterns

Third graders have already learned many spelling patterns (for example, *it, sit, bit, spit, flit*), but they are still acquiring more complex patterns (for example, *-eight, -able*). Awareness of spelling patterns makes word solving more efficient. The lessons included in this category are designed to take advantage of the pattern seeking behaviors children will already have established and/or to show them that patterns are useful in connecting words and decoding multisyllable words. There are many lessons incorporating common and less common spelling patterns in words with more than one syllable.

High Frequency Words

Third graders are continuously adding to the body of high frequency words they can read and write; in the process, they develop systems for learning words rapidly. In third grade, they continue the process of studying high frequency words and begin to monitor their own learning. Rapid recognition of many words, especially the 500 most frequently appearing words in English, frees attention for comprehension and supports fluent reading.

Word Meaning/Vocabulary

It is necessary for children constantly to expand their listening, speaking, reading, and writing vocabularies so that they can comprehend the more complex texts they are reading and produce more interesting writing. This section of the Continuum for grade three describes understandings related to various word categories such as words with multiple meanings, homophones, antonyms, and synonyms. In addition, you will find lessons on particular uses of words, such as figurative language, and on blended words and on basic dictionary skills such as entry words and guide words.

Word Structure

Word structure involves the underlying rules for understanding both simple and complex patterns in words, including syllables, contractions, compound words, plurals, prefixes, affixes, possessives, and abbreviations. Word structure is an important area for third graders, and you will find a large range of lessons from which to select.

Word-Solving Actions

Third graders engage in word solving in very complex ways, using many different sources of information. Readers take strategic actions when they use their phonics knowledge while reading or writing continuous text. These strategies are invisible "in-the-head" actions, although we can infer them from some overt behavior. Children solve words by thinking about sound-to-letter relationships, noticing patterns, and connecting words. They may work on a word left to right or solve it by analogy, thinking about parts of words that can be connected to known words. Often a good speller will make an attempt at a word and then visually examine it to see if it "looks right." Errors in reading new words (often, again, representing several attempts) reveal hypotheses.

Learning Your Way Around the Minilessons

Our goal in presenting a variety of lessons in each category is to provide clear prototypes from which you can create your own lessons (see *Teaching Resources,* Blank Lesson Template), using the Word Study Continuum, that will develop the understandings your students need to experience over time. Although we present the lessons in a standard format, every lesson you teach over years is inherently different because of the conversations you will have with the children you teach. Your students will offer their own examples and make their own connections, and you will enrich their learning as you acknowledge and extend their thinking. Within each category, the lessons are numbered for ease of reference and generally represent a sequence from easier to harder, but the sequence may be altered to fit the needs of the children you are teaching. Easy and hard are relative terms; they refer to students' previous experience, and only you as a teacher know the children's learning background.

If you are new to teaching itself or have not taught word study before, you may want to follow this sequence carefully; the sequence we have suggested works well, and observation of behavior will let you know when concepts are very easy for children and you need to move on. As you implement these lessons, you will not only learn more about children's development of word-solving strategies but also gain invaluable insight into our English linguistic system. Ultimately, feel confident in building your own sequence of explicit lessons that moves your students systematically toward a flexible and powerful range of strategies.

Generative Lesson

early
mid
late

Noticing Silent Letters in Words
Two-Way Sort

Consider Your Children

Children have already encountered silent letters as parts of word patterns (e.g., *walk*) and probably recognize silent *e* since they use it often in interactive and independent writing. They may not understand the principle, however. Take an informal inventory of children's knowledge of silent letters by noticing how often they represent them in their writing. Once children are aware of silent letters, this lesson will expand their knowledge.

Working with English Language Learners

Letters that are not connected with sounds may be confusing to English language learners, especially if they have been taught to expect a direct sound-to-letter relationship. Use this lesson to help them realize that there can be silent letters in words. Help them attend to the larger patterns in words and to see silent letters as part of word parts connected to sounds.

You Need

► Chart paper.
► Markers.

From *Teaching Resources:*
► Two-Way Sort Cards.
► Two-Way Sort Sheets.
► Lesson LS 11 Word Cards.

Understand the Principle

In some words, consonants are silent because the pronunciation has changed over time and the letters are no longer reflected in speech. Other words with silent letters have come into English from other languages. When children understand the principle of silent letters and at the same time work with larger patterns, they gain a better sense of word structure. Some letter combinations such as *sh* or *th* do not have silent letters, but have letters that combine to make a new or unique sound.

Explain the Principle

❝ Some words have consonant letters that are silent. ❞

LS 11
Letter/Sound Relationships

CONTINUUM: LETTER/SOUND RELATIONSHIPS — RECOGNIZING AND USING CONSONANT LETTERS THAT REPRESENT NO SOUND

(115)

Modify the steps for implementing the lesson to fit your own group of children. Much will depend on your children's experience and how well you have taught routines.

plan

teach

We take you through the lesson step by step, suggesting effective language you might use. Sometimes, the lesson is oral only, without written examples. Make frequent use of the pocket chart to hold pictures, letters, and words (or use chart paper on an easel). Occasionally, you may write the principle on the chart before the lesson and generate examples with children during the lesson.

Explain the Principle

❝ **Some words have consonant letters that are silent.** ❞

① Tell the children that you will show them something interesting about words.

② Read the first column of words. Suggested language: "What do you notice about these words?" [Children respond.] "Yes, they each have a *b* at the end, and you do not hear the *b* sound when you say the word. Sometimes words have letters that you do not pronounce."

③ Write *b* at the top of the column.

④ Read the next column of words. "What do you notice about these words?" [Children respond.] "Yes, there is a silent *k* at the beginning of each word." Children may also notice the silent *e* in *knife*.

⑤ Repeat the process with words with silent *l* and silent *t*. Write the silent consonant at the top of each column and title the chart Words with Silent Letters.

⑥ Explain that children will complete a two-way sort, sorting words *with* silent letters and those *without* silent letters.

Words with Silent Letters

b	k
lamb	knot
crumb	know
thumb	knife
	knee
walk	whistle
calf	

In each TEACH section, we provide a sample chart that you and your students might create. Some depict the chart in process; some depict the final result.

We repeat the principle in language suitable for children so that you may refer to it during your teaching.

Children work independently (individually, with partners, in small groups) to apply and practice what they've learned in the lesson.

apply

take
say
sort
write

▸ Have the children use word cards and a Two-Way Sort Card to complete a two-way sort of words *with* silent letters and words *without* silent letters.

▸ Then children write the words on a Two-Way Sort Sheet and circle the silent letter in each word. Read their lists to a partner.

Name: Ashley   Two-Way Sort

Silent letters	No silent letters
Knot	behind
whistle	most
walk	short
know	summer
lamb	next
thumb	
knife	
calf	
knee	
crumb	
knew	
know	
grade	

early
mid
late

LS 11
Letter/Sound Relationships

Each lesson suggests the approximate time of year to teach the lesson. (See Lesson Selection Map.)

share

Have children share one word with a silent letter and add it to the chart.

Ask them to talk about what they have learned about words. You will probably want to reinforce the understanding that the *h* in *sh* is not a silent letter. Rather the two letters combine to create a unique sound.

The lesson routines are identified in concise words on tags that you can post to remind children of what to do. Post the tags where everyone can refer to them as they work. Tags help your children become independent learners.

⑪⑦

Easy-to-use tabbing organization (referenced to the Lesson Selection Map as well as the Month-by-Month Planning Guide) helps you to find and select appropriate lessons for your children.

Use the guidelines to reinforce the principles and help children share their learning. In many lessons, we suggest behaviors to notice and support.

In each Apply section, we provide a photo showing an example of the product or process children will engage in as they practice and apply what they've learned.

Connect learning across the Language and Literacy Framework through interactive read-aloud, shared reading, guided reading, guided writing, and independent writing. Your observations across learning contexts will help you think of specific connections you can bring to your children's attention; add your own notes to enhance the lesson.

We provide a variety of useful bibliographies in *Teaching Resources.*

For each lesson, we provide two suggested read-aloud titles chosen specifically to support the principle and work of each lesson.

Link

Interactive Read-Aloud: Read aloud books that invite curiosity about words and how they work, and point out two or three words containing a silent letter. Examples of appropriate books are:

▶ *Hot Potato: Mealtime Rhymes* by Neil Philip

▶ *The Snail and the Whale* by Julia Donaldson

Shared Reading: Read a variety of poems that children enjoy. After reading the text and discussing it, project the text on a whiteboard or write it on a large chart and ask children to highlight a few words that contain a silent letter.

Guided Reading: During word work, write three or four words on a whiteboard and have children identify the silent letters. Invite them to add one or two more.

Guided/Independent Writing: Help children think about word patterns with silent letters when they write new words.

assess

▸ Observe whether the children are able to identify silent letters in words.

▸ Notice whether the children attempt to include silent letters in the words they spell.

▸ Ask the children to write five words with silent letters. Their degree of success will tell you whether you need to repeat this lesson, expanding the number of words.

Expand the Learning

Repeat the lesson with other patterns that include silent letters: *ghost, ghoul, gnat, bought, would, should, scent, scene, scissors, rhyme, rhino, khaki, calf, talk, calm, faster, listen, whistle, write, wrap, wrist.* (See Lesson LS 15.)

Connect with Home

Encourage the children to read their Two-Way Sort Sheet to family members.

Give children a sheet of lesson word cards (Word Card Template) to take home, cut apart, and sort.

If children need more experience, you can repeat the lesson format using these suggestions for variations, different examples, or more challenging activities.

These are not homework assignments; rather, they are ways you can help family members and caregivers make connections between home and school.

Assess the impact of the minilesson and application in ways that are informal and integral to the work children are doing. For some lessons, we suggest using the more formal and systematic procedures in the Assessment Guide (in *Teaching Resources*) to help you determine children's needs for further lessons.

Irene C. Fountas & Gay Su Pinnell

grade **3**

word study
lessons

TEACHING RESOURCES

- *Assessment Guide*
- *Materials & Routines*
- *Games*
- *Templates*
- *Category Word Cards and Lists*
- *Lesson Word Cards and Lists*
- *Bibliographies*

*first*hand

The Assessment Guide includes more formal, performance-based Assessment Tasks across the Categories of Learning.

We've provided a variety of bibliographies listing hundreds of books categorized for ease of use. Categories include Language Play, Rhymes, Poetry, and Read Alouds.

You will find descriptions of and directions for the materials and daily routines most important for your classroom. These are comprehensive lists of the hands-on materials and activities that undergird effective teaching.

Additionally, look for word cards, templates, and reproducibles to make an array of your own cards and ready-to-use booklets. We include game materials and directions for Lotto, Crazy Eights, Battle, Trumps, and Concentration, among others. We also provide numerous reproducibles for student activities.

Assessment

Lesson Word Cards and Lists

Materials & Routines

Category Word Cards and Lists

Games

Bibliographies

Templates

Get to Know Your Third Grader

Essential Literacy Concepts Every Third Grader Should Know

Third grade is an important year for expanding children's knowledge of the written language system. Third graders, for the most part, are comfortable with many of the conventions of language and are making use of reading and writing for their own purposes. Those who lack confidence will need help to catch up so that they do not lose the accuracy and fluency they need in order to focus on meaning. All third graders will need many opportunities to use their knowledge of words while engaging in the reading and writing of continuous text.

Important concepts about words and how they work are learned and enriched in both direct word study and in reading/writing continuous text. More extensive discussions of third-grade learners may be found in Pinnell & Fountas 1998, Chapter 19, 2001a and 2001b. The expectations inherent in these descriptions are consistent with recommended literacy standards for kindergarten through third grade (New Standards Primary Literacy Committee, National Center on Education and the Economy and the University of Pittsburgh, 1999).

Letters and Sounds

Third graders have also consolidated their knowledge of relationships between letters and sounds, understanding that there is not a direct one-to-one relationship between letters and sounds in English words. They are learning how to map the sounds of the language onto the print system and to expand their understandings to accommodate how words look. They are learning about doubled letters and many different vowel patterns in words such as: *moon, look, boy, oil, cow, house,* and *float.* These are all patterns that third graders may encounter in reading or use in writing, and they are ready to understand the more complex letter/sound relationships that exist. Much of this learning is accomplished by looking at letter/sound relationships within words as children explore them in categories.

Vocabulary

Third graders who are processing grade-level texts with understanding have developed ways of deriving the meaning of many words that are new to them, but direct teaching of words and word parts can accelerate the process. They use context clues to discern the meaning of new words and additional meanings of words they already know. They are also acquiring knowledge of specialized vocabularies as they read nonfiction texts in many content areas. They become acquainted with tools such as dictionaries and expand their ability to make use of references and resources to increase their understanding of word meanings.

Reading Words Fluently

Typically third graders begin the year reading the simple chapter books and shorter informational books on levels L or M (Fountas & Pinnell 2001), and by the end of the year, the expectation is that they will be reading and understanding texts at level O or P. They are advancing a smaller number of text levels than in the earlier grades, but they are sampling a much wider variety of fiction and nonfiction texts and reading more in quantity. Third grade is a good time to build a strong foundation for reading in different genres. As word solvers, they will recognize or rapidly decode the full range of words usually found in texts at grade level.

Writing Words

Third graders are expanding their knowledge of the high frequency words they can write and by the end of the year have made good progress on producing hundreds of conventionally spelled words, with the goal of correctly and automatically spelling and recognizing all of the 500 most frequently used words in English by the time they leave elementary school. They write words fluently, with efficient and legible manuscript and cursive handwriting, and they use their knowledge of letter/sound relationships and word parts to make good attempts at spelling new and more complex words.

Phoneme Chart

We examine forty-four phonemes. The actual sounds in the language can vary as dialect, articulation, and other factors in speech vary. The following are common sounds for the letters listed.

Consonant Sounds

b /b/ box	n /n/ nest	ch /ch/ chair
d /d/ dog	p /p/ pail	sh /sh/ ship
f /f/ fan	r /r/ rose	wh /wh/ what
g /g/ gate	s /s/ sun	th /th/ think
h /h/ house	t /t/ top	th /TH/ the
j /j/ jug	v /v/ vase	ng /ng/ sing
k /k/ kite	w /w/ was	zh /zh/ measure
l /l/ leaf	y /y/ yell	
m /m/ mop	z /z/ zoo	

Vowel Sounds

/ă/ hat	/ā/ gate	/o͞o/ moon	/û/ bird
/ĕ/ bed	/ē/ feet	/o͝o/ book	/ə/ about
/ĭ/ fish	/ī/ bike	/ou/ house	/ä/ car
/ŏ/ mop	/ō/ boat	/oi/ boy	/â/ chair
/ŭ/ nut	/ū/ mule	/ô/ tall	

Literacy Concepts Every Third Grader Should Know

Letters and Sounds—most third grade children are still expanding their ability to:

▶ Use letter-sound information and structural analysis to decode words.
▶ Understand irregular sound correspondences, for example –*eight* for /a/.
▶ Understand the variety of sounds and letters connected to the five vowels.
▶ Understand vowel combinations and their relationships to one or more vowel sounds.
▶ Understand and recognize the sounds connected to vowels in words with *r*.

Vocabulary—most third grade children are still expanding their ability to:

▶ Learn the meanings of new words that they meet while reading texts.
▶ Use context clues to determine the meaning of new vocabulary.
▶ Accurately read a large number of high frequency words.
▶ Understand many specialty words that apply to content areas of study (for example, biology or technology).
▶ Connect words by their meanings, creating categories of information that will help them remember words.
▶ Realize when they don't know the meaning of a word and engage in a search for more information.
▶ Use references and resources to determine the meanings and pronunciations of unknown words.

Reading Words Fluently—most third grade children are still expanding their ability to:

▶ Recognize quickly and automatically most of the words that they meet in reading texts at third grade level (approximately levels M, N, O, and P).
▶ Recognize and solve most irregularly spelled words and words with complex spelling patterns.
▶ Use structural analysis and letter-sound information to solve multisyllable words.
▶ Connect words with similar word patterns—diphthongs, special vowel spellings, and word endings.
▶ Understand and manipulate words by adding or deleting affixes or changing tenses.
▶ Understand and use plurals in reading and writing.
▶ Realize that there can be more than one meaning for words or that two words can mean about the same (synonyms) or about the opposite (antonyms).
▶ Realize that words can be connected by the way they sound or look (homonyms).
▶ Realize the functions of parts of speech—nouns, verbs, adjectives.
▶ Understand the functions of prefixes and suffixes—the way they change the meaning and tense of words as well as their function in the syntax of language.
▶ Understand how to take multisyllable words apart.

Writing Words Fluently—most third grade children are still expanding their ability to:

▶ Write a large number of high frequency words quickly and automatically.
▶ Automatically write words with regular letter/sound relationships and with spelling patterns they know.
▶ Internalize spelling rules as they sort words and examine words in categories.
▶ Apply knowledge of prefixes and suffixes in spelling words.
▶ Spell words with inflectional endings.
▶ Recognize many irregular words, the spelling of which must be memorized.
▶ Demonstrate clear logic in their attempts to spell words so that incorrectly spelled words are close to conventional.
▶ Recognize when a word is incorrectly spelled or needs to be capitalized.
▶ Notice and use spelling patterns.
▶ Recognize most frequently used abbreviations and how to punctuate them.

Processing Strategies in Reading—most third grade children are still expanding their ability to:

- Apply reading strategies to longer stretches of texts and to more difficult texts.
- Recognize a large number of high frequency words and many multisyllable words while reading continuous text and keeping their attention or meaning.
- Use a range of word-solving strategies to take words apart while reading for meaning and to monitor and self-correct their reading.
- Recognize and solve words while at the same time maintaining fluency and phrasing by using their knowledge of language and of punctuation.
- Notice and use punctuation cues (commas, periods, question marks, and quotation marks) to assist in phrased reading.
- Use word-solving strategies in combination with sense of language and meaning in a smoothly orchestrated system.
- Make predictions, inferences, and examples, and cite specific examples in the text to support their thinking.
- Realize when they do not comprehend and go back to search for clarification through examining words, sentences, or longer stretches of text.
- Understand the meaning of words that are used figuratively.
- Apply reading strategies to summarize and compare information in a text.
- Understand how a text is organized as a way of checking on accuracy and understanding.
- Identify themes in texts; identify main ideas and supporting detail.
- Compare and contrast plots and characters across literary works.
- Recognize the characteristics of a range of genres.
- Begin to recognize authors' styles of writing and analyze the writer's craft.

Processing Strategies in Writing—most third grade children are still expanding their ability to:

- Spell correctly in their writing the words they know, including those recently studied and learned.
- Produce writing that is mostly conventionally spelled.
- Write words easily and fluently so that they can produce longer pieces of text.
- Make connections between the texts that they hear, read aloud, or read for themselves and their own writing, including the use of a variety of words and literary language.
- Select appropriate words (for example, transition words and phrases) in the production of varied sentence patterns in their writing.
- Make word choices that convey precise meaning and also make their writing interesting.
- Acquire and use technical words to make their writing more accurate.
- Use simple punctuation (periods, question marks, exclamation marks, quotation marks) in their writing.
- Use a range of spelling strategies while writing continuous text.
- Proofread and edit their writing for conventions such as punctuation, capitalization, choice of verb, and spelling.
- Use references and resources to correct spelling in pieces that they write.
- Revise their writing, including word choice and sentence construction, to make it more interesting or clear.

Processing Strategies in Reading

Third graders will be reading texts that demand a full range of comprehending strategies, including solving words, monitoring and self-correcting reading, searching for essential information, making predictions, sustaining fluency, and adjusting reading for different purposes. They will also begin to understand more sophisticated uses of language, vocabulary that is seldom used in oral language, literary phrases, and metaphor. In reading, they also go beyond the text to make personal connections to ideas they encounter. They bring their knowledge of the world and of other texts to the comprehension of new texts. In the process, they "read between the lines," making inferences to understand what is implied but not stated. Competent readers are able to summarize ideas from text and to make the adjustments in their own understandings as they acquire new information. They can use text features and structures to organize content, draw conclusions, and build knowledge. When reading nonfiction texts, they interpret and draw information from graphics, integrating it with the information from the text body. They also are learning to analyze the literary elements of text and to read critically. They may compare and contrast plots and characters across literary works and recognize the characteristics of different genres. They are learning to recognize authors' styles and to identify important themes in literature.

Processing Strategies in Writing

Third grade writers can produce longer and more varied texts; they write fluently, applying a flexible range of word-solving strategies, although they are still expanding their writing vocabularies and their ability to work with multisyllable words. They are beginning to write in different genres and their compositions reflect their current awareness of the characteristics of genres. They can proofread their writing and are learning to make efficient use of references and resources to assist in this process. They write legibly (although individualistically) because they have internalized efficient habits of handwriting and are developing skill in writing in cursive form. They are becoming more interested in the craft of writing, which involves attention to word choice, sentence structure, and voice. They make connections between their own writing and the texts that they hear, read aloud, or read for themselves, to include using a greater variety of words and literary language. They are learning to select appropriate words (for example, transition words and phrases) in the production of varied sentence patterns in their writing; they may learn and use technical words.

What to Do If Children Are Learning to Speak English

Considering the diversity of our society, it is very likely that you will have children in your class who are learning English as a second or even third language. A third grader may be at any level of knowledge, from just beginning to speak a few words of English, to understanding and speaking the language, but just beginning to read and write in it. Children are fast language learners; usually it takes only a few years for them to learn to speak and become literate in English.

Having English language learners in the classroom requires attention to multilevel learning. You may be required to work with small groups of children to provide simpler lessons and also to add word study to your work with guided reading groups. It is important to understand and value children's language abilities even if they are only beginning to learn English. They know a great deal about language simply because they speak one fluently, although this knowledge will not be at a conscious level. You will want to adjust your teaching to make sure that English language learners have access to everything that can help them learn about letters, sounds, and words. Often, these adjustments are minor and easy to implement, but they are necessary to promote learning on the part of these students. In addition, many of these adjustments may be helpful to many other children in your class.

We have offered some general suggestions for each of four areas—oral language, reading, writing, and phonics instruction. It is obvious that these four areas overlap and are interconnected. Work in one area will tend to support learning in all other areas as well. Each lesson in this book has specific suggestions for helping English language learners acquire understanding of the principle.

You may also want to make use of the picture card sets included in *Phonics Lessons K* or *Phonics Lessons 1* (Pinnell & Fountas 2003) as they are very useful for building vocabulary.

Guidelines: Working with English Language Learners

Oral Language

① Show children what you mean when you give directions. You may need to act out a procedure and have children do it while you coach them. Have them repeat directions to each other or say them aloud as they engage in the activity. Support them during their first attempts rather than expecting independence immediately.

② Give English language learners more "wait and think" time. You could say, "Let's think about that for a minute" before calling for an answer. Demonstrate to students how you think about what you are going to say.

③ Paraphrase and summarize for students. Repeat the directions or instructions several different ways, watching for feedback indicating they understand you. Paraphrase until you can see that they understand.

④ Use pictures and objects that children understand and can connect to their homes and neighborhoods. At the same time, avoid examples that may be completely strange to children and to which they have difficulty bringing meaning.

⑤ Use short, simple sentences in shared reading, guided or interactive writing, and oral conversations. Avoid complex, embedded sentences that children will find hard to follow if they are just learning English. When a complex sentence is used (for example, in read-aloud or shared reading), watch for evidence of confusion on the part of students and paraphrase with simpler sentences when necessary.

⑥ Bring children's familiar world into the classroom through family photos, holiday souvenirs, and objects from home. Expand children's world by bringing in other objects that will give them new experiences.

⑦ Demonstrate using language structures while talking about familiar topics. Involve children in games that require repeating these simple language structures, for example: "My name is _____." "_____ has two brothers and one sister." "It is hot today. _____ likes hot weather." Use question-and-answer formats to increase flexibility. "Who has two brothers?" "Julio has two brothers."

⑧ Make instruction highly interactive, with a great deal of oral language surrounding everything children are learning.

⑨ Plan some activities using children's names (for example, poems that you can say over and over, substituting different names). Be sure that you are pronouncing all children's names correctly and clearly as you draw their attention to the particular word that is a child's name.

⑩ Engage English language learners in repeating and enjoying songs, rhymes, and repetitive chants. Incorporate body movements to enhance children's enjoyment of poetry and help them to remember and understand the language better.

Reading

① Some English language learners will have knowledge of the alphabetic system as it applies to their own languages, but others will not. For those learners, provide an extensive collection of simple alphabet books so that children can encounter the same letters, in the same sequence, with picture examples in different texts.

② Read aloud often to students; in general, it is wise to increase the amount of time that you read aloud and discuss books with students. Be sure that the material you are reading to students is comprehensible, that is, within their power to understand with your support. Remember that English language learners can often understand more than they can perform, and pictures help a great deal.

③ Stick to simple and understandable texts when you read aloud to students. Watch for signs of enjoyment and reread favorites. Rereading books to children will help them acquire and make use of language that goes beyond their current understandings.

④ Be sure that children's own cultures are reflected in the material that you read aloud to them and that they read for themselves. They should see illustrations with people like themselves in books as well as diverse cultures reflected in food, celebrations, dress, holidays, everyday events, and so on.

⑤ Understand that shared reading involves children in a great deal of repetition, often of language that is different from or more complex than they can currently use in speech. This experience gives children a chance to practice language, learn the meaning of the words, and use the sentence structure of English.

⑥ Use a shared reading text over and over, inserting different names or different words to vary it. Rhythmic and repetitive texts are beneficial to English language learners. This repetition will give children maximum experience with the syntax of English and will help them to develop an implicit understanding of noun-verb agreement, plurals, and other concepts. Once a text is well known in shared reading, it can serve as a resource to children. Revisit shared reading texts for examples of language structure and for specific words and their meaning and spelling.

⑦ Include English language learners in guided reading groups even if you have to begin with very simple texts. Guided reading is a very valuable context for working with English language learners because you can scaffold their reading and their language through an introduction that clears up confusion and you can observe them closely to gain information as to the accuracy and ease of their reading. Through observation and discussion, you can find what is confusing to them and respond to their questions.

⑧ Be sure to use oral language, pictures, concrete objects, and demonstration when you introduce stories to help children untangle any tricky vocabulary or concepts. When they are reading in texts for themselves in guided and independent reading, they may encounter words that they can "read" (that is, pronounce using phonics skills) but do not understand.

⑨ In guided reading, help children relate new words to words they already know. During and after reading, check with children to be sure they understand vocabulary and concepts; build into lessons a time when children can bring up any words they did not know.

⑩ Include word work on a regular basis in the guided reading lessons. Make strong connections to what they have been learning in phonics and word study.

Writing

1. Value and encourage children's drawing as it represents thinking and connects their ideas to early writing. Spending a few moments drawing may help them more easily form the language they need.

2. Have children repeat several times the sentence they are going to write so that they will be able to remember it. If the sentence is difficult to remember, that may be a sign that it is too complex for the present level of language knowledge.

3. Focus on familiar topics and everyday experiences in interactive writing so that children can generate meaningful sentences and longer texts. Reread the piece of interactive writing many times, encouraging fluency as children gain control over the language. Consider simplifying the structure or rephrasing the sentence so that it is easier. It is beneficial to work in interactive writing with small groups of English language learners.

4. Guide children to produce some repetitive texts that use the same sentence structure and phrases over and over again, so that they can internalize them.

5. Understand that once a text has been successfully produced in interactive writing and children can easily read it, this text is a resource for talking about language—locating specific words, noticing beginning and ending sounds, noticing rhymes, and so on.

6. Encourage English language learners to write for themselves. Demonstrate how to think of something to write and repeat it so that they remember it. Demonstrate how to say words slowly, providing more individual help and demonstration if needed. Accept language that is not perfect English grammar; children will gradually expand their knowledge.

7. Surround children's independent writing with a great deal of oral language. Talk with them and help them put their ideas into words before they write. Encourage them to tell their stories, share their writing with others, and extend their meanings through talk.

8. Provide a great many models of writing for English language learners—modeled writing, shared reading, charts about people in the room or experiences. Encourage them to reread and revisit these models to help them in their writing. In the beginning, they may use phrases or sentences from charts around the room, varying their own sentences slightly. Gradually, they will go beyond these resources, but models will be a helpful support for a time.

9. Learn something about the sound systems of the children's first languages. That knowledge will give you valuable insights into the way they "invent" or "approximate" their first spellings. For example, notice whether they are using letter/sound associations from the first language or whether they are actually thinking of a word in the first language and attempting to spell it.

10. Accept spellings that reflect the child's own pronunciation of words, even if it varies from standard pronunciation. Show that you notice and value the way they are using knowledge. After all, variety makes language interesting.

Phonics and Word Study

① Help English language learners manipulate magnetic letters and tiles, move pictures around and connect them with words, and work with words and word parts. The application activities connected to lessons will be especially helpful to them because they will be practicing and overlearning the principles you are teaching.

② Be sure that the print for all charts (ABC, name, shared/interactive writing, picture and word, charts for minilessons, etc.) is clear and consistent so that children who are working in another language do not have to deal with varying forms of letters.

③ Make sure your English language learners are not sitting in an area that is peripheral to the instruction (for example, in the back or to the side). It is especially important for these learners to be able to see clearly and hear all instruction.

④ Provide a "rehearsal" by working with your English language learners in a small group before you provide the minilesson to the entire group. Sometimes they may find it more difficult than other children to come up with words as examples; however, thinking for only a few minutes ahead of time will help these learners come up with responses in whole-group settings. It will not hurt them to think about the concepts twice because this repetition will provide greater support.

⑤ Use real objects to represent pictures and build concepts in children's minds. For example, bring in a real lemon that children can touch and smell rather than just a picture of a lemon. When it is not possible to use real objects to build concepts, use clear pictures that will have meaning for children. Picture support should be included whenever possible.

⑥ Be sure to enunciate clearly yourself and accept children's approximations. If they are feeling their own mouths say (or approximate) the sounds, they will be able to make the connections. Sounds and letters are abstract concepts, and the relationships are arbitrary. It will be especially complex for children whose sound systems and alphabets are very different from those of English. They may have trouble saying the sounds that are related to letters and letter clusters.

⑦ Accept alternative pronunciations of words with the hard-to-say sounds and present the written form to help learners distinguish between them. Minimal pairs (sounds that are like each other, have similar tongue positions, and are easily confused, such as *s* and *sh, r* and *l, sh* and *ch, f* and *v*) are often quite difficult for English language learners to differentiate. English language learners often also have difficulty with inflected endings (*s, ed*).

⑧ Speak clearly and slowly when working with children on distinguishing phonemes and hearing sounds in words, but do not distort the word so much that it is unrecognizable. Distortion may confuse English language learners in that it may sound like another word that they do not know.

⑨ Use the pocket chart often so that children have the experience of working with pictures and words in a hands-on way. They can match pictures with words so that the meaning of words becomes clearer.

⑩ Work with a small group of English language learners to help them in the application activity and make your instruction more explicit. Notice concepts that they find particularly difficult and make note to revisit them during word work.

Inside the Classroom: Organizing to Teach

As these schedules demonstrate, ideally, your explicit word study lessons are embedded in a rich language and literacy framework that offers an organized combination of experiences, each of which contributes uniquely to children's literacy development. During the third-grade year, children will have made the transition from active work in centers to the sustained, independent reading and writing required in the reading and writing workshop. Below, we describe a Language and Literacy Framework for Grade Three which features three blocks for learning: Language and Word Study, Reading Workshop, and Writing Workshop (Fountas and Pinnell 2001).

Language and Literacy Framework for Grade Three

Language/ Word Study	30–60 minutes	Select from: ▶ Interactive Read-Aloud ▶ Word Study Lesson, Application Activity, and Sharing ▶ Modeled/Shared Reading ▶ Modeled/Shared Writing ▶ Poetry Sharing/Response ▶ Readers' Theatre/Process Drama ▶ Choral Reading ▶ Interactive Vocabulary ▶ Interactive Edit ▶ Handwriting ▶ Current Events ▶ Test Reading & Writing Lesson
Reading Workshop	60 minutes	▶ Independent Reading—Minilesson, Reading and Conferring, Sharing ▶ Guided Reading—Introduce Text, Read, Discuss the Meaning, Teach for Processing Strategies, Extend the Meaning (optional), Word Work (optional) ▶ Literature Study—Select Books, Prepare, Discuss, Self-Evaluate
Writing Workshop	60 minutes	▶ Independent Writing—Minilesson, Writing and Conferring, Sharing ▶ Guided Writing ▶ Investigations

Language and Word Study

The language/word study block includes a variety of activities designed to immerse children in language and help them learn about it. We recommend about 30 to 60 minutes for the language/word study block, and you will usually be working with the entire group.

Interactive Read-Aloud By hearing written language read aloud, children learn about the structure, or syntax, of written language, which is different in many ways from oral language. Reading aloud is very important for third grade children because the language structures and vocabulary that they meet in books is foundational not only for learning to read for themselves but for expanding their comprehending strategies and background knowledge as they move into more complex texts.

Phonics/Word Study Lesson During the language/word study block, you can take the opportunity to provide a brief, lively minilesson on some principle related to the use of letters, sounds, or words. The minilesson is followed by an application activity that involves exploration of the principle.

The Buddy Study spelling system involves children in a more formal word study process. This system is described in detail in *Word Matters* (Pinnell & Fountas 1998). The five days of word study activities begin with a minilesson focusing on a spelling principle. See *Teaching Resources* for basic framework and forms. Lessons outlining the Buddy Study spelling system can be found in the Word-Solving Actions section.

In Buddy Study, students learn a variety of word learning activities. They engage in an application to practice core words related to the minilesson and personal words selected from the writing.

Modeled/Shared Reading Most third graders no longer need the very basic understandings that younger children acquire through shared reading; but, as children become more competent in reading for themselves, shared reading still offers opportunities to enjoy the sound of language, to use structures unique to written language, to explore deeper meanings, and to support phrased, fluent reading. It is a way to demonstrate and practice fluency and phrasing.

Modeled/Shared/Interactive Writing Modeled writing involves demonstrating the writing process for children. Teachers often "think aloud" about any aspect of writing: for example, word selection, message composition, layout of print, punctuation, word solving, and text organization.

Shared writing involves the composition of a common text by a group of children. Guided by the teacher, they are able to participate in the writing process to develop a meaningful text that may be any genre—for example, a letter, description, story, label, sign, or note.

Interactive writing is usually not used in grade three. It involves a "sharing the pen" process in which children make contributions by coming up to the easel and writing some words and letters (for a detailed description, see McCarrier, Pinnell, & Fountas 2000). In third grade, you may want to use interactive writing when working with English language learners or with children who need a great deal more support in composing and constructing messages.

Interactive Edit An interactive edit is a brief activity (typically no more than five minutes) that focuses on conventions. You work with dictated sentences that present appropriate challenges related to capitalization, punctuation, grammar, or spelling. You can have one child write it correctly on the easel for all to see while the rest use clipboards; or you can display the sentences on a chart, having the students copy and edit them individually or as partners.

Handwriting A five- to ten-minute minilesson once a week on letter formation will improve the quality of student work and make students more conscious of the importance of legible writing. The handwriting lesson includes demonstration and guided practice. For example, one student can write on a chalkboard or flipchart while the others work on their own. Then the children spend time practicing formation of letters, words, and sentences in manuscript or cursive form.

Reading Workshop

Poetry Sharing/Response The students or the teacher read aloud poems that they have rehearsed; sometimes they recite them from memory. After reading or recitation, students talk about what the poem means or how the writer used language.

Readers' Theatre/Process Drama In readers' theatre, two or more people read a piece of writing aloud, usually assuming the roles of the characters and narrator. Students analyze the text and practice their performance so that their voices convey the meaning. "Process" drama involves students in assuming identities as a means of understanding human problems and issues. Rather than acting (as in a play), students are given a framework (often related to literature or social studies) within which they develop their roles. Process drama evolves over time and is a valuable way to help students explore concepts and language in new ways. It often involves reading and writing as background research.

Choral Reading Through rehearsed recitation of prose or poetry, students learn to read together, using intonation, rhythm, and pace to convey meaning.

Interactive Vocabulary Focusing on word meaning, students are involved in thinking about different ways to figure out the meaning of a word. Using a chart or the chalkboard, students focus attention on a few examples that expand the way they think about the meaning of words and help them to make connections between words.

Current Events Students take turns reporting on the issues of the day to each other. Discussions may be linked to previous knowledge and experiences or to works of literature that you read aloud to them. Students prepare for current events sharing so that the presentation is concise, engaging, and informative.

Test Reading and Writing Teachers provide minilessons that help students become more sophisticated in taking reading and writing tests; for example, teaching the structure of multiple-choice and short-answer questions, talking about what questions really ask readers and writers to do, and evaluating possible answers.

Independent Reading The reading workshop block begins with a reading minilesson on any aspect of reading—procedures for the workshop (choosing books, keeping records, using a Reader's Notebook, etc.), reading skills and strategies, or literary aspects of texts. In the lesson, you demonstrate, show, and tell students how to become better readers.

The lesson is followed by a period of silent, independent reading; students must be either reading a book of their choice (with teacher's guidance) or writing about their reading in the Reader's Notebook. The teacher can confer with individuals, sampling oral reading, or work with small groups in guided reading or literature discussion.

The Reader's Notebook is a tool to help students analyze and reflect on their own reading. Students keep lists of books they have read and want to read. They write one thoughtful letter a week to tell the teacher about their thinking as they read. The teacher responds to each letter and also provides minilessons to help students grow in their ability to write about their thinking.

The workshop ends with a brief sharing and evaluation period in which the lesson principle is reinforced and extended and students show how they have used the information while reading. For a detailed description, see Fountas & Pinnell 2003.

Guided Reading Guided reading involves small-group instruction within which teachers provide specific instruction on effective reading strategies. For a detailed description of guided reading, see Fountas & Pinnell 1996, Pinnell & Fountas 1998, Chapter 18, Fountas & Pinnell 2003.

Small reading groups are homogeneous in terms of students' development of a reading process at a particular point in time. Using a gradient of texts organized according to level of difficulty, you select a book that is within the learners' control but that offers a small amount of challenge. You introduce the book, and then each member of the group individually reads the text silently.

While children are reading, you have the opportunity to observe for effective behaviors (including, but not limited to, application of phonics principles) and to interact briefly with children. These interactions can support their application of principles you are teaching in word study. Following the reading, you discuss the meaning of the story and teach for processing strategies.

An optional but important component of a guided reading lesson is called "word work." At the end of the lesson, you spend one or two minutes working with words and word parts. It is preplanned and not related to the text the students have just read. This time gives you the opportunity to revisit principles that have been part of the word study program for students who are having more difficulty. You and the students may work with white dry-erase boards, the chalkboard, word cards, or magnetic letters.

Literature Study In literature study, you work with heterogeneous groups of children who sign up for book discussions, sometimes called "book clubs." Literature discussion gives the opportunity to teach children how to talk with each other about books, sharing their thinking and reaching a great depth of understanding. Also, literature study helps them learn more about literary aspects of texts.

Writing Workshop Block

The writing workshop involves a minilesson on some aspect of writing, a time when children work on their own writing with teacher support, and a sharing time. We recommend about 60 minutes.

Minilesson A writing minilesson is designed to demonstrate specific principles related to the conventions and craft of writing. The first minilessons of the year will be on procedural topics—for example, showing children how to use supplies and engage in the process of producing drafts. A great deal of time is devoted to helping children learn to use a Writer's Notebook to record thoughts, collect language, make lists, sketch, record observations, and so on. This notebook, which is a tool that many writers use, is a resource for authentic writing.

Independent Writing and Conferring Children write independently while you interact with individuals and sometimes with small groups, helping them clarify and expand their messages. Individual conferences are a good time to remind children of what they have learned in the word study minilessons. You will also gather very valuable information that will help you select and design effective and timely word study minilessons.

Guided Writing Most third graders can work more independently in writing than can younger children because they know how to spell so many words. They will, however, need a great deal of help to generate and develop topics and to use skills such as proofreading. When students have learned the routine of working independently and silently, you can begin to bring together small needs-based groups to work on specific aspects of writing.

Sharing and Evaluation In a brief sharing period at the end of the time, children can discuss their writing. Along with a discussion of the meaning and voice of the stories children write, you can take this opportunity to reinforce and extend the learning in your word study minilesson.

Word Study Minilessons That Really Work

Organization, Space, and Materials Make a Difference

When you teach a minilesson, it is very important to do so in a clearly defined space in which all children can see and hear easily. They should be able to sit comfortably on the floor without touching other children. You will want an easel, a small white dry-erase board, markers, magnetic letters, and a vertical magnetic board. You will also need a pocket chart on which you can post letters or words on cards large enough for the whole group to see.

We recommend using black or dark-colored markers on white or cream-colored chart paper. You may want to use colored transparent highlighter tape for emphasis but it is better not to clutter up the examples with color-coding. We want children to look at features—not the color! A random assortment of colors increases the appeal of tasks with magnetic letters without creating an identifier that may distract the learner's attention, which should be directed to the true identifier—the distinctive features of letters. Be sure that all the necessary materials are readily available for students

Basic Principles: Designing/Implementing Effective Minilessons

Designing Effective Minilessons

► Focus on one principle that is appropriate and useful for your students at a particular point in time.

► State the principle in simple, clear terms.

► Think of a few good examples in advance so that you have them ready to show the students.

► Have in mind why you selected the minilesson, which probably will help you connect it to children's work in other components of the language/literacy framework; make connections explicit.

► Consider whether you can connect your minilesson principle to the children's first and last names, for example, endings, consonant clusters, or vowel patterns.

► Design an application activity that students can do independently (after being taught routines) and that will be productive in their learning.

► Design multilevel activities that not only permit advanced students to go beyond the given activity to make more discoveries but also allow children who are less experienced to complete the minilessons.

Implementing Effective Minilessons

► Have all materials organized and quickly available.

► Be sure that all children can see and hear as you demonstrate the principle or write examples on a chart.

► Make a clear statement of the principle as you begin the lesson or clearly state the principle at the end as children come to their own conclusions from examples.

► Use a conversational rather than a lecture style. Promote interaction so children can be active, engaged learners.

► Invite interaction so that children bring their own knowledge to bear on the application of the principle.

► Share examples and add examples from children. (If children are unable to provide some examples, then either the principle is not clearly stated or it is too difficult.)

► Keep minilessons brief; a few examples are enough.

► Make connections to previous word study minilessons or understandings and discoveries made in any other component of the Language and Literacy Framework.

► Check for understanding by asking children to locate and talk about examples.

► Summarize the minilesson by returning to the principle and stating it again.

► Demonstrate the application activity explicitly so that you know children can perform it independently.

► Provide all necessary materials for the application activity in one place—for example, on tables or clusters of tables or in a clearly defined and organized materials center.

► Convene children for a brief sharing period so that they can comment on what they have learned and you can reinforce the principle again. Involve the children in evaluating their work.

Options for Application Activities

1. Present the minilesson to the entire class and then involve all children simultaneously in the application activity. They can work individually or with partners as you circulate around the room. Immediately follow the activity with sharing and evaluation.

2. Present the minilesson to the entire class, but involve children in application activities in small groups that you supervise. Have the rest of the children involved in independent reading/writing activities. Follow the activity with sharing as soon as all groups have worked with you.

3. Present the minilesson to the entire class and explain the application activity. Have children complete it first (simultaneously for the whole group) and then move to reading or writing. Work with small groups in guided reading or writing while children work independently.

to use in the application. If students work at their own tables, arrange materials in a central area or on each table. If the activity is new or difficult, place a model in clear view so that children can check their results. For additional information about the materials, read the Material Description List in *Teaching Resources*.

Classroom Routines for Effective Teaching

Routines refers both to the basic routines of how to live and learn in the classroom (where to store materials or how to participate in a class meeting, for example) and to a series of instructional procedures such as making words, sorting words, and playing word study games that children will use again and again as they learn a range of concepts. Teach the routines carefully when you first begin using word study minilessons. First, demonstrate the activity precisely, and then have everyone do it at once. If you run into a logistical problem (not having enough magnetic letters, for example), ask children to take turns with a partner or in a small group and check each other.

When you know that children can perform the routine on their own, then they can work individually, as partners, or in groups. (You will need to demonstrate the activity again in relation to the particular principle you are exploring in the minilesson.) For a comprehensive overview of routines, see the descriptions and directions in *Teaching Resources;* additionally, you will find many references to routines in the Month-by-Month Planning Guide.

Consider Your Language and Delivery

Minilessons should be conversational. You will want to state the principle clearly at the beginning of the lesson (or at the end, if you think it is appropriate for students to derive it through inquiry and example). Your tone should be that of *"I'm going to show you something interesting about how words work"* or *"I'm interested in what you notice about these words."* Invite children to make connections to words they know. Invite them to contribute further examples and recognize and praise their thinking even if the examples don't quite fit. Always try to understand their thinking and build on a partially correct response. Help them clarify their suggestions as necessary.

Remember that a minilesson is *brief*. Don't let it go on too long. Depending on the particular principle, you'll need only a few examples to make an understanding clear. Your goal is for students to integrate some of these examples into their own thinking so they can connect them to new learning when they are working on their own. At the end of the minilesson, summarize the understanding you are trying to instill and take another moment to restate the principle. Then explain and demonstrate the application activity.

So What Did We Learn? Sharing and Evaluation

After independent work, convene a brief sharing period in which children can discuss the principle and share their examples. Recognizing their independent work gives it value and emphasis. If you have made a chart, refer to it again and restate the principle. You may want to add some of their examples. Recognize children's thinking as they share their ideas. This community meeting is a good way to ask children to evaluate themselves. You can ask how many completed the activity and have them self-evaluate their work. Make further connections with reading and writing in other components of the Language and Literacy Framework.

Grade 3 – Lesson Selection Map

Letter/Sound Relationships LS

early

___ **LS 1** Recognizing Words with Consonant Clusters (Making Words)

___ **LS 2** Identifying Words with Ending Consonant Clusters (Making Words)

___ **LS 3** Recognizing Words with Ending Consonant Digraphs (Consonant Cluster Lotto)

___ **LS 4** Recognizing Words with Beginning and Ending Consonant Digraphs (Go Fish)

___ **LS 5** Recognizing and Using y as a Vowel Sound in Words (Follow the Path)

___ **LS 6** Identifying Words with Different Vowel Sounds (oo, ow, ea) (Connect)

___ **LS 7** Identifying Other Vowel Sounds (oo, oi, oy, ow, aw, au) (Make, Write, Read)

___ **LS 8** Recognizing Long Vowel Patterns (ai, ay, ee, oa, ow, ue, ui, ew) (Crazy Eights)

___ **LS 9** Recognizing Double Consonants in Words (Word Grid Game)

mid

___ **LS 10** Recognizing Consonant Letters with Different Sounds (c, g, th, ch) (Crazy Eights)

___ **LS 11** Noticing Silent Letters in Words (Two-Way Sort)

___ **LS 12** Taking Apart Words with Open Syllables (Two-Way Sort)

___ **LS 13** Taking Apart Words with Closed Syllables (Two-Way Sort)

___ **LS 14** Recognizing Words with r-Influenced Vowel Sounds (Word Search)

late

___ **LS 15** Identifying Silent Letters in Words (Follow the Path)

___ **LS 16** Recognizing Words with the Final k Sound (c, k, ke, ck, que) (Make, Write, Read)

___ **LS 17** Learning about Words with Capital Letters (Capital Detective Lotto)

___ **LS 18** Learning Cursive Handwriting (Handwriting Notebook)

___ **LS 19** Learning Effective Keyboarding for the Computer (Keyboard Practice)

Spelling Patterns SP

early

___ **SP 1** Recognizing Phonograms with Short Vowel Sounds (Word Search)

___ **SP 2** Recognizing Word Patterns with Ending Consonant Clusters (Go Fish)

___ **SP 3** Recognizing Word Patterns with Long Vowel Sounds (Blind Sort)

___ **SP 4** Recognizing Phonograms with Double Vowels (Crazy Eights)

___ **SP 5** Recognizing Word Patterns with the Short o Sound (Battle)

___ **SP 6** Recognizing Word Patterns with Unique Vowel Sounds (Long /ū/) (Word Pairs)

___ **SP 7** Recognizing Word Patterns with Unique Vowel Sounds (Short /oo/) (Blind Two-Way Sort)

mid

___ **SP 8** Recognizing Word Patterns with Unique Vowel Sounds (/ow/) (Making Word Pairs)

___ **SP 9** Recognizing Word Patterns with Vowel Combinations (Connect)

___ **SP 10** Recognizing Phonograms with Double Consonants (Blind Sort)

___ **SP 11** Noticing Word Patterns That Represent Unique Vowel Sounds (Concentration)

___ **SP 12** Recognizing Words with VC Pattern (Four-Way Sort)

___ **SP 13** Recognizing a Vowel Pattern (VCe) in Two-Syllable Words (Three-Way Sort)

___ **SP 14** Recognizing Word Patterns with Double Consonants (Word Grid Game)

___ **SP 15** Recognizing Word Patterns with r-Influenced Vowels (Follow the Path)

late

___ **SP 16** Recognizing Words with the /a/ Pattern (Making Words and Sentences)

___ **SP 17** Recognizing Frequently Appearing Syllables in Word Patterns (Go Fish)

High Frequency Words HF

early

___ **HF 1** Recognizing High Frequency Words (with 3 or More Letters) (Make, Check, Mark)

___ **HF 2** Recognizing High Frequency Words 2 (with 4 or More Letters) (Concentration)

mid

___ **HF 3** Recognizing High Frequency Words 3 (with 5 or More Letters) (Word Grid Game)

___ **HF 4** Recognizing High Frequency Words 4 (High Frequency Lotto)

late

___ **HF 5** Checking Your Knowledge of High Frequency Words (Word Inventory)

___ **HF 6** Connecting High Frequency Words (Go Fish)

Word Meaning/Vocabulary WM/V

early

___ **WM/V 1** Recognizing and Using Compound Words (Making Words)

___ **WM/V 2** Working with Compound Words (Word Sorting)

___ **WM/V 3** Exploring Homophones (Words in Context)

___ **WM/V 4** Connecting Words (Open Word Sort)

___ **WM/V 5** Connecting Concept Words (Word Maps)

___ **WM/V 6** Recognizing and Using Synonyms (Synonyms Match)

___ **WM/V 7** Recognizing and Using Antonyms (Antonyms Concentration)

___ **WM/V 8** Synonyms and Sentences (Go Fish)

mid

___ **WM/V 9** Summary of Synonyms and Antonyms (Lotto)

___ **WM/V 10** Making Decisions about Using Homophones (Homophone Lotto)

___ **WM/V 11** Recognizing Homophones, Synonyms, and Antonyms (Word Grids)

___ **WM/V 12** Recognizing Homographs (Sentence Pictures)

___ **WM/V 13** Connecting Words by Meaning (Word Sorting)

___ **WM/V 14** Learning about Action Words (Verb Search)

late

___ **WM/V 15** Recognizing and Using Action Words (Read Around the Room)

___ **WM/V 16** Learning about Describing Words (Adjective Search)

___ **WM/V 17** Recognizing and Using Describing Words (Read Around the Room)

___ **WM/V 18** Learning about Nouns—Words for People, Places, Things (Noun Search)

___ **WM/V 19** Learning about Nouns, Describing Words, Action Words (Three-Way Sort)

___ **WM/V 20** Exploring Words (Word Maps)

___ **WM/V 21** Recognizing and Using Metaphors and Similes (Making Comparisons)

___ **WM/V 22** Recognizing and Using Blended Words (Matching Words)

___ **WM/V 23** Recognizing and Using Words That Mimic Real Sounds (Labeling)

Word Structure WS

early

___ **WS 1** Summarizing Contractions (Crazy Eights)

___ **WS 2** Recognizing Syllables in Words with Double Consonants (Checkers)

___ **WS 3** Recognizing Words with Open Syllables (Word Plot)

___ **WS 4** Recognizing Words with Closed Syllables (Taking Words Apart)

___ **WS 5** Recognizing Syllables in Words with a Silent *e* Pattern (Syllable Lotto)

___ **WS 6** Recognizing Parts in Compound Words (Compound Rummy)

___ **WS 7** Forming Plurals of Words That Add *es* (Three-Way Sort)

___ **WS 8** Forming Plurals with Words Ending in *y* (Two-Way Sort)

___ **WS 9** Forming Plurals with Words Ending in *f, fe,* or *lf* (Making Words)

___ **WS 10** Noticing and Using Abbreviations (Abbreviation Concentration)

mid

___ **WS 11** Recognizing Syllables in Words with Vowel Combinations (Taking Words Apart)

___ **WS 12** Noticing and Using the Past Tense with *ed* (Trumps)

___ **WS 13** Forming New Words by Adding *-er* (Two-Way Sort)

___ **WS 14** Using Compound Word Parts to Understand Meanings (Battle)

___ **WS 15** Reading Two-Syllable Words with a Vowel and *r* (Checkers)

late

___ **WS 16** Forming Plurals for Words Ending in *o* (Four-Way Sort)

___ **WS 17** Forming Plurals: Summary (Plural Lotto)

___ **WS 18** Identifying Syllables in Multisyllable Words (Connect)

___ **WS 19** Noticing Syllables in Multisyllable Words (Trumps)

___ **WS 20** Forming Comparisons with *-er, -est* (Making Words)

___ **WS 21** Recognizing Words with a Prefix *(un-)* (Making Words)

___ **WS 22** Recognizing Words with a Prefix *(re-)* (Follow the Path)

Word-Solving Actions WSA

early

___ **WSA 1** Learning How to Learn Words: Buddy Study 1 (Choose, Write, Build, Mix, Fix, Mix)

___ **WSA 2** Learning How to Learn Words: Buddy Study 2 (Look, Say, Cover, Write, Check)

___ **WSA 3** Learning How to Learn Words: Buddy Study 3 (Buddy Check)

___ **WSA 4** Learning How to Learn Words: Buddy Study 4 (Making Connections)

___ **WSA 5** Learning How to Learn Words: Buddy Study 5 (Buddy Study Test)

mid

___ **WSA 6** Using Alphabetical Order (List Sheet)

___ **WSA 7** Using Word Parts to Solve Words (Word Grid Game)

___ **WSA 8** Recognizing and Using Syllables (Syllable Race)

___ **WSA 9** Making Connections between Words (Word Ladders)

late

___ **WSA 10** Using Guide Words in a Dictionary (Guide Word Sort)

___ **WSA 11** Using What Is Known to Solve Words (Word Race)

___ **WSA 12** Using a Dictionary to Learn Word Meaning (Word Entry Search)

___ **WSA 13** Expanding Vocabulary through Reading Texts (Learning New Words from Reading)

The Assessment Guide

There is a time to use systematic, planned tasks that are designed to gather information about particular aspects of children's growing word knowledge. Performance-based assessment may involve observation, but it also includes more formal structured experiences in which the tasks are standardized. Standardization of the procedure creates a reliable assessment situation that provides a check on daily observation. The goal is to get a picture of what each student can do independently.

The Assessment Guide includes more formal, performance-based Assessment Tasks across the nine Categories of Learning (six for third grade). You can use these tasks in multiple ways: as diagnostic tools to determine what your students know and need to know; as monitoring tools to help you keep track of your teaching and your students' learning; and as documentation of the teaching and learning you and your students have accomplished over time. You and your colleagues may even decide to place some of the summary sheets in your children's permanent cumulative folders as a way to create a schoolwide record of the word study program.

As noted, the opportunities for informal assessment are embedded in each lesson, in the Assess feature. Look for more formal assessment opportunities across the third grade's six Categories of Learning in the Assessment Guide inside *Teaching Resources.*

The Month-by-Month Planning Guide

The Month-by-Month Planning Guide outlines and describes a year of instructional contexts and ways to organize that instruction—whole-group, independent, and small-group work. It also lists the instructional routines (which include everything from where to store supplies to how to play Syllable Lotto) you will need to teach so that children will be able to complete the application activities. Although you'll teach only a few new routines each month, children's knowledge accumulates. Once a routine (sorting, for example) has been learned, children can use it again and again in different ways. Finally, our yearly plan suggests specific lessons by month, from easier to harder, and lists specific competencies that you can determine through observation and assessment. These simple assessments of what children can do will help you identify children who are having more difficulty and may need repetition or additional word study work in a small group.

This yearly plan is a ladder of support as you work with children over time. Don't worry if your group does not progress in precisely the same way this plan implies. They may learn more rapidly in one area than another, but referring to the plan will help you reflect on areas where you need to invest more instruction.

If you are new to teaching (or new to teaching word study), you may want to follow this month-by-month plan closely. You will learn from the experience and over the year will begin to see how you can adapt the plan for greater effectiveness with your own students and also how you can teach more efficiently.

Every lesson is labeled "early," "mid," or "late" as a guide for selection. Here is a brief look at the meaning of those terms.

Early Third Grade

This section contains a number of summary lessons for concepts that may have been explored in second grade but not fully consolidated by many students. Use these lessons to refresh students' memories of these bodies of knowledge or skip them if your assessment shows they are not needed. The lessons may also be a resource for working with a small group of children who have large gaps in their understanding. If you use a summary lesson, your observation will let you know whether to expand it with more examples or move on to other principles.

Middle Third Grade

The lessons labeled "middle" represent a substantive body of knowledge that helps third graders learn to solve the words they will meet in grade-level texts as well as produce satisfactory pieces of writing. This category includes some very systematic step-by-step explorations of principles in all six categories. You will find generative lessons that you can adapt to design more lessons addressing a particular principle.

Late Third Grade

Later lessons expand children's knowledge to more complex principles. We have included some advanced principles that you may decide are too complex for your third graders at this time. They may help you in meeting the needs of your more advanced students.

Month-by-Month Planning Guide – September

The first month of third grade is a time for establishing the basic classroom routines and for assessing students' strengths and needs. You'll want to use some of the basic assessments in each of the nine areas of learning in order to do an efficient job of selecting lessons. Also, you can start using some of the early lessons and embed assessment within them. After you've used several of these lessons, you will have good feedback on whether students find them easy or difficult. At the same time, establish timeframes and routines for the instructional framework—language/word study, reading workshop, and writing workshop. For word study, establish a daily schedule that includes the structures of (1) minilesson, (2) application, and (3) sharing so that students see it as a predictable structure. Your word study minilesson, application, and sharing should be limited in time; at first, you may even want to use a timer to keep students working efficiently. Read aloud often to establish a community of learners in your room and also to expand students' listening vocabularies and make links to word study. You may wish to begin creating personal poetry anthologies as part of the language/word study block.

Organization of Instruction: *Whole class and independent work as teacher circulates.*

Learning Contexts	New Routines to Teach	Suggested Lessons	Assessment—Students can:
Introduce the three blocks: ▸ Language/Word Study ▸ Reading Workshop ▸ Writing Workshop Use mostly whole-class instruction and independent work. Spend time demonstrating how to use materials and put them away. Establish responsibility for homework. Introduce new tools such as the Word Study Notebook. Establish the procedures for the Buddy Study system and show children how to keep records in folders, find and use forms, and perform all routines. Establish the routine structure of minilesson followed by application activity and ending in group share.	▸ Basic routines for community meeting, individual work ▸ Voice modulation appropriate for various contexts (from silent independent work to community meeting) ▸ Routines for Buddy Study system: *Choose, Write Build; Look, Say, Cover, Write, Check; Buddy Check; Making Connections; Buddy Test* ▸ Making Words ▸ Lotto: Words with Ending Consonant Clusters ▸ Word Search: Phonograms ▸ Go Fish: Words with Ending Consonant Clusters ▸ Make, Check, and Mark High Frequency Words ▸ Using a List Sheet ▸ Highlighting ▸ Using Words-to-Learn Lists ▸ Using a Word Study Notebook ▸ Using forms for Buddy Study activities	**LS 1** Recognizing Words with Consonant Clusters (Making Words) **LS 2** Identifying Words with Ending Consonant Clusters (Making Words) **SP 1** Recognizing Phonograms with Short Vowel Sounds (Word Search) **SP 2** Recognizing Word Patterns with Ending Consonant Clusters (Go Fish) **HF 1** Recognizing High Frequency Words (3 or More Letters) (Make, Check, Say) **WSA 1** Learning How to Learn Words: Buddy Study 1 (Choose, Write, Build, Mix, Fix, Mix) **WSA 2** Learning How to Learn Words: Buddy Study 2 (Look, Say, Cover, Write, Check) **WSA 3** Learning How to Learn Words: Buddy Study 3 (Buddy Check) **WSA 4** Learning How to Learn Words: Buddy Study 4 (Making Connections) **WSA 5** Learning How to Learn Words: Buddy Study 5 (Buddy Study Test)	▸ Perform basic classroom routines. ▸ Use materials as instructed. ▸ Use what they know about a word to solve it. ▸ Recognize and use word parts. ▸ Change a word to make a new word. ▸ Match words with ending consonant clusters. ▸ Recognize words with ending consonant clusters. ▸ Use phonograms with short vowel sounds to solve words. ▸ Perform the basic steps of the five-day word study system.

October

By the second month of school (late September or early October in most places), children should understand the schedule and know how to move quickly from one context to another. They should be able to efficiently use the routines of the five-day Buddy Study system. Continue to observe transitions and implementation of word study routines. You can have the class continue to implement the application activity at the same time right after the minilesson, or you can assign children to use the activity and Buddy Study routines as independent work during a longer period of reading or writing. Continue reading aloud to children and having them make personal poetry anthologies as part of the language/word study block.

Organization of Instruction: *Whole class and independent work as teacher circulates; some small-group work.*

Learning Contexts	New Routines to Teach	Suggested Lessons	Assessment—Students can:
Continue to work on the routines for language/word study, reading workshop, and writing workshop until they are firmly established and students are independent. Use whole-group contexts for minilessons and group share. Children work independently, with partners, or in small groups for the application activity. They work with a partner for the Buddy Study system activities. If materials are not being used correctly, back up and reteach the routines. If the routines of reading workshop are soundly established and students can choose books well and sustain reading for around forty-five minutes, you can begin working with some small groups for guided reading.	▸ Lotto: Words with Ending Consonant Digraphs ▸ Go Fish: Beginning and Ending Consonant Digraphs ▸ Concentration: High Frequency Words ▸ Blind Sort: Patterns with Long Vowel Sounds ▸ Crazy Eights: Phonograms with Double Vowels; Contractions ▸ Making Words: Compound Words ▸ Word Sorting: Compound Words ▸ Checkers: Syllables in Words with Double Consonants ▸ Using Three-Way Sort Cards ▸ Using Three-Way Sort Sheet	**LS 3** Recognizing Words with Ending Consonant Digraphs (Consonant Cluster Lotto) **LS 4** Recognizing Words with Beginning and Ending Consonant Digraphs (Go Fish) **LS 5** Recognizing and Using *y* as a Vowel Sound in Words (Follow the Path) **SP 3** Recognizing Word Patterns with Long Vowel Sounds (Blind Sort) **SP 4** Recognizing Phonograms with Double Vowels (Crazy Eights) **HF 2** Recognizing High Frequency Words 2 (with 4 or More Letters) (Concentration) **WM/V 1** Recognizing and Using Compound Words (Making Words) **WM/V 2** Working with Compound Words (Word Sorting) **WS 1** Summarizing Contractions (Crazy Eights) **WS 2** Recognizing Syllables in Words with Double Consonants (Checkers)	▸ Recognize words with beginning and ending consonant digraphs. ▸ Write and read high frequency words (3-4 letters). ▸ Recognize long vowel sound patterns in words. ▸ Recognize double vowel patterns in words. ▸ Identify, read, and write compound words. ▸ Read and write a variety of contractions. ▸ Identify syllables in words with double consonants.

Month-by-Month Planning Guide – November

By November, students should have settled into the schedule established for language/word study, reading workshop, and writing workshop. It will help to have word study at the same time every day if that is possible. You may want to work with small groups of children who are having difficulty with routines, pacing, and responsibility rather than reteaching the entire group. Continue to read aloud to children to enrich the language base for

word study. By now you will have created several charts that you want to display to remind students to use word study principles. It will help to have a particular place in the room to post the charts. Continue reading aloud to children and having them make personal poetry anthologies as part of the language/word study block.

Organization of Instruction: *Whole class, independent work, small groups.*

Learning Contexts	New Routines to Teach	Suggested Lessons	Assessment—Students can:
Continue to use whole-group contexts for minilessons and group share. Depending on the application activity, children may work individually, with a partner, or in small groups. You may choose to have all students engage in Buddy Study activities and application activities simultaneously. Or, students may rotate to word study center to do the application activity over several days during an independent work time. If they are taking too much time, you may want to have them practice using a timer. By now, students will be independent in reading and writing workshop. Identify some small groups of students who have similar needs and work with them in guided reading and writing.	▸ Connect: Words with *oo, ow, ea* ▸ Battle: Words with Short *o* ▸ Word Pairs: Word Patterns—Unique Vowel Sounds ▸ Blind Two-Way Sort: Word Patterns—Unique Vowel Sounds ▸ Words in Context: Homophones ▸ Open Word Sort ▸ Word Webs: Concept Words ▸ Synonyms Match ▸ Concentration: Antonyms ▸ Word Plot: Words with Open Syllables ▸ Taking Words Apart: Words with Closed Syllables ▸ Lotto: Syllables in Words with Silent *e* ▸ Rummy: Compound Words ▸ Using the Word Pairs Sheet ▸ Using Two-Way Sort Cards and Sheets ▸ Using the Word Web Sheet	**LS 6** Identifying Words with Different Vowel Sounds *(oo, ow, ea)* (Connect) **SP 5** Recognizing Word Patterns with the Short *o* Sound (Battle) **SP 6** Recognizing Word Patterns with Unique Vowel Sounds (Long /oo/) (Word Pairs) **SP 7** Recognizing Word Patterns with Unique Vowel Sounds (Short /oo/) (Blind Two-Way Sort) **WM/V 3** Exploring Homophones (Words in Context) **WM/V 4** Connecting Words (Open Word Sort) **WM/V 5** Connecting Concept Words (Word Maps) **WM/V 6** Recognizing and Using Synonyms (Synonyms Match) **WM/V 7** Recognizing and Using Antonyms (Antonyms Concentration) **WM/V 8** Synonyms and Sentences (Go Fish) **WS 3** Recognizing Words with Open Syllables (Word Plot) **WS 4** Recognizing Words with Closed Syllables (Taking Words Apart) **WS 5** Recognizing Syllables in Words with a Silent *e* Pattern (Syllable Lotto) **WS 6** Recognizing Parts in Compound Words (Compound Rummy)	▸ Read and write words that have unique vowel sounds *(oo, ow, ea)*. ▸ Recognize and use word patterns for short *o*. ▸ Recognize and distinguish between homophones. ▸ Make connections between words using meaning. ▸ Recognize and use synonyms and antonyms. ▸ Recognize and pronounce words with open and closed syllables. ▸ Take apart compound words and derive meaning by looking at the parts.

December

The basic framework of language/word study, reading workshop, and writing workshop should be automatic by now. Keep the schedule predictable and try not to allow holiday programming to disrupt routines too much. Discard or store charts that are no longer valuable references for students to use in word study, reading, or writing. You may want to keep one chart rack that you can quickly flip over to refer to previously used charts—reviewing the principle, connecting to current lessons and/or adding examples. Continue reading aloud to increase students' knowledge of texts and expand vocabulary. Keep a list of books you have shared so that the titles will be easy to recall as you need examples for reading workshop and writing workshop minilessons. These texts will also be sources of examples for word study. December is a good time to move poetry into the reading workshop or writing workshop time. Many teachers decide to have a two-hour "poetry workshop" every two weeks.

Organization of Instruction: *Whole class, independent work, small group.*

Learning Contexts

Continue to work on the routines for language/word study, reading workshop, and writing workshop until they are firmly established and students are independent. Use whole-group contexts for minilessons and group share. Children work independently, with partners, or in small groups for the application activity. They work with a partner for the Buddy Study system activities. If materials are not being used correctly, back up and reteach the routines. If the routines of reading workshop are soundly established and students can choose books well and sustain reading for around forty-five minutes, expand the time you spend working with small groups for guided reading.

New Routines to Teach

- Make, Write, and Read: Words with *oo, oi, oy, ow, aw, au*
- Crazy Eights: Words with Long Vowel Patterns
- Word Grid Game: Words with Double Consonants; High Frequency Words; Synonyms, Antonyms, Homophones
- Making Word Pairs: Word Patterns with Unique Vowel Sounds
- Connect: Words with Vowel Combinations
- Lotto: Synonyms and Antonyms
- Lotto: Homophones
- Three-Way Sort: Plurals
- Two-Way Sort: Plurals-Words ending in *y*
- Making Words: Plurals; Words ending in *f, fe,* or *lf*
- Concentration: Abbreviations
- Using the List Sheet
- Using the Word Pairs Sheet
- Using the Three-Way Sort Sheet
- Using the Two-Way Sort Cards and Sheets

Suggested Lessons

LS 7 Identifying Other Vowel Sounds *(oo, oi, oy, ow, aw, au)* (Make, Write, Read)

LS 8 Recognizing Long Vowel Patterns (Crazy Eights)

LS 9 Recognizing Double Consonants in Words (Word Grid Game)

SP 8 Recognizing Word Patterns with Unique Vowel Sounds (Making Word Pairs)

SP 9 Recognizing Word Patterns with Vowel Combinations (Connect)

HF 3 Recognizing High Frequency Words 3 (with 5 or More Letters) (Word Grid)

WM/V 9 Summary of Synonyms and Antonyms (Lotto)

WM/V 10 Making Decisions about Using Homophones (Homophone Lotto)

WM/V 11 Recognizing Homophones, Synonyms, and Antonyms (Word Grids)

WS 7 Forming Plurals of Words That Add *es* (Three-Way Sort)

WS 8 Forming Plurals with Words Ending in *y* (Two-Way Sort)

WS 9 Forming Plurals with Words Ending in *f, fe,* or *lf* (Making Words)

WS 10 Noticing and Using Abbreviations (Abbreviation Concentration)

Assessment—Students can:

- Read and write words with vowel sounds: *oo, oi, oy, ow, aw, au.*
- Represent long vowel patterns in spelling words.
- Recognize words with double consonants.
- Read and write words with vowel combinations.
- Make plurals for words by adding *s* or *es* and for words ending in *y, f, fe,* or *lf*.
- Use homophones correctly.
- Recognize and use synonyms and antonyms.
- Notice and use abbreviations.

Month-by-Month Planning Guide – January

Continue the schedule for the language/literacy framework. Have students add principles and examples to their Word Study Notebooks if you are using them. An important goal as the year goes on is to encourage students to recall important word study principles as they come up in reading and writing. Drawing examples across the framework will greatly increase students' ability to apply word study principles in the context of reading and writing continuous text. Students can also begin monitoring their own acquisition of high frequency words, highlighting or checking them off as they are learned. Use books you have read aloud for student's first experiences in literature study. In poetry workshop, students select and illustrate poems as well as writing in response to poetry.

Organization of Instruction: *Whole class, independent work, small group.*

Learning Contexts	New Routines to Teach	Suggested Lessons	Assessment—Students can:
Continue implementing all elements of the framework and work for increasing independence. By now students will be accustomed to varying activity between independent and guided reading. If you haven't already done so, begin to implement literature study. A Word Study Notebook can be used depending on students' experiences.	▸ Routines for literature discussion ▸ Crazy Eights: Words with Different Sounds for *c, g, th, ch* ▸ Two-Way Sort: Words with Silent Letters ▸ Lotto: High Frequency Words ▸ Blind Sort: Phonograms with Double Consonants ▸ Concentration: Words with Unique Vowel Sounds ▸ Four-Way Sort: Words with VC Pattern ▸ Three-Way Sort: VC*e* Patterns in Two-Syllable Words ▸ Sentence Pictures: Homographs ▸ Taking Words Apart: Multisyllable Words with Vowel Combinations ▸ Putting Words in Alphabetical Order ▸ Word Grid Game: Word Parts ▸ Using the Four-Box Sheet ▸ Using the Two-Way, Three-Way, and Four-Way Sort Cards and Sheets ▸ Using a Word Study Notebook	**LS 10** Recognizing Consonant Letters with Different Sounds (Crazy Eights) **LS 11** Noticing Silent Letters in Words (Two-Way Sort) **SP 10** Recognizing Phonograms with Double Consonants (Blind Sort) **SP 11** Noticing Word Patterns That Represent Unique Vowel Sounds (Concentration) **SP 12** Recognizing Words with VC Pattern (Four-Way Sort) **SP 13** Recognizing a Vowel Pattern (VC*e*) in Two-Syllable Words (Three-Way Sort) **HF 4** Recognizing High Frequency Words 4 (High Frequency Word Lotto) **WM/V 12** Recognizing Homographs (Sentence Pictures) **WS 11** Recognizing Syllables in Words with Vowel Combinations (Taking Words Apart) **WS 12** Noticing and Using the Past Tense with *ed* (Trumps) **WS 13** Forming New Words by Adding *-er* (Two-Way Sort) **WSA 6** Using Alphabetical Order (List Sheet) **WSA 7** Using Word Parts to Solve Words (Word Grid Game)	▸ Recognize and write words with a wide range of consonant sounds. ▸ Use phonograms with double consonants to read and write words. ▸ Read and write words with patterns VC and VCe in two-syllable words. ▸ Recognize and use homographs in reading and writing. ▸ Read and write one- and two-syllable words that have vowel combinations. ▸ Form past tense using *ed*. ▸ Write words by adding *-er* to base word. ▸ Put a list of words in alphabetical order. ▸ Take words apart to solve them while reading continuous text.

February

By now the schedule and routines will be so firmly established that you will not need to spend much time on giving directions. Continue to work for efficiency. Continue to read aloud to provide resources for minilessons in reading and writing workshop as well as in word study. In reading workshop, students will be participating in independent reading every day.

Work out the schedule over several weeks to provide guided reading and literature discussion. Continue poetry workshop every two or three weeks in the place of reading and writing workshop. Students select and illustrate poems and may write their own poems on the same topics or in the same style as those they like.

Organization of Instruction: *Whole class, independent work, small group.*

Learning Contexts	New Routines to Teach	Suggested Lessons	Assessment—Students can:
Continue to add to the charts on display in the classroom, storing (or letting students take home) those that are no longer needed. Students can record principles and examples in their Word Study Notebooks. Work for increased independence as they monitor their own progress in learning high frequency words from the list of 500. Prompt them to recall principles of word study as they try to solve words in writing and reading workshop. As necessary, revisit principles in the word study component of guided reading.	▸ Two-Way Sort: Words with Open Syllables; Words with Closed Syllables ▸ Word Search: Words with *r*-Influenced Vowels ▸ Word Grid Game: Words with Double Consonants ▸ Follow the Path: Words with *r*-Influenced Vowels ▸ Word Sort: Meaning ▸ Checkers: Two Syllable Words- Vowel + *r* ▸ Syllable Race: Recognizing Syllables in Words ▸ Word Ladders: Making Connections between Words ▸ Using the Two-Way and Three-Way Sort Cards and Sheets ▸ Using the Word Grid Sheet ▸ Using the List Sheet ▸ Using the Word Pairs Sheet ▸ Using the Word Ladders Sheet	**LS 12** Taking Apart Words with Open Syllables (Two-Way Sort) **LS 13** Taking Apart Words with Closed Syllables (Two-Way Sort) **LS 14** Recognizing Words with *r*- Influenced Vowel Sounds (Word Search) **SP 14** Recognizing Word Patterns with Double Consonants (Word Grid Game) **SP 15** Recognizing Word Patterns with *r*-Influenced Vowels (Follow the Path) **WM/V 13** Connecting Words by Meaning (Word Sorting) **WS 14** Using Compound Word Parts to Understand Meanings (Battle) **WS 15** Reading Two-Syllable Words with a Vowel and *r* (Checkers) **WSA 8** Recognizing and Using Syllables (Syllable Race) **WSA 9** Making Connections between Words (Word Ladders)	▸ Take words apart by syllables. ▸ Read and write words that have *r*-influenced vowels. ▸ Put words together that have related meanings. ▸ Identify syllables in words. ▸ Write new words that are connected by familiar parts of a word.

Month-by-Month Planning Guide – March

March is often a time of district or state testing; some districts have a spring vacation in this month. In spite of these circumstances, work for as little disruption as possible in the classroom routines. Be sure to continue reading aloud to students to provide an essential foundation for all of the other components of the framework. Students may want to take inventory of the number of words they can spell on the 500 high frequency words list and set some goals for the end of the year. Continue to make links between word study and their reading and writing of continuous text.

Organization of Instruction: *Whole class, independent work, small group.*

Learning Contexts	New Routines to Teach	Suggested Lessons	Assessment—Students can:
Use guided reading to help students take on more difficult texts and expand their knowledge of genres that are not as familiar to them. Encourage students to notice and discuss examples of word study principles in guided reading. Two lessons refer to cursive handwriting and computer keyboarding. (Depending on your school's curriculum, you may have used one or both of these lessons earlier in the year. If so, continue to have students practice.)	▸ Follow the Path: Words with Silent Letters ▸ Make, Write, Read: Words with /k/—c, k, ke, ck, gue ▸ Capital Detectives ▸ Handwriting Notebook ▸ Keyboard Practice ▸ Word Inventory ▸ Making Words and Sentences: Words with /a/ Pattern ▸ Verb Search: Action Words ▸ Read Around the Room: Action Words; Describing Words ▸ Adjective Search: Describing Words ▸ Using the List Sheet ▸ Using a Word Study Notebook ▸ Using the Word and Sentence Sheet ▸ Using the Words Around the Room Sheet	**LS 15** Identifying Silent Letters in Words (Follow the Path) **LS 16** Recognizing Words with the Final *k* Sound *(c, k, ke, ck, que)* (Make, Write, Read) **LS 17** Learning about Words with Capital Letters (Capital Detective Lotto) **LS 18** Learning Cursive Handwriting (Handwriting Notebook) **LS 19** Learning Effective Keyboarding for the Computer (Keyboard Practice) **SP 16** Recognizing Words with the /a/ Pattern (Making Words and Sentences) **HF 5** Checking Your Knowledge of High Frequency Words (Word Inventory) **WM/V 14** Learning about Action Words (Verb Search) **WM/V 15** Recognizing and Using Action Words (Read Around the Room) **WM/V 16** Learning about Describing Words (Adjective Search) **WM/V 17** Recognizing and Using Describing Words (Read Around the Room)	▸ Read and write words with silent letters. ▸ Read and write words with a variety of spellings for /k/. ▸ Identify words that should be capitalized. ▸ Write accurately in cursive handwriting. ▸ Use efficient movements to write in cursive. ▸ Use efficient keyboarding on the computer. ▸ Read and write words with various spellings for /a/. ▸ Identify verbs. ▸ Identify adjectives.

April

Students continue to participate in all aspects of the language/literacy framework. By now, the work should be efficient, with children showing independence as well as a strong sense of community. It is a good time to introduce some new books for the classroom library to help students develop reading interests that they can take into summer. Have them begin to reflect on their progress over the year as readers, writers, and spellers.

Organization of Instruction: *Whole class, independent work, small groups.*

Learning Contexts	New Routines to Teach	Suggested Lessons	Assessment—Students can:
Use assessment to determine which students need some small-group work in word study to solidify their understanding of principles that should be in place by the end of third grade. Many of the lessons in the last two months cover advanced principles that students will probably meet again in grade four. Set priorities and goals for the end of the year.	▶ Go Fish: High Frequency Words; Frequently Appearing Syllables in Words ▶ Five-Way Sort: Syllables with Short Vowel Patterns in Multisyllable Words ▶ Noun Search ▶ Three-Way Sort: Nouns; Plurals for Words Ending in *o* ▶ Word Maps ▶ Lotto: Plurals ▶ Connect: Syllables in Multisyllable Words ▶ Guide Word Sort: Dictionary Skills ▶ Word Race ▶ Using a Word Study Notebook ▶ Using Three-Way and Five-Way Sort Cards and Sheets ▶ Using the Word Map Sheet	**SP 17** Recognizing Frequently Appearing Syllables in Word Patterns (Go Fish) **HF 6** Connecting High Frequency Words (Go Fish) **WM/V 18** Learning about Nouns—Words for People, Places, Things (Noun Search) **WM/V 19** Learning about Nouns, Describing Words, Action Words (Three-Way Sort) **WM/V 20** Exploring Words (Word Maps) **WS 16** Forming Plurals for Words Ending in *o* (Four-Way Sort) **WS 17** Forming Plurals: Summary (Plural Lotto) **WS 18** Identifying Syllables in Multisyllable Words (Connect) **WSA 10** Using Guide Words in a Dictionary (Guide Word Sort) **WSA 11** Using What Is Known to Solve Words (Word Race)	▶ Read and connect a wide range of high frequency words. ▶ Recognize and connect syllables that appear frequently in word patterns. ▶ Take apart multisyllable words while reading. ▶ Write multisyllable words by breaking them into parts and noticing patterns. ▶ Read and write the full range of plural forms. ▶ Use guide words to locate words quickly in a dictionary. ▶ Solve words by noticing and using anything known about the word.

Month-by-Month Planning Guide – May/June

In most places, the months of May and June mark the end of the school year and students begin a long summer holiday. You may want to engage your students in reflection on their accomplishments and progress during the year. For example, they can look at the number of high frequency words they have learned to spell or go back to principles they have learned. They can examine the pieces of writing they have completed as well as the list of books read. At the same time, be sure that they understand they will continue the basic classroom routine until the end of school and that they should be moving forward in their work across that time.

Organization of Instruction: *Whole class, independent work, small groups.*

Learning Contexts	New Routines to Teach	Suggested Lessons	Assessment—Students can:
Continue whole group, individual and small group instruction. The more you can maintain the regular schedule, the easier it will be for students to remain focused. Perform final assessments for the year and conduct your own evaluation of the degree of learning about word structure, spelling, and vocabulary during the year. If possible, provide Writer's Notebooks, books, journals, or magazines for students to use in the summer.	► Word Grid Game: Multisyllable Words with Long Vowel Patterns ► Making Comparisons: Metaphors and Similes ► Matching Words: Blended Words ► Sorting Words: Word Origin ► Labeling: Words That Mimic Sounds ► Trumps: Syllables in Multisyllable Words ► Making words: Words with *-er, -est*; Words with Prefixes (*un-, re-*) ► Follow the Path: Words with Prefixes (*un-, re-*) ► Word Entry Search: Dictionary Skills ► Learning New Words from Reading ► Using Word Grid Sheets ► Using a Two-Column Sheet	**WM/V 21** Recognizing and Using Metaphors and Similes (Making Comparisons) **WM/V 22** Recognizing and Using Blended Words (Matching Words) **WM/V 23** Recognizing and Using Words that Mimic Real Sounds (Labeling) **WS 19** Noticing Syllables in Multisyllable Words (Trumps) **WS 20** Forming Comparisons with *-er, -est* (Making Words) **WS 21** Recognizing Words with a Prefix *(un-)* (Making Words) **WS 22** Recognizing Words with a Prefix *(re-)* (Follow the Path) **WSA 12** Using a Dictionary to Learn Word Meaning (Word Entry Search) **WSA 13** Expanding Vocabulary through Reading Texts (Learning New Words from Reading)	► Recognize and understand easy metaphors and similes. ► Recognize and read blended words. ► Efficiently find words in a dictionary and gather and report information about a word. ► Read and write words with prefixes *re-* and *un-*. ► Make words by adding *-er* and *-est* to base. ► Demonstrate identifying and understanding new vocabulary while reading a text.

The Word Study Continuum:
Systematic Word Study, Grades 2–8

The Word Study Continuum is the key to the minilessons. Over the course of the school year, you will use it, in concert with the Month-by-Month Planning Guide, the Lesson Selection Map, and continuous assessment, to inform your work. The Continuum comprises nine categories of learning that your students need to develop over time; it is a comprehensive picture of linguistic knowledge. Although there are easier and more complex concepts within each category, we are not suggesting that there is a rigid sequence. Instead, we want to help children develop their abilities along a broad front, often using and learning about several different kinds of information simultaneously.

While instruction and assessment are embedded within classroom activities, both are systematic. Indeed, every aspect of the phonics mimilessons is systematic, including the observation of children, collection of data on what children know about letters, sounds, and words, and the teacher's selection of lessons to fit the specific instructional needs of individual children. Teaching is efficient and systematic when lessons are carefully selected and sequenced to provide what children need to learn next.

The shaded area of the Continuum performs two important functions. First, it serves as a guide for introducing principles to children; second, it helps you understand what principles you can expect your students to fully control and when. You'll notice that the shaded areas cross grade levels. These shaded areas provide broad indicators of expected achievement; however, learning rate and time will vary with individual children as well as for different groups. In general, at grade level (the earliest period of time indicated by shading), you can begin to assess children's knowledge of a specific principle and refer to the principle during reading and writing activities. Additionally, you will select specific lessons that help them expand their knowledge of the chosen principle. At the latest time indicated by shading, take steps to ensure that children fully understand and can use the principle. You may need to increase time spent on lessons related to the principle or work with small groups of children who are still having difficulty.

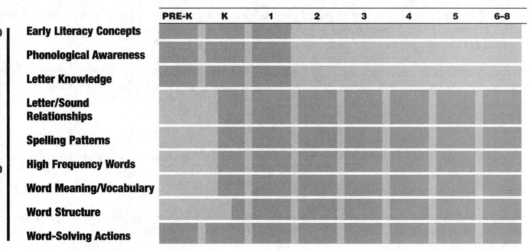

Letter/Sound Relationships

The sounds of oral language are related in both simple and complex ways to the twenty-six letters of the alphabet. Learning the connections between letters and sounds is basic to understanding written language. Children first learn simple relationships that are regular in that one phoneme is connected to one grapheme, or letter. But sounds are also connected to letter clusters, which are groups of letters that appear often together (for example, *cr, str, st, bl, fr*), in which you hear each of the associated sounds of the letters; and consonant digraphs *(sh, ch)*, in which you hear only one sound. Vowels may also appear in combinations *(ea, oa)* in which you usually hear the first vowel *(ai)* or you hear a completely different sound *(ou)*. Children learn to look for and recognize these letter combinations as units, which makes their word solving more efficient. It is important to remember that children will be able to hear and connect the easy-to-identify consonants and vowels early and progress to the harder-to-identify and more difficult letter/sound relationships— for example, letter clusters with two and three letters and those that have more than one sound. You will want to connect initial consonant cluster sounds to the Consonant Cluster Linking Chart (see *Teaching Resources*). It is not necessary to teach every cluster as a separate lesson. We also provide lessons for cursive writing and keyboarding for the computer.

Letter/Sound Relationships

Consonants

Principle	Explanation of Principle
	GRADE 2 · GRADE 3 · GRADE 4 · GRADE 5 · GRADES 6–8 (early/mid/late)
Recognizing and using ending consonant sounds and the letters that represent them: *b, m, t, d g, n, p, f, l, r, s, z, ff, ss, ll, tt, ck*	" You can hear sounds at the end of a word. " " You can match letters and sounds at the end of a word. " " When you see the letter at the end of a word, you can make the sound. " " When you know the sound, you can find the letter. " " You can find a word by saying it and thinking about the ending sound. "
Recognizing similar ending consonant sounds and the letters that represent them	" Words can end with the same sound and letter [*duck, book*]. "
Recognizing and using letters that represent two or more consonant sounds at the beginning of a word: *c, g, th, ch*	" Some consonants or consonant clusters stand for two or more different sounds [*car, city; get, gym; think, they; chair, chorus, chateau*]. "
Recognizing and using consonant clusters that blend two or three consonant sounds [onsets]: *bl, cl, fl, pl, pr, br, dr, gr, tr, cr, fr, gl, sl, sn, sp, st, sw, sc, sk, sm, scr, squ, str, thr, spr, spl, shr, sch, tw*	" A group of two or three consonants is a consonant cluster. " " You can usually hear each sound in a consonant cluster. "
Recognizing and using consonant sounds represented by consonant digraphs: *sh, ch, th, ph* (at beginning of word), *wh*	" Some clusters of consonants stand for one sound that is different from either of the letters. They are called *consonant digraphs*. " " You can hear the sound of a consonant digraph at the beginning or ending of a word. "
Recognizing and using middle consonant sounds sometimes represented by double letters: *bb, cc, dd, ff, ll, mm, pp, rr, ss, tt, zz*	" Sometimes double consonant letters stand for a consonant sound in the middle of a word [*rubber, arrive, coffee, lesson*]. "
	GRADE 2 · GRADE 3 · GRADE 4 · GRADE 5 · GRADES 6–8 (early/mid/late)

©2004 by Irene C. Fountas and Gay Su Pinnell from *Word Study Lessons*

Letter/Sound Relationships, continued

Principle	Explanation of Principle	GRADE 2 early/mid/late	GRADE 3 early/mid/late	GRADE 4 early/mid/late	GRADE 5 early/mid/late	GRADES 6–8

Consonants

Recognizing and using letters that represent consonant clusters [blends] at the end of a word: *ct, ft, ld, lt, mp, nd, pt, rd, rk, sk, sp, st, lf, nt*
" Some words have consonant clusters at the end. "
" You can hear each sound in a consonant cluster at the end of a word. "

Recognizing and using consonant letters that represent no sound: *lamb, know, pick, wrap, gnome, scene, sign, rhyme, khaki, calm, island, listen*
" Some words have consonant letters that are silent [*wrap, gnome, know, climb, honor, who*]. "

Recognizing and using letters that represent consonant digraphs at the end of a word: (making one sound): *sh, th, ch, ck, tch, dge, ng, ph, gh*
" Some words have consonant clusters at the end that make only one sound. "

Recognizing and using letters that represent less frequent consonant digraph sounds at the beginning or ending of a word (making one sound): *gh, ph, (rough, phone, graph)*
" Consonant digraphs stand for one sound that is different from either of the letters. "
" You can hear the sound of a consonant digraph at the beginning or end of a word. "

Understanding that some consonant sounds can be represented by several different letters or letter clusters: final *k* sound: *picnic, unique, make, kayak, duck;* **final *f* sound:** *stiff, cough*
" Some consonant sounds are represented by several different letters or letter clusters. "

Understanding that some consonant letters represent several different sounds: *ch*: *cheese, school, machine, choir, yacht*
" Some consonant letters represent more than one sound. "

Vowels

Hearing and identifying short vowel sounds in words and the letters that represent them
" In some words, *a* sounds like the *a* in *apple* and *can*. "
" In some words, *e* sounds like the *e* in *egg* and *net*. "
" In some words, *i* sounds like the *i* in *igloo* and *sit*. "
" In some words, *o* sounds like the *o* in *octopus* and *hot*. "
" In some words, *u* sounds like the *u* in *umbrella* and *cup*. "

Recognizing and using short vowel sounds at the beginning of words: *at, apple, Andrew*
" Some words have one vowel at the beginning [*apple, at, Andrew*]. "
" The sound of the vowel is *short*. "

Recognizing and using short vowels in the middle of words [CVC]: *hat, bed*
" Some words have one vowel between two consonants [*hat, bed*] and the sound of the vowel is *short*. "

Hearing and identifying long vowel sounds in words and the letters that represent them
" In some words, *a* sounds like the *a* in *name* and *came*. "
" In some words, e sounds like the *e* in *eat* and *seat*. "
" In some words, *i* sounds like the *i* in *ice* and *kite*. "
" In some words, *o* sounds like the *o* in *go* and *boat*. "
" In some words, *u* sounds like the *u* in *use* and *cute*. "

Recognizing and using long vowel sounds in words
" You can hear and say the vowel in words like *make, pail, day*. "
" You can hear and say the vowel in words like *eat, meat, see*. "
" You can hear and say the vowel in words like *I, ice, ride*. "
" You can hear and say the vowel in words like *go, grow, boat*. "
" You can hear and say the vowel in words like *use, cute, huge*. "

early	mid	late	early	mid	late	early	mid	late	early	mid	late		
GRADE 2			GRADE 3			GRADE 4			GRADE 5			GRADES 6–8	

LETTER/SOUND RELATIONSHIPS / LS

Vowels

Principle	Explanation of Principle
Recognizing and using vowels in words with silent e (CVCe): make, take, home A: make, ate, take, came, same, base [Exceptions: are, dance] E: Pete, breeze [Exception: edge] I: bite, bike, five, ice, slime, shine [Exceptions: mince, fringe which have a CVCCe pattern] O: rode, hole, joke [Exceptions: come, some, goose] U: use, cube, cute, fume [Exceptions: judge, nurse]	" Some words end in an e that is silent and the vowel usually has a long sound (sounds like its name). "
Contrasting long and short vowel sounds in words	" A vowel can have a sound like its name [a as in make] and it is called a long vowel sound. " " A vowel can have a sound that is different from its name [a as in apple] and it is called a short vowel sound. "
Recognizing and using y as a vowel sound: happy, family, my, sky, monkey, key	" Y is a letter that sometimes makes a vowel sound. " " Y sounds like /e/ on the end of words like happy, funny, family, monkey, key. " " Y sounds like /i/ in words like my, sky, by. "
Recognizing and using letter combinations that represent long vowel sounds: ai, ay, ee, ea, oa, oe, ow, ue, ui, ew: chair, play, meet, near, roar, toe, blow, blue, suit, new	" Some vowels go together in words and make one sound. " " When there are two vowels [ai, ay, ee, ea, oe, oa, ow, ui, ue, ew], they usually make the sound of the name of the first vowel or a long vowel sound [rain, day, feet, meat, toe, boat, snow, suit, new]. "
Recognizing and using letter combinations that represent other vowel sounds: oo as in moon, look; oi as in oil; oy as in boy; ou as in house; ow as in cow; aw as in paw; ay as in always; au as in autumn	" Some letters go together and make other vowel sounds [autumn, moon, look, boy, oil, cow, house, paw]. "
Recognizing that letter combinations may represent two different vowel sounds: oo–moon, look; ow–snow, cow; ea–bear, meat, break	" Two letters that go together can stand for different sounds in different words [moon, look, snow, cow, meat, break.]"
Recognizing and using vowel sounds in open syllables: [CV]: ho-tel	" Some syllables have a consonant followed by a vowel. " " The sound of the vowel is long [ho-tel, Pe-ter, lo-cal]. " " The first or second syllable can be stressed. "
Recognizing and using vowel sounds in closed syllables: [CVC]: lem-on	" Some syllables have one vowel that is between two consonants. " " The sound of the vowel is short [lem-on; cab-in]. " " The first syllable is stressed. "
Recognizing and using vowel sounds with r: car, first, hurt, her, corn, floor, world, near	" When vowels are with r in words, you blend the vowel sound with r [car, her, fir, corn, hurt, nerve, door, world, near]. "

Letter/Sound Representation

Principle	Explanation of Principle
Learning about words with capital letters	" You use capital letters at the beginning of some words to show the beginning of a sentence or to show a proper noun. "
Forming cursive letters correctly, efficiently, and fluently	" You can write letters smoothly and efficiently in cursive form. "
Using the computer keyboard	" You can use efficient finger movements to type words on the computer. "

Grade columns header/footer:

GRADE 2			GRADE 3			GRADE 4			GRADE 5			GRADES 6–8		
early	mid	late	early	mid	late	early	mid	late	early	mid	late			

Spelling Patterns

One way to look at spelling patterns is to examine the way simple words and syllables are put together. Here we include the consonant-vowel-consonant (CVC) pattern in which the vowel often has a short, or terse, sound; the consonant-vowel-consonant-silent *e* (CVC*e*) pattern in which the vowel usually has a long, or lax, sound; and the consonant-vowel-vowel-consonant (CVVC) pattern in which the vowel combination may have either one or two sounds.

Phonograms are spelling patterns that represent the sounds of *rimes* (last parts of words). They are sometimes called *word families.* You will not need to teach children the technical word *phonogram*, although you may want to use *pattern* or *word part.* A phonogram is the same as a rime, or vowel-bearing part of a word or syllable. We have included a large list of phonograms that will be useful to children in reading or writing, but you will not need to teach every phonogram separately. Once children understand that there are patterns and learn how to look for patterns, they will quickly discover more for themselves.

Knowing spelling patterns helps children notice and use larger parts of words, thus making word solving faster and more efficient. Patterns are also helpful to children in writing words because they will quickly write down the patterns rather than laboriously work with individual sounds and letters. Finally, knowing to look for patterns and remembering them help children make the connections between words that make word solving easier. In column one we list a wide range of phonograms. The thirty-seven most common phonograms are marked with an asterisk.

Spelling Patterns

Phonogram Patterns

Principle	Explanation of Principle
	GRADE 2 (early, mid, late) · GRADE 3 (early, mid, late) · GRADE 4 (early, mid, late) · GRADE 5 (early, mid, late) · GRADES 6–8
Recognizing and using simple phonograms with a VC pattern (easiest): -ad, -ag, -an*, -am, -at*, -ed, -en, -et, -ig, -in*, -it*, -og, -op*, -ot, -ut	" You can look at the pattern (part) you know to help you read a word. " " You can use the pattern (part) you know to help you write a word. " " You can make new words by putting a letter or letter cluster before the word part or pattern. "
Recognizing and using more difficult phonograms with a VC pattern: -ab, -ap*, - ar, -aw*, -ay*, -ed, -eg, -em, -en, -ib, -ip*, -ix, -ob, -od, -ow (blow), -ow (cow), -ug*, -um, -un	" You can look at the pattern (part) you know to help you read a word. " " You can use the pattern (part) you know to help you write a word. " " You can make new words by putting a letter or letter cluster before the word part or pattern. "
Recognizing and using phonograms that end with double letters (VCC): -all*, -ell*, -ill*, oll, -uff	" Some words have double consonants at the end. The sound of the vowel is usually short. "
Recognizing and using phonograms with double vowels (VVC): -eed, -eek, -eel, -een, -eem, -eep, -eer, -eet, -ood, -ook, -ool, -oom, -oon	" Some words have double vowels followed by a consonant. " " Sometimes vowels sound like their name (long sound). " " Sometimes vowels stand for other sounds. "
Recognizing and using phonograms with a vowel-consonant-silent *e* (VCe) pattern: -ade, -ace, -age, -ake*, -ale*, -ame*, -ane, -ape, -ate*, -ice*, -ide*, -ike, -ile, -ime, -ine*, -ite, -ive, -obe, oke*, -ope, -ore	" Some words have a vowel, a consonant, and a silent *e.* The vowel sound is usually the name of the vowel [*a* in *make, e* in *Pete, i* in *ride, o* in *rode, u* in *cute*]. "

GRADE 2 (early, mid, late) · GRADE 3 (early, mid, late) · GRADE 4 (early, mid, late) · GRADE 5 (early, mid, late) · GRADES 6–8

* Indicates most common phonograms.

Spelling Patterns, continued

Principle

Explanation of Principle

Phonogram Patterns

Recognizing and using phonograms with ending consonant clusters (VCC): ack*, -act, -alk; - amp, - and, - ank*, -ant, -ard, -art, -ark, -arm, -ash*, -ask, -ath, -eck, -elt, -elp, -end, -ent, -esh, -est*, -ick*, -igh, -ift, -ing*, -ink*, -ish, -ock*, -old, -ong, -uck*, -ump*, -ung, -unk*, -ush

" Some words have patterns that end with consonant clusters [*mask, lump*]. "

Recognizing and using phonograms with vowel combinations (VVC): -aid, -ail*, -ain*, -air, -ait, -ay*, -aw, -ea, -ead, -eak, -eam, -ean, -eap, -ear, -eat*, -oad, -oak

" Some words have two vowels together (vowel combinations). The vowel sound is usually the name of the first vowel [*stream, road*]. "

Sound to Letter Patterns in Single-Syllable Words

Recognizing and using phonogram patterns with a short vowel sound in single-syllable words: -at, -an, -am, -ad, -ag, -ap, -ack; -ed, -ell, -en, -et, -end, -ent, -est; -it, -in, -ill, -id, -ig, -ing, -ip, -ick, -ish; -op, -ot, -ock, -ug, -un, -ut, -up, -ub, -ump, -unk, -us(s), -ust, -uck

" Some words have a short vowel pattern. You can hear the short vowel sound [*man, best, pick, not, rust*]. "

Recognizing and using phonogram patterns with a long vowel sound in single-syllable words: -ake, -ame, -ate, -ave, -ade, -ace, -age, -ale, -ain, -ane, -ay; -e, -ee, -ea, -ey, -eep, -een, -eet, -eal, -ead, -eam; -ew, -ie, -igh, -ight, -ike, -ide, -ime, -yme, -ine, -ice, -ile, -ite, -ire, -y; -o, -oe, -ow, -oat, -oad, -ole, -old, -oak, -ose, -one; -ule, -use, -uge, -ute.

" Some words have a long vowel pattern. You can hear the long vowel sound [*make, green, pie, coat, few*]. "

Recognizing and using phonogram patterns with vowels and *r* in single-syllable words: -ar, -ark, -air, -are, -arm, -art, -ear, -eart, -er, -ear, -erd, -earn, -eard, -ird, -ir, -or, -ore, -ord, -oor, -our, -orn, -ur, -urse, -urn

" Some words have a vowel pattern with one or two vowels and *r*. "
" When vowels are with *r* in words, you usually blend the sound with *r* [*nurse, third*]. "

Recognizing and using phonogram patterns with the /aw/ sound (as in *saw*) in single-syllable words: -all, -aw, -alk, -aught, -ought, -ost; -ong

" Some words have patterns with vowels that make the /aw/ sound as in *saw*. "
" Several patterns of letters can stand for the sound [*wall, paw, taught, cost*]. "

Recognizing and using phonogram patterns with the /ū/ sound (as in *moon*) in single-syllable words: -oo, -oon, -une; -ew, -ue, -oot, -uit; -ool, -ule; -oom, -oup

" Some words have patterns with vowels that make the /oo/ sound as in *moon*. "
" Several patterns of letters can stand for the long /u/ sound [*tune, suit, soup*]. "

Recognizing and using phonogram patterns with the /oo/ sound (as in *book*) in single-syllable words: -ook, -ood, -ould; -ull, ush

" Some words have patterns with vowels that make the /oo/ sound as in *book*. "
" Several patterns of letters can stand for the sound [*book, could*]. "

Recognizing and using phonogram patterns with the /ow/ sound (as in *cow*) in single-syllable words: -ow; -own; -ound; -ow, -owd; -out, -outh, -our, -ouse

" Some words have patterns with vowels that make the /ow/ sound as in *cow*. "
" Several patterns of letters can stand for the sound [*clown, crowd, hour, mouth*]. "

Spelling Patterns, continued

Sound to Letter Patterns in Multisyllable Words   Sound to Letter Patterns in Single-Syllable Words

Principle

Explanation of Principle

	GRADE 2			GRADE 3			GRADE 4			GRADE 5			GRADES 6–8		
	early	mid	late	early	mid	late	early	mid	late	early	mid	late			

Recognizing and using phonogram patterns with the /oy/ sound in single-syllable words: *-oy; -oil, -oin, -oice, -oise*

" Some words have patterns with vowels that make the /oy/ sound as in *boy*. "
" Several patterns of letters can stand for the sound [*coin, voice, noise*]. "

Recognizing and using more difficult phonogram patterns in single-syllable words (VVCC, VVCe, VCCe, VCCC, VVCCC): *-aint, -aise, -ance, -anch, -arge, -aste, -atch, -each, -ealth, -east, -eath, eave, -edge, -eech, -eeze, -ench, -ight*, -itch, -ooth, -ouch, -ound, -udge, -unch, -aight, -eight,*

" Some words have parts (patterns) that are the same. "
" You can find patterns (parts) that are the same in many words. "
" You can use the pattern you know to help you read (or write) a word. "

Understanding that some words have double consonants in the pattern: *coffee, address, success, accident, mattress, occasion*

" Some words have double consonant letters in the patterns. "

Noticing and using a frequently appearing syllable pattern in multisyllable words: /a/ *alone*

" You see some patterns often in multisyllable words. "
" You see *a* at the beginning of some words and it sounds like the *a* in *alone*. "

Noticing and using frequently appearing syllable patterns in multisyllable words: *-en — enter; o — ago; -er — other; -ar — partner; -at — batter; -it — bitten; -in-winter; -is(s) — whisper; -un-sunny; -be-begin; re-repeat; -or — border; -a-bacon; -y — candy; -ey — monkey; -ble — trouble; -i — pilot; -ur — burden; -um — humble; -ic(k) — chicken; -et — better; -im — simple*

" You see some patterns often in multisyllable words. "
" You can look for the pattern you know to help you read a word. "
" You can think about the pattern you know to help you spell a word. "

Noticing and using short vowel patterns that appear in multisyllable words (other than most frequent): *-ab — absent; -ad — address; -ag — magnet; -age — garbage; -ang — anger; -am — hammer; -an — handle; -ant — gigantic; -ap — happen; -ent — center; - -el(l) — yellow; -ep — pepper; -es — estimate; -ev — seven; -id — middle; -ig — figure; -il(l) — familiar; -ob — hobby or robot; -oc(k) — October; -od — body; -ol — follow; -om — complete; -on — honest; -op — opportunity; -ot — bottom; -ub — rubber; -uc(k) — lucky; -ud — puddle; -uf — muffin; -ug — ugly; -up — puppy; -um — humble; -us — customer; -ut — butter; -uz — puzzle*

" You see short vowel patterns in multisyllable words. "
" Looking for the pattern you know helps you read the word. "
" Thinking about the pattern you know helps you spell the word. "

early	mid	late	early	mid	late	early	mid	late	early	mid	late			
GRADE 2			GRADE 3			GRADE 4			GRADE 5			GRADES 6–8		

SP
SPELLING PATTERNS

©2004 by Irene C. Fountas and Gay Su Pinnell from *Word Study Lessons*

Sound-to-Letter Patterns in Multisyllable Words

Principle	Explanation of Principle

	GRADE 2			GRADE 3			GRADE 4			GRADE 5			GRADES 6–8		

| | early | mid | late | early | mid | late | early | mid | late | early | mid | late | | | |

Noticing and using long vowel patterns that appear in multisyllable words: *-e – beginning; -ee – agree; -ea – reason; -ide – decide; -ire – entirely; -ise – revise; -ive – survive; -ize – realize; -ade – lemonade; -aid – braided; -ail – railroad; -ale – female; -ain – painter; -ate – crater; -ope – antelope; -one – telephone; -oke – spoken; -u – tutor; -ture – future*

" You can see long vowel patterns in multisyllable words. "
" Looking for the pattern you know helps you read and spell the word. "

Noticing and using other vowel patterns that appear in multisyllable words (easier): *-al – always; -au – author; -aw – awfully; -ea – weather; -i – sillier*

" You can see many vowel patterns in multisyllable words. "
" Looking for the pattern you know helps you read and spell the word. "

Noticing and using other vowel patterns that appear in multisyllable words (harder): *-i-e – police; -tion – attention; -sion – tension; -y – reply; -oi – noisy; -oy – enjoy; -ou – about; -ow – power; -oo – booster; -ove – remove; -u – tuna; -ook – looking; -oot – football; -ood – woodpile; -ul(l) – grateful*

" You can see many vowel patterns in multisyllable words. "
" Looking for the pattern you know helps you read and spell the word. "

| | early | mid | late | early | mid | late | early | mid | late | early | mid | late | | | |

	GRADE 2			GRADE 3			GRADE 4			GRADE 5			GRADES 6–8		

High Frequency Words

A core of known high frequency words is a valuable resource as students build processing strategies for reading and writing. Young children notice words that appear frequently in the simple texts they read; eventually, their recognition of these words becomes automatic. In this way, their reading becomes more efficient, enabling them to decode words using phonics as well as the meaning in the text. These words are powerful examples that help them grasp that a word is always written the same way. They can use known high frequency words to check on the accuracy of their reading and as resources for solving other words (for example, *this* starts like *the*). In general, students learn the simpler words earlier and in the process develop efficient systems for learning words. They continuously add to the core of high frequency words they know as they move to late primary and early intermediate grades. Lessons on high frequency words help them look more carefully at words and develop more efficient systems for word recognition.

High Frequency Words

Principle	Explanation of Principle
	GRADE 2 / GRADE 3 / GRADE 4 / GRADE 5 / GRADES 6–8 (early mid late)
Locating and reading high frequency words in continuous text	" When you know a word, you can read it every time you see it. " " You can find a word by knowing how it looks. "
Recognizing and using high frequency words with three or more letters	" You see some words many times when you read. " " Some have three or more letters [*the, and, but, she, like, come, this*]. " " Words you see a lot are important because they help you read and write. "
Recognizing and using high frequency words with five or more letters	" You see some words many times when you read. " " Some have five or more letters [*would, could, where, there, which*]. " " Words you see a lot are important because they help you read and write. "
Noticing patterns and categorizing high frequency words to assist in learning them quickly	" You can notice patterns in high frequency words. " " You can make connections among high frequency words to help you learn them. "
Developing self-monitoring strategies for acquiring a large core of high frequency words	" You can add to the number of high frequency words you can write. " " You can write high frequency words quickly. " " You can check to see how many words you know. "
	GRADE 2 / GRADE 3 / GRADE 4 / GRADE 5 / GRADES 6–8 (early mid late)

Word Meaning/Vocabulary

Students need to know the meaning of the words they are learning to read and write. It is important for them constantly to expand their vocabularies as well as to develop a more complex understanding of words they already know. And they need to have multiple encounters with those words. Word meaning is related to the development of vocabulary—labels, concept words, synonyms, antonyms, and homonyms. The meaning of a word often varies with the specific context and can be related to its spelling.

Accuracy in spelling often requires knowing the meaning of the word you want to write. Comprehension and accurate pronunciation are also related to knowing word meanings. In this section, we include synonyms, antonyms, and homonyms, which may be homographs (same spelling, different meaning and sometimes different pronunciation) or homophones (same sound, different spelling). Knowing synonyms and antonyms will help students build more powerful systems for connecting and categorizing words; it will also help them comprehend texts better and write in a more interesting way. Though students may understand the category, words in the category can be simple or complex. Being able to distinguish between homographs and homophones assists in comprehension and helps spellers to avoid mistakes. We also include work with categorization of words and their relationships as well as figurative language. We introduce basic dictionary skills.

Word Meaning/Vocabulary

Principle	Explanation of Principle															
	GRADE 2			**GRADE 3**			**GRADE 4**			**GRADE 5**			**GRADES 6–8**			
	early	mid	late	early	mid	late	early	mid	late	early	mid	late				
Concept Words Recognizing and learning concept words: color names, number words, days of the week, months of the year, seasons	" A color (number, day, month) has a name. " " Days of the week have names and are always in the same order. " " Months of the year have names and are always in the same order. " " You can read and write the names of colors (numbers, days, months). " " You can find the names of colors (numbers, days, months). "															
Recognizing and using concept words that imply sets and subsets: *countries-states-counties-cities and towns; fruit-apples-pears; liquids-water, milk; president, vice-president*	" Some words represent big ideas or items. You can find words that represent smaller ideas or items related to the big ideas. "															
Related Words Recognizing and using words that are related in many ways: sound, spelling, meaning	" Some words go together because of how they sound: *sleep/slip; sore/soar.* " " Some words go together because of how they look: *read/read.* " " Some words go together because of what they mean: family *(mother-father; sister-brother);* clothing; animals; food; swim, swimmer; hot, cold. "															
Recognizing and using synonyms (words that mean about the same)	" Some words mean about the same and are called synonyms: *begin/start, close/shut, fix/mend, earth/world, happy/glad, high/tall, jump/leap, keep/save, large/big.* "															
Recognizing and using antonyms (words that mean the opposite)	" Some words mean about the opposite and are called antonyms: *hot/cold, all/none, break/fix, little/big, long/short, sad/glad, stop/start.* "															
Recognizing and using homophones (same sound, different spelling and meaning) (It is not necessary to teach children the technical term *homophone*.)	" Some words sound the same but look different and have different meanings: *to/too/two; there/their/they're; hare/hair; blue/blew.* "															
	early	mid	late	early	mid	late	early	mid	late	early	mid	late				
	GRADE 2			**GRADE 3**			**GRADE 4**			**GRADE 5**			**GRADES 6–8**			

Word Meaning/Vocabulary, continued

Principle	Explanation of Principle

Related Words and Word Functions

Recognizing and using homographs (same spelling, different meaning and they may have different pronunciation—heteronym) (It is not necessary to teach children the technical terms *homograph* or *heteronym*.)
" Some words look the same, have a different meaning, and may sound different: *bat/bat, well/well; read/read; wind/wind.* "

Recognizing and using words with the multiple meanings (a form of homograph): *can, beat*
" Some words are spelled the same but have more than one meaning. "

Recognizing nouns (words that represent a person, place, or thing)
" Some words stand for a person, a place, or a thing. They are called *nouns.* "

Recognizing and using action words (verbs)
" Some words tell what a person, object, or animal does. They are called *action words* or *verbs.* "

Recognizing adjectives (words that describe)
" Some words describe a person, place, or thing. They are called *adjectives.* "

Combined and Created Words

Recognizing and using simple compound words: *into, something*
" Some words are made up of two words that are combined. They are *compound* words. "

Recognizing and using compound words with frequently used components: *where, thing, one, every, air,* family names (*grandmother*), *home, walk, some, sun, when, under, body, head, cycle*
" You see some words in many compound words. "

Recognizing and using hyphenated compound words: *jack-in-the-box*
" Some compound words are joined by a hyphen. "

Recognizing and using words that are blended together (portmanteau words): *brunch, horrific, smog, clash, smash, squiggle, o'clock, skylab*
" Some words are made by blending together two words. The meaning of the blended word is related to both parts. "

Recognizing and using words that are made by combining initials: *NATO, UNICEF*
" You can take the first letter from each word in a group of words and put them together to make an *acronym.* "

Recognizing palindromes (words that can be spelled frontward or in reverse) as interesting aspects of language: *mom, noon, radar, madam, Hannah, did, pop*
" Some words can be spelled the same frontward or backward. "

Poetic Uses of Words

Recognizing and using words that are "mixed up" for humorous effect: *spoonerisms* like *dop tog* for *top dog*
" You can mix of the starting letters of words to make up *spoonerisms.* "

Recognizing and using onomatopoetic words: *crash, slush, bang, zoom, whir*
" Some words mimic the sounds they represent. You often see these words in books and poetry. "

Recognizing and using words as metaphors and similes to make a comparison: *light as air, dogged, stormed out*
" You can use words to compare things to make your writing more interesting. "

Recognizing and using idioms or expressions (metaphors that have become traditional sayings and the comparisons are not evident): *raining cats and dogs, sweating bullets*
" Some phrases have a meaning that is different from the words because of tradition. "

Grade columns: GRADE 2 (early mid late), GRADE 3 (early mid late), GRADE 4 (early mid late), GRADE 5 (early mid late), GRADES 6–8

©2004 by Irene C. Fountas and Gay Su Pinnell from *Word Study Lessons*

55

WMV
WORD MEANING/VOCABULARY

Word Meaning/Vocabulary, continued

Principle	Explanation of Principle	GRADE 2			GRADE 3			GRADE 4			GRADE 5			GRADES 6–8		
		early	mid	late	early	mid	late	early	mid	late	early	mid	late			
Making connections to understand words	" You can make connections to help you to understand a word better. "															
Understanding that English words come from many different sources: other languages, technology, place names	" Over many years, English words have been added from many different sources. "															
Understanding that some English words come from names: *hamburger, sandwich*	" Some English words come from the name of a person or a place. "															
Understanding that many English words come from other languages	" Many English words come from other languages. "															
Understanding the concept of Greek and Latin "roots" and their use in learning to pronounce and think about the meaning of a word	" A *root* is a word part from another language that can be found in English words. " " A root can help you pronounce the word and understand its meaning. You can notice the way a word is used to help you think about what it means or how it is pronounced. "															
Understanding that many English words and word parts have Latin roots: *and, bene, cap, ce, cide, cor, cred, dic, duce, equa, fac, fer, form, grac, grad, hab, ject, lit, loc, man, mem, miss, mob, mimr, ped, pens, port, pos, prim, quer, scub, setn, sist, spec, train, tract, val, ven vens, vid, voc*	" Many English words come from Latin. They have Latin 'roots.' "															
Many English words and word parts have Greek roots: *aer, arch, aster, bio, centr, chron, eyel, dem, derm, geo, gram, graph, dydr, ology, meter, micro, phon, photo, phys, pol, scope, sphere, tel*	" Many English words come from Greek. They have Greek 'roots.' "															
		early	mid	late	early	mid	late	early	mid	late	early	mid	late			
		GRADE 2			GRADE 3			GRADE 4			GRADE 5			GRADES 6–8		

Word Structure

Looking at the structure of words will help students learn how words are related to each other and how they can be changed by adding letters, letter clusters, and larger word parts. Being able to recognize syllables, for example, helps readers and writers break down words into smaller units that are easier to analyze.

Words often have affixes, parts added before or after a word to change its meaning. An affix can be a prefix or a suffix. The word to which affixes are added can be a *base* word or a *root* word. A base word is a complete word; a root word is a part that may have Greek or Latin origins (such as *phon* in *telephone*). It will not be necessary for young children to make this distinction when they are beginning to learn about simple affixes, but working with suffixes and prefixes will help children read and understand words that use them as well as use affixes accurately in writing.

Endings or word parts that are added to base words signal meaning. For example, they may signal relationships *(prettier, prettiest)* or time *(running, planted)*. Principles related to word structure include understanding the meaning and structure of compound words, contractions, plurals, and possessives as well as knowing how to make and use them accurately. We have also included the simple abbreviations that students often see in the books they read and want to use in their writing.

Word Structure

Principle	Explanation of Principle
	GRADE 2 early mid late **GRADE 3** early mid late **GRADE 4** early mid late **GRADE 5** early mid late **GRADES 6–8**
Understanding the concept of syllable	" A syllable is a word part you can hear. "
Hearing and identifying syllables	" You can hear the syllables in words. " " You can look at the syllables to read a word. "
Recognizing and using one or two syllables in words	" You can look at the syllables in a word to read it *[horse, a-way, farm-er, morn-ing]*. "
Understanding how vowels appear in syllables	" Every syllable of a word has a vowel. "
Recognizing and using syllables in words with double consonants	" Divide the syllables between the consonants when a word has two similar consonants in the middle *[run-ning, bet-ter]*. "
Recognizing and using syllables ending in a vowel (open syllable)	" When a syllable ends with a vowel, the vowel is usually long *[ho-tel]*. "
Recognizing and using syllables ending in a vowel and at least one consonant (closed syllable)	" When a syllable ends with a vowel and at least one consonant, the vowel sound is usually short *[lem-on]*. "
Recognizing and using syllables with a vowel and a silent *e*	" When a vowel and a silent *e* are in a word, the pattern makes one syllable with a long vowel sound *[hope-ful]*. "
Recognizing and using syllables with vowel combinations	" When vowel combinations are in words, they usually go together in the same syllable *[poi-son, cray-on]*. "
	early mid late **GRADE 2** early mid late **GRADE 3** early mid late **GRADE 4** early mid late **GRADE 5** **GRADES 6–8**

Syllables

WS
WORD STRUCTURE

Word Structure, continued

Syllables

Recognizing and using syllables with vowel and *r*
" When a vowel is followed by an *r*, the *r* and the vowel form a syllable *[cor-ner, cir-cus]*. "

Recognizing and using syllables in words with the the VCC pattern (syllable juncture)
" Divide the word after the first consonant in a consonant blend that joins two syllables in a word *[plas-tic]*. "
" Divide the word after the consonant digraph that joins two syllables in a word [*wish-ful*]. "

Recognizing and using syllables with consonant and *le*
" When a consonant and *le* appear at the end of a word, the consonant and *le* form the final syllable *[ta-ble, ket-tle]*. "

Recognizing and using three or more syllables in words
" You can look at the syllables in a word to read it *[bi-cy-cle, to-geth-er, ev-er-y, won-der-ful, li-brar-y, com-put-er; au-to-mo-bile, a-quar-i-um, un-der-wat-er]*. "

Recognizing and using syllables in words with the VV pattern: *ri-ot; di-et.*
" Divide the word after the long vowel sound in words with two vowels that each contribute a sound. "

Compound Words

Recognizing and understanding simple compound words: *into, itself, myself, cannot, inside, maybe, nobody, outside, sunshine, today, together, upset, yourself, without, sometimes, something*
" Some words are made of two whole words and are called compound words. "

Noticing words as patterns that appear frequently in compound words: *some, thing, side, every, any, one, under, ever, where*
" You see some words often in compound words. "
" You can make connections among compound words that have the same word parts. "

Recognizing and understanding more complex compound words: *airplane, airport, another, anyone, homesick, indoor, jellyfish, skyscraper, toothbrush*
" The word parts in compound words often help you think about the meaning. "

Contractions

Recognizing and understanding contractions using *is* or *has*: *he's, it's, she's, that's, there's, what's, where's, who's*
" To make a contraction, put two words together and leave out a letter or letters. Write an apostrophe where the letter(s) are left out. "
" Many contractions are made with *is* and/or *has*: he + is = he's [He's going to the zoo.]; he + has = he's [He's finished his work.] "

Recognizing and understanding contractions using *will*: *I'll, it'll, he'll, she'll, that'll, they'll, we'll, you'll*
" To make a contraction, put two words together and leave out a letter or letters. Write an apostrophe where the letter(s) are left out. "
" Many contractions are made with *will*: I + will = I'll. "

Recognizing and understanding contractions using *are*: *they're, we're, you're*
" To make a contraction, put two words together and leave out a letter or letters. Write an apostrophe where the letter(s) are left out. "
" Many contractions are made with *are*: they + are = they're. "

Recognizing and understanding contractions using *not*: *aren't, can't, couldn't, didn't, doesn't, don't, hadn't, hasn't, haven't, isn't, mustn't, needn't, shouldn't, wouldn't*
" To make a contraction, put two words together and leave out a letter. Write an apostrophe where the letter(s) are left out. "
" Many contractions are made with *not*: can + not = can't. "

Recognizing and understanding contractions using *have*: *could've, I've, might've, should've, they've, we've, would've, you've*
" To make a contraction, put two words together and leave out a letter or letters. Write an apostrophe where the letter(s) are left out. "
" Many contractions are made with *have*: should + have = should've. "

Grade columns: GRADE 2 (early, mid, late), GRADE 3 (early, mid, late), GRADE 4 (early, mid, late), GRADE 5 (early, mid, late), GRADES 6–8

Word Structure, continued

Principle	Explanation of Principle

GRADE 2 — early mid late · GRADE 3 — early mid late · GRADE 4 — early mid late · GRADE 5 — early mid late · GRADES 6–8

Contractions

Recognizing and understanding contractions using _us: let's_
" To make a contraction, put two words together and leave out a letter or letter(s). Write an apostrophe where the letters are left out. "
" Many contractions are made with _us: let + us = let's [Let's go.]_ "

Recognizing and understanding contractions using _would_ or _had: I'd, it'd, she'd, there'd, they'd, we'd, you'd_
" To make a contraction, put two words together and leave out a letter or letters. Write an apostrophe where the letter(s) are left out. "
" Many contractions are made with _would_ or _had: she + would = she'd; they + would = they'd._ "

Recognizing and understanding multiple contractions using _not_ and _have: shouldn't've; mustn't've; wouldn't've_
" Some contractions put together three words and leave out letters. "
" You write an apostrophe every time a letter is left out. "
" These contractions are usually made with _not_ and _have._ "

Plurals

Recognizing and using plurals that add s: _dogs, cats, apples, cans, desks, faces, trees, monkeys_
" Add _s_ to some words to make them plural. "
" You can hear the _s_ at the end. "

Recognizing and using plurals that add _es_ when words end with _x, ch, sh, s, ss, tch, zz: buzzes, branches, buses, boxes, dishes, foxes, kisses, patches, peaches_
" Add _es_ to words that end with _x, ch, sh, s, ss, tch, zz_ to make them plural. "
" The _s_ at the end sounds like /z/. "

Recognizing and using plurals that add _s_ to words that end in vowel and _y: boys, days, keys, plays, says, valleys_
" Add _s_ to words that end in a vowel and _y_ to make them plural. "

Recognizing and using plurals that add _es_ to words that end in consonant and _y: babies, candies, cities, countries, flies, families, ladies, ponies, skies, stories_
" Change the _y_ to _i_ and add _es_ to words that end in consonant and _y_ to make them plural. "

Recognizing and using plurals that change _f_ to _v_ and add _es_ for words that end with _f, fe, lf: wolves, hooves, lives, scarves, selves, shelves, wives_
" Change _f_ to _v_ and add _es_ to words that end with _f, fe, or lf_ to make them plural. "

Recognizing and using plurals for words that end in a vowel and _o_ by adding _s: radios, rodeos, kangaroos_
" Add _s_ to words that end in a vowel and _o_ to make them plural. "

Recognizing and using plurals for words that end in a consonant and _o_ by adding _es: zeroes, heroes, potatoes, volcanoes_
" Add _es_ to words that end in a consonant and _o_ to make them plural. "

Recognizing and using plurals that change the spelling of the word: _child/children, foot/feet, goose/geese, man/men, mouse/mice, ox/oxen, woman/women_
" Change the spelling of some words to make them plural. "

Recognizing and using plurals that are the same word for singular and plural: _deer, lamb, sheep, moose, salmon_
" Some words are spelled the same in both the singular and plural forms. "

early mid late — GRADE 2 · early mid late — GRADE 3 · early mid late — GRADE 4 · early mid late — GRADE 5 · GRADES 6–8

WS
WORD STRUCTURE

Word Structure, continued

	Principle	Explanation of Principle

GRADE 2 (early, mid, late) · **GRADE 3** (early, mid, late) · **GRADE 4** (early, mid, late) · **GRADE 5** (early, mid, late) · **GRADES 6–8**

Plurals

Recognizing and using plurals that are formed by changing some of the letters of the base word or by adding an unusual suffix: one *ox* – herd of *oxen;* a *medium* – different *media; tooth* – *teeth; goose* – *geese*

" You form some plurals by changing some of the letters of the base word or by adding an unusual suffix. "

Suffixes

Understanding the concept of a suffix

" A suffix is a word part that is added at the end of a word to change its meaning or function in a sentence. "

Understanding that adding a suffix to a word may change the spelling

" Sometimes when you add a suffix to the word, you add or drop letters. "

Understanding that the final *e* is usually dropped when adding suffixes that begin with a vowel or when adding *y* to words: *raced, racing, noisy*

" Drop the *e* before adding a suffix that begins with a vowel when *y* is added. "

Understanding that the final *e* is kept when adding suffixes that begin with a consonant to words: *rarely, careful, careless, likeness, wholesome*

" Keep the final *e* when adding a suffix that begins with a consonant. "

Understanding that the *y* is changed to *i* when adding a suffix that begins with a consonant: *happily*

" Change the *y* to *i* before adding a suffix that begins with a consonant. "

Understanding that when the word part before the suffix ends in *ns*, you add the suffix *-ible:* sensible, responsible

" Add the suffix *-ible* when the part before the suffix ends in *–ns.* "

Understanding that the final *e* is kept when adding the suffix *-able* to words ending in *-ce* or *-ge* ("soft" sound of *c* or *g*): *manageable, traceable*

" Do not drop the final *e* when adding *-able* to words ending in the soft sound of *c* or *g.* "

Understanding that *-able* is added to base words and *-ible* is added to root words: *washable, credible*

" Add *-able* to a base word. Add *-ible* to a root word. "

Suffixes [Verb Endings]

Recognizing and using endings that add *s* to a verb to make it agree with the subject: *skate/skates; run/runs*

" Add *s* to the end of a word to make it sound right in a sentence. "
" She can run. "
" She runs. "
" She can skate. "
" She skates. "

Recognizing and using endings that add *ing* to denote the present participle: *play/playing; send/sending*

" Add *ing* to a word to show you are doing something now. "
" I can *read.* "
" I am *reading.* "
" She can *jump.* "
" She is *jumping.* "

Recognizing and using endings that add *ed* to a verb to make it past tense: *walk/walked; play/played; want/wanted*

" Add *ed* to the end of a word to show that you did something in the past. "
" I can *play* a game today. "
" I *played* a game yesterday. "
" I *want* to play. "
" I *wanted* to play. "

GRADE 2 (early, mid, late) · **GRADE 3** (early, mid, late) · **GRADE 4** (early, mid, late) · **GRADE 5** (early, mid, late) · **GRADES 6–8**

Suffixes [Verb Endings]

Principle	Explanation of Principle	GRADE 2 early/mid/late	GRADE 3 early/mid/late	GRADE 4 early/mid/late	GRADE 5 early/mid/late	GRADES 6–8

Principle / **Explanation of Principle**

Recognizing and using endings that add *d* to a verb ending in silent *e* to make it past tense: *like/liked*
" Add *d* to words ending in silent *e* to make the *ed* ending and show it was in the past. "
" I *like* vanilla ice cream. "
" I *liked* vanilla ice cream but I don't anymore. "

Recognizing and using endings that add *ing* to words that end in *y* to denote the present participle: *carry/carrying; marry/marrying*
" Add *ing* to words that end in *y*. "
" I can *carry* the flag. "
" I am *carrying* the flag. "

Recognizing and using endings that add -*ing* to words of one syllable ending in *y*: *lying, crying, dying, flying, trying*
" Add -*ing* to one-syllable words that end in *y*. "
" I *cry*. "
" I am *crying*. "

Recognizing and using endings that add *ing* to words that end in a single vowel and consonant to denote the present participle: *run/running, bat/batting, sit/sitting*
" Double the consonant and add *ing* to words ending in a single vowel and consonant. "
" I can *run*. "
" I am *running*. "

Recognizing and using endings that add *ing* to a word ending in silent *e* to denote the present participle: *come/coming; write/writing; bite/biting*
" Drop the *e* and add *ing* to most words that end with silent *e*.
" Will she *come*? "
" She is *coming*. "
" I can *write*. "
" I am *writing*. "

Recognizing that *ed* added to a word to make it past tense can sound several different ways
" When you add *ed* to a word, sometimes it sounds like /d/: *grabbed, played, yelled*. "
" Sometimes you change the *y* to *i* and add *ed* and the ending sounds like /d/: *cried, fried, carried*. "
" When you add *ed* to a word, sometimes it sounds like /ed/ (short *e* plus the /d/ sound): *added, landed, melted*. "
" When you add *ed* to a word, it may sound like /t/: *dressed, liked, talked, laughed, walked*. "

Recognizing and using endings that that add *es* or *ed* to verbs ending in a consonant and *y* to form the present or past tense: *cry/cries/cried; try/tries/tried*
" You can add word parts to the end of a word to show when you did something in the present or in the past. "
" Change the *y* to *i* and add *es* or *ed* to words that end in a consonant and *y*. "
" I can *try* to run fast. "
" He *tries* to run fast. "
" We *tried* to run fast in the race yesterday. "

Recognizing and using endings that add *ed* to verbs ending in a single short vowel and consonant or a vowel and double consonant to make it past tense: *grab/grabbed; grill/grilled; yell/yelled*
" You add word parts to the endings of words to show when you did something in the past. "
" Double the consonant before adding *ed* to words ending in a short vowel and one consonant. "
" *Grab* the end of the rope. "
" She *grabbed* the end of the rope. "
" Add *ed* if the word ends with a vowel and a double consonant. "
" She can *yell* loud. "
" She *yelled*, 'Run!' "
" Mom can *grill* the hot dogs. "
" Mom *grilled* the hot dogs. "

Recognizing and using endings add -*er* to a verb to make it a noun: *read/reader; play/player; jump/jumper*
" Add -*er* to a word to tell about a person who can do something. "
" John can *read*. "
" John is a *reader*. "

GRADE 2 early/mid/late	GRADE 3 early/mid/late	GRADE 4 early/mid/late	GRADE 5 early/mid/late	GRADES 6–8

WS
WORD STRUCTURE

Word Structure, continued

Principle	Explanation of Principle
Suffixes [Verb Endings]	
Recognizing and using endings that add -er to a verb that ends with a short vowel and a consonant: *dig/digger; run/runner*	" Double the consonant and add -er when words end in a short vowel and a consonant. " " Sarah can run. " " Sarah is a runner. "
Recognizing and using endings that add r to a verb that ends in silent e: *bake/baker; hike/hiker*	" Add r to words that end in silent e to make the -er ending. " " I like to hike. " " I am a hiker. "
Recognizing and using endings that add -er to a verb that ends in y: *carry/carrier*	" Change the y to i and add -er to words that end in y. " " He can *carry* the mail. " " He is a mail *carrier*. "
Recognizing and using words that change spelling to show past tense: *write/wrote; catch/caught; teach/taught*	" You can change the spelling of some words to show something happened in the past. "
Recognizing and using endings that add -ing to a word that ends in -oe: *hoe/hoeing*	" Add *ing* to a word that ends in *oe*. "
Recognizing and using endings that add an ending that begins with a vowel to a word that ends in c: *picnic–picnicking; traffic–trafficking*	" When you are adding an ending that starts with a vowel to a word that ends in c, put a k after the c. "
Suffixes [Adjectives]	
Recognizing and using endings that show comparison (-er, -est): *cold/colder; hard/harder; dark/darker; fast/faster; tall/taller; rich/richest; thin/thinner/thinnest*	" Add -er or -est to show how one thing compares with another. " " John can run *fast* but Monica can run *faster*. " " Carrie is the *fastest* runner in the class. "
Recognizing and using endings that show comparison for words ending in e: *pale/paler/palest; ripe/riper/ripest, cute/cuter/cutest*	" Add r or st to words that end in silent e to make the -er or -est ending. " " Jolisa has a *cute* puppy. " " Matthew has a *cuter* puppy. " " Jaqual has the *cutest* puppy. "
Recognizing and using endings that show comparison for words ending in a short vowel and a consonant: *red, redder, reddest*	" Double the consonant and add -er or -est to words that end in a short vowel and one consonant. " " The red box is *big*. " " The blue box is *bigger*. " " The green box is *biggest*. "
Recognizing and using endings that show comparison for words ending in y: *scary/scarier/scariest; funny/funnier/funniest*	" Change y to i and add -er or -est to words that end in y. " " Ciera told a *funny* story. " " Kyle's story was *funnier* than Ciera's. " " Amanda told the *funniest* story of all. "
Recognizing and using endings for adjectives that add -ible (added to partial words) and -able (added to whole words): *acceptable, doable, breakable, dependable; horrible, visible.* [Exceptions: *portable, capable, distractible, incomprehensible*]	" Add -ible to partial words or root words. " " Add -able to whole words or base words. " " This is a *horrible* situation. " " He is a *dependable* friend. "

Grade columns header: GRADE 2 (early, mid, late) · GRADE 3 (early, mid, late) · GRADE 4 (early, mid, late) · GRADE 5 (early, mid, late) · GRADES 6–8

Principle	Explanation of Principle	GRADE 2 early mid late	GRADE 3 early mid late	GRADE 4 early mid late	GRADE 5 early mid late	GRADES 6–8

Suffixes [Adjectives]

Understanding that when you add -able to a verb you may change the spelling: *apply–applicable; vary–variable*
" **When you add -able to a verb, change the spelling.** "

Understanding that when you add -able to base words ending in e, you delete the e before adding the suffix: *love–lovable*
" **Delete the final e before adding the suffix -able to base words ending in e.** "

Understanding that when a base word ends in y, you change the y to i before adding the suffix -able: *rely–reliable*
" **Change the y to i before adding the suffix -able to a base word ending in y.** "

Recognizing and using word endings that add -ful (meaning "full of" or "like"): *grateful, graceful, peaceful, handful*
" **Add -ful to words to show they are 'full of something.'** "

Recognizing and using word endings that add *less* (meaning without) and *ness* (meaning condition): add the ending to most words: *sleepless, tireless, joyless; kindness.* Change y to i and add the ending for words that end in vowel + y: *penniless; happiness*
" **Add -less or -ness to words to mean a condition. If the word ends in a vowel and y change the y to i before adding -less or -ness.** "

Recognizing and using adjectives that are formed by adding -ous, -cious, or -tious (full of; characterized by): *joyous, beautious, capatious, spacious, cautious, rambunctious, gracious*
" **Add -ous , -cious, or -tious to words (adjectives) to show they are full of or characterized by something.** "

Recognizing and using nouns that are formed by adding -ic ; -al, -ian, -ial, -cial (like, of the nature of, suitable for): *stoic, hectic, volcanic; hysterical, theatrical; reptilian, artificial*
" **Add -ic, -al, -ian, -ial, or -cial to words (nouns) to show they are like, suitable for or of the nature of something.** "

Suffixes [Adverbs]

Understanding the concept that an adjective (describing word) can become an adverb to tell how something is done: *happy–happily*
" **You can change a describing word to a word that tells how something is done.** "

Recognizing and using adverbs that add -ly (meaning like) to a base word: *sadly, really, carefully, quickly*
" **To show how something is done, you can add -ly to words.** "
" **Words like quickly are called adverbs.** "

Understanding that for most words, you add -ly or -ally to change an adjective to an adverb: *beautiful–beautifully, automatic–automatically*
" **Add -ly or -ally to change a describing word to a word that tells how.** "

Recognizing and using adverbs that end in y and change y to i and add -ly: *happy–happily, noisy–noisily*
" **For words that in y change the y to i and add -ly to make an adverb.** "

Recognizing and using adverbs that end in ic and add al before adding -ly: *tragic–tragically; magic–magically; automatic–automatically; frantic–frantically*
" **For words that end in -ic, add -al before adding -ly to make an adverb.** "

Recognizing and using adverbs that end in e and either keep the e (*sincerely, merely, extremely*) or drop the e (*truly, duly*)
" **Keep the e before adding -ly for some words that end in e.** "
" **Drop the e before adding -ly for some words that end in e.** "

early mid late GRADE 2	early mid late GRADE 3	early mid late GRADE 4	early mid late GRADE 5	GRADES 6–8

Suffixes [Nouns]

Principle	Explanation of Principle

Principle	Explanation of Principle
Recognizing and using nouns that are formed by adding -teen, used to form the suffixes for the cardinal numbers (13 to 19)	" Add -teen to the number word to show ten plus the number. "
Recognizing and using nouns that are formed by adding -er to a verb to indicate "one who" does something: fighter	" You can add -er to a verb to show someone who does something. "
Understanding that you add -ar or -or to some verbs to indicate "one who does something": actor, elevator	" Add -ar or -or to some verbs to show one who does something. "
Understanding that when making a noun by adding -er to a verb that has a short vowel and one consonant, double the final consonant: robber, swimmer, runner, beggar	" Double the consonant on words ending with a short vowel and one consonant before adding the suffix –er to show someone who does something. "
Understanding that when making a noun by adding -er or -ar to a verb that ends in silent e, you drop the e before adding the suffix: writer, rider, liar, burglar	" Delete the e before adding the suffix -er or -ar to words ending in e to show someone who does something. "
Understanding that when making a noun by adding –er to a verb that ends in y, you change the y to i before adding the suffix: worrier, carrier	" Change the y to i for words ending in y before adding the suffix -er to show someone who does something. "
Understanding that when making a noun by adding -er to a verb that ends in hard c, you add a k before the suffix: picnicker, frolicker	" Add k to words ending with hard c before adding the suffix -er to show one who does something. "
Recognizing and using nouns that are formed from adjectives or verbs by adding -tion or -ion: perfect–perfection, contract–contraction, infect–infection	" You can make some verbs into nouns by addition -tion or -ion. "
Recognizing and using nouns that are formed from verbs with silent e by dropping the e and adding -tion : vacate–vacation, define–definition, prepare–preparation, regulate–regulation	" You can make some verbs into nouns with silent e by dropping the e and adding -tion. "
Recognizing and using nouns that are formed from verbs by adding -sion: persuade–persuasion, decide–decision, provide–provision, revise–revision. The silent e and sometimes more of the base word are omitted.	" You can make some verbs into nouns by adding -sion. " " Omit the silent e and sometimes more of the base word. "
Recognizing and using nouns that are formed by adding -ment (a result or product): basement, easement, enchantment	" Add -ment to nouns to mean a result or product. "

Word Structure, continued

Principle	Explanation of Principle	GRADE 2			GRADE 3			GRADE 4			GRADE 5			GRADES 6–8		
		early	mid	late	early	mid	late	early	mid	late	early	mid	late			

Suffixes [Nouns]

Recognizing and using nouns that are formed by adding *-ent* or *-ant* (shows or does): *superintendent, solvent, accountant*
" Add *-ent* or *-ant* to nouns to mean *one who shows or does.* "

Recognizing and using adjectives that are formed by adding *-ent* or *-ant* to indicate "characterized by": *insistent, defiant, radiant*
" Add *-ent* or *-ant* to verbs to describe something or someone. "

Recognizing and using nouns that are formed by adding *-ity* (state or condition of being): *chastity, possibility, entity*
" Add *-ity* to nouns to show the state or condition of being. "

Recognizing and using nouns that are formed by adding *-ence* and *-ance* (act, fact, quality, state, result, or degree): *excellence, conference, hindrance, utterance, remittance*
" To add the suffixes *-ance, -ence, -ant, -ent* to a base word, double the final consonant and add the ending. "

Understanding that when you form a noun by adding *-ance, -ence, -ant,* or *-ent* to a base word ending in *e*, you remove the final *e* from the base word: *observe, observance*
" To add the suffixes *–ance, -ence, -ant,* or *–ent* to a base word ending in *e*, remove the final *e* and the add the suffix. "

Understanding that when you form a noun by adding *-ance, -ence, -ant,* or *-ent* to words ending in *y*, change the *y* to *i* and add the ending: *rely, reliance*
" When you add *-ance, -ence, -ant,* or *-ent* to words ending in *y*, change the *y* to *i* and add the ending. "

Recognizing and using nouns that are formed by adding *-ure* or *-ture* (act, process, or state of being): *legislature, exposure, composure, literature*
" Add *-ure* or *-ture* to nouns to mean 'act, process, or state of being'. "

Prefixes

Recognizing and using common prefixes (*re-* meaning *again*): *make–remake, do–redo, live–relive*
" Add a word part or prefix to the beginning of a word to change its meaning. "
" Add *re-* to the beginning of a word to mean *do again.* "
" I *made* the bed and took a nap. I had to *remake* the bed. "

Recognizing and using common prefixes (*un-* meaning *not* or *the opposite of*): *do–undo, tie–untie, known–unknown, believable–unbelievable*
" Add a word part or prefix to the beginning of a word to change the meaning. "
" Add *un-* to the beginning of a word to mean *not* or *the opposite of.* "
" I don't *believe* it. That is *unbelievable.* "
" I *tied* my shoes and then they came *untied.* "

Recognizing and using more complex prefixes (*im-, in-, il-, dis-, non-* [meaning *not*]): *possible–impossible, valid–invalid, like–dislike, literate–illiterate, legal–illegal*
" Add a word part or prefix to the beginning of a word to change the meaning. "
" Add *im-, in-, il-,* or *dis-* to the beginning of words to mean *not.* "
" That is not *possible.* It is *impossible.* "
" We cannot *cure* the disease. It is *incurable..* "
" It is not *legal.* It is *illegal.* "
" I do not *like* broccoli. I *dislike* broccoli. "

Recognizing and using more prefixes that mean *wrong* (*mis*): *misinform, misinformation, mistake, mishandle, mispronounce*
" Add *mis* before a word to change the meaning. "
" He *pronounced* the word wrong. He *mispronounced* the word. "

	early	mid	late	early	mid	late	early	mid	late	early	mid	late			
	GRADE 2			GRADE 3			GRADE 4			GRADE 5			GRADES 6–8		

Prefixes

Principle	Explanation of Principle
Recognizing and using prefixes that refer to numbers *(uni-, bi-, tri-, cent-, dec-, mon-, mult-, cot-, pent-, poly-, quad-, semi-): uniform, unicycle, unicorn; bicycle, biweekly, biannual; tricycle, triceratops; tricolor*	**"You can add some prefixes to words to refer to numbers."** **"We are all wearing the same uniform."** **"My bicycle has two wheels."** **"My mother has trifocals that have three different lens strengths."**
Recognizing and using prefixes that mean *before (pre-): preface, preamble, preapprove, prearrange, precaution, pregame, prefigure, preplan*	**"Add a prefix to a word to show something happening before."** **"Let's go to the *pregame* ceremony."**
Recognizing and using prefixes that mean *make (en-, em-): enable, entrap, empower, embed, embody*	**"Add the prefix to a word to show making something happen."** **"This money will *enable* me to buy a ticket."** **"The king *empowered* the people to vote."**
Recognizing and using prefixes that mean across *(transportation; translate; transaction)*	**"Add the prefix *trans-* to a word to mean 'across'."**
Recognizing and using prefixes that mean *between* or *together (interaction; interfaith, interfere, intermediate)*	**"Add the prefix *inter-* to a word to mean *between* or *together*."**
Recognizing and using prefixes that mean within or inside *(intra-): intramural, intrapersonal, intravenous*	**"Add the prefix *intra-* to words to mean 'within' or 'under'."**
Recognizing and using prefixes that mean *with* or *together (con-, com-): compose, composition, confer, conference, conceal, concern, compound, compare)*	**"Add the prefix *con-* or *com-* to words to mean 'with' or 'together'."**
Recognizing and using prefixes that mean *under (sub-): submarine, subcategory, subdivision, sublethal, subzero, subculture, subway*	**"Add a prefix to show that something is below or under."** **"I traveled below the streets on the *subway*."**
Recognizing and using prefixes that mean *above (super-); supermarket, superordinate, supervisor, superintendent*	**"Add the prefix *super-* to mean 'above'."**
Recognizing and using prefixes that mean *bad (mal-): malpractice, malcontent, malnourished, malformation, malediction*	**"Add a prefix *mal-* to show that something is bad."** **"The patient died and they suspected *malpractice* by the doctor at the hospital."**
Recognizing and using prefixes that mean *out (ex-): exit, extend, expand, exotic*	**"Add the prefix *ex-* to words to mean 'out'."**
Recognizing and using prefixes that mean *going beyond or through (per-): perform, perhaps, perforate, perceive*	**"Add the prefix *per-* to words to mean 'going beyond or through'."**
Recognizing and using prefixes that mean *around (circum-); circumnavigate, circumvent, circumference*	**"Add the prefix *circum-* to words to mean 'around'."**

GRADE 2			GRADE 3			GRADE 4			GRADE 5			GRADES 6–8
early	mid	late	early	mid	late	early	mid	late	early	mid	late	

Principle	Explanation of Principle														
		GRADE 2			GRADE 3			GRADE 4			GRADE 5			GRADES 6–8		
		early	mid	late	early	mid	late	early	mid	late	early	mid	late			

Prefixes

Recognizing and using prefixes that change form to match the root word (assimilated prefixes): *in- (immigrate, illegal, irregular); ad- (address, approach, aggressive); ob- (obstruct, opportunity); sub- (subtract, suppose, surround); com-(commit, collide, corrode); dis- (distinguish; difference); ex-(expand, expose, eccentric, efficient)*

" When you add some prefixes to change word meaning, you change the spelling of the word. "
" The prefix may become a part of the root word. "

Possessives

Recognizing and using possessives that add an apostrophe and an *s* to a singular noun: *dog–dog's, woman–woman's, girl–girl's, boy–boy's*

" A person, animal, place, or thing can own something. To show ownership, you add *'s* to a word. "
" The collar belongs to the *dog*. It is the *dog's* collar. "
" The ball belongs to the *girl*. It is the *girl's* ball. "
" The *book* has a cover. It is the *book's* cover. "

Recognizing and using possessives for names that end in *s* and singular words that end in *s*—add an apostrophe: *Marcus' papers, Charles' lunch box; the octopus' ink*

" If a name or other object already ends in *s*, just add an apostrophe to show ownership. "
" Here is *Marcus'* lunch box. It belongs to *Marcus*. "

Recognizing and using plural possessives to show that the item belongs to a group—add apostrophe after the *s: boys' game, girls' dresses, dogs' dishes, pigs' houses*

" For a plural noun that ends in *s*, show possession by adding an apostrophe only. "
" The *girls* are getting the jump ropes. The ropes belong to the *girls*. They are the *girls'* jump ropes. "
" Those balls belong to the *boys*. They are the *boys'* balls. "

Understanding that when you make the word *it* show possession, you do not use an apostrophe

" No apostrophe is needed when you use *its* to show possession. "

Recognizing and using plural possessives that do not end in *s*—add apostrophe + *s: women's room, children's party*

" For a plural noun that does not end in *s*, show possession by adding apostrophe + *s*. "

Abbreviations

Recognizing and using common abbreviations: *Mrs., Ms., Mr., Dr., St., Ave., Rd., months of the year, days of the week*

" Some words are made shorter by using some of the letters and a period. They are called *abbreviations*. "

Recognizing and using more complex abbreviations: *state names, weights, Sr., Jr, Ph.D.*

" Some words are made shorter by using some of the letters and a period. They are called *abbreviations*. "

Root Words

Understanding that many English words are derived from other languages: *charade, bouquet*

" Many English words and parts of words come from other languages. "

Recognizing and using word roots from Greek or Latin: *aero, bio, chron, geo, meter, photo, ject, struct, dict, mit, flex, cred, duc, pend, pel, fac, vert*

" Many words and parts of words come from ancient languages called Greek and Latin. You can use Greek and Latin word roots to help you learn the meaning of a word. "

Combining roots from Greek and taking words apart into morphemes: *micro, scope, photo, graph, tele, phon, geo, -meter, -ology, -itis*

" Word roots are sometimes combined to make words. You can notice Greek word roots to understand the meaning of words. "

Understanding that many English words are derived from new inventions, technology, or current events

" The origin of a word can help you learn its meaning. "

early	mid	late	early	mid	late	early	mid	late	early	mid	late			
GRADE 2			GRADE 3			GRADE 4			GRADE 5			GRADES 6–8		

WS WORD STRUCTURE

Word-Solving Actions

Word-solving actions are the strategic moves readers and writers make when they use their knowledge of the language system to solve words. These strategies are "in-the-head" actions that are invisible, although we can often infer them from overt behaviors. The principles listed in this section represent children's ability to *use* the principles in all previous sections of the Continuum.

All lessons related to the Continuum provide opportunities for children to apply principles in active ways; for example, through sorting, building, locating, reading, or writing. Lessons related to word-solving actions demonstrate to children how they can problem-solve by working on words in isolation or while reading or writing continuous text. The more children can integrate these strategies into their reading and writing systems, the more flexible they will become in solving words. The reader/writer may use knowledge of letter/sound relationships, for example, either to solve an unfamiliar word or to check that the reading is accurate. Rapid, automatic word solving is a basic component of fluency and important for comprehension because it frees children's attention to focus on the meaning and language of the text.

Word-Solving Actions

Explanation of Principle

Principle	Explanation of Principle
Using What Is Known to Solve Words	
Recognizing and spelling known words quickly	" You can read or write a word quickly when you know how it looks [*the*]. " " When you know how to read some words quickly, it helps you read fast. " " When you know how to write some words quickly, it helps you write fast. "
Using letter/sound knowledge to monitor reading and spelling accuracy	" You can use what you know about letters and sounds to check on your reading (and writing). "
Using parts of known words that are like other words: *my, sky; tree, try; she, shut*	" You can use parts of words you know to read or write new words. "
Using what you know about a word to solve an unknown word: *her, mother*	" You can use what you know about words to read new words. "
Taking Words Apart to Solve Them	
Solving words by thinking about the order of the sounds and letters	" You can figure out how to spell new words by thinking about the order of the sounds and letters. "
Changing beginning letters to make new words: *sit, hit; day, play*	" You can change the first letter or letters of a word to make a new word. "
Listening for sounds to write letters in words	" You can say words slowly to hear the sounds. " " Hearing and saying the sounds helps you write words. "
Changing ending letters to make new words: *car, can, cat*	" You can change the last letter or letters of a word to make a new word. "
Changing middle letters to make new words: *hit, hot; sheet, shirt*	" You can change the middle letter or letters of a word to make a new word. "
Using letter/sound analysis from left to right to read a word	" You can read words by looking at the letters and thinking about the sounds from left to right. "

GRADE 2 — early mid late | GRADE 3 — early mid late | GRADE 4 — early mid late | GRADE 5 — early mid late | GRADES 6–8

Word-Solving Actions, continued

Principle	Explanation of Principle	GRADE 2 early / mid / late	GRADE 3 early / mid / late	GRADE 4 early / mid / late	GRADE 5 early / mid / late	GRADES 6–8
Noticing and using word parts (onsets and rimes) to read a word: *br-ing*	" You can use word parts to solve a word. " " You can look at the first and last parts of a word to read it. "					
Changing the onset and rime to make a new word: *bring, thing; bring, brown*	" You can change the first part or the last part to make a new word. "					
Adding letters to the beginning or end of a word to make a new word: *in, win; bat, bats; the, then*	" You can add letters to the beginning of a word to make a new word. " " You can add letters to the end of a word to make a new word. "					
Adding letter clusters to beginning or end of a word to make a new word: *an, plan; cat, catch*	" You can add letter clusters to the beginning or end of a word to make a new word. "					
Removing letters or letter clusters from the beginning of words: *sit, it; stand, and; his, is*	" You can take away letters at the beginning of a word to make a new word. "					
Removing letters from the end of a word to make a new word: *and, an; Andy, and; kite, kit*	" You can take away letters at the end of a word to make a new word. "					
Recognizing and using word parts (onsets, rimes) to read a word: *br-ing; cl-ap*	" You can notice and use word parts to read (or write) a new word. " " You can look at the first part and last part to read a word. "					
Taking apart compound words or joining words to make compound words: *into, sidewalk, sideways*	" You can read compound words by finding the two smaller words. " " You can write compound words by joining two smaller words. "					
Removing letter clusters from the end of a word to make a new word: *catch, cat*	" You can take away letter clusters from the end of a word to make a new word. "					
Removing the ending from a base word to make a new word: *sit, sits, sitting; big, bigger, biggest*	" You can take off the ending to help you read a word. "					
Learning to notice the letter sequence to spell a word accurately	" You can make a word several times to learn the sequence of letters. "					
Studying features of words to remember the spelling	" You can look at a word, say it, cover it, write it, and check it to help you learn to spell it correctly. "					
Noticing and correcting spelling errors	" You can write a word, look at it, and try again to make it 'look right.' " " You can notice and think about the parts of words that are tricky for you. " " You can write words to see if you know them. "					
Breaking down a longer word into syllables in order to decode manageable units: *for-got-ten*	" You can divide a word into syllables to read it. "					

		early / mid / late	early / mid / late	early / mid / late	early / mid / late	
		GRADE 2	GRADE 3	GRADE 4	GRADE 5	GRADES 6–8

Making Connections between and among Words to Solve Them

Principle	Explanation of Principle
Connecting words that start the same: *tree, tray*	" You can connect the beginning of the word with a word you know. "
Connecting words that end the same: *candy, happy*	" You can connect the ending of the word with a word you know. "
Connecting words that mean the same or almost the same: *wet, damp*	" You think about the words that mean almost the same. "
Connecting words that have the same pattern: *light, night; running, sitting*	" You can connect words that have the same letter patterns. "
Connecting words that sound the same but look different and have different meanings: *blew, blue*	" You can read words by noticing that they sound the same but look different and have different meanings. "
Connecting words that rhyme: *fair, chair*	" You can think about words that rhyme. "
Connecting words that look the same but sometimes sound different, and have different meanings: *read, read*	" You can read words by remembering that some words look the same but sometimes sound different and have different meanings. "
Connecting and comparing word patterns that look the same but sound different: *dear, bear*	" You can read words by remembering that some words have parts or patterns that look the same but sound different. "
Connecting and comparing word patterns that sound the same but look different: *said, bed*	" You can read words by remembering that some words have parts or patterns that sound the same but look different. "
Using dictionary entries	" Dictionary entries have many different kinds of information about a word. "
Connecting words that are related to each other because they have the same base or root word: *direct, directs, directed, direction, misdirect, directional*	" You can make lists of words that have the same base or root word but different suffixes or prefixes. The words have different but related meanings. "

Using Word Roots to Determine Meaning and Pronunciation

Principle	Explanation of Principle
Understanding the concept of analogy and its use in discovering relationships between and among words	" Some words are related to other words in specific ways. " " You can think about how words are related and think of other words that are related in the same way. "
Understanding that common Greek roots are related to the meaning of words	" You can use the meaning of some common Greek roots to help you think about the meaning of English words. "
Using Latin roots to understand the meaning of words	" You can use the meaning of some Latin roots to help you think about the meaning of some English words. "
Using word history to learn about words	" You can learn about the spelling of a word by knowing its history. The history of words is called *etymology* (e.g. *boc* is Old English for *book*). "

Grade bands across top and bottom: GRADE 2 (early, mid, late), GRADE 3 (early, mid, late), GRADE 4 (early, mid, late), GRADE 5 (early, mid, late), GRADES 6–8

Principle

Explanation of Principle

	GRADE 2			GRADE 3			GRADE 4			GRADE 5			GRADES 6–8		
	early	mid	late	early	mid	late	early	mid	late	early	mid	late			

Using Strategies to Determine the Meaning of a Word

Understanding that the context of the sentence, paragraph, or whole text helps determine the meaning of a word

" When you read a word but don't know what it means, you can think about the meaning of the sentence to figure it out. "

Understanding that word parts help you learn what a word means

" You can think about the meaning of parts of words to help you understand a new word. "

Spelling Strategies—Ways of Studying and Remembering the Spelling of Words

Using syllables to remember the spelling of a word

" You can notice the syllables in a word to help you remember its spelling. "

Using the whole words within compound words to remember the spelling

" You can notice the two whole words in a compound word to help you remember the spelling and think about the meaning. "

Using letter/sound order to help in spelling a word

" You can use the order of sounds and letters in a word to spell a word or check on your spelling. "

Using the letter patterns in words to help you remember the spelling

" You can notice the letter patterns in words to help you remember their spelling. "

Using "hard parts" of a word to help you remember its spelling

" You can concentrate on the "hard" part of a word to help you remember how it is spelled. "

Using "look, say, cover, write, and check" to help you remember how a word is spelled

" You can look at a word, say it, cover it, write it, and then check it to help you remember how it is spelled. "

Using special devices to help in remember the spelling of a word: *friends to the end; a bear bit my ear*

" You can make up a phrase or rhyme to remind you (or help you remember how to spell) how to spell tricky words. Memory helpers are called *mnemonic devices*. "

Making a first attempt in the process of spelling a word

" When you are not sure how to write a word, try it first and see if it looks right. "

Using the dictionary to learn how to spell a word

" You can use the dictionary to learn how to spell a word or to check on your spelling. "

Remembering and applying principles to solve words

" You can figure out how to spell new words by thinking about principles you know. "

Using an acronym to help in remembering a phrase or sentence: *pin–personal identification number*

" You can take the first letter from each word in a group and put them together to form an *acronym*. "

Using word history to assist in spelling a word

" You can figure out how to spell a word by thinking about the history of the word or its meaning. "

early	mid	late	early	mid	late	early	mid	late	early	mid	late			
GRADE 2			GRADE 3			GRADE 4			GRADE 5			GRADES 6–8		

WSA
WORD SOLVING ACTIONS

Word-Solving Actions, continued

Principle	Explanation of Principle	GRADE 2			GRADE 3			GRADE 4			GRADE 5			GRADES 6–8
		early	mid	late	early	mid	late	early	mid	late	early	mid	late	
Using "spell-check" to check and correct your spelling	" You can use spell-check to check and correct your spelling. "													
Asking for help when you have used all the strategies you know	" When you have used all your strategies, ask for help in spelling a word. "													
Using resources to learn about word meanings	" You can use a dictionary, glossary or thesaurus to help you think about the meaning of a word. "													
Understanding when to use a dictionary to assist in spelling and make writing efficient	" You can tell when you need to use a dictionary to learn how to spell a word: When it doesn't 'look right' the way you have spelled it. When you are not sure exactly what it means. When you want a more interesting synonym. "													
Understanding alphabetical order and how to use it in references and resources	" You can use alphabetical order to locate words in a dictionary, glossary, or thesaurus. " " You can use alphabetical order to find or organize information. "													
Distinguishing between the multiple meanings of words	" When you look up a word in the dictionary, you will need to choose which meaning is right for the word you have used. "													
Noticing and using syllable divisions in a dictionary	" You can find syllable divisions in a dictionary entry. "													
Becoming a collector of interesting words (developing the Word Study Notebook)	" You can collect interesting words. "													
Noticing and using accent marks to help in pronouncing a word	" You can use accent marks in a dictionary entry to help you pronounce a word. "													
Noticing and using guide words to locate words in a dictionary	" You can use guide words to help you find words quickly in a dictionary. "													
Using the pronunciation guide in a dictionary	" The pronunciation guide in the dictionary helps you know how to say a word. "													
Using the dictionary to discover word history	" You can find a word's history in the dictionary entry. "													
Recognizing and using the different types of dictionaries: general, specialized (synonyms, abbreviations, theme or topic, foreign language, thesaurus, electronic dictionaries)	" There are different kinds of dictionaries and you use them for different purposes. "													
		early	mid	late	early	mid	late	early	mid	late	early	mid	late	
		GRADE 2			GRADE 3			GRADE 4			GRADE 5			GRADES 6–8

Letter/Sound Relationships

The sounds of oral language are related in both simple and complex ways to the twenty-six letters of the alphabet. Learning the connections between letters and sounds is basic to understanding written language. Children first learn simple relationships that are regular in that one phoneme is connected to one grapheme, or letter. But sounds are also connected to letter clusters, which are groups of letters that appear together (for example, *cr, str, st, bl, fl*), in which you hear each of the associated sounds of the letters; and consonant digraphs (*sh, ch*), in which you hear only one sound. Vowels may also appear in combinations (*ea, oa*) in which you usually hear the first vowel (*ai*) or you hear a completely different sound (*ou*). Children learn to look for and recognize these letter combinations as units, which makes their word solving more efficient. It is important to remember that children will be able to hear and connect the easy-to-identify consonants and vowels early and progress to the harder-to-hear and more difficult letter/sound relationships—for example, letter clusters with two and three letters and those that have more than one sound. You will want to connect initial consonant cluster sounds to the Consonant Cluster Linking Chart (see *Teaching Resources*). It is not necessary to teach every cluster as a separate lesson. In this section, we also provide lessons for cursive writing and keyboarding for the computer.

Connect to Assessment

See related LS Assessment Tasks in the Assessment Guide in *Teaching Resources:*

- ▶ Writing Words with Beginning Consonant Clusters

- ▶ Writing Words with Ending Consonant Clusters

- ▶ Writing Consonant Clusters within Words

- ▶ Reading Words with Consonant Clusters

- ▶ Reading and Writing Words with Vowel Clusters

- ▶ Noticing Double Consonants in Words

Develop Your Professional Understanding

See *Word Matters: Teaching Phonics and Spelling in the Reading/Writing Classroom* by G.S. Pinnell and I. C. Fountas. 1998. Portsmouth, NH: Heinemann.

Related pages: 48–52, 90–93, 120–121, 123, 146–147, 245–246.

Recognizing Words with Consonant Clusters

Making Words

Consider Your Children

In this lesson, the children read a variety of words with *l* clusters, *r* clusters, *s* clusters, and *tw*. Some clusters have three letters (*scr, squ, thr, spr, spl, shr, sch*). If children have not had experience with this variety of two- and three-letter consonant clusters, you may wish to begin with a limited number of clusters, and then introduce others in subsequent lessons.

Working with English Language Learners

Once English language learners understand that some consonants often appear in pairs or groups of three, they will more easily notice consonant clusters in words. Knowing these larger parts of words gives students better access to the words they read and spell. Remember that it might be difficult for some children to hear or say the sounds represented by some letters (e.g., *s* and *r*), so they may need to give more attention to the visual features of the word—how it *looks* as well as the sound-to-letter relationships.

You Need

► Highlighter tape or highlighter.

► Pocket chart.

From *Teaching Resources:*

► Pocket Chart Card Template.

► List Sheets.

► Category Word Cards, Onsets and Rimes. (Select the *s, l, r,* and *tw* onsets.)

Understand the Principle

A cluster is made of two or three consonants blended together with each sound represented. Consonant clusters at the beginning of words are also called *onsets*. Clusters are often labeled as categories —*l* clusters (*bl, cl, fl, gl, pl, sl, spl*), *r* clusters (*br, dr, cr, pr, tr, fr, thr, spr, shr*) and *s* clusters (*sl, sn, sp, st, sw, sc, sk, sm, scr, squ, spr, spl, shr, sch*). Another cluster is *tw*. Realizing that consonants often appear together in words makes reading and writing more efficient.

Explain the Principle

" A group of two or three consonants is a *consonant cluster.* "

" You can usually hear each sound in a consonant cluster. "

CONTINUUM: LETTER/SOUND RELATIONSHIPS — RECOGNIZING AND USING CONSONANT CLUSTERS THAT BLEND TWO OR THREE CONSONANT SOUNDS (*ONSETS*)

(75)

plan

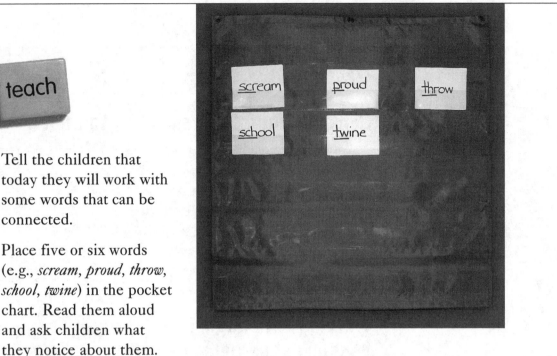

Explain the Principle

" A group of two or three consonants is a *consonant cluster*. "

" You can usually hear each sound in a consonant cluster. "

① Tell the children that today they will work with some words that can be connected.

② Place five or six words (e.g., *scream, proud, throw, school, twine*) in the pocket chart. Read them aloud and ask children what they notice about them. They will respond that each begins with two or three consonants. Underline the consonant clusters in each.

③ Point out that you can usually hear each consonant sound and that they are blended together. In some words the consonants together make one sound such as the *ch* in *school* and the *th* in *throw*.

④ Suggested language, "A group of two or three consonants is a consonant cluster. You can hear each sound in a consonant cluster. In some clusters, two consonants make one sound."

⑤ Invite the children to give a few more examples. Point out that a consonant cluster is sometimes called a *consonant blend*. Use highlighter tape or a highlighter to mark the cluster and show that every word includes a first part starting with a consonant or consonant cluster (the cluster, or *onset*) and a last part (the rest of the word, or *rime*).

⑥ Explain to the children that they will use the Onset and Rime Cards to make twenty words with different beginning clusters, which they will write on a List Sheet. Finally, they will read their complete list to a partner.

make
write
read

► Have the children make twenty words with different beginning clusters using the Onset and Rime Cards.

► Have them write the words on a List Sheet.

► Then they read their lists to a partner.

bl	ot		pr	ank
cl	oud		tr	end
fl	oor		fr	ock
gl	ass		thr	one
pl	ot		spr	ing
sl	am		shr	ift
spl	ash		sl	ed
br	unch		sp	ark
dr	ip		sw	ift
cr	am		sc	one

Name: Andrew

1. blot
2. cloud
3. floor
4. glass
5. plot
6. slam
7. splash
8. brunch
9. drip
10. cram
11. prank
12. trend
13. frock
14. throne
15. spring
16. shrift
17. sled
18. spark
19. swift
20. scone

LIST SHEET

Have the children read their consonant cluster lists to a different partner. Invite them to talk about what they learned about consonant clusters. They can add new examples to the class chart.

Link

Interactive Read-Aloud: Read aloud books that have a variety of words beginning with consonant clusters. Here are two examples:

▸ *Some Smug Slug* by Pamela Edwards

▸ *Autumnblings* by Douglas Florian

Shared Reading: Read aloud a variety of poems with words that begin with consonant clusters. On the first reading, cover the cluster with a stick-on note and invite children to identify the missing letters.

Guided Reading: As students are reading texts, prompt them to "look at the first part" when they are trying to solve unknown words with consonant clusters. You may want to show them how to cover the last part of the word to help them start the word.

Guided/Independent Writing: When students are writing new words with consonant clusters, remind them to say and write the letter for each sound in the cluster.

assess

▸ Dictate about ten words with a variety of consonant clusters to determine how easily students can write them.

▸ Have students read the same list of words from a typed sheet.

▸ Notice how quickly students take words apart as they read them.

Expand the Learning

Have the children play Consonant Cluster Lotto to review the variety of consonant clusters. (See Directions for Lotto in *Teaching Resources*.)

Connect with Home

Send home a set of Onset and Rime Cards for students to cut out. Have them glue the word parts on plain paper to make twenty words and read them to family members.

Identifying Words with Ending Consonant Clusters

Making Words

Consider Your Children

Initial consonant clusters and digraphs tend to be easier than those that are final clusters. The ending clusters are often learned most easily when they are part of a rime (*ard* as in *card*). Most clusters are represented in this lesson; those that are not taught appear infrequently in only a few words, such as *milk, help*. This lesson focuses on consonant clusters (blends) in which you can hear both sounds. If children find this principle very easy, you may want to expand the lesson to include words that end in digraphs combining it with Lesson LS 3.

Working with English Language Learners

Be sure that English language learners understand the concept of consonant clusters at the beginning of words. They can use examples they know and make connections with the same clusters at the end of a word. Reinforce this principle during the word work component of guided reading or when working with a small group for added practice. Have children use magnetic letters to build words and then to physically separate the ending clusters so that they notice them. Accept approximate pronunciations and provide many opportunities for children to say the words.

You Need

▸ Chart paper.

▸ Markers.

▸ Magnetic letters.

From *Teaching Resources:*

▸ Word Pairs Sheets.

▸ Lesson LS 2 Word Cards.

Understand the Principle

A consonant cluster is made up of two consonants together. In ending consonant clusters, each consonant sound is pronounced and blended together. There are also final consonant digraphs, such as *ch, ng, sh, th* (*which, swing, cash, cloth*).

Explain the Principle

❝ Some words have consonant clusters at the end. ❞

❝ You can hear each sound in a consonant cluster at the end of a word. ❞

CONTINUUM: LETTER/SOUND RELATIONSHIPS — RECOGNIZING AND USING LETTERS THAT REPRESENT CONSONANT CLUSTERS (BLENDS) AT THE END OF THE WORD

79

plan

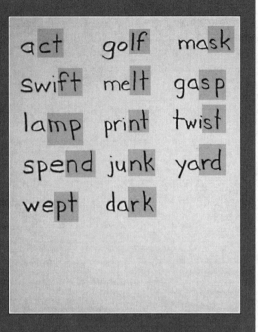

Explain the Principle

" Some words have consonant clusters at the end. "

" You can hear each sound in a consonant cluster at the end of a word. "

① Explain to the children that you are going to help them learn more about consonant clusters.

② Write words on the chart that show a variety of ending consonant clusters. Suggested language: "You have been noticing consonant clusters at the beginning of words. What do you notice about these words?"

③ Have the children read each word aloud as you highlight or underline the ending cluster.

④ Children will notice that there are consonant clusters at the end of words. Some endings may be surprising to them.

⑤ Explain that many words have consonant clusters at the end.

⑥ Tell the children that they will use word cards and magnetic letters to make ten pairs of words, each pair with a different ending cluster. They will then write their pairs on a Word Pairs Sheet.

take
make
write
highlight

- ▸ Have the children choose a word card, make the word with magnetic letters, and write it on a Word Pairs Sheet.

- ▸ For each word, children write another word with the same ending cluster and then highlight the clusters.

- ▸ Children repeat this for ten pairs of words, each pair with a different ending cluster.

drift	
camp	
bend	
kept	
elf	
belt	

Name: Jeff — Word Pairs Sheet
Date:

drift	—	lift
camp	—	ramp
bend	—	send
kept	—	leapt
elf	—	shelf
belt	—	kilt
ant	—	pant
card	—	hard
bark	—	ark
ask	—	task
gasp	—	lisp
chest	—	rest

Have children read their lists to a partner and add a few more examples to the chart. Ask children to discuss what they have learned about words.

Observe for comments such as:

- ▸ In consonant clusters you hear the sound of every letter.

- ▸ Do all three-letter consonant clusters start with *s*?

- ▸ There are a lot of words with consonant clusters using *st*.

- ▸ Consonant clusters can be at the beginning, the end, or the middle of a word.

Link

Interactive Read-Aloud: Read aloud books that have words with ending clusters. Suggested titles are:

- ▸ *Birdsong* by Audrey Wood
- ▸ *Jumpity-Bumpity* by Kay Chorao

Shared Reading: Select a variety of poems that include words with ending consonant clusters or digraphs. Use an overhead projector to highlight several of them.

Guided Reading: During word work, write some words with ending clusters on the whiteboard and then call for quick recognition.

Guided/Independent Writing: When children write new words, encourage them to analyze each sound in the ending cluster.

assess

- ▸ Dictate ten words with ending clusters or a sentence with many words ending with consonant clusters.
- ▸ Notice how quickly the children write the words as well as the degree to which they successfully represent final consonant clusters.

Expand the Learning

Repeat the lesson with ending consonant digraphs. To make the activity more challenging, combine consonant clusters of both types in the activity.

Connect with Home

Ask the children to look through magazines, catalogs, and newspapers and cut out words in large print that have final consonant clusters. They can glue five words on a sheet of paper and then write a sentence using each word.

Recognizing Words with Ending Consonant Digraphs

Consonant Cluster Lotto

Consider Your Children

This lesson reviews a variety of ending consonant sounds, some of which have complex spellings. You can include all of them in the lesson or select those you want to work with first and add the others in a subsequent lesson. The Lotto game may be familiar to children, in which case you do not need to demonstrate it.

Working with English Language Learners

This lesson helps English language learners review the principle of consonant digraphs. You may need to remind children of words with digraphs at the beginning as well as at the end of words. They will need to use words that are meaningful to them. Playing Lotto should be a familiar routine for them. If not, play the game with children the first time to be sure they know the routine and the words used. During guided reading, have children search a page to find examples of words with ending consonant clusters.

You Need

- Chart paper.
- Markers.
- Index cards.

From *Teaching Resources:*
- Directions for Lotto.
- Four-by-Four Lotto Game Boards.
- Lesson LS 3 Word Cards.

Understand the Principle

Consonant clusters, which can occur at the beginning, within, or at the end of words, also include consonant digraphs. In some consonant clusters you can hear each sound (*rust*). In consonant digraphs, two letters combine to make one sound (*graph*). The letters *gh* sometimes function as silent letters (*night, sigh*). The *ch* cluster and *tch* differ only by the extra *t*, as they represent the same sound. The *tch* combination occurs only with a vowel before the consonant (*catch*), while *ch* can have either (*lunch, rich*)

Explain the Principle

" Some words have consonant clusters at the end that make only one sound. "

CONTINUUM: LETTER/SOUND RELATIONSHIPS — RECOGNIZING AND USING LETTERS THAT REPRESENT CONSONANT DIGRAPHS AT THE
END OF A WORD (*SH, TH, CH, CK, TCH, DGE, NG, PH, GH*)

83

plan

teach

Explain the Principle

" **Some words have consonant clusters at the end that make only one sound.** "

① Tell the children that you are going to help them learn more about the last parts of words.

② Write *brush, cloth, much, duck, latch, edge, song, graph, tough* on the chart, leaving room for a few words under each. Read the words aloud and ask children what they notice about the ending letters of each one. Underline the consonant digraph as they discuss each of the nine patterns.

③ Suggested language: "Some words have consonant clusters at the end that make only one sound." Write this statement across the top of the chart.

④ Invite children to provide a second example for each pattern. Underline the cluster as you write them on the chart. Remind children that they will have to attend to both the way words sound and the way they look.

⑤ Tell children that they will play Consonant Cluster Lotto with words having these ending patterns.

⑥ Demonstrate the game with one or two children if the routine is new. Each player has a Lotto game card. Players take turns drawing word cards, reading the words and searching for a word on their card that has the same ending consonant cluster. If they find a match, they cover the space with a game marker. The first player to cover the entire card wins the game.

> Some words have consonant clusters at the end that make only one sound.
>
> brush   edge
> cloth   song
> much   graph
> duck   tough
> latch

take
read
match
cover

apply

► Have the children play Consonant Cluster Lotto in groups of two to four.

► After playing, they write three words on an index card and highlight the ending digraph.

► Have children bring their cards to sharing and contribute to the group's learning.

LOTTO

tough	change	watch	lock
rich	sing	bath	stock
ledge	dish	rash	cloth
rock	much	swing	edge

brush

share

Ask the children to suggest one more word for each pattern on the chart and review the lesson principle.

Observe for comments like:

► A digraph can be at the beginning or end of a word.

► The two letters in a digraph make only one sound.

► There are more consonant clusters that you hear all the sounds than there are digraphs.

► If you add *tub* to *bathtub*, the digraph will be in the middle of the word.

Link

Interactive Read-Aloud: Read aloud a variety of books with words that have ending consonant clusters, such as:

▸ *Waterhole Waiting* by Jane Kurtz and Christopher Kurtz

▸ *Slowly, Slowly, Slowly, Said the Sloth* by Eric Carle

Shared Reading: Have the children find words with ending consonant clusters in a familiar poem that you have placed on an overhead projector.

Guided Reading: When the children come to an unknown word with a consonant cluster, prompt them by asking, "Do you know another word that ends like that?"

Guided/Independent Writing: Encourage the children to refer to the chart you made in this lesson when they edit for spelling.

assess

▸ As a quick assessment, dictate nine words, one with each pattern. Alternatively, dictate a sentence with words having several of the patterns.

▸ Observe the children's ability to write words with ending consonant clusters.

▸ As an alternative, have them read a typed list of words and then highlight consonant clusters.

Expand the Learning

Create Lotto cards that include all the ending consonant clusters.

Alternatively, create Lotto cards that include beginning and ending consonant clusters (including digraphs) for a comprehensive review.

Connect with Home

Have the children take home the Lotto game cards and word cards to play the game with a family member. As an alternative, children can make their own game cards to share with their families.

Recognizing Words with Beginning and Ending Consonant Digraphs

Go Fish

Consider Your Children

Children may already have experience with the simpler consonant digraphs (*sh, ch, wh, th*). The consonant digraph *ph* may be more challenging. Consonant digraphs found at the end of words are part of the *rime,* or spelling pattern.

Working with English Language Learners

Depending on the phonological systems of their native language, children may find it difficult to say sounds represented by some consonant digraphs. Pronunciation will not be a problem if children have many experiences with words and learn to use the visual features when problem solving. Help children by providing one or two familiar examples for each digraph so that they can make connections with unfamiliar words. Show children how the words are connected by using oral and print examples. If children's experiences are limited, teach a lesson on beginning consonant digraphs first, and then teach lessons on ending consonant digraphs. Instead, you may prefer to limit the number of digraphs you use.

You Need

► Chart paper.

► Markers.

From *Teaching Resources:*

► Directions for Go Fish.

► Go Fish Game Cards made from Lesson LS 4 Word Cards and Deck Card Template.

Understand the Principle

Consonant digraphs comprise two letters that make one sound, which is usually different from either of the letters. The cluster *wh* is unique. *Wear* and *where* are close, but slightly different in pronunciation (depending on local dialects), but *wh* has another associated sound, as in *who.* The *th* digraph has two sounds as in *there* and *thought* and may be followed by *r* as in *throw.* The final *ch* may be spelled with *tch* as in *catch.*

Explain the Principle

❝ Some clusters of consonants stand for one sound that is usually different from either of the letters. They are called *consonant digraphs.* ❞

❝ You can hear the sound of a consonant digraph at the beginning or ending of a word. ❞

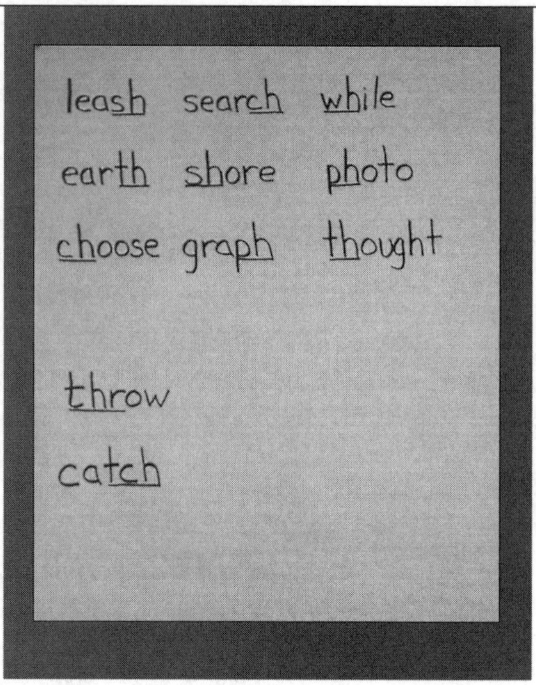

plan

teach

The chart reads:

leash   search   while
earth   shore   photo
choose   graph   thought

throw

catch

Explain the Principle

" Some clusters of consonants stand for one sound that is usually different from either of the letters. They are called *consonant digraphs.* "

" You can hear the sound of a consonant digraph at the beginning or ending of a word. "

① Explain to the children that you are going to help them think about consonant digraphs at the beginning and ending of words. Have children read the words that you have written on the chart.

② Invite one student at a time to underline the consonant digraphs in each word. Suggested language: "What do you notice about each of the digraphs?" They will likely respond that each makes one sound that is different from either of the consonants.

③ Write *throw* and *catch* on the chart to show that sometimes a third letter is part of the pattern. Summarize with: "You can hear the sound of a consonant digraph at the beginning or ending of a word."

④ Explain to the children that they will play Go Fish with words having consonant digraphs at the beginning or at the end of the word.

⑤ Demonstrate how to play with initial and ending consonant digraphs. Give each player six cards. Players take turns saying a word they have on a card and asking another player whether he has a card with a word that begins or ends with the same consonant digraph. If the other player has one, the first player takes that card and makes a pair on the table. If no one has a match, then the player says "Go Fish" and the first player takes a card from the deck. The first player to run out of cards wins the game.

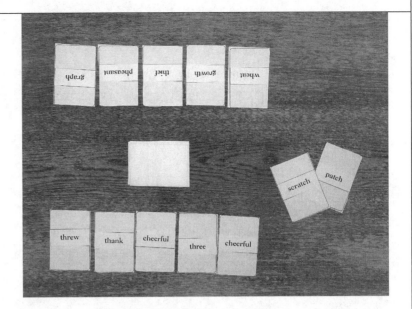

ask
match

apply

- ▸ Have the children play Go Fish in pairs or small groups.
- ▸ Players take turns asking for cards and making matches. The first player to run out of cards wins the game.

share

After playing, children look for an example that is not already on the group chart or that helped them read a new word. They write it on a stick-on note and place it on the right place on the chart.

Invite children to suggest three or four more words with consonant digraphs to add to the chart. Ask them to talk about what they have learned about words.

Children may have noticed that words like *mother* and *fishing* have consonant digraphs in the middle.

Link

Interactive Read-Aloud: Read aloud books that have many words with beginning or ending consonant digraphs, such as:

- ▶ ***Where Once There Was a Wood*** by Denise Fleming
- ▶ ***Drat the Fat Cat*** by Pat Thompson

Shared Reading: Select a variety of poems with words that have beginning or ending consonant digraphs. Use an overhead projector to display the poems. Have students find and highlight words with beginning or ending consonant digraphs in the poem.

Guided Reading: As children are reading new words with consonant digraphs, prompt them to read the first or last part of the word and notice the digraph.

Guided/Independent Writing: During word work, have children make and mix words with consonant digraphs. Emphasize quick construction of the words.

assess

- ▶ Notice whether the children's writing of words includes beginning or ending consonant digraphs. Select a few to dictate so that you can do a quick assessment of students' control of this principle.

Expand the Learning

Repeat the lesson adding word cards for words that have consonant digraphs within them, such as *washer, kitchen, telephone, fisherman, catcher, father, mother, brother, whether, hatched, biography, rushed, watches, dishes, coaches, teacher, birthday, dishwasher, lunchbox.*

Connect with Home

Send home a deck of word cards for students to play Go Fish with a family member.

Recognizing and Using y as a Vowel Sound in Words

Follow the Path

Consider Your Children

If the children already understand this letter/sound relationship, then you may not need to review it. In this lesson the word list contains a variety of words with the long vowel sound of /ē/ or /ī/, which are represented with a *y* or with a vowel and *y*.

Working with English Language Learners

Understanding that a letter can represent several different sounds depending on its place in a word is an important concept for children who are learning to speak, read, and write English. Some languages may be more regular than English in its letter/sound relationships; others may not use an alphabetic system. The examples you use to illustrate the sounds represented by *y* should be easy words that English language learners can understand and perhaps read and write. Establish the concept firmly with these easier examples. In the beginning, remove any words that children do not understand.

You Need

► Pocket chart.
► Paper.
► Dice or number cards.

From *Teaching Resources:*
► Pocket Chart Card Template (with a selection of words ending in *y*).
► Directions for Follow the Path.
► Lesson LS 5 Word List.
► Two-Column Sheets.

Understand the Principle

In a one syllable word, *y* functions as a vowel sound and usually sounds like a long /ī/. In multisyllable words it usually sounds like a long /ē/ when it appears at the end of words. In still others, it may represent the short /i/ sound in *cymbals*. It often functions as the letter representing the vowel sound in a syllable.

Explain the Principle

" *Y* is a letter that sometimes makes a vowel sound. "

" *Y* sounds like /ē/ on the end of words like *happy, funny, family, monkey, key.* "

" *Y* sounds like /ī/ in words like *my, sky, by.* "

plan

Explain the Principle

" *Y* is a letter that sometimes makes a vowel sound. "

" *Y* sounds like /ē/ on the end of words like *happy, funny, family, monkey, key.* "

" *Y* sounds like /ī/ in words like *my, sky, by.* "

① Explain to the children that they will look at some words with *y* in them. Place *why, family, dry, happy, funny, tidy, sky, fly, cuddly* in the pocket chart in random order.

② Ask children what they notice about the *y* in each word. They will likely say that the *y* is at the end of the words and that it sometimes sounds like long /ē/ and other times sounds like long /ī/.

③ Invite children to sort the words into two columns. They will notice that the one-syllable words have a *y* that sounds like long /ī/ and in the multi-syllable words the *y* sounds like long /ē/.

④ Explain to children they will play Follow the Path. Each time they toss the dice, they move the number of spaces shown, read the word in the space, and then use it in a sentence.

⑤ When they finish the game, children will write two columns of words on a Two-Column Sheet. In the first column they write three words with a long /ī/ sound at the end; in the second column they write three words with a long /ē/ sound at the end.

throw
move
read
say
write

apply

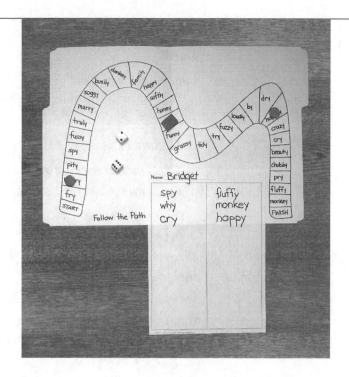

► Have the children play Follow the Path in groups of two to four.

► They roll the dice, move that number of spaces, read the word in the space and then use it in a sentence.

► Finally, using a Two-Column Sheet they write three words with a long /ī/ sound in the first column and three words with a long /ē/ sound in the second column.

share

Have the children swap lists and read one another's words. Then they use each of the partner's words in a sentence.

Ask students to discuss what they have learned about the letter *y* in words. Watch for comments like these:

► *y* can sound like /ē/ or /ī/ at the end of a word.

► In two syllable words, it sounds like long /ē/ at the end.

throw
move
read
say
write

apply

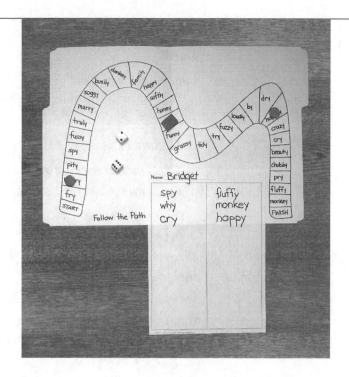

► Have the children play Follow the Path in groups of two to four.

► They roll the dice, move that number of spaces, read the word in the space and then use it in a sentence.

► Finally, using a Two-Column Sheet they write three words with a long /ī/ sound in the first column and three words with a long /ē/ sound in the second column.

share

Have the children swap lists and read one another's words. Then they use each of the partner's words in a sentence.

Ask students to discuss what they have learned about the letter *y* in words. Watch for comments like these:

► *y* can sound like /ē/ or /ī/ at the end of a word.

► In two syllable words, it sounds like long /ē/ at the end.

Link

Interactive Read-Aloud: Read aloud books that have many words ending in *y*. Here are two examples:

- ▸ *Elephant Games* by Brad Bagert
- ▸ *Read Anything Good Lately*
  by Susan Allen and Jane Lindaman

Shared Reading: Read aloud and enjoy poems and then ask children to find three or four words ending with *y* and have them tell the vowel sound they hear. Place highlighter tape on the words.

Guided Reading: During word work, write a few words ending in *y* on the whiteboard and call for quick recognition.

Guided/Independent Writing: As students write words ending in *y*, they name the vowel sound it represents.

assess

- ▸ Observe how quickly and accurately children read words ending in *y*.
- ▸ Dictate and have children write three to five words ending in *y* to assess children's control of the principle.

Expand the Learning

Have children create Word Searches for one another, selecting words from the lesson list. (See Directions for Word Search in *Teaching Resources*.)

Connect with Home

Give children a photocopy of the lesson word list and a blank Word Card Template to take home. They can use the list to make word cards that they place face down in a pile. Children take one card at a time and create two columns of words, one with words having a *y* with long /ē/ sound, and another with words having the long /ī/ sound.

Identifying Words with Different Vowel Sounds: oo, ow, ea

Connect

Consider Your Children

Children should have a strong control of basic letter/sound relationships so they can turn their attention to more complex patterns, including vowel combinations that represent different sounds. Be sure that children are familiar with the concept that letters and letter clusters can represent more than one sound, depending on the word (gown, grown) and also that they have solid knowledge of letter/sound relationships for vowels. In this lesson the children learn a new routine for the Connect card game.

Working with English Language Learners

Be sure that English language learners have worked with vowel patterns and know a core of words in each category before they begin to play this new game. You may wish to work with small groups the first time students use this new and more complex routine. The game requires them to notice vowel patterns quickly. Review the word cards, reading them several times to be sure children are familiar with the words before they play the game.

You Need

▶ Pocket chart.

▶ Index cards.

From *Teaching Resources:*

▶ Pocket Chart Card Template.

▶ Directions for Connect.

▶ Connect Game Cards made from Lesson LS 6 Word Cards and Deck Card Template. Include several "wild cards" of your choosing in each deck.

Understand the Principle

Letter combinations can represent different sounds and children need to learn the options so they can try alternate sounds if needed when reading. *Ea* can sound like a long /ā/ as in *break, steak* or a short /e/ as in *bread. Lead* and *read* can have both sounds of *ea*. The same *oo* sound in *book* is represented by *ould* in *could, would, should*. The same *oo* sound in *boot* is represented by other letter combinations in *grew, new, you, group*.

Explain the Principle

❝ Two letters that go together can stand for different sounds in different words: *moon, look, snow, cow, meat, break*). ❞

CONTINUUM: LETTER/SOUND RELATIONSHIPS — RECOGNIZING THAT LETTER COMBINATIONS MAY REPRESENT TWO DIFFERENT VOWEL SOUNDS

plan

Explain
the Principle

" Two letters that go together can stand for different sounds in different words: *moon, look, snow, cow, meat, break.* "

① Tell the children they will learn about letters that stand for different sounds. Randomly place one word with each sound in a pocket chart.

② Ask children to make pairs of words that have matching letters.

③ Have them say what they notice when they read each pair. They will notice that the words have some of the same letters but they stand for different sounds.

④ Invite the children to add another word or two that fits each sound pattern.

⑤ Tell the children you will teach them a card game that uses words with letters that stand for different sounds.

⑥ Demonstrate the Connect card game with one or two children. Deal the word cards evenly to the players. One player lays down a card and reads it. The next player must follow suit by playing and reading another word with the same letters and sound. The next player does the same. If a player does not have a match to follow suit (same letter and same sound), he cannot discard and picks up all the cards played in the round. A wild card can match any other card. If all players lay down a matching card, the pile is moved to the side and not played again. The object of the game is to run out of cards.

take
sort
read
write

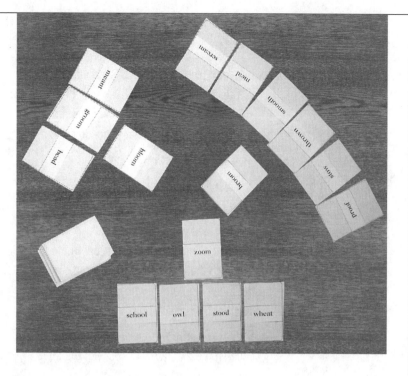

► Children play Connect in groups of two to four players. The first player to discard all cards wins the game. If time is limited, the player with the fewest cards at the end wins the game.

► After playing, children write on an index card one word pair in which the vowel pair *looks* the same but *sounds* different. They bring their cards to share with the group.

Have the children share examples of word pairs that look the same but sound different.

Invite the children to add one more example to each section of the chart.

Invite them to talk about what they learned about words. They may notice that sometimes vowels that go together have the same sound but different letters (*week, weak*) and sometimes vowel pairs have the same letters but different sounds (*moon, look*).

Link

Interactive Read-Aloud: Read aloud books that feature words with the letter patterns, *ea, ow, oo*. After reading, help the children notice two or three of the words. Suggested titles are:

- ▸ *A Chill in the Air* by John Frank
- ▸ *Rain Romp* by Jane Kurtz

Shared Reading: Select a variety of poems that includes words with the letter patterns *ea, ow, oo*. Have children read the poem the first time with the letter patterns covered. Ask them to predict the pattern while you uncover it to confirm their predictions.

Guided Reading: After reading a text, have children point to a few words with the letter patterns *ea, ow, oo*.

Guided/Independent Writing: In the editing process, have children notice words with the letter patterns *ea, ow, oo*.

assess

- ▸ Observe the children's correct use of the patterns in their writing.
- ▸ Notice how fluently the children read words with these letter patterns.

Expand the Learning

Create a new deck of cards with a different variety of words.

Have children create their own Word Searches for a partner to complete. (See Directions for Word Searches in *Teaching Resources*.)

Connect with Home

Send home a deck of Connect cards. Children can teach family members how to play.

As an alternative, children can create their own Connect card decks to share with family members. Give them copies of the Deck Card Template (see *Teaching Resources*).

Identifying Other Vowel Sounds: oo, oi, oy, ow, aw, au

Make, Write, Read

Consider Your Children

After the children are flexible with single consonants and consonant clusters in a variety of positions and have good knowledge of basic vowel patterns, they can develop more systematic knowledge of other vowel combinations. In this lesson, they work to organize their knowledge by creating categories. Start with examples they know.

Working with English Language Learners

This lesson, and others that you adapt from it, will help English language learners expand their knowledge of more complex words. Begin with simple examples. Most of the words in this lesson are one syllable, but in reading and writing point out two- and three-syllable words with the same patterns. In thinking about connecting to home, be sure that the words children take home on their List Sheets are words they understand and can read. Work with small groups to be sure children understand the task of making a crossword puzzle. If this is too complex, have the children take home word cards with simple sentences on the back that they can read.

You Need

▶ Pocket chart.

▶ Magnetic letters.

From *Teaching Resources:*

▶ Pocket Chart Card Template.

▶ List Sheets (two per child).

▶ Lesson LS 7 Word Cards.

Understand the Principle

You often see the letter combinations *oo, oi, oy, ow, aw,* and *au* in words. They represent unique vowel sounds. The *oo* can represent a longer (*moon*) or shorter (*took*) sound; *ow* can represent a long *o* (s*now*) or another sound (*cow*). The *ow* sound can also be represented by *ou* (*round*). The short *o* sound can be represented with *ough* as in *thought* or *cough*. Children will notice that sometimes a consonant is paired with a vowel to create a unique vowel sound.

Explain the Principle

" Some letters go together and make other vowel sounds (*autumn, moon, look, boy, oil, cow, house, paw*). "

plan

teach

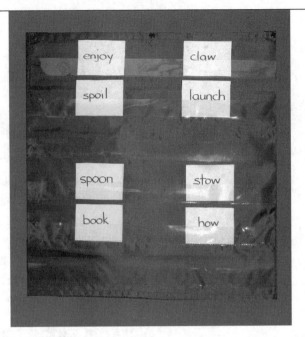

Explain the Principle

" **Some letters go together and make other vowel sounds (autumn, moon, look, boy, oil, cow, house, paw).** "

① Tell the children you will help them notice more about letters and sounds. Place these word cards in a pocket chart: *enjoy, spoon, book, claw, stow, launch, spoil,* and *how.*

② Suggested language: "You have been studying vowel sounds. Some letters go together but sound different in different words (such as the two sounds of *ow* and *oo*). Different vowel combinations can make the same sound (such as the *oy* in *enjoy* and *oi* in *spoil*). As you read these words, think about the vowel sounds."

③ Ask children to read the words aloud with you. Place the pairs of words together, with children suggesting which pairs go together.

④ Ask the children what they notice about each pair of words. They will say that some have the same vowel sound (*enjoy, spoil,* and *claw, launch*) but different letters. Others have the same letters and different sounds (*book, spoon* and *how, stow*).

⑤ Explain the principle to the children. Suggested language: "Some letters go together and stand for other vowel sounds."

⑥ Tell the children they will select five word cards with each pattern, make each word with magnetic letters, and then write the words on a List Sheet. Finally, they read their word lists to a partner.

take
make
write
read

► Have children select five word cards with each pattern.

► Taking one card at a time for each of the sound and letter patterns, they make each word with magnetic letters and then write the words on a List Sheet. Since each List Sheet has only twenty spaces, children need two sheets each to write the thirty words they made.

► Finally, they read their lists to a partner.

Invite children to read their lists to a different partner. Have them suggest words to add to the class chart and explain how the new words relate to the words already on the chart.

Explain that when you are working with vowels that go together, you can connect words by how they look (*how, know*) or how they sound (*how, sound*).

Link

Interactive Read-Aloud: Read aloud books that have a variety of words with the lesson letter patterns, such as:

▸ *Pocketful of Nonsense* by James Marshall

▸ *Four Famished Foxes and Fosdyke* by Pamela Edwards

Shared Reading: As you read poems displayed on the overhead projector, highlight the words with letter patterns *oo, oi, oy, ow, aw, au.*

Guided Reading: After reading a text, have children locate and read a word with one of the vowel patterns.

Guided/Independent Writing: When children write new words, remind them to think about vowel patterns to help them with correct spelling.

assess

▸ Examine the children's writing to notice words in which the children have misspelled the vowel combinations. Analyze the categories and revisit those that are challenging.

▸ Notice how quickly children read words with the vowel patterns.

Expand the Learning

Have children play Concentration with the lesson word cards. (See Directions for Concentration in *Teaching Resources*.)

Connect with Home

Send home the List Sheets for children to read to family members.

Recognizing Long Vowel Patterns:
ai, ay, ee, ea, oa, ow, ue, ui, ew

Crazy Eights

Consider Your Children

Children should have good control of simple letter/sound relationships and basic phonogram patterns. In this lesson, children learn to play Crazy Eights so that they can play it with different principles. In this version of the game, vowel patterns that represent four different long vowels are used.

Working with English Language Learners

English language learners may have some words with long vowel patterns in their speaking vocabularies but not realize that the sounds are represented by two vowels instead of one. Once they understand this principle, their word solving will become more efficient and their spelling will improve. Crazy Eights gives them the opportunity to examine words many times, noticing and remembering the vowel patterns. Use the word work component of guided reading to reinforce the principle and help children use magnetic letters to build words with vowel patterns.

You Need

▸ Pocket chart.

From *Teaching Resources:*

▸ Pocket Chart Card Template.

▸ Directions for Crazy Eights.

▸ Crazy Eights Game Cards made from the Lesson LS 8 Word Cards and Deck Card Template. Include four cards with a Crazy Eight on them.

Understand the Principle

Usually vowel combinations represent the long sound of the first vowel. Sometimes a consonant is paired with the vowel to represent the long vowel sound. In this lesson two patterns represent long /ā/ (*ai, ay*), two represent long /ē/ (*ee, ea*), two represent long /ō/ (*oa, ow*) and three represent long /ū/ (*ue, ui, ew*). Long /ī/ patterns such as *ie* in pie and *igh* in *might* are not included.

Explain the Principle

❝ Some vowels go together in words and make one sound. ❞

❝ When there are two vowels (*ai, ay, ee, ea, oa, ow, ue, ui, ew*) they usually make the sound of the name of the first vowel or a long vowel sound. ❞

plan

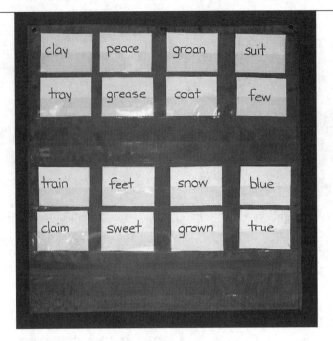

Explain the Principle

" Some vowels go together in words and make one sound. "

" When there are two vowels (*ai, ay, ee, ea, oa, ow, ue, ui, ew*) they usually make the sound of the name of the first vowel or a long vowel sound. "

① Explain to the children that you are going to help them notice more about vowel patterns. Place eight word cards in two rows across the pocket chart.

② Hold the remaining eight cards in your hand. Hold up one card at a time and have children read it, and then place it under the word with the same vowel sound. (Note that a word with *ai* can be placed under a word with *ay* because it has the same vowel sound.)

③ Explain that letter combinations can represent the long vowel sounds. If the vowel *i* is mentioned, explain that *tie* and *night* both contain patterns with the long *i* sound. The letters *ew* represent a long /ū/ sound, not the sound of long /ē/.

④ Tell children they are going to play the Crazy Eights card game. Each player gets eight cards. Place the remaining deck face down, with one card turned up beside the deck. The first player reads the card that is face up, puts down one of his cards with the same long vowel sound, and reads it. If the player does not have a card that matches, he can discard a Crazy Eight card, which functions as a free card. Otherwise, the player draws cards until he finds a match to put down. The first player to discard all his cards wins the game.

⑤ Demonstrate and explain the game with two children until everyone understands how to play the game.

read
match
take card
put down pair

▸ Have the children play Crazy Eights in groups of three or four.

▸ After playing, children write two words representing different vowel sounds on a stick-on note and place it in the appropriate column on the chart.

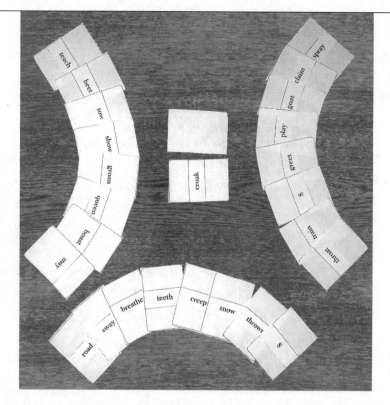

Have children retrieve their stick-on notes and invite them to use their notes to give a few more examples for each category on the chart. Ask the children to share what they learned about words.

Link

Interactive Read-Aloud: Read aloud a variety of books with long vowel patterns, such as:

- ▸ *A. Nonny Mouse Writes Again!* by Jack Prelutsky
- ▸ *Bringing the Rain to Kapiti Plain* by Verna Aardema

Shared Reading: Select poems that have words with long vowel patterns to read with your students. After reading, say a word and then find another word with the same sound represented by a letter pattern.

Guided Reading: During word work, write a few words on the whiteboard, varying the long vowel pattern.

Guided/Independent Writing: Have children notice words that have long vowel patterns in their writing.

assess

- ▸ As children read, notice their ability to read words with long vowel patterns quickly.
- ▸ Dictate a few words with long vowel patterns for children to write. Analyze their words to determine their control of the letter patterns.

Expand the Learning

Add words with long *i* vowel patterns (e.g., *igh*) to the deck. Also include multisyllable words with long vowel patterns, such as *crayon, renew, cashew, avenue, repair, raincoat, mermaid, explain, ideal, disappear*.

Connect with Home

Send home a deck of Crazy Eights cards so that the children can play the game with family members.

Alternatively, send home copies of the Deck Card Template with words on them for students to cut out and make the Crazy Eights card deck.

Recognizing Double Consonants in Words

Word Grid Game

Consider Your Children

In this lesson, children focus on words with two similar consonants in the middle. The lesson includes a range of double consonants, some of which are doubled prior to adding an ending (e.g., *setting*). Be sure to include a complete range of double letters on the word cards. Children should have good control of basic one-syllable patterns prior to teaching this principle.

Working with English Language Learners

Double consonants that are similar are not detectable in pronunciation, but they are easy to notice when children look at words. English language learners may need to see and say words many times to notice the double letters and to understand the appropriate syllable to stress. Have children build words with magnetic letters so that the details are clear. They will be more likely to remember the double consonant if they search for two *l*'s, for example. Work with children in a small group when they begin to use word grids so that you can help them understand the task.

You Need

▶ Chart paper.

▶ Markers.

▶ Index cards.

From *Teaching Resources:*

▶ Directions for Word Grids.

▶ Word Grid Template.

▶ Word Grid Game Cards made from Lesson LS 9 Word Cards and Deck Card Template.

Understand the Principle

The double consonant pattern includes a variety of consonant letters, usually within two-syllable words. The syllable division is between the two consonants and most often the stress is on the first syllable (*cof-fee, ar-rive*). Sometimes the stress is on the second syllable but not often (*des-sert, hel-lo*). Noticing double consonants will help children take apart and read words.

Explain the Principle

" Sometimes double consonant letters stand for a consonant sound in the middle of a word (*rubber, arrive, coffee, lesson*). "

CONTINUUM: LETTER/SOUND RELATIONSHIPS — RECOGNIZING AND USING MIDDLE CONSONANT SOUNDS SOMETIMES REPRESENTED BY DOUBLE LETTERS

107

plan

slipper mitten lesson ladder follow
zipper fatten message hidden dollar
dessert   balloon
pollute

Explain the Principle

" Sometimes double consonant letters stand for a consonant sound in the middle of a word (*rubber, arrive, coffee, lesson*). "

① Tell the children that you are going to help them learn more about spelling patterns.

② Write *slipper, mitten, lesson, ladder, follow* across the top of the chart and have children read the words. Suggested language: "What do you notice about these words?"

③ Students will notice the double consonants. They will notice that each has two syllables, and that the first syllable is usually stressed.

④ Ask children to think of other words with double consonant letters in the middle and write each below the word with the same consonants.

⑤ Write *balloon, pollute, dessert* in the columns and have children read them aloud and listen for the stress. Help children notice that the stress is sometimes (but not often) on the second syllable. Tell them they will see more double letters in the words they will use in today's game.

⑥ Explain that when children see double consonants, they can divide the word between the two consonants to help them read the word. They can remember double consonants to help them write words correctly. Suggested language: "Sometimes double consonant letters stand for a consonant sound in the middle of a word."

⑦ Show children how to play the Word Grid Game. The first player takes a card, reads it aloud, looks for a word on his grid that contains the same double consonant, then reads the word on his grid and crosses it out. He turns the card over and the next person takes a turn. The goal is to cross out all the words on the grid.

take
read
find
cross out

write
divide
underline

The word grid shows the following words:

giggle	smelly	puppet	fellow	funny	slipper	pollute	possess	narrow	afford
shallow	bottle	raccoon	fatten	happen	mitten	stopper	village	sadden	ribbon
hammock	wedding	buzzer	attic	puppy	sitter	hidden	hollow	getting	dollar
blossom	glitter	rabbit	happy	gutter	puzzle	letter	hello	matter	cellar
coffee	pepper	collect	buffet	accident	gallon	baggy	suggest	tennis	juggle
zipper	button	beggar	bonnet	channel	common	gossip	passage	yellow	willow
jogger	hammer	apple	spelling	supper	muffin	rotten	critter	follow	pillow

effort

- ▸ Children play the Word Grid Game in pairs or groups of three.
- ▸ After playing, they write two words on an index card, indicate where those words can be divided, and underline the syllable that is stressed.
- ▸ They bring their cards to sharing.

Select a double consonant pattern and have each child read one word with the same letters from his grid or index card. You may wish to add one or two examples to the chart. Children can share the words on their index cards, explaining the syllable division and pronunciation.

Link

Interactive Read-Aloud: Read aloud a variety of books with words that have double consonants, such as:

- ▶ *Street Rhymes Around the World* by Jane Yolen

- ▶ *The Horrible Holidays* by Audrey Wood

Shared Reading: After enjoying poems, have children find two or three words with double consonants. Ask them which syllable is stressed.

Guided Reading: During word work, write a few words with double consonants on the whiteboard and draw a line between them. Ask children to read the words and tell which syllable is stressed.

Guided/Independent Writing: Point out words with double consonants. As children edit, have them find words that need two consonants in the middle.

assess

- ▶ Observe children's correct use of double consonants when they write.

- ▶ You may want to dictate a few words as a quick assessment. Notice children's ability to take apart words with double consonants.

Expand the Learning

Have children create Word Grids for one another. Create a new variety of words on the grids so the children can play a new game.

Give children completed grids and ask them to read across the lines to a partner to practice fluent reading of words with double consonants.

Connect with Home

Send home the completed Word Grids for children to practice reading aloud to family members. They can highlight or circle the double consonants they find.

Recognizing Consonant Letters with Different Sounds: c, g, th, ch

Crazy Eights

Consider Your Children

Children should have strong control of consonant sounds so that they can attend to the more complex letter/sound relationships that are presented in this lesson. The two sounds of *c*, *g*, and *th* may be more familiar than the three sounds of *ch*.

Working with English Language Learners

This lesson helps children learn words that often present spelling challenges. At first it might be difficult for children to understand that in English, letters and letter clusters can represent two or even three different sounds. They may find it confusing that just as they have learned *ch* as in *children* and *reach*, they find words like *character*. Children may be learning some new vocabulary words during this lesson and as they play the game. Be sure they understand the meaning of the words you use for the Crazy Eights. Use the word work component of guided reading or work with small groups to sort words that begin the same, but have different sounds.

You Need

▶ Pocket chart.

From *Teaching Resources*:

▶ Pocket Chart Card Template.

▶ Directions for Crazy Eights.

▶ Crazy Eights Game Cards made from the Lesson LS 10 Word Cards and Deck Card Template. Include four cards with a Crazy Eight on them.

Understand the Principle

The letters *c*, *g*, *th*, and *ch* can represent different phonemes depending on the words in which they appear. Sounds can be represented by different letters and letters can represent different sounds. Children need to learn how to attend to the visual patterns in words to become more sophisticated in their spelling.

Explain the Principle

" Some consonants or consonant clusters stand for two or more different sounds: *car, city; get, gym; think, they; chair, chorus, chateau.* "

CONTINUUM: LETTER/SOUND RELATIONSHIPS — RECOGNIZING AND USING LETTERS THAT REPRESENT TWO OR MORE CONSONANT SOUNDS AT THE BEGINNING OF A WORD

111

plan

teach

Explain the Principle

❝ Some consonants or consonant clusters stand for two or more different sounds: *car, city; get, gym; think, they; chair, chorus, chateau.* ❞

① Tell the children that you will help them think about letters that can stand for different sounds.

② Write one word with each sound on the chart. Ask children to read each word and have them compare the two sounds of *c*, two sounds of *g*, two sounds of *th*, and the three sounds of *ch*. Help them notice that the *ch* in chateau comes from the French language.

> ### Consonants with more than one sound
>
> **c** cabin   circle   gigantic
>   city   circle   voice
>
> **g** gas   gorge   gigantic
>   gym   gorge   gigantic
>
> **th** think three   length
>   they   gather this
>
> **ch** chair   attach   chip
>   chorus chord
>   chateau machine

③ Place words such as *circus, gigantic, machine, gorge, circle, gather, length, voice, attach, pathway* in the correct columns. Discuss the words that have two *c*s or *g*s and those with the *g* or *ch* in places other than the beginning.

④ Summarize the principle: "Some consonants or consonant clusters stand for two or more different sounds."

⑤ Tell children they are going to play the Crazy Eights card game. Give each player eight cards and place the remaining deck face down, with one card turned up beside the deck. The first player reads the card that is face up, puts down a card with the same *c*, *g*, *th*, or *ch* sound, and reads it. Note that words like *circle, circus, gigantic, gorge* can be used for either sound. If the player does not have a card that matches, he can discard a Crazy Eight card, which functions as a free card. Otherwise, the player draws cards until he finds a match to put down. The first player to discard all her cards wins the game.

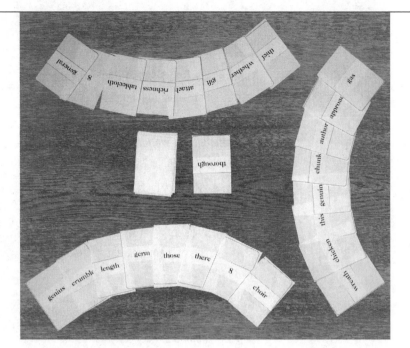

read
match
put down pair

apply

▸ Children play the Crazy Eight card game in groups of three or four.

▸ Players make and discard matches with words that have the same *c*, *g*, *ch*, or *th* sound. The first player to discard all her cards wins.

share

Invite the children to provide one more example for each sound to place on the chart.

Invite them to discuss what they have learned about consonants and how they represent sounds. You may want to add more words to the chart.

Link

Interactive Read-Aloud: Read aloud books with a variety of words that have consonant letters that represent different sounds such as:

- ▶ *Sometimes I Wonder if Poodles Like Noodles* by Laura Numeroff

- ▶ *Once I Was ...* by Niki Clark Leopold

Shared Reading: Read poems with words having consonants that represent two sounds. After reading and enjoying the poem, make a list of the words.

Guided Reading: When children are solving unknown words, have them substitute the different sounds the consonants represent until they recognize the word.

Guided/Independent Writing: During the editing process, have children notice words with consonants that stand for different sounds.

assess

- ▶ As a quick assessment, dictate three or four words with consonants that have different sounds.

- ▶ Notice how children pronounce words with the two sounds of *c, g, th* or the three sounds of *ch.*

- ▶ Observe children's oral reading to determine whether they attempt different pronunciations (the alternative sounds) in a flexible way when they encounter new words.

Expand the Learning

Select a different variety of words for the card game. To make it more challenging, select more words that have the consonant letters in places other than in the beginning position and those that have more than one syllable (e.g. *magic, orange, danger, dungeon*).

Connect with Home

Send home the Crazy Eights card game for children to play with family members.

As an alternative, send home a sheet of lesson word cards that children cut apart and use to play Concentration. (See Directions for Concentration in *Teaching Resources.*)

Noticing Silent Letters in Words

Two-Way Sort

Consider Your Children

Children have already encountered silent letters as parts of word patterns (e.g., *walk*) and probably recognize silent *e* since they use it often in interactive and independent writing. They may not understand the principle, however. Take an informal inventory of children's knowledge of silent letters by noticing how often they represent them in their writing. Once children are aware of silent letters, this lesson will expand their knowledge.

Working with English Language Learners

Letters that are not connected with sounds may be confusing to English language learners, especially if they have been taught to expect a direct sound-to-letter relationship. Use this lesson to help them realize that there can be silent letters in words. Help them attend to the larger patterns in words and to see silent letters as part of word parts connected to sounds.

You Need

▶ Chart paper.

▶ Markers.

From *Teaching Resources:*

▶ Two-Way Sort Cards.

▶ Two-Way Sort Sheets.

▶ Lesson LS 11 Word Cards.

Understand the Principle

In some words, consonants are silent because the pronunciation has changed over time and the letters are no longer reflected in speech. Other words with silent letters have come into English from other languages. When children understand the principle of silent letters and at the same time work with larger patterns, they gain a better sense of word structure. Some letter combinations such as *sh* or *th* do not have silent letters, but have letters that combine to make a new or unique sound.

Explain the Principle

❝ Some words have consonant letters that are silent. ❞

CONTINUUM: LETTER/SOUND RELATIONSHIPS — RECOGNIZING AND USING CONSONANT LETTERS THAT REPRESENT NO SOUND

plan

Explain
the Principle

" Some words have
consonant letters
that are silent. "

① Tell the children that you will
show them something
interesting about words.

② Read the first column of words.
Suggested language: "What do
you notice about these words?"
[Children respond.] "Yes, they
each have a *b* at the end, and
you do not hear the *b* sound
when you say the word.
Sometimes words have letters
that you do not pronounce."

③ Write *b* at the top of the column.

④ Read the next column of words. "What do you notice about these words?"
[Children respond.] "Yes, there is a silent *k* at the beginning of each word."
Children may also notice the silent *e* in *knife*.

⑤ Repeat the process with words with silent *l* and silent *t*. Write the silent
consonant at the top of each column and title the chart Words with Silent
Letters.

⑥ Explain that children will complete a two-way sort, sorting words *with* silent
letters and those *without* silent letters.

Words with Silent Letters

b   k
lamb   knot
crumb   know

thumb   knife

            knee
    l   t
walk   whistle
calf

apply

take
say
sort
write

► Have the children use word cards
and a Two-Way Sort Card to
complete a two-way sort of words
with silent letters and words
without silent letters.

► Then children write the words
on a Two-Way Sort Sheet and
circle the silent letter in each
word. Read their lists to a
partner.

Name: Ashley   Two-Way Sort

Silent letters	No silent letters
knot	behind
whistle	most
walk	short
know	summer
lamb	next
thumb	
knife	
calf	
knee	
crumb	
knew	
know	
grade	

share

Have children share one word with a silent letter and add it to the chart.

Ask them to talk about what they have learned about words. You will
probably want to reinforce the understanding that the *h* in *sh* is not a silent
letter. Rather the two letters combine to create a unique sound.

Link

Interactive Read-Aloud: Read aloud books that invite curiosity about words and how they work, and point out two or three words containing a silent letter. Examples of appropriate books are:

- ▸ *Hot Potato: Mealtime Rhymes* by Neil Philip
- ▸ *The Snail and the Whale* by Julia Donaldson

Shared Reading: Read a variety of poems that children enjoy. After reading the text and discussing it, project the text on a whiteboard or write it on a large chart and ask children to highlight a few words that contain a silent letter.

Guided Reading: During word work, write three or four words on a whiteboard and have children identify the silent letters. Invite them to add one or two more.

Guided/Independent Writing: Help children think about word patterns with silent letters when they write new words.

Expand the Learning

Repeat the lesson with other patterns that include silent letters: *ghost, ghoul, gnat, bought, would, should, scent, scene, scissors, rhyme, rhino, khaki, calf, talk, calm, faster, listen, whistle, write, wrap, wrist.* (See Lesson LS 15.)

Connect with Home

Encourage the children to read their Two-Way Sort Sheet to family members.

Give children a sheet of lesson word cards (Word Card Template) to take home, cut apart, and sort.

assess

- ▸ Observe whether the children are able to identify silent letters in words.
- ▸ Notice whether the children attempt to include silent letters in the words they spell.
- ▸ Ask the children to write five words with silent letters. Their degree of success will tell you whether you need to repeat this lesson, expanding the number of words.

Taking Apart Words with Open Syllables

Two-Way Sort

Consider Your Children

In this lesson the children learn about open syllables and learn how to listen for the part that is stressed. Children should be very familiar with single-syllable words with common patterns. Select an equal number of word cards with a stressed first syllable and a stressed second syllable for the sort.

Working with English Language Learners

Varying pronunciation of English words may be a barrier to children's understanding the principle of the lesson as well as their ability to sort the words. Model pronunciation and give children a chance to repeat the words. They will be able to hear your pronunciation and connect it to each word, even if they cannot pronounce it exactly as you do. Clapping the words while saying them may be helpful. Use magnetic letters to build the words, and then pull the letters apart to show the two syllables.

You Need

► Pocket chart.

From *Teaching Resources:*

► Pocket Chart Card Template.

► Two-Way Sort Cards.

► Two-Way Sort Sheets.

► Lesson LS 12 Word Cards.

Understand the Principle

An open syllable ends in a vowel and the mouth is open after you say it (*la-zy, sea-son*). Understanding this principle helps readers take apart words with more than one syllable. When they see a new word, they can try the first part as an open syllable with a long vowel sound, and if it isn't correct, they can try a short vowel sound in a closed syllable *(rob-in)*. In this lesson, they work with the words with an open syllable and practice identifying which syllable is stressed.

Explain the Principle

❝ Some syllables have a consonant followed by a vowel. ❞

❝ The sound of the vowel is *long* (*ho*-tel, *Pe*-ter, *lo*-cal, *re*-ward, *po*-lice, *du*-ty). ❞

❝ The first or second syllable can be stressed. ❞

CONTINUUM: LETTER/SOUND RELATIONSHIPS — RECOGNIZING AND USING VOWEL SOUNDS IN OPEN SYLLABLES

plan

Explain the Principle

66 **Some syllables have a consonant followed by a vowel.** 99

66 **The sound of the vowel is *long* (*ho*-tel, *Pe*-ter, *lo*-cal, *re*-ward, *po*-lice, *du*-ty).** 99

66 **The first or second syllable can be stressed.** 99

① Tell the children you will help them think about sounds and syllables in words.

② Place the word cards *before* and *lazy* at the top of two columns of a pocket chart. Then place *reason* under *lazy* and *police* under *before*.

Ask children what they notice about all the words. They will likely tell you that each word has two syllables. Lead them to notice where they hear the syllable breaks, marking the break with a line. Point out that the final sound of the first syllable is a long vowel sound.

③ Select two more word cards, *deny* and *silent*, and place *deny* under *police* and *silent* under *reason*.

④ As you read each column of words, ask children what they notice about each column. They should notice that the stress is on the first syllable in the first column and on the second syllable in the second column.

⑤ Suggested language: "Some syllables have a consonant followed by a vowel. The sound of the vowel is long." Remind them that the stress can be on either syllable and explain that the syllable ending with a vowel is called an *open syllable* because your mouth is open when you finish saying it.

⑥ Tell children that they will practice reading words with open syllables and thinking about which syllable is stressed. They will put *lazy* and *before* at the top of a Two-Way Sort Card and do a two-way sort. They will read each word card, listen for the syllable that is stressed and put the word under *lazy* if the first syllable is stressed or under *before* if the second syllable is stressed. They continue until they have sorted twenty words. Then they write the sort on a Two-Way Sort Sheet, drawing a slash at the end of the first syllable in each word.

take
read
say
sort
write
mark

▸ Have the children
say and sort the
word cards, listening
for the syllable that
is stressed.

▸ Children then write
the sort on a Two-
Way Sort Sheet and
mark the syllable
break in each word.

lazy	before
rumor	repair
cocoa	police
china	promote
shiny	reduce
zebra	deny
clover	beyond
solo	
bacon	
even	
spicy	

Name: Jack   Two-Way Sort

la/zy	be/fore
ru/mor	re/pair
co/coa	po/lice
chi/na	pro/mote
shi/ny	re/duce
ze/bra	de/ny
clo/ver	be/yond
so/lo	
ba/con	
e/ven	
spi/cy	

Have the children read their word sorts to a partner, emphasizing the
correct syllable stress. They can add new examples to the columns of the
class chart.

Have the children use selected words in sentences or read a series of
sentences you have prepared. Emphasize correct syllable stress.

Link

Interactive Read-Aloud: Read aloud books that have many words with open syllables, such as:

- *Fix-It Duck* by Jez Alborough
- *Work Song* by Gary Paulsen

Shared Reading: Prior to the first reading of a poem, cover the second syllable of a few words that have open syllables and have the children predict the word. Then uncover the word to confirm their predictions.

Guided Reading: During word work, write a few words with open syllables on a whiteboard for children to read quickly.

Guided/Independent Writing: When children write new two-syllable words, encourage them to say and clap each syllable and then write it.

assess

- Notice how easily children take apart words with open syllables.
- Give children a list of ten words to read, marking the first syllable in each word.

Expand the Learning

Engage the children in a two-way sort that includes a different variety of words with open syllables.

In the texts they're reading, have children find ten two-syllable words that have open syllables.

Connect with Home

Have children take home a sheet of word cards to cut up and sort with family members.

As an alternative, have them search a magazine to find ten two-syllable words with open syllables.

Taking Apart Words with Closed Syllables

Two-Way Sort

Consider Your Children

This lesson should follow Taking Apart Words with Open Syllables (LS 12). Children will learn that some words have an open first syllable and others have a closed first syllable.

Working with English Language Learners

It will help English language learners to hear you say the words and then pay close attention to their own mouths as they repeat the pronunciation. Work with children as they say and sort the words so that they hear your pronunciation the first time they perform this task. You may want to have them sort the words three times, each time saying the words but sorting more quickly. This will help them overlearn a set of words so that they internalize the principle.

You Need

▸ Pocket chart.

From *Teaching Resources:*

▸ Pocket Chart Card Template.

▸ Two-Way Sort Sheets.

▸ Lessons LS 13 and LS 12 Word Cards.

Understand the Principle

A closed syllable is a vowel between consonants, with the syllable ending in a consonant. The mouth is closed after saying the syllable. It helps readers when they notice and try a syllable as open and closed when reading new words. Usually, the first syllable is stressed in a word with a closed first syllable, while in words with an open syllable, the first or second syllable can be stressed.

Explain the Principle

❝ Some syllables have a vowel that is between two consonants. ❞

❝ The sound of the vowel is *short* (lem-*on,* cab-*in*). ❞

❝ The first syllable is stressed. ❞

CONTINUUM: LETTER/SOUND RELATIONSHIPS — RECOGNIZING AND USING VOWEL SOUNDS IN CLOSED SYLLABLES

plan

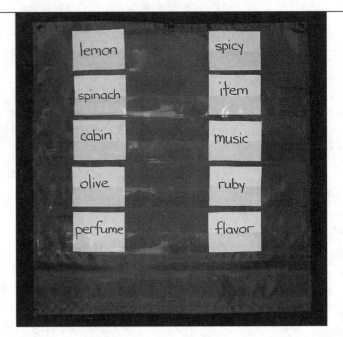

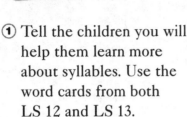

Explain the Principle

" Some syllables have a vowel that is between two consonants. "

" The sound of the vowel is *short* (lem-*on*, cab-*in*). "

" The first syllable is stressed. "

① Tell the children you will help them learn more about syllables. Use the word cards from both LS 12 and LS 13.

② Place *lemon*, *spinach*, and *cabin* in the first column of a pocket chart. Ask the children to read the words and tell what they notice about the first syllable in each word. They will likely tell you that the first syllable ends in a consonant and that the sound of the vowel is short. Help them see that when they finish saying the first syllable, their mouths are closed.

③ Then place *spicy*, *item*, and *music* in the second column. From the previous lesson they should know that each has an open first syllable. In these examples the first syllable is stressed but there are other words in which the second syllable is stressed.

④ Next take a few more word cards, such as *olive*, *ruby*, *perfume*, and *flavor* and have children place them in the correct column.

⑤ Tell children that they will write *lemon* and *spicy* at the top of a Two-Way Sort Sheet. They will take and read twenty word cards and write the words below *lemon* if the first syllable is closed or under *spicy* if the first syllable is open. Then they read their sort to a partner.

apply

say
sort
write
read

▶ Have the children say, sort, and write twenty words with open and closed syllables on a Two-Way Sort Sheet. Then they read their sorts to a partner.

Name: Kieran   Two-Way Sort

lemon	spicy
wagon	propose
talent	repair
shovel	promote
parent	return
admire	below
confuse	hotel
control	beside
indeed	beyond
robin	
forget	
confess	
until	

Two-Way Sort Sheet

share

Have children suggest a few more words to place in the sort on the pocket chart.

Have each child read one closed syllable word from their sorts. You may want to add more examples to the class chart.

Link

Interactive Read-Aloud: Read aloud books that have two-syllable words with open and closed syllables, such as:

- ► *Lunchtime for a Purple Snake* by Harriet Ziefert
- ► *Ella Sarah Gets Dressed* by Margaret Chodos-Irvine

Shared Reading: Following the reading of a poem, have children draw a slash to show the syllables in a few words with open and closed syllables.

Guided Reading: After reading a text, have the children find a word with an open and one with a closed syllable.

Guided/Independent Writing: Help children think about open and closed syllables when constructing new words.

assess

- ► Notice how easily children take apart words with open or closed syllables.

- ► Dictate three to five words with open and closed syllables to assess the children's control of the principle.

Expand the Learning

Have children do a blind sort with open and closed syllables. One child takes a card and reads it without allowing the other child to see it. The second child points to the column in which it belongs, and the first child places it in the column.

Connect with Home

Send home a sheet of word cards with open and closed syllables for children to cut up and sort with family members.

Recognizing Words with r-Influenced Vowel Sounds

Word Search

Consider Your Children

Children may be familiar with the basic patterns of a single vowel with *r*, but less familiar with the other patterns. All the words in this lesson are single syllable. For an additional challenge, include multisyllable words (see sample list in Expand the Learning). Children will enjoy creating Word Searches for each other after completing the one in this lesson.

Working with English Language Learners

Words with vowels influenced by *r* may be particularly difficult for some children to say. Model pronunciation, yet accept children's approximations. If children have trouble understanding the concept of a word search, then have them build the word with magnetic letters and then place the letters over the letters in the boxes. This makes the word "pop out" and easier for them to see, illustrating the activity.

You Need

▶ Chart paper.
▶ Markers.
▶ Enlarged word search for demonstration.

From *Teaching Resources:*

▶ Directions for Word Searches.
▶ Word Search Templates.
▶ Word Search made from the Word Search Template and Lesson LS 14 Word List.
▶ Large chart of LS 14 Word List for student reference.

Understand the Principle

The letter *r* occurs with a variety of other letters and influences the vowel sound. The simplest combinations are *ar, er, ir, ur, or,* but *r* also occurs with other letter patterns, such as *door, your, rose, world, near, nerve, warm, square.* Children need to become flexible in reading a variety of vowel patterns with *r*. After working with one-syllable words, have children work with two-syllable words with *r*-influenced vowels. Quick and automatic recognition of the vowel and *r* pattern will help students read with greater fluency.

Explain the Principle

❝ When vowels are with *r* in words, you blend the vowel sound with *r* (*car, her, first, corn, hurt, nerve, door, world, near*). ❞

plan

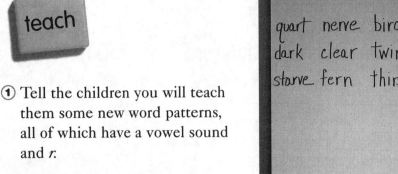

Explain the Principle

" When vowels are with *r* in words, you blend the vowel sound with *r* (*car, her, first, corn, hurt, nerve, door, world, near*). "

① Tell the children you will teach them some new word patterns, all of which have a vowel sound and *r*.

② Select a variety of word cards with *r* and give one to each child. Have each child read the card while you write it quickly on a chart, placing words with similar patterns under one another and pointing out how the *r* influences the vowel sound.

③ Suggested language: "When vowels are with *r* in words, you blend the sound with *r*."

④ Show your enlarged word search. Suggested language: "There is a list of words at the bottom, all of which have vowels that are influenced by *r*s." Read the list with the group. "I am looking for *turn*. I see *turn*, so I will circle it. Now I am looking for *beard*; I see it vertically so I will circle it. I will continue to look for each word on the list. Words can be left to right, top to bottom, vertically, or diagonally in the grid. I will put a check next to each word I circle until I find all the words."

⑤ Suggested language: "Today you will do a word search, which is like a word hunt. You will search for certain words in a puzzle. First you will complete a word search that I made. Then you will use a blank Word Search Template and the word list on this chart to make your own word search for a partner to complete."

⑥ "Let's read through this list together [read list with students]. First, list at least eight words on the bottom. Place them in the grid, one letter in each box. The words can be written across, down, diagonally, or bottom to top. Then fill in the empty spaces with other letters to make the words harder to find. Give your word search to a partner and challenge him to find all the words."

read
find
circle
check
make

► Have the children complete the word search you created.

► Then they use the Word List and a blank Word Search Template to create one of their own for a partner to solve.

► They swap and solve searches with a partner.

Point to random words for the group to read. Consider reproducing a few of the word searches for the class to do for homework.

Notice how quickly students can recognize and pronounce words with *r*.

Link

Interactive Read-Aloud: Read aloud books with words that have *r*-influenced vowels. Here are two titles to consider.

- ► *Month by Month a Year Goes Round* by Carol Diggory Shields
- ► *Cows Can't Fly* by David Milgrim

Shared Reading: Invite children to highlight words with *r*-influenced vowels in poems you have read together.

Guided Reading: When children have difficulty with a word that has an *r*-influenced vowel, suggest that they try a pattern that they know. For example, for *curtain*, "Could it be like the *-ur* in *turn*?"

Guided/Independent Writing: During the editing process, encourage children to check for words having vowel patterns with *r*.

assess

- ► Notice how the children take apart words with *r* and a vowel or vowels.

- ► Dictate three to five words with vowel patterns with *r* to assess the children's control of patterns.

- ► Have students read a passage with a good sampling of words with vowels plus *r*. At most levels these will be easy to find. Notice the ease with which students read these words.

Expand the Learning

Repeat the lesson with two-syllable words that have vowels and *r*, such as: *barber, carpet, alarm, garbage, market, partner, sparkle, prepare, careful, repair, dairy, merry, alert, perfect, gerbil, learner, nearby, yearly, cheerful, sincere, dirty, birthday, admire, coral, florist, ignore, curtain, turkey, surely, person, squirrel, normal, important, purple, urgent, surprise.*

Connect with Home

Have children take home a blank Word Search Template and Word List and make a word search for family members to complete.

Identifying Silent Letters in Words

Follow the Path

Consider Your Children

Children need strong control of letter/sound relationships prior to this lesson. Many different letters can be silent in words, so attention to the visual pattern is critical. Some silent letters are more common than others. Be sure that children understand the concept of silent letters related to both vowels and consonants. While Lesson LS 11 helped children begin to notice silent letters, this lesson will help them create categories to organize their knowledge. They also work with more challenging letter patterns.

Working with English Language Learners

Silent letters in words can be especially challenging to children who are learning to speak, read, and write English. Once children grasp the idea, they are more likely to notice words with silent consonants when they read. You can build their knowledge of words in this category by keeping a group chart or individual lists that they can refer to as part of the word work component of guided reading. For accurate word solving, children should think about how a word *looks* as much as they do about the sounds of its letters. Learning about silent letters is a good way to help children make this shift.

You Need

▶ Chart paper.

▶ Markers.

▶ Index cards.

From *Teaching Resources:*

▶ Directions for Follow the Path.

▶ Follow the Path Game Cards made from Lesson LS 15 Word Cards and Deck Card Template.

Understand the Principle

It is important for children to notice letter patterns as they develop their reading vocabularies and spelling skills. There are numerous examples of letters that are part of letter patterns but do not represent a sound, for example *lamb, gnome, pick, scene, sign, rhyme, khaki, calm, island, listen, whole, ballet, honor.* Notice that silent letters occur at any place within the words. Frequently consonant letters are silent because over time spellings stayed the same and pronunciations changed. Letters can also be silent because they came from other languages. Some people actually pronounce letters that others consider silent (e.g., *often*).

Explain the Principle

" Some words have consonant letters that are silent (*wrap, gnome, know, climb, honor, who*). "

CONTINUUM: LETTER/SOUND RELATIONSHIPS — RECOGNIZING AND USING CONSONANT LETTERS THAT REPRESENT NO SOUND

plan

Explain the Principle

" Some words have consonant letters that are silent. (*wrap, gnome, know, climb, honor, who*). "

① Tell the children that you will help them think about how words sound and how they look.

② Have a variety of words with silent letters written on the chart. Ask children to read them. Talk about the meanings of any that are unfamiliar words.

③ Ask children to say each word and think about how it sounds and how it looks. They will notice letters that are silent. Have children highlight the letters that are silent.

④ Suggested language: "You can see that many different letters can be silent in words. Some words have consonant letters that are silent. Begin to notice patterns with silent letters in words."

⑤ Tell children they will play Follow the Path. They roll a die, draw a word card, say the word, tell the silent letter or letters, and then move the number of spaces rolled. The first player to reach FINISH wins the game.

Words with Silent Letters

gnat	knew
design	wry
wrench	latch
write	answer
wrung	listen
back	yacht
knee	comb
sack	rhino
pitch	whose
could	adjust

read
say
move
write

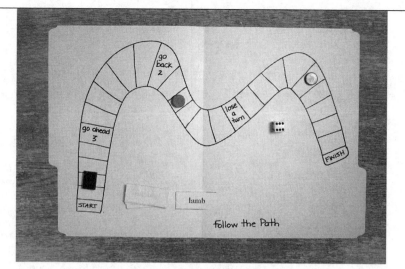

follow the Path

▸ In groups of two to four, children play Follow the Path with words having silent letters.

▸ After playing, children write on an index card two interesting words with silent consonants that were new to them or that they like. They bring their cards to sharing.

Have the children give a few more words to add to the Words with Silent Letters Chart. They can share interesting new words from their index cards.

Invite children to talk about what they have learned about silent letters.

You will probably need to reinforce the understanding that the *wh* in *whose* makes a unique sound. It is the *e* that is the silent letter.

Link

Interactive Read-Aloud: Read aloud books that invite interest in words. Help children notice a few words with silent letters. Here are two suggested titles:

- *A Fine, Fine School* by Sharon Creech
- *Ghosts for Breakfast* by Stanley Terasaki

Shared Reading: Mark one or two words with silent letters after reading and enjoying favorite poems. Have the children highlight the silent letters and add the words to the class chart.

Guided Reading: During word work, spend a few minutes looking at three to five words with silent letters.

Guided/Independent Writing: As children edit for spelling, have them look for patterns with silent consonants.

assess

- Dictate one or two sentences with words that have silent letters. Ask the children to underline the silent letters in the words.
- Notice how quickly children perform the task.

Expand the Learning

Use a different variety of words with silent letters for the Follow the Path game.

Have children find ten words with silent letters in the classroom and make a list on a Words Around the Room Sheet to share with the class. (See *Teaching Resources*.)

Connect with Home

Invite the children to have family members help them find five words with silent letters on signs, in the newspaper, or in magazines. Children share their list of words with the class.

Recognizing Words with the Final k Sound: c, k, ke, ck, que

Make, Write, Read

Consider Your Children

Children should have strong control of basic phonogram patterns in one syllable words (e.g., *ark, cake, plaque*) prior to this lesson. In this lesson children learn about the final *k* sound in words having more than one syllable (e.g., *panic*). Discuss the meaning of some of the words to be sure children understand them.

Working with English Language Learners

If possible, collect a few words in children's first languages that have the sound of *k* (for example, *Enrique* or *quiero* in Spanish). Have children notice the different letters that are used to represent the /k/ sound. For examples, select words that are in children's listening and speaking vocabularies. Building words with magnetic letters helps them make connections between sounds and letter patterns. Repeat the application for this lesson during the word work component of guided reading.

You Need

▶ Chart paper.

▶ Markers.

▶ Magnetic letters.

From *Teaching Resources:*

▶ List Sheets.

▶ Lesson LS 16 Word Cards.

Understand the Principle

The sound of /k/ can be represented by *c, k, ke, ck,* or *que*. Some representations are more common than others. The *c* in *ck* is considered a silent letter. Children need to think about the ways the /k/ sound is represented in two-syllable words.

Explain the Principle

❝ Some consonant sounds are represented by several different letters or letter clusters. ❞

CONTINUUM: LETTER/SOUND RELATIONSHIPS — UNDERSTANDING THAT SOME CONSONANT SOUNDS CAN BE REPRESENTED BY SEVERAL DIFFERENT LETTERS OR LETTER CLUSTERS

plan

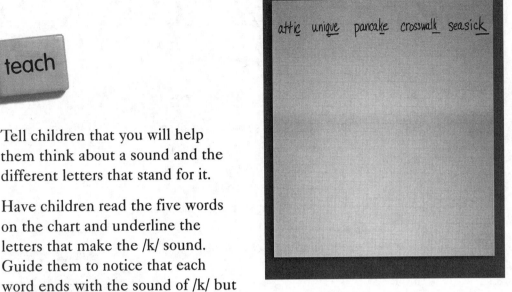

attic unique pancake crosswalk seasick

Explain the Principle

" Some consonant sounds are represented by several different letters or letter clusters. "

① Tell children that you will help them think about a sound and the different letters that stand for it.

② Have children read the five words on the chart and underline the letters that make the /k/ sound. Guide them to notice that each word ends with the sound of /k/ but is spelled differently. Ask children to suggest another example for each spelling, such as *music, antique, cupcake, cornstalk, attack, back,* and *chick.*

③ Suggested language: "You can see that some consonant sounds are represented by several different letters or letter clusters that stand for the /k/ sound." Repeat the process with a few more words such as *panic, plaque, bike, talk,* and *duck.*

④ Tell the children that they will select four words with each of the five patterns, make them with magnetic letters, then write them on a List Sheet and read their lists to a partner.

select
make
write
read
read

▶ Have the children select, make, and write a total of twenty words with the five different representations of the /k/ sound.

▶ They read their words after writing them. Some children may think of and write words that are not on the cards.

▶ When they have finished the whole list, they read it to a partner.

attic	hammock
unique	network
turnpike	clambake
attack	pancake
gimmick	magic
music	seasick
boutique	frantic
earthquake	cupcake
potluck	opaque

unique

Name: Edwinna A.

1. attic   11. hammock
2. unique   12. antique
3. turnpike   13. network
4. attack   14. clambake
5. gimmick   15. pancake
6. crosswalk   16. magic
7. music   17. seasick
8. boutique   18. frantic
9. earthquake   19. cupcake
10. potluck   20. opaque

LIST SHEET

Invite the children to add one more word to each category on the class chart. They may think of words that were not included in the word card set.

Children may also bring up words like *rocket* that have the pattern in the middle of the word. If so, write them and highlight the pattern.

They may mention words like *park*, in which *r* and *k* are blended, or *act* in which *c* and *t* are blended. Make sure they can hear and identify both sounds in the blend.

Link

Interactive Read-Aloud: Read aloud books that have words that represent the /k/ sound in different ways. Here are some titles to consider:

▶ *Duck for President* by Doreen Cronin

▶ *Black Cat* by Christopher Meir

Shared Reading: As you revisit poems, point out words ending with the /k/ sound and talk about how they are represented with letters. Underline the letters in the text and add words to the class chart.

Guided Reading: During word work, write three or four words ending in the /k/ sound with a variety of letter patterns on a whiteboard.

Guided/Independent Writing: Teach children how to notice word endings that sound like /k/ and remind them to check their spelling during the editing process.

assess

▶ Dictate five or six words with the /k/ sound to assess the children's control of the letter patterns.

Expand the Learning

Help children notice other sounds that can be represented different ways in words (e.g., *stiff*, *cough*).

Have children create a word search with words ending in the /k/ sound, using all five varieties of letter patterns. (See Directions for Word Searches in *Teaching Resources*.)

Connect with Home

Have the children work with family members to find five words ending with the /k/ sound in catalogs, magazines, or newspapers.

As an alternative, children can create word searches for family members to solve.

Learning about Words with Capital Letters

Capital Detective Lotto

Consider Your Children

Children learn the differences between upper case (capital) letters and lower case (small) letters early, but it takes many years to learn their relevance for different kinds of nouns as well as how they function in sentences. Even competent adult writers sometimes misuse these conventions. Use this lesson with children who have had exposure to capitalization and discussed it during shared writing and in writer's workshops. Children may have done some editing of their writing and know that all kinds of names are capitalized. Select familiar people, places, things, or sentences to write in the squares of the Lotto Board to make the game enjoyable. The game is played like Lotto, using a die.

Working with English Language Learners

Capitals perform similar functions in English as in most children's native language(s). Even if children are reading at very early levels in English, they can notice words that have capital letters and learn about their functions. For the Apply exercise, use texts that are within their control—proper nouns will be simpler and sentences will be shorter and easier to work with.

You Need

► Selected paragraphs from a text of *Amber Brown* or other text on a large chart or on a transparency.

► Die (sides read: *person, place, thing, free, free, sentence*).

From *Teaching Resources:*

► Directions for Lotto.

► Three-by-Four Lotto Game Cards (with names of familiar persons, places, things, and beginnings of sentences).

Understand the Principle

Capitalization of words is a convention that children will use when they proofread and edit their own writing. Sometimes children are confused (which might detract from comprehension) by the capital letters they see in titles or place names. Capitalized words form a unit that names a person, place, or thing. In general, capital letters are useful because they contribute to fluency and comprehension, so it's important that children become sensitive to their functions.

Explain the Principle

" You use capital letters at the beginning of some words to show the beginning of a sentence or to show a proper noun (name of a person, place, or thing). "

teach

Explain the Principle

" **You use capital letters at the beginning of some words to show the beginning of a sentence or to show a proper noun (name of a person, place, or thing).** "

> Amber Brown Is Feeling Blue
>
> I, Amber Brown, realize that when someone says "I don't want to nag you," they're going to nag you.
> And Brenda does. "Do your homework. You don't want to get into trouble with Mrs Holt again for not doing it, do you?"
> That's a lot of "Do's about my homework...a lot of do-do.
> I sigh. "Oh, OK."
> Brenda says, "I'll go downstairs and finish the dishes. And then I've got to study for a civics test. Call me if you need help."
> I take out my notebook. I've got to figure out a project on the Middle Ages.
> I start planning.

① Tell children that they will look for and talk about words that begin with capital letters.

② Suggested language: "You know that some words begin with capital letters. What kinds of words are those?"

③ Children may suggest names of people or places. They may also refer to the first word in a sentence or the word after a period or question mark.

④ Suggested language: "Today you will be capital detectives. First you will look for a word with a capital letter in a story. Then you will tell why the word is capitalized. It might be the name of a person, place, or thing. Or, it might be the beginning of a sentence. Listen and follow along with your eyes while I read the first paragraph. Don't say anything out loud, but find a word with a capital letter and try to think of the reason that word is capitalized."

⑤ Select and write two or three paragraphs from *Amber Brown* or another familiar text on a chart or show them on a transparency. It has a variety of capitalized words, some of which are challenging, such as the name of a period of history. (If this text is too difficult, select a different one that is an easy one for the class.) You can also read the text to children before they work on it, but it must be within a range that they can process.

⑥ Have children report on the capitalized words they find. Point out that book and newspaper titles can have several words, and that all of them are capitalized (except for words like *a* and *the* unless they are the first word). The *Middle Ages* is a specially identified time in history (like the Civil War) Proper nouns must name a person, place, or thing. The *Middle Ages* is an example of a *thing*. You may wish to point out that this author also italicized newspaper titles.

⑦ Tell the children they will play a game similar to Lotto called Capital Detectives. Children will roll a die and cover matching examples on their game card.

read
explain
cover

▶ Children play Capital Detective Lotto.

▶ Each player has a card that has squares randomly marked with familiar names of a person, place, thing, or beginning of sentence. Players take turns rolling the game die and finding matching examples on their card.

▶ Each player reads the label on the die and the example on his card and tells how they are the same and why they are capitalized. If the other players agree, then he covers the square with a marker or slip of paper. If a player is incorrect or cannot find an example that matches the die, then he passes. The first player to cover all the squares on his card wins the game.

Children come to group share with one example of a capitalized word to share with the group.

Ask children to summarize what they have learned about capitalizing words. You may want them to check their own writing for more examples.

Link

Interactive Read-Aloud: Read aloud books that have a variety of proper nouns. After reading, have children discuss what words in the story would be capitalized. Here are two suggested titles:

- ▶ *The Name Jar* by Yangsook Choi
- ▶ *A Book of Letters* by Ken Wilson-Max

Shared Reading: After reading a poem, revisit it to look at proper nouns and discuss why they are capitialized. Children may notice that sometimes each line of a poem is capitalized even though it is not a complete sentence.

Guided Reading: Prompt children to notice capitalized words and to explain why they are capitalized. Help children notice tricky structures, such as book titles. Informational texts may have many capitalized words. Children may not realize, for example, that some processes or products are capitalized because they are named after an individual.

Guided/Independent Writing: Have children proofread their writing for use of words with capital letters each time they write.

assess

- ▶ Observe children's writing behavior to determine whether they apply what they know about capitalization to their own writing.

- ▶ Dictate two or three sentences that include a few words that require capitals. Analyze the results to learn the types of capitals for which you need to plan more lessons.

Expand the Learning

Repeat this lesson and focus on other capitalization principles, such as words in a title, first word in dialogue, and so forth.

Repeat this lesson with other examples of people, places, and things.

Connect with Home

Have children take home a reproduced portion of the text you used for this lesson. They can circle words with capital letters and explain to a family member why each word is capitalized.

Children can play Capital Detective Lotto with family members.

18 Learning Cursive Handwriting

Handwriting Notebook

Consider Your Children

In this lesson students learn how to form cursive letters. Teach several letters in a lesson, and if that is too much, then introduce only one or two letters at a time. As soon as you have introduced enough letters, work the letters into words to practice. As soon as possible, give children a simple sentence or two to write. Help children understand that letters should slant slightly to the right. You will need to decide the timing of this lesson as it relates to your school's curriculum. For this lesson you may want to have children use lined paper at first to gain control of proportions. When children have gained control, have them try unlined paper.

Working with English Language Learners

Many English language learners already know how to write the letters of an alphabetic language system in manuscript, and some may have cursive skills. With English words, however, they will use letters in a different order than they are accustomed. If children have just begun writing English words, begin with manuscript print and then move to cursive. Assess writing skills and, if necessary, form small groups for daily writing practice. If children learn efficient movements, they will become fluent more quickly. Demonstrate as you use language that describes the movements. Have children use large movements if needed.

You Need

► Whiteboard or chalkboard.

► Marker or chalk.

► Clipboards and paper.

► Handwriting Notebook.

► Lined paper.

From *Teaching Resources:*

► Suggested Order for Learning Cursive Forms.

► Cursive Form Chart, Upper Case, Lower Case.

► Verbal Path for Lower Case Letters and Verbal Path for Upper Case Letters.

Understand the Principle

Children learn to write more quickly when they move from manuscript to cursive form. Cursive letters are formed with a more continuous movement that *slants to the right* as it flows. Practice in larger form makes it easier to form letters in a smaller size. Even though handwriting develops as an individual style, it is important to establish the habit of efficient movements.

Explain the Principle

" You can write letters smoothly and efficiently in cursive form. "

---

plan

Explain the Principle

" **You can write letters smoothly and efficiently in cursive form.** "

① Show an enlarged *abc* chart in cursive form. Tell the children you will help them learn how to make letters in cursive form.

② On a large surface such as a large whiteboard or chalkboard, form the letter *a*. As you form it, use simple words (a verbal path) that will guide the learning (*pull back, around, up, down, and swing up*). Make a few large cursive *a*s, then erase them and start again. Explain that the movement should be smooth and continuous and that writing in cursive should help them write faster. Also show them how the letters slant to the right so it flows.

③ Have children move the finger in the air to mirror your movement. An alternative is to have them use small notebooks or paper on a clipboard to practice the formation.

④ Repeat the process with *c, o,* and *d*, giving children a few minutes to practice a line of the letters on their lined paper.

⑤ Next show the children how to join the letters by "going up and over" each time. Have them make a line of *coad, acod, ocda, doac* so they can practice smooth, continuous writing. Ask them to circle their best group of letters.

⑥ Explain that today they will practice one line of each letter (*a, o, c, d*) and one line of each group (*coad, acod, ocda, doac*) in their Handwriting Notebook.

tag
write
circle

▶ Use the lined
paper with good
solid space
between lines.
The paper your
school provides
for third graders
will work for this
lesson as well.

Name: Amanda

a a a a a a a   coad coad

c c c c c c c   acod acod

o o o o o o o o   ocda ocda

d d d d d d   doac doac

▶ Have children practice one line of each letter and each group of letters on
lined paper or in their Handwriting Notebook. Reinforce the importance of a
slant to the right.

▶ They circle the best formation in each line.

share

Invite each child to make a letter or group of letters on a chalkboard or
whiteboard while the other children make the formation in the air or on
paper on their clipboards.

Link

Interactive Read-Aloud: Read aloud books that feature some cursive handwriting. Show the children the cursive forms after reading the story or part of the text. Here are a few suggested titles:

- ▶ *Amber Brown Is Not a Crayon* by Paula Danziger
- ▶ *Plantzilla* by Jerdine Nolen

Shared Reading: On an overhead, show a poem in written cursive formation to help children develop ease in reading cursive writing.

Guided Reading: When introducing books that have some parts written in cursive (e.g., *Amber Brown*), point out the cursive writing and read those parts with children.

Guided/Independent Writing: Work with children in small groups when they need guided support forming cursive letters.

assess

- ▶ Assign children to write in cursive form for particular tasks. Observe how fluently, efficiently, and proportionally the letters are formed.

Expand the Learning

Repeat the lesson to review *a, c, o,* and *d* and add *g* and *q*.

Teach the lesson with four other letters that begin the same way (*e, i, t, j*).

Continue the lessons with (*p, s, u, w*), (*b, f, l, h, k*) (*m, n, v, x, y, a*) and *r*.

Repeat the lesson with groupings of upper case letters. Refer to the Cursive Form Chart for efficient formation.

Connect with Home

Send home the Cursive Form Chart for children to use as a reference when they practice writing at home (see *Teaching Resources*). The Verbal Path information may also be helpful to family members.

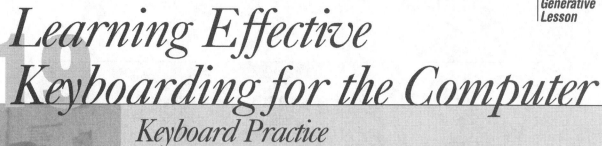

Learning Effective Keyboarding for the Computer

Keyboard Practice

Consider Your Children

If children have had opportunities to use computers, then they already have considerable experience in the general operations of them. More than likely, they know how to turn a computer on and off, use simple programs, navigate with a mouse, and so on. However, they are not likely to be able to keyboard efficiently. You may wish to begin with a brief demonstration and explanation to the whole class, and then work with a small group as they learn to use the computer keyboard. If available, children can use small portable keyboards for a large group lesson.

Working with English Language Learners

If English language learners know the names of the letters, then they can easily learn efficient keyboarding. Computer skills are advantageous when children are expanding their control of English. When typing simple words, phrases and sentences, they are practicing writing English words and gaining fluency with keyboarding. If their native language uses the same alphabet, they can type words in that language as well. Provide concrete demonstrations that children can easily see and let them practice the operation immediately afterward.

You Need

▸ Enlarged version of computer keyboard (hard copy or transparency).

▸ Small portable keyboards or facsimiles (for group lesson).

▸ Computer keyboards (available for practice).

From *Teaching Resources:*

▸ A Sequence of Effective Keyboard Learning.

Understand the Principle

Effective use of the computer keyboard is an asset to children in becoming fluent, efficient users of technology. It may seem awkward to them at first, and they will be tempted to use the "hunt and peck" method. However, if they learn keyboarding early, then it becomes automatic, allowing more attention to composing messages, stories, and reports. Fluent keyboarding allows a writer to put thoughts down quickly and leads to greater productivity in writing as well as in Internet research.

Explain the Principle

" You can use efficient finger movements to type words on the computer. "

plan

Explain the Principle

" You can use efficient finger movements to type words on the computer. "

① Tell children that they will learn a skill that will help them type faster on the computer. Suggested language: "You already know how to use a computer. Today you will begin practicing the finger movements that will help you type faster."

② Children each have a portable keyboard or keyboard facsimile for this first practice session. Suggested language: "I'm going to show you the finger movements now. We will practice them for about 10 minutes every day this week."

③ Highlight the *home row* on the enlargement or transparency. Suggested language: "It is important to remember that your eight fingers rest on the home row most of the time. Your thumbs are on the space bar. Let's identify each finger. On your right hand, hold up your index finger, then your middle finger, then your ring finger, and then your little finger. These names will help you follow directions. Now put them on the home row of keys—index finger on J, middle finger on K, ring finger on L, little finger on the semicolon/colon. Just touch the keys lightly. Your thumb barely touches the space bar. Now put your left hand on the *home row*—index finger on F, middle finger on D, ring finger on S, little finger on A. Your thumb is in the air, ready to touch the space bar when needed."

④ Have students type: *jkl* [space] *jkl* [space] *jkl* [space] *jkl* [space]. Then repeat with the left hand: *asdf* [space] *asdf* [space] *asdf* [space] *asdf* [space]. Have students practice using the home row to practice random combinations of the letters. You can give them an exercise to follow, but also encourage them to use the correct finger when striking each key in the home row.

⑤ Suggested language: "You will use those same four fingers to strike the other keys. Sometimes you will reach up or out with the index finger. Look at your keys. Which letters do you think the index finger can easily reach?" Children will respond by suggesting *RTGV* for the left hand and *UYHNM* for the right hand. Explain that each finger will always strike the nearest keys and that each finger always returns to its place in the home row.

⑥ Introduce the finger movements as indicated in A Sequence of Effective Keyboard Learning (see *Teaching Resources*) and have students practice daily to gain fluency.

place fingers
type

► Students practice keyboarding on portable computer keyboards or take turns at a computer. There will be some drill when learning this skill because you want them to become very familiar with the home row. Children

may tire of the repetition, so if they seem comfortable, go on to introduce new keys, each time having them practice until they are comfortable.

share

Have children demonstrate how quickly their fingers can find the home row. Discuss the idea that while they are learning, they should work for accuracy, smoothness, and comfort rather than speed. The more they practice using accurate finger movements, the faster they will be able to type on the computer.

Link

Interactive Read-Aloud: Read aloud books that illustrate using different fonts to emphasize ideas in writing. Here are a few suggested titles:

- ▶ *Dear Mrs. La Rue: Letters from Obedience School* by Mark Teague
- ▶ *Click, Clack, Moo: Cows That Type* by Doreen Cronin

Shared Reading: When reading poetry, point out different keyboarding options that make the poem more interesting; for example, white space is created deliberately by touching *Enter.*

Guided Reading: When reading informational text, point out specialized uses of the computer to create interesting layouts.

Guided/Independent Writing: As soon as children develop some keyboard fluency, encourage them to type their writing pieces or to compose directly on the keyboard. If children develop the skill of composing while typing, they will have a faster way of producing text. Some writers prefer cursive or manuscript writing for some pieces and use the computer for others.

assess

- ▶ Collect children's practice documents to assess their accuracy.

- ▶ Observe children to determine the degree to which they are using efficient keyboarding. Some may have become quick with the "hunt and peck" method and have established habits that are hard to overcome. You may decide that finger movements can be the child's choice rather than a requirement. Remember that efficient keyboarding benefits children.

Expand the Learning

Continue offering minilessons and practice time for the eight steps outlined on the Sequence of Finger Movements for Effective Computer Keyboarding (see *Teaching Resources*). Monitor children's progress and work with those who find the process more difficult.

Give children the choice of typing poems to include in their poetry anthology.

Establish e-mail capability among the members of your class. Remind children to keyboard correctly when writing their messages.

Connect with Home

If children have access to a computer at home, encourage them to practice for at least five minutes each day.

Let children take home their keyboard facsimile to show family members the finger movements.

Spelling Patterns

One way to look at spelling patterns is to examine the way simple words and syllables are put together. Here we include the consonant-vowel-consonant (CVC) pattern in which the vowel often has a short, or terse, sound; the consonant-vowel-consonant-silent *e* (CVC*e*) pattern in which the vowel usually has a long, or lax, sound; and the consonant-vowel-vowel-consonant (CVVC) pattern in which the vowel combination may have either one or two sounds.

Phonograms are spelling patterns that represent the sounds of *rimes* (the last parts of words). They are sometimes called *word families* because they have similar patterns. You will not need to teach children the technical word *phonogram*, although you may want to use *pattern* or *word part*. A phonogram is the same as a rime or vowel-bearing part of a word or syllable. We have included a large list of phonograms that will be useful to children reading or writing, but you will not need to teach every phonogram separately. Once children understand that there are patterns and learn how to look for patterns, they will quickly discover more for themselves.

Knowing spelling patterns helps children notice and use larger parts of words, thus making word solving faster and more efficient because less attention is required. Patterns are also helpful to children in writing words because they will quickly write down the patterns rather than laboriously work with individual sounds and letters. Finally, knowing to look for patterns and remembering them help children make the connections between words that make word solving easier. The thirty-seven most common phonograms are marked with an asterisk.

Connect to Assessment

See related SP Assessment Tasks in the Assessment Guide in *Teaching Resources:*

▶ Reading Words with Phonogram Patterns

▶ Writing Words with Phonogram Patterns

Develop Your Professional Understanding

See *Word Matters: Teaching Phonics and Spelling in the Reading/Writing Classroom* by G.S. Pinnell and I. C. Fountas. 1998. Portsmouth, NH: Heinemann.

Related pages: 65, 82, 95, 120–121.

Recognizing Phonograms with Short Vowel Sounds

Word Search

Consider Your Children

Use this lesson only if children need more practice with words having one syllable and a short vowel sound. The words in this lesson contain a variety of phonogram patterns; many include consonant clusters in the first or last part of the pattern. You may want to select particular patterns from the set to include in the word search.

Working with English Language Learners

Short vowels may be tricky for English language learners because they often vary in pronunciation and are sometimes hard to identify. Work with students to read each word several times so that they can hear, say, and see the visual forms. Draw their attention to the vowel in the middle. Have them practice with very simple examples until you are sure that they understand the task. Pair children in such a way that you are reasonably sure that partners will use known words in the word search. Remember that children cannot successfully search for a word if they do not recognize it and that they should understand the words for the exercise to be meaningful.

You Need

► Pocket chart.

► Magnetic letters.

► Enlarged Word Search for demonstration.

From *Teaching Resources:*

► Pocket Chart Card Template.

► List Sheets.

► Directions for Word Searches.

► Word Search Template.

► Lesson SP 1 Word Cards.

Understand the Principle

Flexibility and automaticity in reading one-syllable words with short vowel sounds is important for fluent, phrased reading of text. If readers have strong control of these phonogram patterns in single-syllable words, then they will more easily read multisyllable words with short vowel patterns. Vowel sounds are most easily learned when they are part of a word part or pattern.

Explain the Principle

❝ Some words have a short vowel pattern. You can hear the short vowel sound (*man, best, pick, not, nut*). ❞

CONTINUUM: SPELLING PATTERNS — RECOGNIZING AND USING PHONOGRAM PATTERNS WITH A SHORT VOWEL SOUND IN SINGLE-SYLLABLE WORDS

plan

Explain the Principle

" Some words have a
short vowel pattern.
You can hear the
short vowel sound
(*man, best, pick,
not, nut*). "

① Tell the children
that you will help
them think about
spelling patterns
they know. Have
*nest, glad, bring,
clock, shut* placed
across the top of
the pocket chart.

② Use a pile of
large word cards
showing words
with each vowel
sound. Hold up one card at a time, have children read it, and place it in the
column with words having the same vowel sound. Continue until you have
two or three examples of each.

③ Ask children what they notice about the middle sound in every word. They
will observe that the vowel sound is short in every pattern. Have children
read pairs to attend to the middle sound.

④ Explain that they will select a word card and make the word with magnetic
letters. They will write the word on the List Sheet until they have made
twenty words. Remind them that they should include at least two words
with each vowel.

⑤ Show an enlarged version of the Word Search Template with a list of ten
words below the grid. Demonstrate how to place one letter at a time in each
box, making each word from left to right, right to left, up, down, or diagonally.
After all the words are placed, fill in the empty boxes with random letters.

⑥ Tell children that they will use the words on the List Sheet to make a word
search for a partner to complete. The partner finds and circles each word
and then places a check next to each on the list below.

apply

take word
make word
write word

list words
write on grid
fill in boxes
give to partner

▸ Children take a word card and then make the word with magnetic letters.

▸ They write the word on the List Sheet. They continue until they have twenty words. They read over their words and select ten for the word search.

▸ Using the words they selected, children create a word search grid by writing ten words on the empty grid (left to right, right to left, up-down, or diagonally) and then filling in the empty squares with other letters.

▸ They give the word search to a partner to solve.

share

Have the children read their word lists to different partners.

They can add one more example to each column on the class chart.

Invite the children to share comments about the words.

Link

Interactive Read-Aloud: Read aloud books that have many words with short vowels in single syllables. Write two or three of the words on a whiteboard after reading and enjoying the book. Suggested titles are:

- *Lunch Money* by Carol Shields
- *The Llama Who Had No Pajama* by Mary Ann Hoberman

Shared Reading: Cover the last part (the rime or pattern) of some words with stick-on notes before children read a poem with you. Have them predict the patterns. Uncover each word to confirm the children's predictions.

Guided Reading: During word work, write some words with the spelling patterns one at a time quickly on a whiteboard to develop quick recognition.

Guided/Independent Writing: As children edit, have them check words with patterns they know.

assess

- Give a quick dictation test of five to ten words with a variety of the short vowel spelling patterns. Observe to see how quickly and accurately students write words.

- Have students individually read five to ten words with a variety of short vowel spelling patterns.

- Observe how quickly children recognize patterns in words as they read.

Expand the Learning

Repeat the lesson with other patterns having short vowel sounds (e.g., *ag, ab, ed, eg, et, em, in, it, ix, ib, ig, ob, og, od, ug, um*) or with words having the short vowel patterns in two-syllable words (e.g., *funny, gladly, shutter, spotted, platter*).

Connect with Home

Have the children create a word search for family members to try. Encourage the children to teach a family member how to create a word search.

Have the children take home a photocopy of SP 1 Word Cards. After cutting them apart, they can work with family members to sort the words by short vowel sounds.

Recognizing Word Patterns with Ending Consonant Clusters

Go Fish

Consider Your Children

In this lesson, children work with a wide variety of words that end with double consonants or consonant clusters *(ck, ll, mp, nd, nt, nk, ng, lt, sh, st, sk, ff, th, ch, ft)*. Help children notice each complete phonogram pattern.

Working with English Language Learners

With experience in early grades, English language learners may be familiar with consonant clusters, especially those at the beginning of words. If they are not, work with them in a small group (or the whole group if appropriate) to introduce the concept of consonants together at the beginning of words *(swim)*. They may not have looked for these clusters at other places in words; however, once you point out the pattern it will be rather easy for them to notice familiar clusters at the ends of words. Work with words that children understand (at least in spoken language) and are able to read.

You Need

► Pocket chart.

From *Teaching Resources:*

► Pocket Chart Card Template.

► Directions for Go Fish.

► Go Fish Game Cards made from Deck Card Template and Lesson SP 2 Word Cards.

► List Sheets.

Understand the Principle

Many words end with two consonant letters that are blended together *(st)* or make a unique sound *(ch)*. Some words end in two consonant letters that are the same *(ff, ll)*. Children need to learn the complete phonogram pattern, that is, the vowel and consonants (for example, *-uch, -est*). Consonant clusters will include groups of letters in which you can hear all sounds (ca*rd*, be*st*) or those that make a unique sound (*bring*, *bank*).

Explain the Principle

" Some words have patterns that end with consonant clusters *(mask, lump)*. "

SP 2
SPELLING PATTERNS

plan

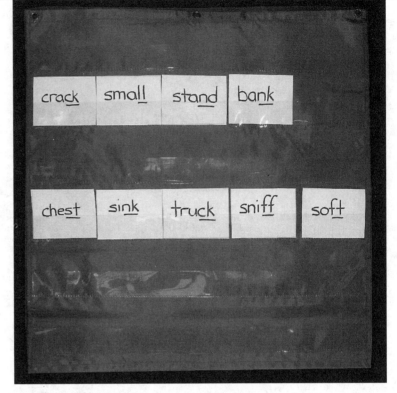

Explain the Principle

" Some words have patterns that end with consonant clusters (*mask, lump*). "

① Explain that you will help children notice more about spelling patterns.

② Place *crack, small, stand, bank* in a pocket chart. Ask children what pattern they notice. Help them summarize that each word has a consonant cluster at the end. Highlight the consonant clusters by underlining them.

③ Place a few more word cards in the chart for the children to read. Again, highlight each ending consonant cluster.

④ Suggested language: "A consonant cluster is two letters that often appear together in a word. Sometimes you hear two or three sounds." Ask children to identify the consonant clusters in *swim, sting, string,* and *tree* and have children identify the sounds and letters. Also mention that for some consonant clusters you hear only one sound *(child, show, truck, song)*. "Today you are going to look at consonant clusters in different places in a word."

⑤ Tell the children that they will play Go Fish with words that have ending consonant clusters. They will try to make pairs of words that end with the same consonant cluster. Then they will list twenty words with ending consonant clusters on a List Sheet.

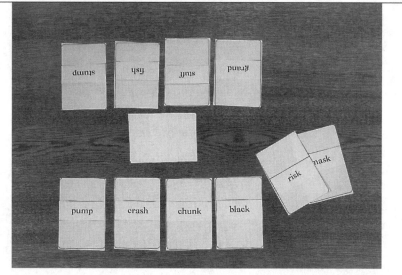

say word
ask for match
make pair or
take card
write words

▸ Have children play Go Fish in groups of three or four.

▸ They make pairs of words with the same ending consonant clusters.

▸ Then they list twenty words with ending consonant clusters on a List Sheet.

They can suggest a few more words with ending consonant clusters to add to the chart.

Ask children to read their word lists to a partner.

Invite the children to talk about what they noticed about the words they worked with today.

Link

Interactive Read-Aloud: Read aloud books that have many words with ending consonant clusters. Here are two suggested titles:

- ▶ *The Spider and the Fly* by Mary Howitt
- ▶ *Peg and the Whale* by Kenneth Oppell

Shared Reading: Display a poem on an overhead projector that includes words with final consonant clusters. Cover the phonogram patterns on the first reading of the text and ask children to predict the patterns. Then show the words.

Guided Reading: On a whiteboard show a variety of words with phonogram patterns ending with consonant clusters and call for quick recognition.

Guided/Independent Writing: Have children reread and edit their writing for spelling, noticing words ending with consonant clusters.

assess

- ▶ Notice how efficiently readers use phonogram patterns ending with consonant clusters.

- ▶ As a quick assessment, dictate six to ten words with phonograms ending with consonant clusters.

- ▶ Observe how quickly students are able to write the clusters.

Expand the Learning

Repeat the lesson with other phonogram patterns ending with consonant clusters. (See full list of phonograms in Pinnell and Fountas, *Word Matters*, Appendix 15.)

Have children make a word search with words that have phonograms with ending consonant clusters.

Connect with Home

Send home a deck of word cards so that children can play Go Fish with family members.

Alternatively, you can send home photocopied sheets of word cards along with several photocopied sheets of the Deck Card Template. Children and their family members can make their own deck of cards to play Go Fish.

Recognizing Word Patterns with Long Vowel Sounds

Blind Sort

Consider Your Children

In this lesson, children engage in a blind sort and learn to notice phonogram patterns that represent long vowel sounds. Select the patterns you want to work with from the chart. Repeat the lesson so that children experience a wide variety of the forty-nine different patterns listed. When children use *oe* and *ow*, or *ee* and *ea* patterns in the same sort, they will notice that the same sound can be spelled different ways.

Working with English Language Learners

With word study in previous grades, English language learners should already be accustomed to looking for patterns in words. If they have more experience, work with them to review the concept of phonograms. These larger units will help them better understand English because attention is drawn to its structural patterns and more obvious letter/sound relationships. For example, looking for a one-to-one relationship between sounds and letters is not as helpful in decoding *stain* as is knowing that *-ain* represents the long /ā/ and the /n/ sound. These larger units of words, once learned, will help students read and spell words more quickly. If students are learning patterns slowly, consider limiting each lesson to two patterns.

You Need

▶ Pocket chart.

From *Teaching Resources:*

▶ Pocket Chart Card Template.
▶ Category Word Cards, Onsets and Rimes.
▶ List Sheets.
▶ Three-Way Sort Cards.
▶ Three-Way Sort Sheets.

Understand the Principle

A *phonogram* is a useful word part for readers and writers to use when taking apart or constructing unfamiliar words. It contains the vowel-bearing part of a word. A phonogram can be as short as two letters (*no, be*) or it can be longer (*-ight*). Recognizing phonograms is more efficient than using letter-by-letter attention. For example, the pattern *ow* can represent a long /ō/ vowel sound (as in *grow*), or a different sound, as in *cow*.

Explain the Principle

" Some words have a long vowel pattern. You can hear the long vowel sound (*make, green, pie, coat, few*). "

CONTINUUM: SPELLING PATTERNS — Recognizing and Using Phonogram Patterns with a Long Vowel Sound in Single-Syllable Words

plan

teach

Explain the Principle

" Some words have a
long vowel pattern.
You can hear the
long vowel sound
(*make, green, pie,
coat, few*). "

1. Tell the children they will
learn more about word
patterns and their vowel
sounds.

2. Show *huge, cute*, and *new* one
word at a time. Have the
children read each word
and listen for the pattern
they hear at the end (*-uge,
-ute, -ew*). Place each word
at the top of a column in a
pocket chart.

3. Once these key words have been placed in the pocket chart, read the other
words one at a time. Have children listen to the word and tell you where on
the chart to place each card. They will sort by sound first and then look at
the pattern when you place the card. When you have finished, children will
have sorted the words into three categories. Discuss what they notice about
the words. Suggested language for summary: "All patterns have a long /ū/
sound. Some patterns have a vowel, a consonant, and a silent *e*."

4. Repeat this process with words having *-ain, -ay*, and *-age* patterns.

5. Suggested language: "Some words have a long vowel pattern. You can hear
the long vowel sound." For a few words, cut the onset from the rime on
each word to show its parts. Explain that you can put the pattern and the
first part together to make a word.

6. Tell the children they will use Onset and Rime Cards to make twenty words
with long vowel patterns and write the words on a List Sheet. Then partners
will place three key words (*huge, cute, new* or *train, play, cage*) in the top row
on a Three-Way Sort Card and do a blind sort, taking turns being the word
card reader and not showing the word, while the partner points to where the
word belongs. Each child then writes the sort on his Three-Way Sort Sheet.

apply

- make words
- write list
- place key words
- partner reads
- partner points
- place card
- switch roles
- write sort

▸ Children make twenty words with the rimes and patterns you select and write the words on a List Sheet.

▸ Partners then complete a blind sort on a Three-Way Sort Card. They place three key words on the top row. One partner reads a word and the other points to its place in the sort.

▸ Each child writes the completed sort on a Three-Way Sort Sheet.

Name: Lisa   Three-Way Sort

train	play	cage
stain	gray	stage
brain	tray	wage
drain	say	page
grain	pray	rage
sprain		

share

Have the children read their word sorts to a different partner. They can then add new words to the categories on the class chart.

Link

Interactive Read-Aloud: Read aloud rhyming books that engage children in thinking about a variety of sound and letter patterns. Here are a few suggested titles:

- *Songs Are Thoughts* by Neil Philip
- *Rush Hour* by Christine Loomis

Shared Reading: Read a variety of poems together on the first reading. Cover the rime on some words with long vowel patterns and have children predict the letter pattern.

Guided Reading: When children come to unknown words, prompt them to use the pattern by thinking of other words they know. For example, ask: "Do you know another word like that?"

Guided/Independent Writing: Teach children to check for patterns when they edit their writing for spelling.

assess

- As you read children's writing, make note of the long vowel patterns that are challenging so that you can use them in lessons.
- Dictate six to ten words with long vowel patterns as a quick assessment. Notice how quickly children write the vowel patterns.

Expand the Learning

Repeat this lesson with three or four other long vowel patterns (see Continuum) to help ensure that children control a wide variety of patterns.

Place a few words in the sort that do not fit any of the three patterns. Children will place these words outside the three columns.

Connect with Home

Send home a sheet of word cards for children to sort with family members.

As an alternative, children can ask a family member to help them search magazines and newspapers for words that contain the spelling patterns studied in the lesson.

Recognizing Phonograms with Double Vowels

Crazy Eights

Consider Your Children

These phonograms are complex, so be sure that children have strong control of basic long and short vowel sounds as well as simple phonograms. In this lesson, they learn the fourteen double-vowel rimes, or ending patterns, in words.

Working with English Language Learners

Double vowels are an easy pattern to recognize in print but pose difficulties when children spell words. Just as they connect single vowels to a sound, it helps English language learners to connect double vowel patterns to a sound. These vowel combinations are a complex feature of English, so expect children to achieve accurate spelling over time rather than immediately. As they work more with these phonogram patterns, children will automatically notice them in words they read and might begin checking them in words they write.

You Need

► Pocket chart.

► Index cards.

From *Teaching Resources*:

► Pocket Chart Card Template.

► Directions for Crazy Eights.

► Crazy Eights Game Cards made from Lesson SP 4 Word Cards and Deck Card Template.

Understand the Principle

Phonogram patterns are useful for children to learn since they help readers link words that are similar. In the patterns used in this lesson, the double vowels sometimes represent a long vowel sound (*feet*) and at other times they represent a unique sound (*broom*). All the patterns in this lesson have two *o*'s or two *e*'s followed by a single consonant. The vowels *o* and *e* are the only vowels doubled in words. Children need to distinguish between the two different sounds represented by two *o*'s (*wood, food*).

Explain the Principle

66 Some words have double vowels followed by a consonant. 99

66 Sometimes vowels sound like their name (long sound). 99

66 Sometimes vowels stand for other sounds. 99

CONTINUUM: SPELLING PATTERNS — RECOGNIZING AND USING PHONOGRAMS WITH DOUBLE VOWELS (VVC)

plan

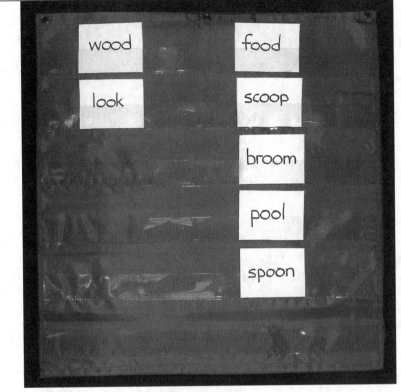

Explain the Principle

" **Some words have double vowels followed by a consonant.** "

" **Sometimes vowels sound like their name (long sound).** "

" **Sometimes vowels stand for other sounds.** "

① Tell the children you will help them learn more about spelling patterns. Place *feed, heel, screen, sweep, steer, meet* in the pocket chart.

② Have children read the words and tell what they notice about the middle sound. Suggested language: "Some words have double vowels followed by a consonant. Sometimes the vowel pattern sounds like its name; it is the long sound."

③ Remove these word cards and insert *wood, food, look, pool, broom, spoon,* and *scoop* in the appropriate columns in the chart (see chart above). Have children read them and help you sort them by sound. Help the children notice the words that have a middle sound like *wood (look)* or a middle sound like *food (pool, broom, spoon, scoop).* Suggested language: "Sometimes the vowel pattern stands for other sounds." Ask them to suggest any other *oo* words to add to either column.

④ Explain to the children that they will play Crazy Eights with spelling patterns. They will make pairs of words that have the same ending pattern and same vowel sound. If the children do not know how to play the game, demonstrate with one child. One card is placed face up next to a face down deck. Each player lays down a card that has the same vowel sound. A Crazy Eight card is a wild card. If they do not have a match, they draw from the deck until they have a match to put down. The object of the game is to run out of cards.

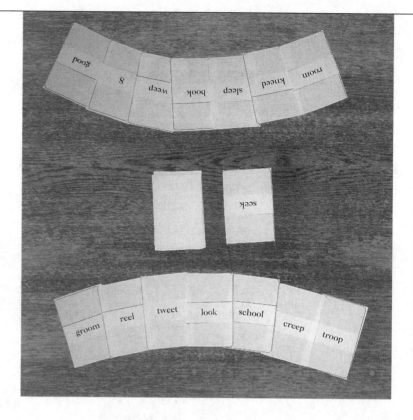

read word

match vowel sound

put card or draw card

write word

► In groups of two to four, children play Crazy Eights with word cards showing a variety of double-vowel spelling patterns.

► Each player begins with eight cards and matches pairs of words with the same ending pattern. The Crazy Eight card serves as a wild card.

► The first player to have no cards in her hand wins the game.

► After playing, children make note on an index card of one pair of words they matched. They bring their index cards to sharing.

Go around the circle, inviting children to share one pair of words they matched. Ask the children if they have any words they would like to add to the pocket chart. Interesting words like *coop* may come up. A *coop* for chickens or birds has a sound like *broom*, but a *coop* grocery store has two syllables because it is an abbreviation of *cooperative*.

Link

Interactive Read-Aloud: Read aloud books that have many words with double vowel phonograms. Here are two suggested titles:

▶ *The War Between the Consonants and Vowels* by Priscilla Turner

▶ *How Are You Peeling?* by Saxton Freymann and Joost Elffers

Shared Reading: Read a variety of poems with double vowel phonograms. After enjoying the text, have children identify two or three of them and highlight the pattern with a marker.

Guided Reading: As children try to solve unknown words, prompt them to notice and use spelling patterns. Ask, "Do you know another word like that?" or "Do you see a part that can help you?"

Guided/Independent Writing: During the editing process, encourage children to check words that fit double vowel patterns they know.

assess

▶ As children read texts, observe how quickly they read phonograms with double vowel patterns.

▶ Notice how well children's written work reflects their control of double vowel phonogram patterns.

▶ Notice their use of patterns in two-syllable words, such as *succeed* or *cartoon*.

Expand the Learning

As a challenge, add a few two-syllable words with double vowel patterns to the Crazy Eights Card Deck (*succeed, cartoon, workbook, carpool*).

Have children play Phonogram Lotto. Write words with the fourteen different patterns (*eed, eek, eel, eem, een, eep, eer, eet, ood, ook, ool, oom, oon, oop*) on Lotto Game Cards and Word Cards (see Directions for Lotto in *Teaching Resources*).

Connect with Home

Send home decks of Crazy Eights cards for children to play the game with family members. You may choose to send home copies of word cards and Deck Card Templates so children can make their decks with family members.

Recognizing Word Patterns with the Short o Sound

Battle

Consider Your Children

In this lesson children work with a variety of phonogram patterns, some of which are phonetically irregular and more complex. You can make the Battle game more or less challenging by selecting particular words from the Word Cards. Examine assessment results, children's writing, or your observations of their reading to inventory their awareness of simple or more complex phonogram patterns.

Working with English Language Learners

Subtle differences in the pronunciation of vowel sounds might be difficult for English language learners. This lesson gives them practice hearing and saying a variety of words that have a vowel sound similar to short *o*, yet have different spellings. These sounds may have slight variations but they are similar enough to be categorized as having the short /o/ sound. This lesson helps children realize that the sounds of English relate to many different spellings. If the examples in this lesson are too complex, then introduce only two or three spellings at one time. Revisit these patterns during word work.

You Need

▸ Pocket chart.

From *Teaching Resources:*

▸ Pocket Chart Card Template.

▸ Directions for Battle.

▸ Battle Game Cards made from Lesson SP 5 Word Cards and Deck Card Template.

Understand the Principle

Phonogram patterns are very useful to readers and writers. All the spelling patterns here include the short /o/ sound, though the pattern may be phonetically regular (*ost, ong*) or may have a more complex letter sound relationship (*all, aw, alk, aught, ought*). Children need to learn the complex irregular patterns and use their knowledge to construct new words.

Explain the Principle

" Some words have patterns with vowels that make the /aw/ sound as in *saw*. "

" Several patterns of letters can stand for the sound (*wall, paw, taught, cost*). "

CONTINUUM: SPELLING PATTERNS — Recognizing and Using Phonogram Patterns with the /aw/ Sound in Single-Syllable Words

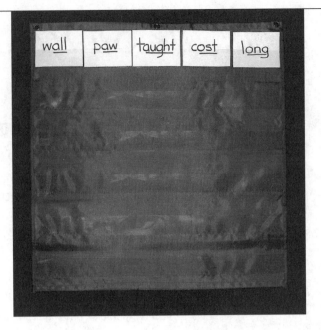

Explain the Principle

" Some words have patterns with vowels that make the /aw/ sound as in *saw*. "

" Several patterns of letters can stand for the sound (*wall, paw, taught, cost*). "

① Explain to the children that you will be helping them learn more about spelling patterns. Place *wall, paw, taught, cost, long* in the first row of a pocket chart.

② Have children read each word as you underline the spelling pattern that contains the short /o/ sound.

③ Invite the children to think of other one-syllable words with the short /o/ sound in the pattern. Write each word on a blank card, place it in the correct column, and underline the pattern. If they suggest words that have other patterns with the short /o/ sound, create a new column. Continue the process with a variety of words so they can see the various patterns that represent the short /o/ sound.

④ Demonstrate how to play Battle. Deal the entire deck face down to two players. Explain that short /o/ phonograms are the trump card, the card that always wins. The first player turns over one card and reads it. Then the second player does the same. The player whose card has the short /o/ phonogram pattern (the trump) takes both cards and places them aside in his discard pile. If both players have the trump (short /o/ phonogram pattern), neither gets the cards and play continues. If neither card has the feature, the cards remain and players continue turning over cards until a card with a short /o/ pattern appears. The pile may build high and the player who takes it will get all the cards. The player with the most cards in his discard pile wins the game.

deal cards
turn card
read word
turn card
read word
take cards
or continue
repeat
write

- Have children, in partners, play Battle.

- Word cards with the short /o/ phonogram pattern are the designated feature or trump.

- The player with the most cards in her discard pile wins the game at the end.

- After playing, children write two words with a short /o/ phonogram pattern to bring to sharing and contribute to the group discussion.

Have the children read their two words and have each suggest a word with a short /o/ phonogram pattern that you add to the class chart. Encourage words with a variety of patterns.

Link

Interactive Read-Aloud: Read aloud books that include words with short /o/ patterns. After enjoying the text, point out several of the words and write them on a chart. Here are two suggested titles:

- ▸ *A Frog in the Bog* by Karma Wilson
- ▸ *I Am the Dog, I Am the Cat* by Donald Hall

Shared Reading: Select a variety of poems with words that have short /o/ phonogram patterns. Before placing them on an overhead, cover the final part (rime) of a few words and have children predict the spelling pattern. Observe to learn whether they are offering predictions within the categories they know (*-aw, -augh, -aught, -ost*).

Guided Reading: During word work name some words with short /o/ phonogram patterns and have children make them quickly with magnetic letters.

Guided/Independent Writing: Call attention to the variety of short /o/ phonogram patterns that children use in their writing.

assess

- ▸ Dictate four to six words with short /o/ phonogram patterns to assess children's control of the patterns.
- ▸ Observe how flexible children are when taking apart specific words with short /o/ phonograms while reading.

Expand the Learning

Add some two-syllable word cards with the short /o/ phonogram pattern (*dollar, baseball, hallway, seesaw, chalkboard, thoughtful, frosty, longest, thoughtless, talker, beanstalk, fallen, caller, drawer, lawful, costly, frosted*).

Connect with Home

Send home a deck of cards with short /o/ words for children to play Battle with family members.

Have the children search for examples of the spelling patterns in magazines and newspapers. They can bring these to class to share.

Recognizing Word Patterns with Unique Vowel Sounds: Long /ū/

Word Pairs

Consider Your Children

Some students may think that the long /ū/ sound is regular (as in *cute*). In fact, representations of long /ū/ is highly varied. In this lesson students work with twenty-nine different spelling patterns that represent the long /ū/ sound. You can choose to focus on three or four patterns or all of them, depending on children's strengths and needs. You may wish to work with the patterns that have a vowel, consonant and *e* together as a group.

Working with English Language Learners

The complex range of spellings in this lesson may be difficult for English language learners. Be sure that they can read and understand the words that you use as examples. Have children review examples of words with the long /ū/ sound. They may be surprised to find so many different spellings related to this sound and also that there is a slight variation in pronunciation (*moon, cute*). Consider having them begin with words having the vowel + consonant + *e* pattern. During word work, create a chart that students can read together and reference as they encounter new words in texts.

You Need

▶ Pocket chart.

From *Teaching Resources*:

▶ Pocket Chart Card Template.

▶ Category Word Cards, Onsets and Rimes (select rimes with *oo, oon, une, oo, ood, ew, ue, oot, uit, ool, ume, use, uge, ute, ub, uce, uke, une, ude, ure, ule, oom, oup, ooze, ooth, uel, oose, uth*).

▶ Word Pairs Sheets.

▶ Lesson SP 6 Word Cards.

Understand the Principle

Knowing spelling patterns helps readers and writers learn many different words. The long /ū/ sound can be represented by twenty-nine different letter combinations, or patterns. Notice that the sound can be /oo/ (*tune, suit*) or /ū/ (*mule*). Many of the patterns are constructed with a vowel, consonant, and *e* (*fuse, cure*). Words can end with *o* (*to, who*) or two o's (*too*) and represent the same sound.

Explain the Principle

" Some words have patterns with vowels that make the /ū/ sound as in *moon*. "

" Several patterns of letters can stand for the long /ū/ sound (*tune, suit, soup*). "

CONTINUUM: SPELLING PATTERNS — RECOGNIZING AND USING PHONOGRAM PATTERNS WITH THE /ū/ SOUND (AS IN *MOON*) IN SINGLE-SYLLABLE WORDS

plan

Explain the Principle

" Some words have patterns with vowels that make the /oo/ sound as in *moon*. "

" Several patterns of letters can stand for the long *u* sound (*tune, suit, soup*). "

① Tell the children that they will learn more about spelling patterns.

② Put *suit, grew, roof, sure* in a column on a pocket chart. Ask children to read each word as you

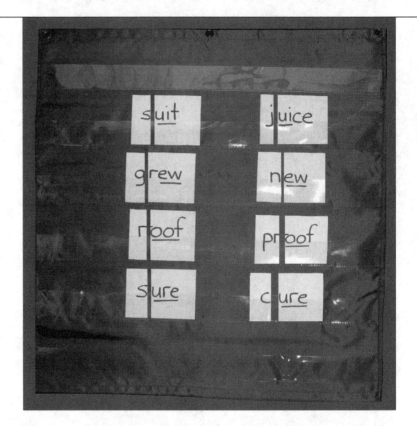

underline its spelling pattern. Then ask children to think of another word that has the same pattern (e.g., *cure, proof, new, juice*) and place it to the right. If children can handle additional patterns, continue with four more patterns at a time (e.g., *oon, oot, oup, ute*).

③ Next, cut the word apart into *onset* (beginning part) and the rime (ending part). Place it back in the chart (*s-uit, gr-ew, r-oof, s-ure*). Notice that words with the *ui* pattern can be cut again for more flexible use of the pattern.

④ Summarize the lesson with the principle. Suggested language: "Some words have patterns with vowels that make the /oo/ sound, as in *moon*. Several patterns of letters can stand for the long /ū/ sound."

⑤ Explain that children will have a pile of single-consonant or consonant-cluster onset cards and a pile of rimes, or ending parts, of words. Children use the word parts to make fifteen different words and then write them on the left column of a Word Pairs Sheet. In the right column, they write another word with the same pattern and then underline the long /ū/ pattern in each.

apply

make
write
underline
read

▸ Children use Onset and Rime Cards to make fifteen words.

▸ They write them in the left column of a Word Pairs Sheet. In the right column, children write another word with the same pattern and then underline the long /ū/ pattern in each.

▸ Children can read their list of word pairs to a partner.

Name: Reneé L.		Word Pairs Sheet
proof	—	roof
crude	—	rude
school	—	tool
groom	—	gloom
bloom	—	room
screw	—	chew
fruit	—	suit
scoot	—	hoot
brood	—	mood
noon	—	soon
hoop	—	snoop
scoop	—	coop
cue	—	clue
glue	—	true
blue	—	due

pr oof
cr ude
sch ool
gr oom
fr uit
br ood
n oon
sc oop
bl ue

share

Invite each child to read a word pair from his list as you write the words on a chart and underline the pattern that represents the long /ū/ sound.

Have children say words slowly to hear the very small differences in the pronunciation of the vowel sound in words like *suit*, *cute*, and *cure*. Invite them to discuss the similarity in pronunciation as well as the differences.

Link

Interactive Read-Aloud: Read aloud books that contain words with the long /ū/ sound. Here are a few suggested titles:

▶ *And If the Moon Could Talk* by Kate Banks

▶ *Rabbit Moon* by Patricia Hubbell

Shared Reading: After enjoying a poem, underline two or three words with a long /ū/ pattern. Add them to the class chart.

Guided Reading: During word work, have children use magnetic letters to make four or five words with a long /ū/ pattern. Then have them write the words.

Guided/Independent Writing: Have the children reread their writing and check for spelling patterns they know.

assess

▶ Have the children use magnetic letters to make six to ten words with the long /ū/ sound to determine control of various patterns.

▶ Give children a list of about twenty words that includes (mixed with others) a variety of six to ten words with long /ū/ patterns. They read the words and circle those that have the long /ū/ sound.

Expand the Learning

Repeat this lesson with a different selection of spelling patterns.

Give children three key words to write on the top of a Three-Way Sort Sheet. Have them write as many words as they can with the same pattern as each key word.

Connect with Home

Give the children a Word Grid Sheet with a variety of words with long /ū/ patterns. Have them read the words aloud several times to family members to increase their speed in recognition.

Recognizing Word Patterns with Unique Vowel Sounds: Short /oo/

Blind Two-Way Sort

Consider Your Children

Children should understand that the sound connected to vowels can vary. They should be able to compare and contrast the shorter /oo/ sound in this lesson with the long /ū/ sound in the previous lesson. In this lesson they study five different spelling patterns with the /oo/ sound.

Working with English Language Learners

Have English language learners begin with examples they know and understand (*blue, fun, food, book*) and then add the more complex examples of these sounds. Working with a limited number of sounds in words with different spelling patterns helps children learn visual patterns. Even if they do not remember every example, they learn about possible spellings that represent a particular vowel sound. Read aloud the words to be sorted, so that children have the opportunity to hear, say, and see the words they will sort.

You Need

▸ Pocket chart.

From *Teaching Resources:*

▸ Pocket Chart Card Template.
▸ Two-Way Sort Cards.
▸ Two-Way Sort Sheets.
▸ Lesson SP 7 Word Cards.

Understand the Principle

Some words contain letters that represent the long /ū/ sound (*suit, few, tune*). Others have a shorter sound (*book* and *could*). The letters *oo*, *u* and *ou* can represent a short /oo/ sound. A short /oo/ sound can also be represented by a *u* as in *push* or *pull*. The *oo* and *ou* pattern can represent other sounds as in *food* and *house*.

Explain the Principle

" Some words have patterns with vowels that make the /oo/ sound as in *book*. "

" Several patterns of letters can stand for the sound (*book, could*). "

CONTINUUM: SPELLING PATTERNS — RECOGNIZING AND USING PHONOGRAM PATTERNS WITH THE /OO/ SOUND (*AS IN BOOK*) IN SINGLE-SYLLABLE WORDS

plan

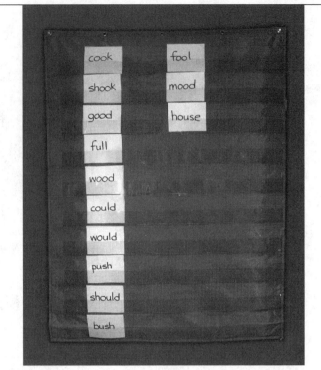

Explain the Principle

" Some words have patterns with vowels that make the /oo/ sound as in *book*. "

" Several patterns of letters can stand for the sound (*book, could*). "

① Tell the children they will learn some more spelling patterns.

② Place *cook, shook, good, full, wood, could, would, push* in one column in a pocket chart. Ask children what they notice about all of the words. They will notice that they have the same vowel sound.

③ Show *should, fool, mood, house, bush* one at a time, and ask if they belong. Guide children to notice that *fool, mood,* and *house* have a different sound and do not belong in the first column. You can place them in a second column. Help children understand that patterns *ook, ood, ould, ull, ush* represent a unique vowel sound that is similar. Suggested language: "Some words have patterns with vowels that make the /oo/ sound as in *book*. Several letter patterns can stand for the sound (*book, could*)."

④ Explain to the children that they will read word cards and complete a blind sort with a partner using *push* and *?* (question mark) at the top of a Two-Way Sort Sheet. One partner takes a word card and reads it without showing the word. The other child points to *push* or *?* (question mark) to indicate that the word on the card has the same vowel sound as *push* or it does not. Partners continue through all the word cards. Then they remove the cards, shuffle them, and reverse roles. Then each child writes the sort on a Two-Way Sort Sheet.

take
say
sort
write

▸ Have partners complete a blind sort, where they say and sort words with unique vowel sounds. Then they switch roles.

▸ Finally they each write the sort on a Two-Way Sort Sheet.

Name: Gage   Two-Way Sort

push	?
bush	mouse
would	food
full	soup
look	

share

Have the children read their sorts to a different partner.

Ask children to share any words that were difficult for them. You may want to add a few more words to the pocket chart.

Link

Interactive Read-Aloud: Read aloud books that have words with unique vowel sounds. Point out one or two of the words after reading. Here are a few suggested titles:

- ▸ *Bus Route to Boston* by Maryann Cocca-Leffler
- ▸ *A Pocketful of Poems* by Nikki Grimes

Shared Reading: In poems you have previously read, use highlighter tape to mark one or two words with the patterns used in the lesson.

Guided Reading: When children come to difficult words, encourage them to use patterns they know. Ask, "Do you know another word like that?"

Guided/Independent Writing: Encourage writers to think of patterns they know when they edit for spelling. Encourage them to refer to the group charts in the classroom as a resource.

assess

- ▸ Give children magnetic letters and observe how quickly they make words with the patterns.
- ▸ Observe how quickly children use patterns to solve unknown words as they read.

Expand the Learning

Have children make a Word Search with words from this lesson (see *Teaching Resources*).

Repeat the lesson with words that have two syllables: *cookbook, rosebush, wooden*, and *bookworm.*

Connect with Home

Have the children take home a sheet of word cards and a Two-Way Sort Sheet to complete a blind sort at home with family members. They can glue the word cards to the sheet to bring to class to share.

Recognizing Word Patterns with Unique Vowel Sounds: /ow/

Making Word Pairs

Consider Your Children

Children should have good control of basic common phonogram patterns as a foundation for the understandings to be developed in this lesson. Children will work with fourteen different spelling patterns that represent the /ow/ sound in single-syllable words. You can use all the patterns or select particular ones to work with.

Working with English Language Learners

This group of phonograms challenges English language learners but helps them realize that larger visual patterns of words relate to sounds. Once they know about this category (/ow/ as in *cow*), they can add spellings that fit within it. Developing these understandings will probably be an ongoing process for several years. Start with simple examples that children understand and gradually expand their repertoire. During word work, reinforce their understanding by having students write or build words.

You Need

▶ Pocket chart.

From *Teaching Resources*:

▶ Pocket Chart Card Template.

▶ Category Word Cards, Onsets and Rimes (*ow, own, ound, owl, out, owd, ounce, oul, ount, ouch, outh, oud, our, ouse*).

▶ Word Pairs Sheets.

Understand the Principle

The letters *ow* and *ou* are followed by various consonants to represent several different spelling patterns. The *ow* can represent the entire phonogram or spelling pattern (as in *cow* or *how*) or it can be part of the pattern (*howl, clown*). It is helpful for children to learn the complete pattern.

Explain the Principle

❝ Some words have patterns with vowels that make the /ow/ sound, as in *cow*. ❞

❝ Several patterns of letters can stand for the sound. ❞

CONTINUUM: SPELLING PATTERNS — RECOGNIZING AND USING PHONOGRAM PATTERNS WITH THE /OW/ SOUND (AS IN *COW*) IN SINGLE-SYLLABLE WORDS

plan

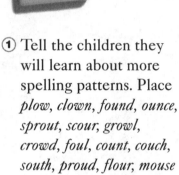

Explain the Principle

66 Some words have
patterns with
vowels that make
the /ow/ sound, as
in *cow*. 99

66 Several patterns of
letters can stand for
the sound. 99

① Tell the children they
will learn about more
spelling patterns. Place
*plow, clown, found, ounce,
sprout, scour, growl,
crowd, foul, count, couch,
south, proud, flour, mouse*
in a pocket chart.

② Have the children read
each word as you
underline the
phonogram.

③ Ask the children what
they notice about the
words. They will see that each has the /ow/ sound represented by *ow* or *ou*,
which is usually followed by consonant letters (except for *ow* in *plow*).

④ Suggested language: "Some words have patterns with vowels that make the
/ow/ sound as in *cow*. Two different letter patterns can be used for this
sound. They are *ou*, as *loud* and *ow* as in *cow*."

⑤ Tell the children they will make words with the /ow/ sound. They will use
Onset and Rime Cards to make fourteen words (one with each of the
fourteen phonograms), which they write in the first column of a Word Pairs
Sheet. Then they make a second word with the same pattern and write it in
the second column. They circle the phonogram pattern and read their words
to a partner.

make
write
circle
read

apply

▸ Have the
children make
fourteen words
with Onset and
Rime Cards,
and then write
the words on a
Word Pairs
Sheet.

sh	out
s	our
tr	out
pr	oud
pl	ow
pr	owl
gr	ound
sl	ouch
gr	ouch
h	ow

Name: Jeremy   Word Pairs Sheet
Date: _____

tout	→	shout
flour	→	sour
sprout	→	trout
loud	→	proud
meow	→	plow
fowl	→	prowl
wound	→	ground
pounce	→	ounce
pouch	→	slouch
vouch	→	grouch
now	→	new
douse	→	spouse
our	→	scour
spout	→	pout

▸ For each word, children make another word with the same phonogram
pattern. They circle the phonograms and read the words to a partner. If they
are in doubt about whether they have created a real word, they can check
with the chart or a simple dictionary.

share

Have children read their word pairs to a different partner.

Show a spelling pattern and have the children share other words that have
that pattern. Add their words to the class chart.

Link

Interactive Read-Aloud: Read aloud books that have words with the /ow/ sound in the pattern. Point out one or two words after reading and enjoying the book. Two examples of such books are:

- ► *Bein' with You This Way* by W. Nikola-Lisa
- ► *Slithery Jake* by Rose-Marie Provencher

Shared Reading: After sharing a poem on a chart, have children highlight with tape two or three words with the /ow/ sound.

Guided Reading: After reading a text, ask children to turn to a particular page and locate two or three words with /ow/ patterns.

Guided/Independent Writing: Remind children to think about patterns they know as they reread and edit their work. Guide them to use the class charts as a resource.

assess

- ► Observe children's written stories to assess their control of spelling patterns with /ow/.
- ► Dictate three to five words with the /ow/ pattern to assess children's control.

Expand the Learning

Have the children create Word Ladders with /ou/ or /ow/ by changing the beginning or ending consonants (see *Teaching Resources*).

Create a Follow the Path game board with words that have the /ow/ sound.

Connect with Home

Give the children ten words with the /ow/ patterns and have them create a Word Search for family members to complete.

Children can challenge a family member to see who can create the longest Word Ladder using words with the /ow/ patterns (see *Teaching Resources*).

Recognizing Word Patterns with Vowel Combinations

Connect

Consider Your Children

In this lesson, children work with a variety of vowel patterns. Select fifty-two words with the particular vowel patterns that children need to learn or practice. There are two different groups of words from which to select. In Group One, children distinguish phonograms with *ai* and *ea*; Group Two includes phonograms with *oa, ee, ay,* and *aw* letter combinations. To make this lesson less challenging, select fewer patterns.

Working with English Language Learners

This lesson focuses on some of the more complex vowel combinations that pose a spelling challenge to children. It will help English language learners to say each word several times. If they have difficulty, have them build the words with magnetic letters and then say them slowly, noticing and touching the double vowels. If Connect is a new game for children, play it with a small group so that you are sure they understand the task.

You Need

▸ Magnetic letters.

▸ Cookie sheet or magnetic whiteboard.

From *Teaching Resources*:

▸ Directions for Connect.

▸ Connect Game Cards made from Lesson SP 9 Word Cards and Deck Card Template. (Use either Group 1—*ai* and *ea*—or Group 2—*oa, ee, ay,* and *aw*.)

Understand the Principle

It is very helpful when reading and writing to know spelling patterns. The vowel patterns *ai, ea* and *oa, ee, ay,* and *aw* that are included in the phonograms of this lesson represent the long sound of the first vowel. The *ea* pattern can also represent the long /ā/ sound (*great*) but can also represent the short /e/ sound (*bread*). In the phonograms *ay* and *aw*, the *w* and the *y* function as vowels in the combinations even though they are consonant letters.

Explain the Principle

" Some words have two vowels together (vowel combinations). The vowel sound is usually the name of the first vowel (*stream, road*). "

CONTINUUM: SPELLING PATTERNS — RECOGNIZING AND USING PHONOGRAMS WITH VOWEL COMBINATIONS (VVC)

plan

Explain the Principle

❝ Some words have two vowels together (vowel combinations). The vowel sound is usually the name of the first vowel (*stream, road*). ❞

① Explain to the children that they will learn to notice more patterns in words. Make *sneak* with magnetic letters and have children read it. Point out the pattern *eak*. Change *sn* to *p* and have children read *peak*.

② Repeat this process with *jail, trail; maid, paid; bait, wait; clean, mean; pea, flea; heap, leap; bead, lead; fear, dear; hair, fair; neat, wheat.* Help the children notice that each word has two vowels together.

③ Suggested language: "Some words have two vowels together. The vowel sound is usually the name of the first vowel."

④ Invite children to suggest more examples of words with the *aid, ail, ain, air, ait, ea, ead, eak, eam, ean, eap, ear, eat* patterns, and make them with magnetic letters. Point out the vowel sound in each.

⑤ Demonstrate the card game Connect with two children. Deal the cards evenly between two players. The first player lays down a word card face up and reads it. The second player must match it by laying down a card with the same phonogram (e.g., *-eam*). A wild card can be substituted for a match. If the second player is able to make a match, the third player must also make a match. If any player does not have a match, he picks up all the cards discarded by the other player(s). If all players have been able to make a match after one round of turn-taking, then the discard pile is moved to the side and not played again. The first player to discard all his cards wins the game.

apply

read
match
take

▶ Children play Connect in groups of three or four.

▶ They take turns laying down a card, reading it, and inviting the other players to lay down a card with the same phonogram. A player without a match picks up all the cards.

▶ The first player to discard all his cards wins the game.

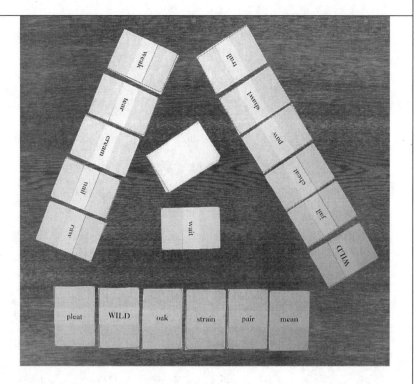

share

Invite the children one at a time to make a few words with the phonogram patterns on a magnetic board. The other children read the word, identify the phonogram pattern, and then change something to make a new word.

Link

Interactive Read-Aloud: Read aloud a variety of books with words having phonogram patterns included in this lesson. Here are a few suggested titles:

▶ *Who's Been Sleeping in My Porridge?* by Colin McNaughton

▶ *A Pup Just for Me* by Ed Young

Shared Reading: Read several poems with words having phonograms with long vowel patterns. After enjoying the poems, give children a photocopy and have them underline the words with long vowel phonograms.

Guided Reading: Help children use their knowledge of word patterns. Ask, "Do you know another word like that?" or "Do you know the last part?" or "Do you see a part that you know?"

Guided/Independent Writing: Remind children to check for the correct spelling by thinking about spelling patterns they know.

assess

▶ As a quick assessment, dictate six words with a variety of long phonogram patterns.

▶ Notice how quickly children recognize or analyze words with long vowel patterns.

Expand the Learning

Repeat this lesson with the set of word cards not used, or mix all the cards to include other phonogram patterns.

As a challenge, include two-syllable words with the phonogram patterns (e.g., *rainbow, season*).

Connect with Home

Send home a deck of Connect cards for children to play the game with family members. You may want to send home sheets of word cards along with several photocopies of the Deck Card Template so children can create a deck with family members.

Recognizing Phonograms with Double Consonants

Blind Sort

Consider Your Children

Use this lesson when children can read and write double consonant spelling patterns in one-syllable words and they are ready to apply their knowledge to words with two syllables. For examples, use only words that are in children's oral vocabularies. As children sort words, they will put words with long vowel sounds in a separate column. Notice that the double consonant is often at the end of the base word *(taller)* but is sometimes in the middle of a whole word *(muffin)*.

Working with English Language Learners

Use words that English language learners have in their speaking or listening vocabularies and also have examined in written form. Have children practice reading each word slowly and clearly (although not exaggerated) so that they can do the activity more easily. Work with small groups to be sure that children understand the prcedure for blind sorting of words.

You Need

► Pocket chart.

From *Teaching Resources*:

► Pocket Chart Card Template.

► Three-Way Sort Cards.

► Three-Way Sort Sheets.

► Lesson SP 10 Word Cards.

Understand the Principle

The short vowel pattern in one-syllable words with double consonants should be under control so that readers can now look for and use the pattern in words with more than one syllable. Children need to learn that sometimes a double consonant follows the short vowel sound in one- or two-syllable words. The vowel sound can be long *(roll)*, but this occurs only with *o*. A double consonant can appear at the end of a one-syllable word or within a two-syllable word.

Explain the Principle

" Some words have double consonants at the end. The sound of the vowel is usually short. "

CONTINUUM: SPELLING PATTERNS — RECOGNIZING AND USING PHONOGRAMS THAT END WITH DOUBLE LETTERS (VCC)

plan

Explain the Principle

" **Some words have double consonants at the end. The sound of the vowel is usually short.** "

① Tell the children they will learn more about spelling patterns in words. Place *taller, yellow, pillow, troll,* and *muffin* in the top row in a pocket chart. As you place each word, ask children to read it aloud.

② Invite children to tell what they notice about all the words. Suggested language: "What do you notice about the letters and sounds in each of these words?" Children will notice that each has a double consonant, one has one syllable, and others have two syllables. The double consonant appears at the end of the base word or in the middle of a word. The sound of the vowel is short, except with *troll,* which is long *o.* Repeat the process adding one or two more words to each column (*spill, smallest, spelling, dollar, stuffing*).

③ Tell children that they will do a blind sort using a Three-Way Sort Card. The three categories will be words with a short vowel sound and double consonant at the end *(doll)*, words with a short vowel sound and double consonant in the middle *(caller)*, and words with a long vowel sound *(troll)*. They place the key words (*doll, caller,* and *troll*) at the top of the columns. One partner reads the word and the other points to the correct column. Then the word is placed in the column. Then they reverse roles. Demonstrate the process with a few words (*smell, yellow, roll*). Finally they each write the sort on a Three-Way Sort Sheet.

listen
point
check
write

Three-Way Sort Card:

doll	caller	troll
spill	filling	toll
bell	selling	yellow
swell	shellfish	poll
gruff	bellman	fellow
still	bluffing	droll
doll		

Three-Way Sort Sheet:

Name: Natalie T.   Three-Way Sort

doll	caller	troll
spill	filler	toll
bell	selling	poll
swell	shellfish	droll
gruff	bellman	
still	bluffing	
doll	yellow	
	fellow	

► Have the
children do a
Blind Sort with
a partner, using
a Three-Way
Sort Card.

► One partner
draws a card and reads it aloud without showing it to the other partner. The
second partner points to the correct column and then places the card in that
column. Finally each child writes the sort on a Three-Way Sort Sheet.

► Children read their Three-Way Sort Sheets to one another and bring their
sheets to sharing.

Invite children to read their Three-Way Sort Sheet to a different partner.
Ask children to share any words they find difficult to place.

Link

Interactive Read-Aloud: Read aloud a variety of books that have words with double consonants. After reading, point out two or three of the words. Here are a few suggested titles:

- ▶ *If You Give a Moose a Muffin* by Laura Numeroff
- ▶ *Hey Little Ant* by Phillip and Hannah Hoose

Shared Reading: Read aloud poems that have words with double consonants. Have children circle them on a photocopy.

Guided Reading: During word work, use magnetic letters to make a few words having double consonants.

Guided/Independent Writing: Have children notice and edit the spelling of words having double consonant patterns.

assess

- ▶ Observe a two-way blind sort to assess children's ability to read words with double consonants.

- ▶ Dictate a few words with double consonants to assess children's knowledge of the patterns.

Expand the Learning

Have children sort words that have *o* and a double consonant according to its long or short vowel sound.

Have children say and sort the word cards in a Two-Way Sort for one- and two-syllable words (see *Teaching Resources*).

Connect with Home

Give children a set of word cards with words that have double consonants to cut and sort at home.

Have children use words with double consonants to create a Word Search for family members (see *Teaching Resources*).

Noticing Word Patterns That Represent Unique Vowel Sounds

Concentration

Consider Your Children

In this lesson, children learn to notice seven phonogram patterns with the /oi/ sound. Be sure that children have previously worked with many phonograms and other word patterns and that they understand the concept. To make the lesson more challenging, include about fourteen word cards with *ou*.

Working with English Language Learners

As English language learners continue to explore vowel sounds that are represented by many different spellings, they will make deeper connections between spelling and sound. This activity helps them decode and write words. The more they work with patterns like *oin,* and *oice,* the more readily they will recognize them as they read and the more alternatives they will consider as they write. During word work, write examples on a whiteboard and have children suggest other words that have the sound of *oy,* as in *boy.*

You Need

▸ Pocket chart.

▸ Marker or highlighter.

▸ Index cards.

From *Teaching Resources*:

▸ Pocket Chart Card Template.

▸ Directions for Concentration.

▸ Concentration Game Cards made from Lesson SP 11 Word Cards and Deck Card Template.

Understand the Principle

The letters *oy* and *oi* represent the /oi/ sound in seven different letter patterns (*-oy, -oil, -oin, -oice, -oint, -oist, -oise*). Help children read and write the patterns as a unit, noticing that usually the /oi/ is followed by other consonants in the pattern.

Explain the Principle

❝ Some words have patterns with vowels that stand for the /oi/ sound as in *boy.* ❞

❝ Several patterns of letters can include the sound (e.g., *coin, voice, noise* or *boy, toy*). ❞

CONTINUUM: SPELLING PATTERNS — RECOGNIZING AND USING PHONOGRAM PATTERNS WITH THE /OI/ SOUND IN SINGLE-SYLLABLE WORDS

plan

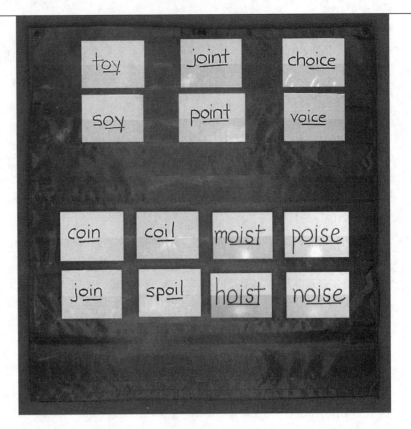

Explain the Principle

" Some words have patterns with vowels that stand for the /oi/ sound as in *boy*. "

" Several patterns of letters can include the sound (e.g., *coin, voice, noise* or *boy, toy*). "

① Tell the children that you will show them more spelling patterns.

② As you place *toy, soy, joint, point, coil, spoil, moist, hoist, choice, voice, poise, noise, coin,* and *join* in the pocket chart, ask a volunteer to highlight or underline each phonogram.

③ Invite children to suggest a few words to add to the chart.

④ Tell children they will play Concentration in small groups. Demonstrate how to play the game if it is new to them. Explain that they put all the cards face down on a table. They take turns turning a card over, reading it, and then turning over a second card and reading it. The goal is to match pairs of words with the same phonogram pattern. The player with the most pairs wins.

apply

turn
turn
match

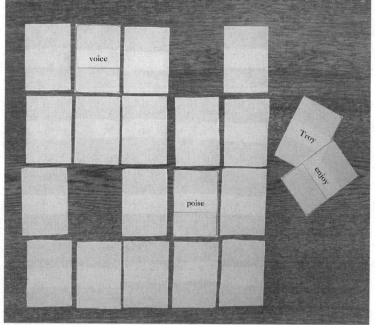

- ▸ Have the children play Concentration in groups of three or four.

- ▸ Players take turns trying to make word pairs with the same phonogram. The player with the most pairs wins the game.

- ▸ Have children record one word pair on an index card to bring to share.

share

Invite children to share one word pair they made in the game.

Add a few new words to the class chart.

Point out that you might not always know whether a word with the /oi/ sound is spelled with *oy* or *oi*, but you have narrowed it down to two options. You can try the word and see it it looks right.

Link

Interactive Read-Aloud: Read aloud books that have words with the /oi/ sound. Point out one or two of the words after reading. Here are a few suggested titles:

- ▶ **Where Does Joe Go?** by Tracey Campbell Pearson
- ▶ **Farfallina and Marcella** by Holly Keller

Shared Reading: Prior to reading a poem on the overhead projector, cover a few words that have the selected phonogram patterns. After children predict a word, uncover it to confirm its spelling.

Guided Reading: Use the whiteboard during word work to review words with /oi/ spelling patterns.

Guided/Independent Writing: Encourage children to use spelling patterns to edit their writing as they reread. Have them circle words they want to work on and then help them think of patterns they know.

assess

- ▶ Dictate six to ten words with different spelling patterns (using vowel pairs) to assess children's control.

- ▶ Give children a list of ten to twenty words with different spelling patterns. Observe them individually as they read the words. Then ask them to circle all the words with the /oi/ sound.

Expand the Learning

Include a larger variety of phonogram patterns in the Concentration game card deck.

Have children use magnetic letters to make twenty words with the /oi/ pattern. Then have them write them on a List Sheet.

Connect with Home

Send home a deck of Concentration cards so that children can play the game with family members.

Have children search magazines and newspapers or words with one of the /oi/ spelling patterns.

Recognizing Words with VC Pattern

Four-Way Sort

Consider Your Children

In this lesson, children gain quicker control of more difficult phonogram patterns in two-syllable words. Be sure that children can use easier patterns in one-syllable words (see Lesson SP 1) with flexibility. They should have developed a habit of looking for patterns and easily recognizing them.

Working with English Language Learners

Be sure that English language learners work with words that are part of their speaking and/or listening vocabularies and are familiar to them in written form. Provide many opportunities for them to hear, see, and say the words before they try them on their own. Since pronunciation can be tricky, help children notice the visual aspects of words as they say them. Replace unfamiliar words with recognizable examples.

You Need

▶ Pocket chart.

From *Teaching Resources*:

▶ Pocket Chart Card Template.

▶ Four-Way Sort Cards.

▶ Four-Way Sort Sheets.

▶ Lesson SP 12 Word Cards.

Understand the Principle

When vowels are combined with certain other letters (e.g., *w* and *y*), they represent a variety of unique sounds and patterns. The *aw* sounds like short *o*, the *ay* sounds like long *a*, the *ow* can sound like long *o* or it can represent a unique sound, as in *cow*. When these letter patterns are part of two-syllable words, they are more challenging for the reader to detect and use.

Explain the Principle

❝ You can look at the pattern (part) you know to help you read a word. ❞

❝ You can use the pattern (part) you know to help you write a word. ❞

❝ You can make new words by putting a letter or letter cluster before the word part or pattern. ❞

CONTINUUM: SPELLING PATTERNS — RECOGNIZING AND USING MORE DIFFICULT PHONOGRAMS WITH A VC PATTERN

plan

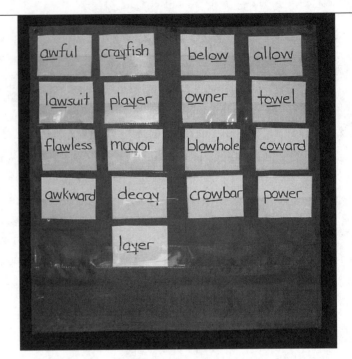

Explain the Principle

" You can look at the pattern (part) you know to help you read a word. "

" You can use the pattern (part) you know to help you write a word. "

" You can make new words by putting a letter or letter cluster before the word part or pattern. "

① Tell the students they will work with letter patterns they know, but this time the patterns are in two-syllable words.

② Have aw*ful*, c*ray*fish, *bel*ow, and *all*ow in the top row of a pocket chart.

③ Hold up a few more word cards, one at a time, inviting children to notice each pattern. Then place the card in the correct column.

④ Continue until you have four or five examples of each.

⑤ Highlight the vowel combinations by underlining them. Explain to the children that looking at the pattern in a word helps them read it.

⑥ Tell children that they will sort word cards using a Four-Way Sort Card. They will read each word card and place it in the correct column until they have placed twenty words. They then write the sort on a Four-Way Sort Sheet and read it to a partner. Suggested language: "You can look at the pattern you know to help you read a word."

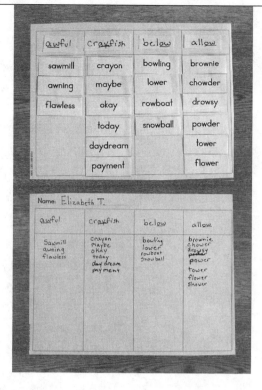

take
say
sort
write

- ▸ Have the children sort at least twenty words on a Four-Way Sort Card using the key words aw*ful*, cr*ay*fish, be*l*ow, and a*ll*ow at the top of the card.
- ▸ Then they write their sort on a Four-Way Sort Sheet and read their lists to a partner.
- ▸ Have children read their Sort Sheets to a partner in preparation for sharing.

share

Have children read their sorts to a different partner. Ask children if there are any words they would like to add to the class chart.

Write about ten multisyllable words on cards. One at a time, show the word to the children and then quickly cover it. Children test themselves to see how quickly they can detect a pattern. Uncover the word again so they can check their quick recognition.

Link

Interactive Read-Aloud: Read aloud books that have a variety of word patterns (*ay*, *ow*, *aw*). Point out some of these words. Here are a few suggested titles:

- ▸ *Tell Me a Story, Mama* by Angela Jackson
- ▸ *Mary Had a Little Jam* by Bruce Lansky

Shared Reading: On an overhead projector share poems and have children highlight words with the *ay*, *aw*, or *ow* patterns.

Guided Reading: After reading and discussing a text, have children turn to specific pages and locate two or three words with the *aw*, *ay*, or *ow* pattern.

Guided/Independent Writing: When children become pattern seekers, they are able to edit their spelling more effectively. Encourage them to notice the *aw*, *ay*, and *ow* patterns in their spelling checks.

assess

- ▸ Observe the children's use of *ay*, *ow*, and *aw* patterns in daily writing.
- ▸ Notice how easily the children take apart words with the *ay*, *ow*, and *aw* patterns as they read.

Expand the Learning

Have the children list on a large chart other two-or three-syllable words they find with the *aw*, *ow*, or *ay* pattern.

Have the children create a Word Search with words that have the *aw*, *ay*, or *ow* pattern (see *Teaching Resources*).

Connect with Home

Have the children take home a sheet of word cards and sort them with family members.

Children can work with a family member to create Word Ladders of words using the *aw*, *ay*, and *ow* patterns (see *Teaching Resources*).

Recognizing a Vowel Pattern (VCe) in Two-Syllable Words

Three-Way Sort

Consider Your Children

In this lesson, the principle is basic, but the words have more than one syllable. Children should have strong control of basic long and short vowel phonograms so they can take apart two syllable words with a silent *e* pattern. The VC*e* pattern appears in the first or last syllable of the word. In the sort, a few words do not fit the pattern at all. Remember there will always be exceptions to any generalization.

Working with English Language Learners

Quickly review this basic pattern in one-syllable words as you begin this lesson. It is important that English language learners have good control of the basic principle and be able to recognize examples of it. To support pronunciation, say each multisyllable word aloud and have students look at it and repeat it aloud. Observe students as they sort words to be sure they understand the task.

You Need

► Pocket chart.

From *Teaching Resources:*
► Pocket Chart Card Template.
► Three-Way Sort Cards.
► Three-Way Sort Sheets.
► Lesson SP 13 Word Cards.

Understand the Principle

Many vowel patterns occur frequently in words. A common phonogram is the vowel-consonant-silent *e* pattern, which is learned early. When the pattern is part of a multisyllable word, it becomes more challenging for readers to notice. Both syllables contain a vowel sound, with one part containing the vowel-consonant-silent *e* pattern. Often, words with VC*e* in the first syllable are compound words.

Explain the Principle

" Some words have a vowel, a consonant, and a silent *e*. The vowel sound is usually the name of the vowel (*a* in *make*, *e* in *Pete*, *i* in *ride*, *o* in *rode*, *u* in *cute*). "

plan

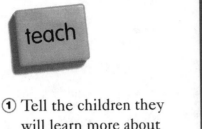

Explain the Principle

" Some words have a vowel, a consonant, and a silent *e*. The vowel sound is usually the name of the vowel (*a* in *make*, *e* in *Pete*, *i* in *ride*, *o* in *rode*, *u* in *cute*). "

① Tell the children they will learn more about vowel spelling patterns in more two-syllable words. Have them read *homework, erase, beside, arrive, safety,* and *grapefruit* in the pocket chart.

② Ask what they notice about the words. They will note that all of them have two syllables and each has a silent *e*.

③ Help them notice that the word part with the silent *e* can be the first or second syllable and that the vowel sound in the syllable is usually the name of the vowel.

④ Sort the words in two columns, depending on where the VC*e* pattern appears. Suggested language: "Some words have a vowel, a consonant, and a silent *e*. The vowel sound is usually the name of the vowel." Show them *seven* and help them recognize that it does not fit the pattern.

⑤ Tell children that often words with VC*e* in the first syllable are compound words. Point out examples on the chart.

⑥ Explain that children will sort words, placing them on a Three-Way Sort Card below the three key words *homework, beside,* and *seven*. Children then write their sorts on a Three-Way Sort Sheet, highlighting the VC*e* pattern in each word in the first two columns. Then the children read their lists to a partner.

take
read
sort
write
circle
read

▸ Have children sort at least twenty words on a Three-Way Sort Card with key words *homework, beside, seven.*

▸ Ask them to write their sort on a Three-Way Sort Sheet and circle the VC*e* pattern in each word.

▸ Have children read their lists to a partner.

Name: Abe   Three-Way Sort

homework	beside	seven
notebook	suppose	freedom
rosebush	dislike	forget
lonesome	excite	camel
homesick	awake	
sidewalk	arose	
iceberg	recite	
baseball	polite	
skateboard	survive	
	pollute	

Have the children suggest a few more words for the pocket chart.

Review some of the more difficult words that contain the VC*e* pattern but do not fit the pattern, such as *camel.*

If there is time, have partners look at a list of ten to twenty words. They see how quickly they can detect and underline or highlight VC*e* patterns in multisyllable words.

Link

Interactive Read-Aloud: Read aloud books that have a variety of words with the VC*e* spelling pattern. Point out several of them after reading and enjoying the text. Here are a few suggested titles:

▸ *ABC Discovery* by Izhar Cohen

▸ *The Old Woman Who Named Things* by Cynthia Rylant

Shared Reading: Read aloud a poem on an overhead projector. Have children notice and circle the VC*e* pattern in several words.

Guided Reading: During word work, write a few two-syllable words that have a VC*e* pattern for children to take apart quickly.

Guided/Independent Writing: When children edit their writing, remind them to check their spelling of words with a VC*e* pattern.

assess

▸ Dictate four to six words that fit the VC*e* pattern to assess children's control. Notice how quickly they write the pattern.

▸ As children read texts, observe how quickly they take apart two-syllable words with the VC*e* patterns.

Expand the Learning

Repeat the lesson with a different batch of word cards to develop fluent reading of two-syllable words.

Have children play Follow the Path with words having the VC*e* pattern (see *Teaching Resources*).

Connect with Home

Send home a sheet of word cards for children to cut, sort, and glue on a sort sheet.

Create a Follow the Path game for children to play with a family member. (See *Teaching Resources.)* As an alternative, children can create their own Follow the Path game to share with a family member.

Recognizing Word Patterns with Double Consonants

Word Grid Game

Consider Your Children

Children need strong control of one-syllable words and basic phonogram patterns prior to this lesson. In this lesson, they read multisyllable words with double consonants in the pattern. They should be able to quickly identify double consonants visually and automatically identify syllables.

Working with English Language Learners

This collection of examples helps English language learners benefit from the visual features and patterns of words. Double consonants are easy for them to notice once they know to look for this pattern. It is also important that they know the meaning of the words and make their best attempt to pronounce them. Dividing words into syllables so that children can hear both parts will help them pronounce the word and understand it when they hear or read it.

You Need

▸ Pocket chart.

From *Teaching Resources*:

▸ Pocket Chart Card Template.

▸ Directions for Word Grids.

▸ Word Grid Template.

▸ Word Grid Game Cards made from Lesson SP 14 Words Cards and Deck Card Template.

Understand the Principle

Many words have double consonants as the dividing point between the syllables. Children need to learn how to take words apart (by dividing between the two consonants) and how to write words with a two-consonant pattern. Knowledge of this convention will help them in writing and also sharpen their awareness of syllables in words and words with double consonants.

Explain the Principle

" Some words have double consonant letters in the pattern. "

CONTINUUM: SPELLING PATTERNS — UNDERSTANDING THAT SOME WORDS HAVE DOUBLE CONSONANTS IN THE PATTERN

plan

Explain the Principle

" Some words have double consonant letters in the pattern. "

① Tell the children you will help them think about letter patterns in words.

② Place *coffee, address, success, accident, matters, occasion* in the pocket chart. Have the children read each word.

③ Suggested language: "What do you notice about the pattern in each word?"

④ Encourage them to listen to the parts in each word and notice that each has two syllables with double consonants. Each word can be divided between the two consonants.

⑤ Explain that noticing where to divide the word helps them think about how to write it. Continue adding other words, asking them to read them, notice the double consonants, and think about where to divide the words.

⑥ Tell the children they will play the Word Grid game. Players take turns drawing a card, saying the word, and crossing it out on their Word Grid if it appears. The first player to cross out all the words wins the game.

take
say
cross out

▶ Have the children play the Word Grid Game in groups of two to four.

▶ Players take turns drawing a card, saying the word, and crossing it out on their Word Grids if it appears.

▶ The game continues until one player has crossed out all the words on her Word Grid.

▶ Children look at their grids to suggest more words during sharing.

Have the children suggest a few more words with double consonants to add to the pocket chart.

For every word one student suggests, another can tell where to divide the word.

gallon

blizzard	spelling	better	coffee	ladder	bottle	cabbage	fellow	success	sadden
follow	foggy	dollar	button	narrow	burrow	kitten	banner	attic	skinny
madden	pillow	gallon	yellow	fatten	pattern	supper	ballot	silly	apple
funny	effort	happen	accident	mattress	puddle	rabbit	office	flipper	wrapper
blossom	glasses	carry	errand	traffic	cottage	scribble	message	wallet	marry
merry	tunnel	rattle	cattle	occasion	occupy	dipper	battle	slipper	worry
address	village	rubber	muffin	dresses	hurry	sorry	soccer	blubber	furry

Link

Interactive Read-Aloud: Read aloud books that have words with double consonant patterns. Here are some suggested titles:

- ▸ *Penny Lee and Her TV* by Glen McCoy
- ▸ *Alexander and the Terrible, Horrible, No Good, Very Bad Day* by Judith Viorst

Shared Reading: After several readings of a poem, have children highlight one or two words with the double consonant pattern.

Guided Reading: When children encounter unfamiliar words with double consonants in texts, prompt them to look at the first part of the word and then the last part or parts. During word work, use the whiteboard to quickly write words with double consonants and have children read them, notice the pattern, and divide them.

Guided/Independent Writing: During the editing process, prompt children to think about and check for words that have double consonants.

assess

- ▸ Observe how fluently children read words with double consonants.
- ▸ Notice how accurately children spell words with a double consonant pattern or dictate several words to assess their knowledge.

Expand the Learning

Have children play the Word Grid Game again with a different set of words on their grid.

Have children read and sort the word cards according to the double consonants in them.

Connect with Home

Send home Word Grids and word cards for children to play with family members.

Children can search for words with double consonants in magazines and newspapers and bring examples to class to share.

Recognizing Word Patterns with r-Influenced Vowels

Follow the Path

Consider Your Children

In this lesson, children work with a variety of words that have phonograms with vowel sounds influenced by the letter *r*. Although children may have been exposed to *r*-influenced vowels, the concept (and associated spellings) are complex. Select words for the lesson that are an appropriate challenge for children.

Working with English Language Learners

The sound of *r* is a challenge for many English language learners, especially if that sound is not present in their own language or if they pronounce the sound in another way. Words with *r* are especially tricky because they influence the sound of the vowel or vowel cluster before the *r*. Looking at the larger patterns in words and connecting them with the pronunciation will help students understand and work with these words. Use words that are in students' oral vocabularies even though this may be the first time they are seeing them in print. Help them notice visual features of the words. During word work have students build some of these words with magnetic letters or practice writing them on paper or a whiteboard.

You Need

▶ Magnetic letters.

▶ Cookie sheet or magnetic whiteboard.

▶ Die or number cube.

From *Teaching Resources*:

▶ Directions for Follow the Path.

▶ List Sheets.

▶ Lesson SP 15 Word List.

Understand the Principle

When vowels are with *r*, the vowel sound is usually changed. One or two vowels may occur with *r* in the phonogram pattern. The simpler patterns include *ar, ir, or, er, ur*, but other patterns pose greater challenges. Some patterns represent a long vowel sound with *r* (*tire*). Patterns include *ar, ark, arm, ard, arl, art, arf, arp, arch, ar-e, air, are; er, ere, ear, eart, eer, earn, eard, erd, er-e; ir, ire, or, oor, ore, our, orn, ord, oar; ur, ure, urse, urn*.

Explain the Principle

❝ Some words have a vowel pattern with one or two vowels and *r*. ❞

❝ When vowels are with *r* in words, you usually blend the sound with *r* (*nurse, third*). ❞

---

plan

Explain the Principle

" Some words have a vowel pattern with one or two vowels and *r*. "

" When vowels are with *r* in words, you usually blend the sound with *r* (*nurse*, *third*). "

① Tell the children you will help them notice the letter *r* when it is in many different spelling patterns.

② Make words such as *care, cart, heart, heard, beard, herd, torn, burn* with magnetic letters. Have children suggest another word that sounds like each one you make, and make it or write it to the right.

③ Help children notice the *r* and listen for the sound in the pattern.

④ Suggested language: "Some words have a vowel pattern with one or two vowels and *r*. When vowels are with *r*, you blend the sound with *r*."

⑤ Explain how to play the Follow the Path game and demonstrate it with one or two children. Taking turns, players roll a die, move that number of spaces, read the word in the space and use it in a sentence. The first player to reach Finish wins the game. Then children list twenty words that have one or two vowels and *r* on a List Sheet and underline the pattern.

apply

roll
move
read
use
list
underline

▶ In groups of
two to four,
children play
Follow the
Path with
words that
have one or
two vowels
with *r*.

Follow the Path

march
where
perch
pour
stern
chirp
spear
storm
work
harp
pearl verse park
your
twirl
here
clerk
wire
warm
START

nerve first
smart there
turn fern
herd
pure
swirl
flirt
skirt
shirt
FINISH

Follow the Path

▶ Then they list twenty words that have one or two vowels and *r* on a List
Sheet and underline the pattern.

▶ Children prepare for sharing by thinking of one word as an example.

share

Have each child suggest one word while you list them on a chart. Then
have the children read their List Sheets to a partner.

Invite children to discuss words that *look* similar at the end but which vary
in pronunciation.

Link

Interactive Read-Aloud: Read aloud a variety of rhyming books that have phonogram patterns with *r*. Here are a few suggested titles:

- ▶ *"I Heard," Said the Bird* by Polly Berien Berends

- ▶ *Dear World* by Takayo Noda

Shared Reading: Read poems that have words with *r*-influenced vowels. After enjoying the poem, give children a copy. Have them mark the words and read them to a partner.

Guided Reading: During word work, write several words with *r*-influenced vowel sounds on a whiteboard to help children develop quick recognition and flexibility with the patterns.

Guided/Independent Writing: Have children reread their writing and check the spelling patterns with *r*-influenced vowels.

assess

- ▶ Dictate four to six words with *r*-influenced vowels to assess children's control.

- ▶ Notice how quickly and accurately children recognize words with *r*-influenced vowels.

Expand the Learning

Select particular patterns and have children complete a Two- or Three-Way Sort, listening for the vowel sounds to complete the columns.

Repeat this lesson with *r*-influenced vowel patterns in words with more than one syllable, such as those shown here: *oyster, peculiar, circular, turquoise, failure, cleaner, slower, similar, thinner, coward, doctor, pasture, treasure, creature, capture, personal, thirsty, service, alert, prefer, turkey, perhaps, surround, modern, concert, teacher, nature, power, powder, shower*

Connect with Home

Send home a sheet of *r*-influenced vowel word cards for children to sort with family members.

Recognizing Words with the /ə/ Pattern

Making Words and Sentences

Consider Your Children

In this lesson children learn to read multisyllable words that begin with the syllable *a*. Use words that children already know or explain the meaning of new words. Be sure to use them in context so that children have a good understanding of their meanings.

Working with English Language Learners

The part *a* at the beginning of a word is prominent in many multisyllable words. Begin with simple examples that students understand (e.g., *along, about*). Have children say each word to notice the unique sound of the vowel at the beginning. Have them notice where the emphasis is placed, that is, on the syllable after the *a*. Gradually expand children's knowledge of words with these patterns by adding those that they encounter in oral or written language. Use words in sentences to help children understand their meaning and function. During word work, review the principles and examples in this lesson.

You Need

► Chart paper.
► Markers.

From *Teaching Resources:*
► Word and Sentence Sheet (two per student).
► Lesson SP 16 Word Cards.

Understand the Principle

The word part *a* forms a syllable in many words, so it is useful for children to notice it. Usually the part is not stressed when it appears as a syllable by itself and its sound is often short. There are words that begin with *a* but have other letters attached to the syllable (*av* in *avenue*).

Explain the Principle

❝ You see some patterns a lot in multisyllable words. ❞

❝ You see *a* at the beginning of some words and it sounds like the *a* in *alone*. ❞

CONTINUUM: SPELLING PATTERNS — NOTICING AND USING A FREQUENTLY APPEARING SYLLABLE PATTERN IN MULTISYLLABLE WORDS
(/ʌ/ AS IN *ALONE*)

(213)

plan

① Tell the children that they will learn more about parts in words. Have *alone, away, again* written on chart paper.

Explain the Principle

❝ You see some patterns a lot in multisyllable words. ❞

❝ You see *a* at the beginning of some words and it sounds like the *a* in *alone*. ❞

② Have children read each word with you and ask what they notice about them.

③ Guide children to notice that each word begins with *a*, the *a* has the same sound, each word has two syllables, the *a* is a syllable by itself, and it is not stressed.

④ Help children understand that the word part *a* appears in many words and ask them to suggest additional examples for the chart. Be sure to talk about the meaning of any new words.

⑤ Tell children that they will make ten words that start with the word part *a* and write each word in a sentence (e.g., *a* and *jar* make *ajar, I saw that the door was ajar, so I went in*).

make
say
write
use

► Have the children make, say, and write ten words starting with the unaccented syllable *a*.

► Children record their words on a Word and Sentence Sheet and write a sentence for each.

► Have children choose one sentence to share with the class.

Name: Aaron

Word	Sentence
alone	Her mother was alone in the store.
afar	Star was shiniy from afar.
alive	I was so happy my fish was alive!
ajar	the teacher left the closet door, ajar.
agree	Finally the class agreed on a songi
another	My sister asked it bring anothe friend
afraid	I'm not afraid of the dark.
ago	Columbus arived in America long ago!
abrupt	The car made an abrupt stop.
asleep	My puppy fell asleep on my lap!

Word and Sentence Sheet

Invite each child to read a sentence they wrote as you list the words that begin with *a* on a chart.

Invite children to discuss the meaning of words; for example, *asleep* is connected to *sleep* by meaning, as is *alone* to *lone* and *lonely*. It is harder to get the meaning of *ago* by looking at word parts.

Link

Interactive Read-Aloud: Read aloud books that have words that begin with unstressed *a*. Write a couple of the words on a chart. Here are a few suggested titles:

- ▸ *One Monday Morning* by Uri Shulevitz
- ▸ *Sheila Rae the Brave* by Kevin Hankes

Shared Reading: Select and read poems with words that start with *a*. On the second reading underline the words that start with the *a* syllable.

Guided Reading: During word work use a whiteboard and review some words that begin with the unstressed *a* syllable.

Guided/Independent Writing: As children write new words that begin with *a*, have them think about whether the *a* stands alone as an unstressed syllable.

assess

- ▸ Working with each student individually, provide an *a* and a few of the word cards from the lesson, and ask them to read the words. Observe the ease with which students construct and read the words.

Expand the Learning

Repeat this lesson and include words that start with *a* in a stressed syllable, or a stressed syllable with other letters (*affluent, aggravate, alligator, ammunition, annual, appear, arrest, arid, acid*). Have children complete a Two-Way Sort to distinguish the two types of words.

Connect with Home

Create a Word Grid for children to take home and read to family members (see *Teaching Resources*).

Recognizing Frequently Appearing Syllables in Word Patterns

Go Fish

Consider Your Children

Prior to this lesson, children need to have experience with common and less common phonogram patterns in single-syllable words and open and closed syllables. In this lesson, they develop flexibility with common parts of words. You may wish to teach the first eight word parts in this lesson and the second eight parts and final six parts in consecutive lessons. Select particular word parts for the card game.

Working with English Language Learners

Go Fish requires children to notice quickly the parts of multisyllable words and to combine this understanding with the word itself. Review the word list to make sure children understand that they need to recognize patterns. Work toward quick recognition by using the same examples several times. During guided reading word work you can offer additional practice.

If children have difficulty with a large number of examples, limit the lesson to three or four word parts until the principle is established.

You Need

► Chart paper.

► Markers.

From *Teaching Resources:*

► Directions for Go Fish.

► Go Fish Game Cards made from SP 17 Word Cards and Deck Card Template.

Understand the Principle

If children gain good control of the word parts included in this lesson, they can use their knowledge to solve many multisyllable words. The word parts in this lesson (*en, ar, in, o, at, is, er, it*) appear in a variety of words having more than one syllable. Children may have good control of some of the parts in one-syllable words, but noticing the parts in multisyllable words often presents a greater challenge.

Explain the Principle

" You see some patterns often in multisyllable words. "

" You can look for the pattern you know to help you read a word. "

" You can think about the pattern you know to help you spell a word. "

---

plan

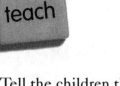

Explain the Principle

" You see some patterns often in multisyllable words. "

" You can look for the pattern you know to help you read a word. "

" You can think about the pattern you know to help you spell a word. "

① Tell the children they will learn more about word parts that help them read longer words.

② Write *enter, ago, other, partner, batter, bitten, winter, whisper* one at a time on a chart, allowing room for two or three other words. As you write each word, underline the word part you want children to notice and ask them to tell another multisyllable word that has the same part, such as *entrance, cargo, mother, carton, matter, mitten, finish, blister*. Help the children understand the principle. Suggested language: "You can look for a particular pattern you know to help you read a word." Explain that thinking about patterns also helps you write a word.

③ If children are ready for more examples, repeat this process with another eight word parts: *sunny, began, repeat, border, bacon, candy, monkey, trouble*.

④ Next create a chart with six more: *pilot, burden, humble, chicken, better, simple*.

⑤ Explain to children that they will play Go Fish in small groups. Demonstrate how to play the game, with each player having six cards and making pairs that have the same word parts. The first person to run out of cards wins the game.

enter   ago   other

entrance   cargo   mother

partner   batter   bitten

carton   matter   mitten

winter   whisper

finish   blister

apply

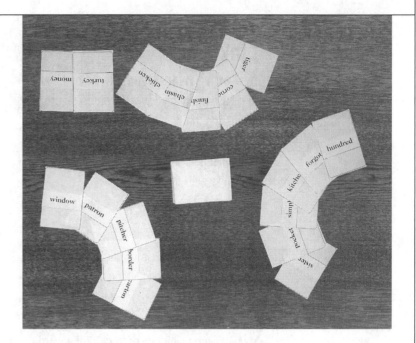

read
ask
match

▸ Have groups of three or four children play Go Fish.

▸ Taking turns, each player asks another for a card that matches a word part in her hand. If no match is made, she must draw a card from the pile.

▸ Matching pairs are set aside. The first player to run out of cards wins the game.

share

Invite the children to suggest one more word for each word part taught in the lesson and add it to the chart.

Invite the children to share what they found interesting about the words. With parts like *-in* and *-it*, students may be thinking they are looking for "a little word." It is best to avoid this language because it can be misleading (for example, *me* in *welcome* is not helpful).

Link

Interactive Read-Aloud: Read aloud books that have many multisyllable words. After discussing the book, write two or three words on a whiteboard and help children notice the parts that help them read the word. Here are a few suggested titles:

- ▸ *Away from Home* by Anita Lobel
- ▸ *The Hat* by Jan Brett

Shared Reading: Use a variety of poems with multisyllable words. Underline a word part in some of the words.

Guided Reading: During word work, write several words with two or three of the word parts to help encourage quick solving.

Guided/Independent Writing: Encourage children to say new multisyllable words slowly and to think about each word part as they write it.

assess

- ▸ Dictate several multisyllable words with the word parts to assess children's ability to use them.

- ▸ Observe how quickly readers process multisyllable words and which parts are tricky for them.

Expand the Learning

Repeat this lesson with more word parts and a wider variety of examples.

Write the words in a Word Grid so children can either practice reading them or play the game (see *Teaching Resources*).

Connect with Home

Send home a Word Grid with multisyllable words for children to practice with family members.

As an alternative, send home a deck of Go Fish cards so children can play with a family member.

High Frequency Words

A core of known high frequency words is a valuable resource as students build their reading and writing processes. Young children notice words that appear frequently in the simple texts they read; eventually, their recognition of these words becomes automatic. In this way, their reading becomes more efficient, enabling them to decode words using phonics as well as the meaning in the text. These words are powerful examples that help them grasp that a word is always written the same way. They can use known high frequency words to check on the accuracy of their reading and as resources for solving other words (for example, this starts like the). In general, students learn the simpler words earlier and in the process develop efficient systems for learning words. They continuously add to the core of high frequency words they know as they move to late primary and early intermediate grades. Lessons on high frequency words help them look more carefully at words and develop more efficient systems for recognition.

Connect to Assessment

See related HF Assessment Tasks in the Assessment Guide in *Teaching Resources:*

▶ Reading Words with Phonogram Patterns

▶ Writing Words with Phonogram Patterns

Develop Your Professional Understanding

See *Word Matters: Teaching Phonics and Spelling in the Reading/Writing Classroom* by G.S. Pinnell and I. C. Fountas. 1998 Portsmouth, NH: Heinemann.

Related pages: 35–41, 44–49, 88–91, 116, 172–174, 209–213, 240–245

Recognizing High Frequency Words 1 (with 3 or More Letters)

Make, Say, Check, Mix

Consider Your Children

Take an inventory of the words children write correctly so you can focus on those they need to learn. Be sure children understand that once they know how to read and write a word, they are expected to use it accurately. Also, be sure that students have many opportunities to read high frequency words in continuous text such as stories, poems, rhymes, and songs. In this lesson you will want to include some words already known and others that are partially known or not known. This lesson includes some easier high frequency words that can serve as the base for learning more difficult ones.

Working with English Language Learners

Use easy examples that English language learners understand and use in their oral language. Remember that high frequency words such as articles (*an, the*) are abstract rather than concrete. A child's native language syntax may be quite different from English; in fact, counterpart words may not exist in some cases. Give children opportunities to hear and say the high frequency words in sentences.

You Need

▶ Magnetic letters.

▶ Cookie sheet or magnetic whiteboard.

▶ Index cards.

▶ Markers.

From *Teaching Resources*:

▶ Make, Say, Check, Mix Sheet.

▶ High Frequency Words List (choose words appropriate for your children).

Understand the Principle

Children need many ways of learning and remembering words. You will find that many high frequency words do not reflect regular phonics principles. When words are consistent with phonics principles, have children use their understanding of letter/sound relationships. When words are not regular, they can be learned through memory of visual features. Children can use parts of words they know to help them learn new high frequency words (*bring, down, brown*).

Explain the Principle

" You see some words many times when you read. "

" Some have three or more letters. "

" Words you see a lot are important because they help you read and write. "

plan

Explain the Principle

" You see some words many times when you read. "

" Some have three or more letters. "

" Words you see a lot are important because they help you read and write. "

① Tell the children they will learn more about words they use often as writers or see frequently as readers.

② Make a few high frequency words with magnetic letters on the board, one word at a time. Help children notice the ways they can use phonics skills and letter patterns to remember how a word looks.

③ Ask volunteers to suggest ways they will remember how to read or write a word, trying to elicit from them helpful ideas. For example, with *because* they might notice the *be* "part" and that *au* together sounds like a short *o*, the *s* sounds like a *z*, and that a silent *e* is at the end of the word.

④ Mix up the letters and make the word again, emphasizing the important phonics and visual or meaningful units that help children learn the word.

⑤ Next, write the word on an index card and use a highlighter to mark a part they want to remember.

⑥ Repeat the process with several other words, using examples that come from the words most children need to learn. Remind children of how each word will be like other words (e.g., be*cause* and be*fore*, *caught*).

⑦ Explain that today children will work with high frequency words. Using a Make, Say, Check, Mix Sheet, children write a word, say it, and make and mix it three times with magnetic letters, each time placing a check mark on their sheet. Children then write the word again and highlight any tricky part they want to remember.

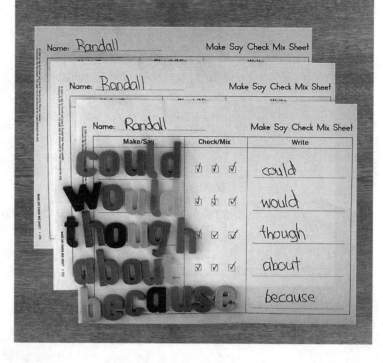

read
mix
make
check
write
highlight

▸ Have the children use the Make, Say, Check, Mix process to practice fifteen different words from the High Frequency Words List.

▸ Ask children to write one word on an index card and highlight the tricky part, then bring the card to group share.

Have each child in the group hold up her card, say the word, and show the highlighted part. Point out other words that have similar parts.

Link

Interactive Read-Aloud: Read aloud books with high frequency words. Write several of the words on a whiteboard and talk about ways to remember them. Here are some suggested titles:

- ▶ *These Hands* by Hope Lynne Price
- ▶ *Rosie's Roses* by Pamela Edwards

Shared Reading: Show poems and chants on a chart or overhead so that children can read many high frequency words. Have children use markers or highlighter tape to mark the tricky parts in a few of the words.

Guided Reading: When children come to tricky high frequency words, remind them of other words that have the same or some of the same features. Show them how they can use parts of high frequency words they know to figure out new words.

Guided/Independent Writing: Hold children accountable for spelling correctly the words they know how to write. Remind them to use words and word parts they know to write new words.

assess

- ▶ Review children's work and notice the high frequency words they do not know. Then, work these words into your minilessons.
- ▶ Notice how quickly children recognize words as they read.

Expand the Learning

Have students select another fifteen words with which to work on the Make, Say, Check, Mix Sheet.

Give students a deck of cards (Deck Card Template in *Teaching Resources*) with high frequency words. Have partners take turns turning a card and reading the word as quickly as they can.

Connect with Home

Encourage students to take home their Make, Say, Check, Mix Sheet and make each word again with magnetic letters or letter cards.

Recognizing High Frequency Words 2 (With 4 or More Letters)

Concentration

Consider Your Children

Some words appear frequently so children will read and write them often. They will need to use their knowledge of how sounds are represented by letters and how some words do not sound the way they look. Keep an ongoing inventory of high frequency words that are known, almost known, and not known so you can focus on those requiring more attention. (See Assessment in *Teaching Resources*.) Make a list of the selected words that you will focus on in this lesson.

Working with English Language Learners

Help English language learners become very familiar with a core of easy high frequency words before taking on more difficult ones. Be sure that the base of known words is solid before expanding the word list. Observe children to be sure that they are not simply producing the words mechanically, without thinking about them or noticing visual features. Use words in sentences and, if needed, work with a small group to provide the practice that will help children rapidly and automatically recognize words.

You Need

▶ Chart paper.

▶ Markers.

▶ Word Study Notebooks.

From *Teaching Resources:*

▶ Directions for Concentration.

▶ Concentration Game Cards made from High Frequency Words List and Deck Card Template (choose words appropriate for your children by including some known words, many words almost known, and some not yet known that you will attend to in the lesson).

Understand the Principle

Some high frequency words are easier to read than others. Having solid knowledge of easy known words provides a powerful resource in learning new words. For example, if a child knows *the*, it helps with *there, they, their;* if he knows *could* it helps with *would, should*. Help children understand that the goal is quick, fluent recognition of words when reading and quick, accurate construction of words when writing.

Explain the Principle

" You see some words many times when you read. "

" Some have four or more letters. "

" Words you see a lot are important because they help you read and write. "

CONTINUUM: HIGH FREQUENCY WORDS — Recognizing and Using High Frequency Words with Four or More Letters

plan

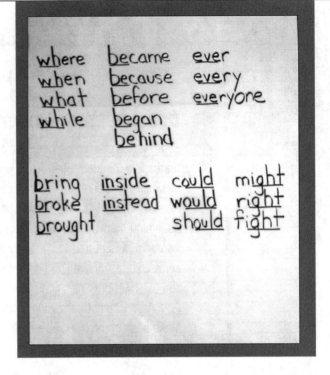

Explain the Principle

" You see some words many times when you read. "

" Some have four or more letters. "

" Words you see a lot are important because they help you read and write. "

① Explain to children that they know many high frequency words and that they can use parts of some known words to help them learn others.

② Suggested language: "You can notice patterns in the high frequency words you know. Connecting these patterns will help you learn them."

③ Write *where, when, what, while* in a list on chart paper.

④ Ask children what they notice. When they say that all the words begin with *wh*, underline the letters in each word. Explain that knowing some high frequency words helps you learn others.

⑤ Continue the process with other word groups, such as *became, because, before, began, behind; ever, every, everyone; bring, broke, brought; inside, instead; could, would, should; couldn't, wouldn't; might, right, fight.*

⑥ Tell children they will work with words that are alike. Using the High Frequency Word Cards, they find five pairs of words that have parts that are alike and write them in their Word Study Notebooks.

⑦ Children then play Concentration in groups of three or four. Players take turns turning over two cards and reading them aloud. If they match, they take the pair. If they do not match, they turn them face down again. The player with the most matches wins the game.

find
write

turn
say
match

▶ Have the children play Concentration using high frequency words. They turn over and read two cards with the goal of finding two that match.

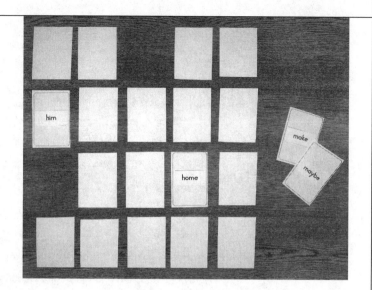

▶ The player with the most pairs wins the game.

Have children read three high frequency words from their Word Study Notebooks to a partner, telling the partner what to remember about the word. Make a group chart of the words children think are the trickiest to remember, highlighting the difficult part of each with a marker.

Link

Interactive Read-Aloud: Read aloud books that have simple text and high frequency words. After reading, mention several of the high frequency words that appeared and write them on a chart. Suggested titles are:

- ▶ *I Walk at Night* by Lois Duncan
- ▶ *Right Outside My Window* by Mary Ann Hoberman

Shared Reading: After enjoying a poem, highlight two or three longer high frequency words, each with four to seven letters.

Guided Reading: Remind children that there are many words they know and can read quickly. During word work, have children make and mix three or four words quickly. Then have children write them to develop fluency.

Guided/Independent Writing: Remind children to write words they know how to spell correctly each time they use them. During conferences, place a check mark by or underline a few words you know a child can spell so he can self-correct.

assess

- ▶ Notice how fluently children read high frequency words in text.
- ▶ Observe how quickly and accurately they write high frequency words.
- ▶ For a more systematic assessment, dictate a list of high frequency words.

Expand the Learning

For more challenge, have children play Concentration with high frequency words that have four, five, or more letters. (See Lesson HF3.)

Create a Follow the Path game with high frequency words (see *Teaching Resources*).

Reteach the lesson with words the children did not write correctly on the High Frequency Word Assessment.

Connect with Home

Send home a pack of Concentration cards with high frequency words. You may want to send photocopies of the Deck Card Template and Word Cards so children can create their own deck.

Invite the children to make a deck of high frequency cards with words they have not yet mastered. They can play the game with family members to develop their knowledge.

Recognizing High Frequency Words 3 (with 5 or More Letters)

Word Grid Game

Consider Your Children

Determine which words most children know, those they almost know, and those not yet known to help you select words for the lesson. Have children keep a High Frequency Words List in their Word Study Notebooks. Children can highlight the words they spell correctly as an ongoing record of accomplishment. Create a Word Grid that includes mostly words that are in the "almost known" or "not known" categories, along with some known words.

Working with English Language Learners

Searching Word Grids provides valuable practice and the opportunity for English language learners to "over-learn" a core of high frequency words as they search for words by noticing visual features. This activity promotes quick word recognition. You may want to work with small groups to be sure children understand the task.

You Need

▶ Chart paper.

▶ Markers.

▶ Enlarged High Frequency Word Grid.

From *Teaching Resources:*

▶ Directions for Word Grids.

▶ High Frequency Words List.

▶ Word Grid Template (to make Word Grids with selected words from High Frequency Words List).

▶ Word Card Template (to make Word Cards with some words on Word Grid and some not on Word Grid).

Understand the Principle

Some high frequency words are easy to read and others are more difficult. Some are phonetically regular (*across, begin*) and others are not (*friend, again*). Words that are not phonetically regular demand that children notice how the words look. Help children develop a range of flexible strategies for reading and writing high frequency words so that, in turn, they can read and write them fluently.

Explain the Principle

❝ You see some words many times when you read. ❞

❝ Some have five or more letters. ❞

❝ Words you see a lot are important because they help you read and write. ❞

CONTINUUM: HIGH FREQUENCY WORDS — RECOGNIZING AND USING HIGH FREQUENCY WORDS WITH FIVE OR MORE LETTERS

plan

teach

Explain the Principle

" You see some words many times when you read. "

" Some have five or more letters. "

" Words you see a lot are important because they help you read and write. "

① Tell children you will help them notice the letters in high frequency words with five or more letters.

② Write four or five high frequency words on chart paper. Invite children to read the words and tell what they notice about how they look. Help children notice similarities between or among words. Remind them to think about the number of syllables, the sounds they hear, and the patterns they notice. For some words, a mnemonic device may be helpful (e.g., *friends* to the *end*).

③ Be sure children understand that their goal is to learn the spelling pattern and to read and write the word quickly and accurately every time they see or use it in text.

④ Show the enlarged High Frequency Word Grid. Demonstrate how to search for words by reading across and down the grid.

⑤ Explain to children that partners will practice reading word grids to one another. Then children play the High Frequency Word Grid game in groups of four.

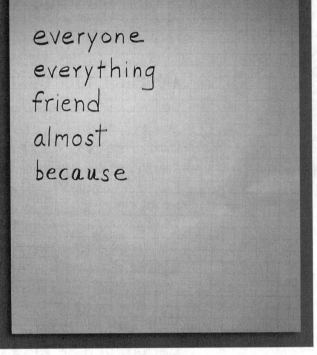

everyone
everything
friend
almost
because

everyone	favorite	could	became	right	great	together	people	almost	through
either	second	since	under	picture	however	certain	friend	watch	should
reason	shown	behind	special	often	house	light	thought	begin	whole
across	several	caught	would	everything	space	world	outside	without	those
night	believe	change	through	never	paper	scared	enough	going	between
person	almost	wrote	picture	again	instead	school	family	wrong	other
morning	maybe	during	inside	large	teach	having	because	found	always

apply

read
take
say
cross out

▸ Partners read their word grids to one another.

▸ Then groups of four play the High Frequency Word Grid game. One player takes a turn drawing a word card, saying it aloud, looking for it on his grid, and crossing it out if it appears.

▸ Then the next player takes a turn, and so on. The first player to cross out all words on his grid wins the game.

share

Invite children to talk about the words that are trickiest for them and to tell how they will remember these words.

Children read their word grids to a different partner to develop their fluency.

Link

Interactive Read-Aloud: Read aloud books that include many high frequency words. After enjoying the books, point out how fluently you read the words because you recognized them quickly. Suggested titles are:

▸ *Inside Mouse, Outside Mouse* by Lindsay Barrett George

▸ *A Beastly Story* by Bill Martin, Jr.

Shared Reading: Read a variety of poems with high frequency words having five or more letters. Have children highlight some of them with a marker and tell what they will remember about them.

Guided Reading: As children solve new words, encourage them to use parts of high frequency words they know (e.g., *begin, behind; everyone, everything*).

Guided/Independent Writing: As children construct words, help them use known parts of high frequency words to solve and write new words.

assess

▸ Notice how quickly children read high frequency words with five or more letters.

▸ Dictate six to ten words used in the lesson to assess children's understanding.

Expand the Learning

Have children play the High Frequency Word Grid game with a different selection of words on the grid.

Alternatively, create a variety of grids that are tailored to individual children. Consider teaching children how to create their own Word Grids.

Connect with Home

Send home individualized word grids so children can play the High Frequency Word Grid game with family members.

Send home a blank grid and have children write the words they know they want to learn.

They can give it to a family member to find the hidden words.

4 *Recognizing High Frequency Words 4*

High Frequency Word Lotto

Consider Your Children

When selecting words for the Lotto game, use your knowledge of the high frequency words children need to learn. Words with five or more letters can be very challenging, so children need repeated practice. Continue to monitor how to spell high frequency words. Lotto is a game that children can play frequently and independently with one other.

Working with English Language Learners

You may want to prepare Lotto Game Cards with mostly simple words that children know or "almost know." You can limit the words by repeating a word twice or even three times on a Lotto Game Card. Children may cover a word only once at any turn. Remember that children need many experiences with a word before they can read or write it quickly and without conscious thought; English language learners may need even more experiences.

You Need

▶ Whiteboard.

▶ Markers.

▶ Paper and pencil (for each child).

From *Teaching Resources*:

▶ Directions for Lotto.

▶ Three-by-Four Lotto Game Boards (with words selected from High Frequency Words List).

▶ Lotto Game Cards (made from words selected from High Frequency Words List and Word Card Template).

Understand the Principle

Quick, automatic recognition of many words is important for fluent reading. When children notice particular features of words, they can learn them more easily. Writing words is helpful because it requires children to slow down and attend to a specific letter sequence. The Buddy Study system (see Lessons WSA 1 to WSA 5) is also beneficial because it teaches children how to learn words.

Explain the Principle

" You see some words many times when you read. "

" Some have five or more letters. "

" Words you see a lot are important because they help you read and write. "

CONTINUUM: HIGH FREQUENCY WORDS — RECOGNIZING HIGH FREQUENCY WORDS WITH FIVE OR MORE LETTERS

plan

teach

Explain the Principle

❝ You see some words many times when you read. ❞

❝ Some have five or more letters. ❞

❝ Words you see a lot are important because they help you read and write. ❞

① Tell the children that you will help them learn more high frequency words. Explain that today's words are even more challenging because they are either longer or more difficult.

② Suggested language: "Words you see a lot are important because they help you read and write."

③ On a whiteboard quickly write one word, inviting children to tell what they notice about it. Underline the tricky parts, erase the word, and write it again quickly. Continue this process with several words.

④ Then have children write each of the words, explaining that it is not a race, but that you want them to write each letter of a word from left to right continuously and without stopping. Proceed word-by-word, writing the word on the whiteboard for them to check. If a word is not written correctly, children cross out and fix their word, underlining the part that is tricky for them.

⑤ Tell children they will practice reading high frequency words by playing High Frequency Word Lotto. If necessary, demonstrate how to play. The first player to cover all the words on her Lotto Game Card wins the game.

take
say
cover

- ▸ Have children play High Frequency Word Lotto in groups of two to six.
- ▸ In turn, each player draws a word card, reads it aloud, and checks for a match on his Lotto Game Card.
- ▸ The first player to fill his Lotto Game Card wins.

Have children write the words they learned to read fluently, and then read them to a partner.

Invite the children to share ways they are remembering tricky words.

Link

Interactive Read-Aloud: Read aloud books with simple text and many repeated high frequency words. After enjoying the book, write two or three words on a whiteboard and have children notice how they look.

- ▸ *Clementine* by Ann Owen
- ▸ *Elizabeth's Doll* by Stephanie Stuve-Bodeen

Shared Reading: Select a poem that has high frequency words with five or more letters. Cover the words before children read the poem for the first time. Invite children to predict each word as you read. After reading the entire poem once, read it again, uncovering each word after the children tell you the letter sequence.

Guided Reading: During word work, have the children make and mix three or four high frequency words. Then have them write the words.

Guided/Independent Writing: Remind children to reread their writing and check the spelling of high frequency words.

assess

- ▸ Dictate six to ten words to children so you can assess their control of particular high frequency words having five or more letters.

- ▸ On a regular basis, review children's highlighted Individual High Frequency Words List (see Assessment in *Teaching Resources*) to see if their control of the words is expanding. The Individual High Frequency Words List provides a way for students to keep track of their own learning. They have a copy in their word study folders. Over several days the teacher tests students on these words. They

highlight words they know and choose others for working with during Buddy Study. This record can be passed up the grades.

Expand the Learning

Have children play High Frequency Word Lotto with game cards that have a different variety of words.

Alternatively, have children select words they need to learn to place on the Lotto Game Cards.

Connect with Home

Send High Frequency Words Lotto home so that children can play the game with family members.

Photocopy each child's highlighted High Frequency Words List and send it home periodically so that children can share their increasing knowledge.

Checking Your Knowledge of High Frequency Words

Word Inventory

Consider Your Children

Use this lesson once children have worked with high frequency words in many different ways. In this lesson, you and the children take inventory of words that are well under control and those that need more teaching and practice. Select an appropriate list of high frequency words, and over several days dictate about twenty each day. Highlight the words spelled correctly on the lists and return them to the children. The lists can also be used for Words to Learn in the Buddy Study System (see Lessons WSA 1 to WSA 5).

Working with English Language Learners

Self-assessing what they know and taking charge of their own learning benefits English language learners, but this requires a complex series of tasks. Work with children in a small group to be sure they understand the purpose of keeping their own word lists. In this lesson, you begin with an incorrect example, so be sure to choose a word that children know well and can see the error in spelling.

You Need

- Whiteboard.
- Marker.
- Index cards.
- Magnetic letters.

  From *Teaching Resources:*
- High Frequency Words List.
- Make, Say, Check, Mix Sheet.

Understand the Principle

It is important for children to be able to write a large number of words quickly and accurately. Fluency in writing high frequency words is acquired when children have worked with them in many different ways. For example, they have made them with magnetic letters, written them, sorted them, and so on. It is important for children to know which words they can write accurately and which need more work.

Explain the Principle

" You can add to the number of high frequency words you can write. "

" You can write high frequency words quickly. "

" You can check to see how many words you know. "

CONTINUUM: HIGH FREQUENCY WORDS — DEVELOPING SELF-MONITORING STRATEGIES FOR ACQUIRING A LARGE CORE OF HIGH FREQUENCY WORDS

239

plan

thear

ther

there

Explain the Principle

" You can add to the number of high frequency words you can write. "

" You can write high frequency words quickly. "

" You can check to see how many words you know. "

① Explain to the children that you will help them think about words they know how to write and those they almost know or do not yet know.

② Show a sample High Frequency Word List with known words for one child highlighted. Explain to the children that they can keep track of words they know and need to know by highlighting those they can write accurately.

③ Write *thear* on a whiteboard and use it in a sentence: *There is a cloud in the sky*. Think aloud and demonstrate that what you have written does not look right, so you will try it again. Write *ther*. Think aloud again. Suggested language: "This does not look right either, so I'll try writing it once more." Write *there*. Explain that when a word does not look right, you can write it different ways until it does look right. Then show how to check the word on the High Frequency Words List.

④ Tell children that they will work with words they do not yet know how to write correctly. Children select fifteen unknown words from their Individual High Frequency Words List and write them on an index card. Using a Make, Say, Check, Mix Sheet, they make each word with magnetic letters, mix it and remake it until they have made it three times. They place a check mark in the box each time they make it. Then they write the word and highlight any tricky part they want to remember.

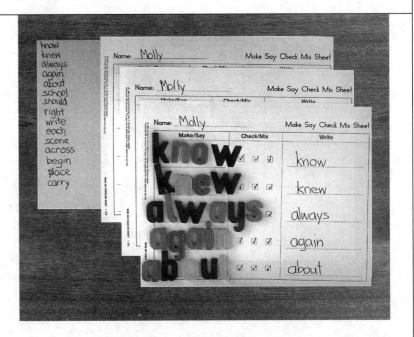

make
check
write

▶ Children select fifteen unknown words from their Individual High Frequency Words List and write them on an index card.

▶ Using a Make, Say, Check, Mix Sheet, they make each word with magnetic letters, mix it and remake it until they have made it three times. They place a check in the box each time they make it, then write the word and highlight any tricky part they want to remember.

In groups of three, have children tell two words they worked on and what they want to remember about how to write them.

Link

Interactive Read-Aloud: Read aloud books that keep the children interested in how words sound and how they look. Here are some suggested titles:

- ► *Song of the North* by Frank Asch
- ► *Word Wizard* by Cathryn Falwell

Shared Reading: After enjoying poems with children, notice something interesting about a few of the high frequency words and mark them with a highlighter or highlighter tape.

Guided Reading: During word work, think aloud as you write some high frequency words that children need to learn. Have them quickly write several of the words.

Guided/Independent Writing: Ask the children to mark the words that might be incorrect and then use their word lists to check them.

assess

- ► Observe how children write high frequency words in their daily writing so you can help them keep an accurate inventory on their High Frequency Words List.

Expand the Learning

Have the children create their own High Frequency Word Grid for reading practice (see Directions for Word Grid Game in *Teaching Resources*). Each child's grid will contain the particular words he needs to learn.

Have the children create a Concentration card deck by making pairs of index cards with high frequency words they need to learn. Then they find a partner and play Concentration with the card deck.

Connect with Home

Photocopy each child's High Frequency Word Inventory to send home or to share during family conferences.

Have children take home their individual High Frequency Word Grids and practice reading them to family members.

Connecting High Frequency Words

Go Fish

Consider Your Children

Children are learning to monitor their own learning of high frequency words. In this lesson children learn that they can use their foundational knowledge of some high frequency words to help them with others. A high frequency word pretest or reliance on a record of known high frequency words will help ensure that instructional time focuses on those words most useful to children.

Working with English Language Learners

Go Fish provides extensive practice, which helps English language learners build a core of known words. Vary the game by having children use words in sentences to help them clarify meaning. Remember that if children do not understand the words, then the lesson is meaningless and students will forget them. Work with them in a small group to model saying each word aloud, using it in a sentence, and discussing its meaning.

You Need

▶ Magnetic letters.

▶ Index cards (one for each child).

From *Teaching Resources:*

▶ Directions for Go Fish.

▶ Go Fish Game Cards made from words from High Frequency Words List and Deck Card Template.

Understand the Principle

About one hundred high frequency words account for approximately 50 percent of the words in print, so it is very useful for children to have quick recognition of them. The less effort children need to recognize these words as they read, the more fluently they can process print and give attention to word meaning. Since many high frequency words have similar word parts, children can use their knowledge to solve many other words.

Explain the Principle

❝ You can notice patterns in high frequency words. ❞

❝ You can make connections among high frequency words to help you learn them. ❞

CONTINUUM: HIGH FREQUENCY WORDS — NOTICING PATTERNS AND CATEGORIZING HIGH FREQUENCY WORDS TO ASSIST IN LEARNING THEM QUICKLY

plan

Explain the Principle

" **You can notice patterns in high frequency words.** "

" **You can make connections among high frequency words to help you learn them.** "

① Explain that you will help children learn how to read and write some words quickly. Remind them that some words are used very often and if they learn them well, they can quickly read and write them in text.

② Suggested language: "There are many words you know how to read and write quickly. Today you will learn more words."

③ Make *any* with magnetic letters. Suggested language: "There are many words you see often when you read. Some of them have three or four letters." Point out that *any* has three letters. "You can see *an* at the beginning and a *y* at the end that sounds like /ee/." Make *ever, from, once* with magnetic letters. Ask children what they notice about each word. Guide them to notice sound and letter patterns.

④ Continue this process with each of the "almost known" or "unknown" words selected for this lesson. Ask children to share what they notice and want to remember about each word.

⑤ Tell children that they will play Go Fish with high frequency words. They will make matches of words with similar parts. If necessary, demonstrate how to play the game. When children finish the game, they will list on an index card three high frequency words they learned and bring the card to group share. Children should be prepared to tell a partner how they will remember each word.

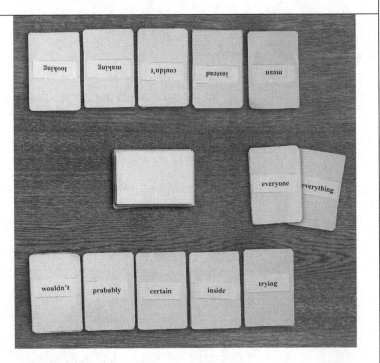

find
connect
ask
match
write

▸ Have children play Go Fish in pairs or small groups.

▸ When the game ends, children write three high frequency words they learned on an index card to bring to group share. Children should be prepared to tell a partner how they will remember each word.

Children choose one word from their individual lists and tell a partner how to remember it.

Invite children to suggest pairs of game words that had similar parts (e.g., *there*, *where*). Write the pairs on a chart, underlining the similar parts. Remind children that they can use parts of words they know to help them write other words.

Link

Interactive Read-Aloud: Read aloud books that create interest in words that are alike and help children make connections between them. Here are a few suggested titles:

- ▶ *Behind the Mask* by Ruth Heller
- ▶ *Snow, Snow: Winter Poems for Children* by Jane Yolen

Shared Reading: All poems will have a variety of high frequency words. After reading and enjoying a poem, have children point out pairs of words that have similar parts.

Guided Reading: After the lesson, use magnetic letters to make several pairs of high frequency words that have similar parts.

Guided/Independent Writing: When working with children while they reread their writing, point out high frequency words that have similar parts for them to notice.

assess

- ▶ Observe children's ability to use parts of known high frequency words to write or read other words.

- ▶ Dictate three to five high frequency words and ask children to write another word with a matching part for each.

Expand the Learning

Repeat this lesson with a different variety of words for the Go Fish game cards.

Have children make Word Ladders with high frequency words (see Directions for Word Ladders and Word Ladder Template in *Teaching Resources*).

Connect with Home

Send home the deck of cards so that children can play Go Fish with family members.

Invite children to make four Word Ladders with family members (see Directions for Word Ladders and Word Ladder Template in *Teaching Resources*).

Word Meaning/Vocabulary

Students need to know the meaning of the words they are learning to read and write. It is important for them constantly to expand vocabulary as well as to develop a more complex understanding of words they already know. And they need to have multiple encounters with those words. Word meaning includes the development of vocabulary, as well as special uses of words and connections between and among words. The meaning of a word often varies with the specific context and can be related to its spelling.

Accuracy in spelling often requires knowing the meaning of the word you want to write. Comprehension and accurate pronunciation are also related to knowing word meanings. In this section, we include synonyms, antonyms, and homonyms, which may be homographs (same spelling, different meaning and sometimes different pronunciation) or homophones (same sound, different spelling). Knowing synonyms and antonyms will help students build more powerful systems for connecting and categorizing words; it will also help them comprehend texts better and write in a more interesting way. Though students may understand the category, words in the category can be simple or complex. Being able to distinguish between homographs and homophones assists in comprehension and helps spellers to avoid mistakes. We also include work with categorization of words and their relationships as well as figurative language. We introduce basic dictionary skills.

Connect to Assessment

See related WM Assessment Tasks in the Assessment Guide in *Teaching Resources:*

- ▶ Reading Category Words
- ▶ Identifying Action Words and Describing Words
- ▶ Understanding Concept Words
- ▶ Understanding Antonyms
- ▶ Understanding Synonyms
- ▶ Understanding Homographs
- ▶ Writing Homophones
- ▶ Compound Words

Develop Your Professional Understanding

See *Word Matters: Teaching Phonics and Spelling in the Reading/Writing Classroom* by G. S. Pinnell and I. C. Fountas. 1998 Portsmouth, NH: Heinemann.

Related pages: 60–62, 78–81, 96–99, 105

Recognizing and Using Compound Words

Making Words

Consider Your Children

Compound words are easy for children to understand; they typically have had experience with many of them. If they have not formally studied compound words, introduce the principle by using simple examples such as *sunshine*. Begin with words that are in children's speaking vocabularies and then branch out to include words that they may not have thought about, but for which they can easily derive the meaning (for example, *everybody* and *everywhere*).

Working with English Language Learners

Understanding the concept of compound words will be very helpful to English language learners once they have added meaningful examples to their speaking and listening vocabularies. Work with children in small groups during shared reading, guided reading, and writing and identify easy examples that are meaningful to them. Have children locate compound words in the text and then write them on the board so that children can take them apart to see the two words that were put together.

You Need

▶ Chart paper.

▶ Markers.

From *Teaching Resources:*

▶ List Sheets.

▶ Lesson WM/V 1 Word Cards.

▶ Category Word Cards, Compound Words List

Understand the Principle

In English compound words are often the result of words juxtaposed so often that they become one word. Understanding compound words helps young readers and writers since the component parts of such words provide the foundation for finding the meaning. Often, but not always, the meaning of compound words relates to the meaning of the two individual words. You may want to refer to the extensive list of compound words organized by components in *Teaching Resources*.

Explain the Principle

❝ Some words are made up of two words that are combined. They are called *compound words*. ❞

❝ You see some words in many compound words. ❞

plan

teach

Explain the Principle

" Some words are made up of two words that are combined. They are called *compound words*. "

" You see some words in many compound words. "

① Explain to the children that they are going to learn about compound words. Read *sidewalk*, *sunlight*, *into*, and *haircut* aloud.

② Suggested language: "What do you notice about the words on the chart?" Children will likely respond that "there are two words put together." Suggested language: "All of these words are *compound* words. That means that they are made up of two words that are combined. Here are some more words."

③ Write the words *everyday*, *everybody*, and *everything* on the chart and ask children what they notice. Children will notice that they all begin with *every*. Suggested language: "Yes, they all begin with the same word, *every*. Many compound words are made from words like *every* or *any*. Look at these words." Write *anybody*, *anyone*, *anywhere* on the chart.

④ Ask children if they know any other words that are often part of compound words. If they do not respond, suggest *in* (*inside*, *into*, *indoors*), *bath* (*bathtub*, *bathrobe*, *bathroom*), or *black* (*blackboard*, *blackberry*, *blackbird*, *blacktop*) to get them thinking. Children might suggest words, such as Chinese food, that are not truly compound words but that they associate with a concept. Listen to their ideas, and explain that they are two separate words and are not compound words. You may comment that these would be good compound words.

⑤ After adding to the list of compound words, remind the children that each example shows two words put together and that sometimes understanding the smaller words will help them understand the meaning of the compound word.

sidewalk
sunlight
into
haircut

everyday
everybody
everything

anybody
anyone
anywhere

⑥ Explain to the children that they are going to make compound words with two word cards and then write the compound words on a List Sheet. Have them make twenty compound words. Remind the children that the words must be real. Be sure they know that some words (like *every* or *in*) can be used more than once. After they write their words, have them read each word to a partner.

take cards
make words
write words
read list

▶ Have the children put together two word cards to make twenty compound words. Children write their words on a List Sheet and then read them to a partner.

door	play	rain	sea
doorbell	playground	rainfall	seashore
doorknob	playroom	raindrop	seaweed
doorway	playmate	rainstorm	seafood

Name: Abby

Have the children read their lists of compound words to a different partner or the group. Be prepared for some creative suggestions. You can always check the dictionary.

Children might offer compound words that are not recognized words, for example *peanut butter* or *macaroni cheese*. Explain that these are two separate words, but as these words are used over a long period of time, they may become compound words.

They might also suggest compound words such as *minivan* that are comprised of words that do not usually stand alone (i.e., *mini*), but are used as prefixes.

Link

Interactive Read-Aloud: Read aloud books that feature compound words and guide children to discuss them. Here are two titles to consider.

- ▸ *Face to Face with the Dog: Loyal Companion* by Valerie Tracqui
- ▸ *The Worrywarts* by Pamela Edwards

Shared Reading: After reading poems or rhymes, have children locate and divide two or three compound words.

Guided Reading: After children have read a text, write a few compound words on a whiteboard. Have the children talk about the component parts and how they are helpful in thinking about the meaning of the word.

Guided/Independent Writing: When conferring with children, point out any compound words they have used in their own writing.

assess

- ▸ Make a list of five to ten compound words and have each child read them.
- ▸ After children have read the compound words, ask them to talk about what they mean. Observe to find evidence of children's ability to think about the meaning of words by noticing their component parts.

Expand the Learning

Have children construct compound word ladders such as this.

within
inside
sidewalk
walkways
wayside
sideways

Children can also brainstorm word families that use compound words. This example uses *snow*.

snowball
snowflake
snowman
snowplow
snowshoe
snowstorm

Refer to the Compound Word List in *Teaching Resources* to expand the range of words used.

Connect with Home

Have the children enlist their family members in looking for compound words. They may find some that are commonly used at home: *bathroom, stovetop, raindrop, doghouse, dishtowel, doorbell.*

Working with Compound Words

Word Sorting

Consider Your Children

This lesson should follow other lessons that help children understand the concept of compound words. Children should have a repertoire of compound words that they can recognize and break down into their component parts. In this lesson, children apply principles to more examples and connect words by studying categories of compound words. For this lesson we have selected words that represent very concrete images.

Working with English Language Learners

Understanding the concept of compound words helps children find word meaning. They can look for the two words that make the compound word and use them as a clue to find meaning. Help children understand meaning by talking about the words and using them in sentences. Give children opportunities to repeat the words and make them with magnetic letters. This allows them to break the compound words into smaller words and then put them together again. Use simple examples that clearly illustrate the principle.

You Need

- Chart paper.
- Markers.

From *Teaching Resources:*
- Four-Way Sort Cards.
- Four-Way Sort Sheets.
- Lesson WM/V 2 Word Cards.
- Category Word Cards, Compound Words List.

Understand the Principle

Word solving is more efficient when children can recognize and use large units. Compound words are a good way to illustrate this principle. For simple compound words, children will readily recognize the component parts. This lesson helps them group compound words into categories. They will learn that some smaller words appear frequently in compound words; quickly recognizing these words as components of compound words will help them become more automatic in word solving.

Explain the Principle

" Some words are made up of two words that are combined. They are *compound words*. "

" You see some words in many compound words. "

CONTINUUM: WORD MEANING/VOCABULARY — RECOGNIZING AND USING COMPOUND WORDS WITH FREQUENTLY USED COMPONENTS.

plan

Explain the Principle

" Some words are made up of two words that are combined. They are *compound words.* "

" You see some words in many compound words. "

① Tell the children that they are going to learn more about compound words. Suggested language: "Compound words are made up of two words that are put together. There are some smaller words that appear often in compound words. Thinking about these smaller words will help you learn many compound words."

Compound Words			
air	fire	hair	snow
airport	fireplace	hairdo	snowball
airline	fireman	hairbrush	snowman
airtight	firefly	haircut	snowflake
airmail	fireworks		snowstorm
airport			snowplow

② Write the word *air* at the top of column 1. Suggested language: "Many compound words have the smaller word *air* in them. Can you think of some?" Children may respond with words like *airport* or *airline.* You can add *airtight, airmail,* and *airport.*

③ Suggested language: "All of these words have the word *air* in them. Their meanings are related but different. What differences do you see?" Children can talk about the different meanings of the words in the column.

④ Repeat the demonstration with *fire, hair,* and *snow.*

⑤ Explain to the children that they are going to sort compound words. They can look for the smaller words in the compound words and place them into categories on the Four-Way Sort Card. Tell them that they will have different words than the ones on the chart. Explain that they should write their words on the Four-Way Sort Sheet, read them to a partner, and then bring their list to share with the group.

take word
sort word
write word
read word

door	play	rain	sea
doorbell	playground	rainstorm	seashore
doorknob	playmate	rainfall	seafood
doorway	playroom	raindrop	seaweed

Name: _____

door	play	rain	sea
doorbell	playground	rainstorm	seashore
doorknob	playmate	rain	seafood
doorway	playroom	raindrop	seaweed

doorstep

seaside

doorstop

doormat

- ▸ Have the children take and sort compound words on the Four-Way Sort Card.

- ▸ Have them write the compound words in categories on the Four-Way Sort Sheet.

▸ Have the children choose a list of related words to share with the class.

Children bring their lists of words to sharing. Have children compare the ways they sorted words.

In a group discussion, address any problems children had sorting words. Talk about the meaning of some of the words they sorted.

Link

Interactive Read-Aloud: Help children notice the compound words in books you read aloud. Some suggested books to read are:

- ▸ *Under the Sea from A to Z* by Anne Doubilet
- ▸ *The Hunterman and the Crocodile* by Baba Wague Diakite

Shared Reading: Help the children notice the compound words in poems that you are using for shared reading. Use a highlighter marker or highlighter tape.

Guided Reading: During the word work component of the lesson, write compound words on the board and invite children to make more words with the parts.

Guided/Independent Writing: Encourage the children to use compound words appropriately in place of words they write as separate words. Help them understand that words that are used together over many years sometimes are put together as compound words.

assess

- ▸ Notice the ease and fluency with which children sort words and write them.
- ▸ Conduct a quick check by having children read a list of five to ten compound words. Have them select several words and talk about what they mean.

Expand the Learning

Create a wall chart to collect and display compound words. Arrange the words in families.

Repeat the lesson with more compound words. Some possible sorts are:

bed: bedroom, bedspread, bedtime, bedroll

night: nightfall, nightgown, nightmare, nighttime

tooth: toothbrush, toothpick, toothpaste

any: anybody, anyone, anything, anytime, anywhere

every: everybody, everything, everywhere

grand: grandchildren, granddaughter, grandfather, grandmother, grandson

over: overboard, overcast, overlook, overhead

Find additional words in the Compound Words List in *Teaching Resources.*

Connect with Home

Have the children take home a set of word cards to sort with family members.

Children can search for compound words in magazines and bring examples to class to share.

Exploring Homophones
Words in Context

Consider Your Children

Use this lesson for children who have not explored homophones. If your students have more experience you may not need to teach this lesson. The reading vocabulary that most children have acquired includes many homophones but children may not have noticed them. In fact they may interchange simple homophones in their writing not realizing that spelling varies for different meanings. This concept is difficult because often one spelling can have different meanings. Children might not always be able to distinguish between two words that sound the same, but knowing that the pairs exist is a first step. Their awareness will increase and they can use a dictionary to check spellings and meanings.

Working with English Language Learners

Homophones are especially difficult for English language learners, but once they grasp the concept, the visual spelling can be helpful to them in sorting out the different words and what they mean. Begin with very simple homophones and provide many opportunities for children to use them in meaningful sentences. Engage them in shared reading and/or read aloud to children and, without interrupting the story, point out homophones in context. Ask the children to predict the spelling of the word in question. English language learners will need a great deal of experience with homophones in context before they can easily distinguish between them.

You Need

▸ Chart paper to make class chart of "A Call from Auntie."

▸ Markers.

From *Teaching Resources*:

▸ Homophone Pairs List.

▸ Homophones Sentence Sheet.

Understand the Principle

Once children understand the principle that words may sound the same but look different and have different meanings, they will be more likely to notice them and be careful when using them in writing. While children may not always select the correct spelling, they will gradually build a repertoire of homophone pairs to watch for as they read and write.

Explain the Principle

" Some words sound the same but look different and have different meanings. "

plan

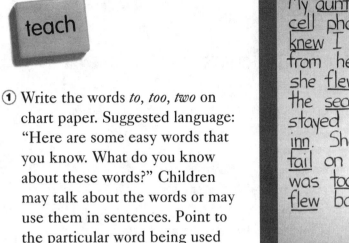

> A Call From Auntie
> My aunt called me on her
> cell phone because she
> knew I would like to hear
> from her. She said that
> she flew in a plane over
> the sea to Maine. She
> stayed two nights at an
> inn. She ate a lobster
> tail on a pier, but there
> was too much rain so she
> flew back here.

Explain the Principle

" Some words sound the same but look different and have different meanings. "

① Write the words *to, too, two* on chart paper. Suggested language: "Here are some easy words that you know. What do you know about these words?" Children may talk about the words or may use them in sentences. Point to the particular word being used and emphasize its spelling.

② Introduce *new* and *knew* in the same way and have children use them in sentences.

③ Suggested language: "When you write, you want to be sure to choose the correct spelling of each word or your meaning might not be clear." If children know the stories about Amelia Bedelia, remind them of the trouble that Amelia gets into because she thinks of the wrong word even though it sounds the same.

④ Read aloud *A Call from Auntie.* Briefly discuss what the sentences describe.

⑤ Next show a chart of the text with blank cards (or stick-on notes) over the underlined homophones so that they do not show. Suggested language: "When I wrote this story I thought very hard about the spelling of many words. Blank cards show where I had to choose between two words that sound the same but are spelled differently. I had to think about the meaning and which spelling to write."

⑥ Suggested language: "The first sentence starts with *my aunt*. Which of these words is the correct spelling for a person in your family?" Point to *aunt* and *ant* on the Homophone Pairs List and ask children to choose the right word by predicting the spelling. (Some children may pronounce the *au* in aunt differently rather than as a homophone for *ant*. If this is the case, then either recognize two pronunciations or skip the word.)

⑦ Remove the blank card and check children's predictions. Work through several more sentences in the same way, reading the complete sentence each time, having children select the correct spelling, and then checking their predictions.

⑧ Suggested language: "Today you are going to work with words that sound the same but look different and have different meanings. You will choose the correct spelling for a word in the sentence and then check your answer."

| read sentences |
| choose word |
| write word |
| check sentence |
| write own sentence |

▸ Children work with ten sentences on the Homophone Pairs Sheet, each with one or two blanks for which they choose the correct word from homophone pairs posted on a chart.

▸ Children write the word in the blank and then check it.

▸ Then children choose one homophone pair. Each student writes a sentence for each word and brings the sentence to sharing. Children may choose homophone pairs that are not included in the Homophone Pairs Sheet, providing a challenge to more advanced students.

Homophone Sentence Strips

I can only eat _one_ pizza.

He knocked at the door. I said, "Come _in_."

Do you have the _right_ answer?

The storyteller told a _tale_ of adventure.

The rabbit had a fluffy _tail_.

I bought this hat at a good _sail_.

Next _week_ we will have a vacation.

My friend's name is _Jim_.

Is today _your_ birthday?

We _won_ the game because we played well.

Children share the homophone pair they have selected for their own sentences and talk about what made it interesting or tricky. They read their sentences to a partner.

Ask children to talk about what they have noticed about words that sound the same but look different and have different meanings.

Link

Interactive Read Aloud: Read aloud books that feature homophones, such as:

- ▸ *Amelia Bedelia Goes Camping* by Peggy Parish
- ▸ *Amelia Bedelia Plays Ball* by Peggy Parish

Shared Reading: Engage children in reading poems that feature homophones and have them highlight those words with a marker.

Guided Reading: During word work, write homophone pairs on the board; discuss them and use them in oral sentences.

Guided/Independent Writing: When children want to write a word that is part of a homophone pair, especially pairs that children often confuse (*would* and *wood*), ask them to stop and think about the two spellings and what the words mean.

assess

- ▸ After several days give children the same set of sentences used in the lesson. Have children identify the accurate word of the homophone pair. This exercise will document how well children learned the particular homophones.

Expand the Learning

You can adjust the difficulty of this lesson by decreasing or increasing the number of sentences (or the number of pairs) with which children work or by selecting a different set of homophones.

Create a chart titled *Words That Sound the Same but Are Spelled Differently*, and have children be on the lookout for more pairs to add to it.

Connect with Home

Have children take home homophone word cards to cut apart and match.

You may want to send home these directions so that family members can help children make sentences with the words.

Dear Family,

We are learning about words like *blue* and *blew*. These words sound the same, but they are spelled differently. They have different meanings, so it helps to use them in sentences. You can help your child match these words and then use them in sentences, such as *The wind blew hard. I have blue shoes.*

Class Teacher

Connecting Words
Open Word Sort

Consider Your Children

In this lesson you will teach children a technique for seeing the relationships between and among words. In an open sort, children create and label the categories. Use very simple words and categories if this is the first time children sort words. Also, limit the number of categories and/or the number of words. If students are experienced sorters, then increase the complexity. While the emphasis in this lesson is on sorting words by meaning, you will want to recognize other criteria children use to sort, for example, how words look or sound.

Make this first sorting experience easy and obvious; later, you can vary the samples so that there is more than one way to sort the words.

Working with English Language Learners

Some English language learners may lack the labels even for simple items and will have trouble reading the words and sorting them into categories. Word sorting can help them if they understand the task sort and start with easy words that are concrete. Making connections will help them create richer definitions for words. Use pictures and words if needed, then gradually remove the pictures. Start with only two categories and just a few words in each.

You Need

▸ Pocket chart.

From *Teaching Resources*:

▸ Pocket Chart Card Template.

▸ Two-Way Sort Sheets.

▸ Lesson WM/V 4 Word Cards.

Understand the Principle

Word sorting is an effective technique for helping children think about the meaning of words and understand them more deeply. Placing words into categories helps children attend to the meaning of words.

Explain the Principle

" Some words go together because of what they mean. "

CONTINUUM: WORD MEANING/VOCABULARY — RECOGNIZING AND USING WORDS THAT ARE RELATED IN MANY WAYS

plan

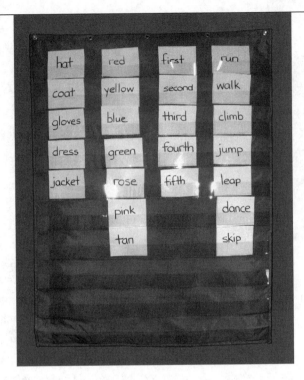

Explain the Principle

" **Some words go together because of what they mean.** "

① Explain to the children that they will put words in groups by thinking about what the words mean.

② Place some words in random order in a column on the left half of the chart. Leave room on the right side for children to take words from the left column and make categories on the right.

③ Suggested language: "I have some words on the chart today. Some of these words go together. Can you see some words that belong together for some reason?" Help children identify the categories as things you wear, colors, number or position words, and ways to move.

④ Have the children take turns suggesting or placing words together into categories. Ask them to label their categories or talk about why they put certain words together. If they suggest visual aspects of words (such as first letters), recognize that way of connecting words. Remind them to think about the meaning of the words.

⑤ Explain to the children that today they will sort more words. If they find any words that they do not know how to group, they can put them aside to sort later. Children select categories, sort the word cards, and then write the words on the Two-Way Sort Sheet. Then they write a label for the categories at the top of each column.

Name: Mohammed	Two-Way Sort
color	things we wear
blue	coat
pink	dress
red	gloves
green	hat
rose	jacket
tan	
yellow	

read word
sort words
write category label

apply

▸ Have the children say and sort the word cards. You may wish to add other words that fit the categories.

▸ For each category, children write the words on a Two-Way Short Sheet, and then they write a label describing each column.

share

Have the children bring their word sorts to group share and read them to a partner.

Ask the children to talk about what they have learned about words by sorting them. You may wish to collect and review their word sorts.

Link

Interactive Read-Aloud: Read aloud books that increase children's awareness of how words are connected by meaning. These titles are suggested.

> ► *G is for Goat* by Patricia Polacco
>
> ► *Teach Us, Amelia Bedelia* by Peggy Parish

Shared Reading: Mention a category (for example, words that mimic sounds or words that describe how something looks) and have the children find words in a poem or piece of familiar material that they have used for shared reading.

Guided Reading: When children encounter an unfamiliar word, help them connect it by meaning to some words that they already know (for example, a new way of moving through water as in *gliding*).

Guided/Independent Writing: Suggest to the children that they can increase the variety of words they use in their compositions by thinking of words that are connected to the words they usually use.

assess

> ► Observe the children as they sort words and ask them to talk about what they are thinking. This will give you an idea of how they are thinking about words.

Expand the Learning

Have the children sort the word cards that they set aside during the lesson sort.

Expand the categories of words and make it possible to sort them in several different ways. For example:

Words about numbers: *one, two, three, four, five, fifth, fourth, third, second, first*

Words about moving: *walk, ride, run, creep, dive, swim, splash, fly*

Animal words: *turtle, dog, cat, horse, bird, horse, fish, duck*

The same words can be sorted like this:

Live/move on land: *run, walk, ride, creep, fly, gallop, turtle, dog, cat, horse, bird*

Live/move in the water: *swim, dive, splash, fish, duck, turtle (both categories)*

Position words: *first, second, third, fourth, fifth*

Number words: *one, two, three, four, five*

Connect with Home

Have the children take home words to sort. As they build their collections of words, they can create new categories and sort in different ways.

Connecting Concept Words
Word Maps

Consider Your Children

This lesson is placed early in the year to help children begin forming categories for connecting words. You can choose any category of words for this lesson, so coordinate it with your science or social studies curriculum as a means of developing content vocabulary. The purpose is to help children begin the process of relating words by meaning. For the first lesson, choose a topic with which children have concrete experience, as well as many opportunities to talk about the topic and listen to stories about it.

Working with English Language Learners

Connecting words is a good way to help children expand their English vocabularies. Begin with familiar subject areas and topics, using words that children have encountered in books you read to them and in conversation in the classroom. Provide opportunities for English language learners to use words in meaningful sentences. You may wish to work with them in a small group and to simplify the word map, perhaps using fewer words, to be sure they understand the task. Before beginning the application, test whether children can read the words and eliminate any that are too difficult. Then create word maps about simple subjects (for example, *activities we do at school*) until you are sure children understand the concept.

You Need

▸ Chart paper.

▸ Markers.

From *Teaching Resources*:

▸ Word Map Sheets.

▸ Lesson WM/V 5 Word Cards.

Understand the Principle

Helping children connect words by meaning will help them build networks of information and expand their vocabularies. Reading in content areas is often difficult because children lack the background knowledge (including concepts and individual vocabulary words) to understand the material. Developing categories for specific and technical vocabulary will support children's comprehension, especially when reading informational texts.

Explain the Principle

" Some words represent big ideas or items. You can find words that represent smaller ideas or items related to the big ideas. "

plan

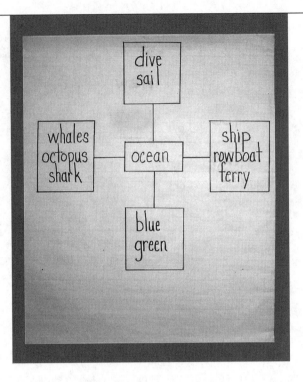

Explain the Principle

" Some words represent big ideas or items. You can find words that represent smaller ideas or items related to the big ideas. "

① Explain to the children that they will learn how to make word maps in order to connect words by meaning. Have a blank chart with the word *ocean* in the center.

② Suggested language: "We have been talking about the ocean, and today you are going to work with some of the words that we have been using."

③ "The word in the center is *ocean*. What are some of the ocean words we have talked about this year?" Invite children to suggest words (*whale, shark, sail*), but do not write anything yet.

④ When children have generated a productive list of words, tell them that they can make a map to show how these words relate to the word *ocean*.

⑤ If your group is inexperienced in relating words, then make a simple map by putting *ocean* in the middle and arranging all the individual words around it, with lines toward the center. If your group is more experienced, then encourage them to subcategorize words as described below.

⑥ Suggested language: "*Ocean*" is a big idea and the words you have been using describe smaller ideas related to ocean." Select one child's word, for example, *whales* and place it to the left. Ask: "Are there any words that go with whales?" Children may offer words like *shark, octopus*. Write the words under *whales* and draw a line to ocean. Suggested language: "Whales, octopuses, and sharks are all animals that live in the sea." Then select another word (for example, *ship*), and ask children for other words that go with it. Group these words and draw a line to *ocean*.

⑦ Continue making the map by placing categories of words. Have children discuss why they are grouping some words together. If you have time, children can suggest labels for their groups of ocean words. Some words may simply appear alone rather than being grouped. The completed word map will be a model that children can refer to.

⑧ Tell the children that they are going to sort ocean words into groups. After they sort the words, they will work with a partner to make an ocean word map to bring to sharing.

read word

sort word

make a word web

▸ Have the children work with a partner and sort the ocean word cards into smaller categories.

▸ Partners then write *ocean* in the middle of a Word Web Sheet. They write the words in each category to make a final map. Children can draw circles around their categories and/or label them.

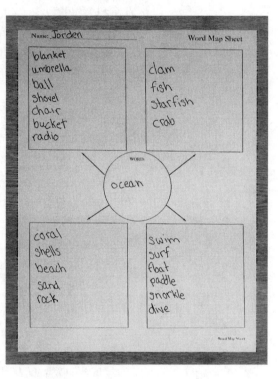

Partners bring their word maps to share with the group.

Children may compare the different maps and the ways children have made their subcategories.

Link

Interactive Read-Aloud: As you read aloud informational books, find words that are big ideas and categorize related words by making a word map. Some examples are:

▶ *Names for Snow* by Judi Beach

▶ *How Much Is a Million?* by David M. Schwartz

Shared Reading: Have the children read aloud poems about different topics. Invite them to help you make a list of the related words and then create a categorized word map.

Guided Reading: In discussing selections that children have read, point out words that are related to larger concepts or ideas by creating a quick map in the extension part of the lesson.

Guided/Independent Writing: If you have made some word maps in content areas, prompt the children to use them as resources for writing. Prompt the children to use word connecting as a strategy to compose informational writing.

assess

▶ Observe the children as they sort words to notice how quickly they can put them into categories.

▶ Look at the word maps to see the kind of thinking children have done as they placed words into categories.

▶ Have the children do a simple individual word map to see if they understand the concept.

Expand the Learning

Create word maps in different content areas to help children build vocabulary knowledge they need.

Connect with Home

Children may take turns taking home the class word maps to share.

Give children the assignment of creating a word map for *activities I do at home, things in my house,* or another home-related topic.

Recognizing and Using Synonyms

Synonyms Match

Consider Your Children

Use this lesson to provide a review of the concept of synonyms and to increase the children's knowledge of good examples. If the children have not learned the term *synonym*, this lesson will familiarize them with that language and help them quickly generate synonym pairs. You may want to start with limited sets of synonyms that you are sure children know, and then increase the number and complexity of the examples over several days.

Working with English Language Learners

English language learners may have found it a challenge to learn one word to express a particular meaning. Finding two words for a concept presents an additional challenge, yet it will help them greatly expand their English vocabularies. Be sure that you begin with very easy words that are in children's oral vocabularies. Work with students in a small group to repeat the words several times, use them in sentences, and talk about what they mean. As they understand more, work from the base of a word they know well and then bring in the synonym. Observe them closely as they match synonyms. If you can, give children some synonyms in their own language or pictures of words to illustrate the principle.

You Need

▶ Pocket chart.

From *Teaching Resources*:
▶ Pocket Chart Card Template.
▶ Word Pairs Sheets.
▶ Lesson WM/V 6 Word Cards.
▶ Category Word List, Synonyms.

Understand the Principle

Making connections between words is essential if children are to create the webs of meaning that will expand their vocabularies. Synonyms offer a beginning way to help children see that words are connected by meaning. Though the principle of the relationship is easy to understand, the range of words that can be connected by meaning is extensive.

Explain the Principle

" Some words mean about the same and are called *synonyms*. "

plan

Explain the Principle

" Some words mean about the same and are called *synonyms*. "

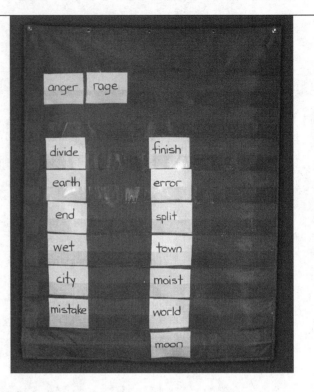

① Explain to the children that they will work with *synonyms*. Suggested language: "Does anyone know what a *synonym* is?" If the children have had some experience, they may suggest a definition.

② Place *anger* and *rage* in the pocket chart. Suggested language: "*Anger* and *rage* are synonyms because they have about the same meaning."

③ Make two columns of words. The left column lists five to six words; the right column lists six to eight synonyms and distracters. Suggested language: "Can you find a synonym for *divide* and match it?"

④ Work through the words, finding the synonym from the column on the right and placing it next to the word that has about the same meaning.

⑤ When all the synonyms have been matched, have the children generate a few more synonym pairs. Write the word pairs on cards and add them to the matches.

⑥ Sometimes children offer words that are related in meaning but are not the *same* in meaning (for example, *hot* and *warm*). Use your judgment as to whether to accept these pairs as evidence of beginning understanding. You may wish to place these word pairs aside as words that are closely related in meaning but are not actual synonyms.

⑦ Explain to the children that they will find synonym matches and choose two pairs to share with a partner. Make this application more challenging by including distracter words that do not form synonym pairs. You might wish to provide extra blank cards so that children can add their own synonyms.

apply

take card
match word
write words

- Have the children work with lesson word cards to make fifteen pairs of synonyms.
- They write their pairs on a Word Pairs Sheet.
- Then they choose two interesting word pairs to bring to sharing.

Name: Shane   Word Pairs Sheet
Date:

add	—	total
arrive	—	reach
anger	—	rage
ask	—	question
baby	—	infant
begin	—	start
below	—	under
call	—	yell
close	—	shut
dislike	—	hate
divide	—	split
earth	—	world
end	—	finish
error	—	mistake
fat	—	chubby

share

Have the children share their two selected synonym pairs with a partner.
Children may suggest new synonym pairs, which you can show in a class chart.

Link

Interactive Read-Aloud: Read aloud books that will help children learn how to notice synonyms. You might invite children to give two or three synonyms for interesting words as you need. These titles are suggested:

▸ *Earth and You: A Closer View* by J. Patrick Lewis

▸ *I Like Cats* by Patricia Hubbell

Shared Reading: Have the children find and highlight synonyms in a piece of shared reading. Or suggest a word and ask children to scan a poem to find a synonym.

Guided Reading: Using a text children are reading, hold up a card with a word on it and ask them to search for a synonym. Discuss the meaning of the word pairs and whether the synonym fits well into the sentence without changing its meaning.

Guided/Independent Writing: Take a piece of writing and create a chart or transparency. Highlight a few appropriate words and ask the children to think of synonyms that could be substituted to make the writing more interesting. In a minilesson, help children see where they can cross out a word and replace it with a more interesting synonym.

assess

▸ Observe children during sharing to notice whether they were able to select synonym pairs.

▸ Notice the variety and complexity of the pairs they choose.

▸ Give children a page of words and ask them to write synonyms for each one.

Expand the Learning

Repeat the lesson with a different variety of synonyms to expand children's vocabularies. (See Synonym List in *Teaching Resources*.)

Mix synonym and antonym Lesson WM/V 6 Word Cards. Children match them and decide whether they mean the same or the opposite.

Connect with Home

Have the children take home a sheet of words that they can cut apart and use to make synonym pairs.

Alternatively, have children find and write five pairs of synonyms with family members.

Recognizing and Using Antonyms

Antonyms Concentration

Consider Your Children

Most children are familiar with words that have opposite meanings and may have examined them formally in a word study program. In this lesson, you will review the concept of antonyms and expand children's repertoires of examples. Be sure that you are using words that children already have in their speaking, reading, or writing vocabularies. Remember, though, that when working mostly with known words, children can often learn new words.

Working with English Language Learners

English language learners will benefit from connecting words that mean the opposite. Keep this lesson simple by using easy examples and words that children understand and can read (*hot/cold* or *smooth/rough*) until you are sure that they understand the principle. Work with childen individually or in a small group to create picture labels, act out meanings of words, or use words in sentences. If you can, give children some antonyms in their own language to illustrate the principle.

You Need

► Chart paper.

► Markers.

► Index cards.

From *Teaching Resources*:

► Concentration Game Cards made from Lesson WM/V 7 Word Cards and Deck Card Template.

► Directions for Concentration.

► Category Word List, Antonyms.

Understand the Principle

A student's vocabulary and deeper understanding of word meanings will be enhanced by the study of antonyms. Students can expand their knowledge of examples of antonyms as they learn more about the principle. Studying synonyms and antonyms forms a foundation for understanding analogy, an area of knowledge that appears frequently on proficiency tests.

Explain the Principle

❝ Some words mean about the opposite and are called *antonyms*. ❞

CONTINUUM: WORD MEANING/VOCABULARY — RECOGNIZING AND USING ANTONYMS (WORD THAT MEAN THE OPPOSITE)

plan

fast	slow
good	bad
above	below
dirty	clean
inside	outside

Explain the Principle

66 **Some words mean about the opposite and are called *antonyms*.** 99

① Explain to the children that they are going to learn about words that mean the opposite. Place several antonym pairs on the chart and ask children to read them.

② Suggested language: "What do you notice about these words?" Children may respond that each pair of words means the opposite and may come up with the word *antonyms*. If not, you can introduce it.

③ Suggested language: "Words that mean the opposite, or almost the opposite, are called *antonyms*." Have the children say the word. "Can you think of any more words that mean the opposite?" Children can offer examples and/or you can propose a word and ask them to think of a word that means the opposite.

④ Continue until you have about ten or fifteen antonym pairs. Some of them can be matched in different ways, for example, *lose* as the opposite of either *win* or *find* and *slow* as the opposite of either *quick* or *fast*. Accept the different ways children put words together if they are opposites.

⑤ After you have generated a list, have children read the antonym pairs.

⑥ Explain to children that they will play Antonym Concentration. Limit the game at first to the words you have presented in the lesson. Children place all the cards face down on a table. In turn, they flip one card over, read it aloud, and then turn over another card and see whether it means the opposite (is an antonym). The player with the most pairs wins. After the game, have each child write three pairs of antonyms on an index card to bring to share.

mid
late

apply

| turn card |
| turn card |
| match pair |
| write three pairs |

► In groups of two to four players, children play Antonym Concentration.

► Then they list three antonym pairs on an index card to bring to group share.

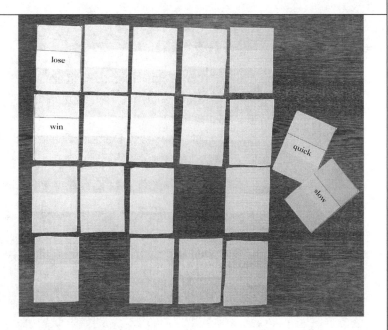

share

Using their index cards, have the children share and discuss the antonym pairs in groups of three.

Have them help add a few more examples to the class list. Encourage them to provide interesting words.

WORD MEANING/VOCABULARY

275

Link

Interactive Read-Aloud: Read aloud books that feature antonyms. Help children notice how antonyms are used to create contrasts that help them learn. Examples of appropriate books are:

- ▸ *Under, Over, by the Clover* by Brian Cleary
- ▸ *The Emperor's Old Clothes* by Kathryn Lasky

Shared Reading: Engage the children in shared reading of poems that feature contrasts. Pull out (or generate) a list of antonyms from the contrasts they find. Alternatively, select a few words and have the children generate antonyms as you list them.

Guided Reading: Prompt children to notice antonyms after reading a text. Work with a few antonyms on a whiteboard during the word work segment of the lesson.

Guided/Independent Writing: Help children understand how to use contrasts in their writing and to think of antonym pairs that help make their meaning clear.

assess

- ▸ Observe the children as they play Antonym Concentration and identify those who need some extra help.
- ▸ Give the children a list of ten words and ask them to write an antonym for each one.

Expand the Learning

Repeat the lesson with a different variety of antonym pairs as children learn more of them (see Antonym List, *Teaching Resources*).

Set up a board or chart where children can post or write antonym pairs that they have discovered through reading, writing, or conversation.

Children may enjoy making an Antonym Book with words that mean the opposite on the left and right pages. They can write the words and illustrate them.

Connect with Home

Have children take home the antonym pairs they have listed to read to family members.

Create sets of antonym word cards for children to take home, cut apart, and match. They can play Antonym Concentration with family members.

8 *Synonyms and Sentences*

Go Fish

Consider Your Children

Use this lesson to help children remember both the concept of synonyms and some examples. The lesson will also help them understand the finer shades of meaning that they find in words. Often synonyms do not have exactly the same meaning and children read to choose between them to express a more precise meaning. Children should work mostly with words that they already know, but they may acquire a few new words as they connect synonyms.

Working with English Language Learners

The concept of synonyms will give English language learners a tool to use in expanding their speaking, reading, and writing vocabularies. Connecting words they know to new words will help them realize how English is structured. Realize that many English language learners will make mistakes as they try to use synonyms interchangeably. Provide opportunities for children to work with easy synonyms that are in their speaking vocabularies. If you can, give children some synonyms in their own language to illustrate the principle.

You Need

► Chart paper.
► Markers.
► Index cards.

From *Teaching Resources*:
► Go Fish Game Cards made from Lesson WM/V 8 Word Cards and Deck Card Template.
► Directions for Go Fish.

Understand the Principle

Understanding synonyms can accelerate the expansion of children's speaking, reading, and writing vocabularies. Making connections among words that mean the same or almost the same gives children more choices in writing. Using synonyms enhances comprehension when children connect a known word to a new word that has about the same meaning.

Explain the Principle

" Some words mean about the same and are called *synonyms*. "

plan

Explain the Principle

" **Some words mean about the same and are called** *synonyms.* "

① Place several sets of synonyms on the chart and ask children what they notice about the words. You may need to read the words with the children.

② Even if they do not know all the words, children will notice that some pairs mean the same or almost the same.

Synonyms

happy	glad
all	every
ask	question
anger	rage
start	begin
little	small

It's time to _____ our work.

Mom tried to ___ the car.

③ Suggested language: "That's good. Words that mean about the same are called *synonyms*." Write the word *synonyms* and have children say the word aloud.

④ Ask the children to generate more pairs of synonyms. If they have difficulty, suggest some easy words like *start* and *little* and have them offer synonyms.

⑤ Suggested language: "Synonyms can often be used interchangeably. Let's try it with a sentence." Write *It's time to ____ our work*. Have children read the sentence with both *start* and *begin*. "They mean the same, don't they?"

⑥ Suggested language: "You have to think about how you are using the synonym to be sure it makes sense. Try this sentence." Write *Mom tried to ____ the car*. Have the children read the sentence with both *start* and *begin*. Help them notice that although *start* fits, the word *begin* does not.

⑦ Discuss the idea that synonyms mean almost the same and that their meaning also depends on how they are used in sentences. Generate several more pairs of synonyms and have children try them in sentences.

⑧ Tell the children that they will play Go Fish with synonyms. Include in the game synonyms you know children will recognize because they are easy or children have worked with them. If you include a few more difficult synonyms, with which children have little experience, then review those pairs at the end of the lesson.

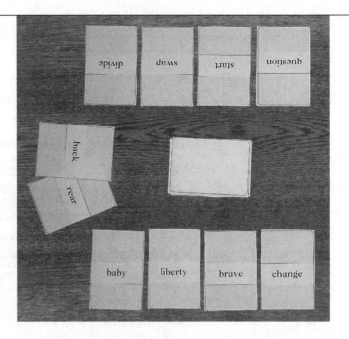

ask
match word or
take card
say sentence
choose pair
write pair

▸ Have partners play a version of Go Fish. Players match synonyms and then use both words in the same sentence before laying down the synonym pair.

▸ If both synonyms do not fit the exact meaning of the sentence, the player should create another sentence. The first player to have no cards in her hand wins. Players can play the game more than once if time allows.

▸ After the game, have each child choose a synonym pair to write on an index card and bring to share.

Have the children share their synonym pairs by using them both in the same sentence.

Add some of these synonyms to the class chart.

Children may want to discuss the fact that homographs can be tricky (*close/shut; close/near*).

Link

Interactive Read-Aloud: Read aloud books that will help children learn how to notice synonyms as you read the text. Examples are:

- *Quilt Alphabet* by Lesa Cline-Ransome
- *Willie Wins* by Almira Astudillo-Gilles

Shared Reading: Have the children tape a synonym over one or two words in a poem or other text and then reread the text with the new words. They can discuss whether the meaning changes a little.

Guided Reading: When the children come to a word and are not sure of the meaning, suggest a synonym and write the two words. Have children try substituting the synonym in the sentence in place of the new word.

Interactive/Guided Writing: When the children are composing a text, encourage them to vary their word choice by using synonyms.

Independent Writing: When the children share their writing, ask if any synonyms could be used to make sentences more interesting. They will have to be thoughtful here because a substitution may change the meaning too much.

assess

- ▶ Observe the children as they play Go Fish and identify those who have difficulty either identifying synonyms or making sentences with them.

- ▶ Have the children write a list of as many synonym pairs as they can within a five-minute limit. Look at the results for the accuracy of matches, the number of pairs produced, and their variety.

Expand the Learning

Repeat the lesson with additional synonyms (see Category Word List, Synonyms).

Set up a Synonym Board with words on cards. Children can continually add to the board and may create sets of two or three words that mean almost the same.

Connect with Home

Send home a deck of synonym word cards for children to match at home or to play Go Fish with family members.

Summary of Synonyms and Antonyms

Lotto

Consider Your Children

Use this lesson after the children understand the concepts of synonym and antonym and can easily identify matching pairs. This lesson will require them to switch quickly from one to the other quickly and will help to develop flexibility in thinking about word meanings. Children should have a good repertoire of examples of both synonyms and antonyms before participating in this lesson.

Working with English Language Learners

English language learners should have previous experience talking about synonyms and antonyms and creating pairs as examples. For shared reading, use rhymes with which they are very familiar before asking children to locate antonyms or synonyms. Even if a rhyme is very simple, you can specify a word and say, "Find an antonym [synonym]."

You Need

▶ Synonym and antonym charts made in previous lessons.

▶ Shared reading chart—"Old and New" poem with synonyms and antonyms.

▶ Index cards.

▶ Highlighter tape.

From *Teaching Resources*:

▶ Lotto Game Cards made from Lesson WM/V 9 Word Cards and Deck Card Template.

▶ Three-by-Four Lotto Game Boards.

▶ Directions for Lotto.

Understand the Principle

Understanding the meaning of words that mean the same or opposite will build a foundation that will help children continue to derive word meanings all of their lives. Analogy, for example, is often an exercise on standardized tests and is based on the relationships between and among words. Being able to switch flexibly between synonyms and antonyms will expand children's thinking about words.

Explain the Principle

" Some words mean about the same and are called *synonyms*. "

" Some words mean about the opposite and are called *antonyms*. "

plan

Explain the Principle

" **Some words mean about the same and are called** *synonyms.* "

" **Some words mean about the opposite and are called** *antonyms.* "

① Explain to the children that they are going to work with synonyms and antonyms.

② Suggested language: "You know about *synonyms*, words that mean about the same, and you also know about *antonyms*, words that mean about the opposite. Today you are going to be looking for both synonyms and antonyms."

> **Old and New**
>
> I have a great new pair of jeans.
> They are navy and very cool.
> I like to wear my dark blue jeans
> Everywhere in school.
> I have an old pair of blue jeans.
> They're a light and faded blue.
> But I wear my old blue jeans
> More than I wear the new.
> I have a wonderful new pair of shoes.
> They're clean and chocolate brown.
> I like to wear my great new shoes
> Everywhere in town.
> I have a pair of running shoes.
> They're old with dirty laces.
> I wear my old shoes less unless
> I want to win the races.

③ Read the poem "Old and New" to the children and have them join in as they learn it. (Many different poems could be used for this lesson. Choose several that children like to read.)

④ Using a highlighter, have children locate and highlight words that mean the same and words that mean the opposite. Alternatively, you can make a list of synonym and antonym pairs that appear in this rhyme.

⑤ Children can substitute other words that mean the same or opposite in the poem. Don't worry about sustaining the rhyme. This is simply an exercise to stretch children's thinking.

⑥ Tell children that they are going to play Lotto with synonyms and antonyms. A match can be a word that is either the same or the opposite of the card drawn, but children must state whether it is a synonym or antonym. The player who covers all of the words on her card first is the winner. After playing the game, children write one synonym pair and one antonym pair on an index card to bring to share.

apply

take card
say word
match word
tell synonym or antonym
cover space

► In groups of two to four, have the children play Lotto with synonyms and antonyms. Be sure the children understand that they are to read the words and specify the relationship between them.

lose | begin / finish | cry
city | close | absent
girl | give | come
big | ask | dislike / hate

► After playing, children write one pair of synonyms and one pair of antonyms on an index card to bring to sharing. They write their initials on their cards.

share

Have the children share their synonym and antonym pairs with a partner.

Invite the children to talk about what they have noticed about words through exploring synonyms and antonyms.

Children turn in the pairs they have written on index cards. You can quickly examine these cards to determine how well children understand the concepts and the range of examples they understand.

Link

Interactive Read-Aloud: Read aloud books that include many synonyms and antonyms or read books and pause two or three times to invite synonyms or antonyms for interesting words. Here are some titles:

- ▶ *Big and Little* by William Jay Smith
- ▶ *Amos and Boris* by William Steig

Shared Reading: Have the children tape a synonym or antonym over a word in a poem that you are using for shared reading. Have them talk about how the new word changes the meaning.

Guided Reading: When the children have read a selection, go back to locate a few synonyms or antonyms in the text. Write the pairs on a whiteboard.

Guided/Independent Writing: Help children use synonyms to make their writing more interesting or use antonyms to create contrasts.

assess

- ▶ Observe the children as they play Lotto to determine how quickly and easily they find the synonyms and antonyms. Note any creative responses they offer, such as a word that is a synonym for one word and an antonym for another.

- ▶ Give the children a list of ten word pairs and ask them to identify quickly whether they mean the same or opposite.

Expand the Learning

Introduce the "opposite" version of the rhyme used to begin the lesson. Give children a reproduced version and have them list antonyms and synonyms they find.

Old and New

I have a good old pair of jeans.
They are faded and not so cool.
I wear my dull old blue jeans.
When I go to school.
I have a great new pair of jeans.
They're very sharp and bright.
And I wear my new blue jeans
When I want to look just right.
I have a good old pair of shoes.
They're worn and chocolate brown.
I wear my old brown shoes
Everywhere in town.
I have a great new pair of shoes.
They're white with awesome laces.
I wear my new shoes when I want
To win the running races.

Connect with Home

Send home a collection of word cards and ask the children to match both synonym and antonym pairs as quickly as they can with family members.

Children can take home word cards and Lotto Game Cards to play with family members.

Making Decisions about Using Homophones

Homophone Lotto

Consider Your Children

Use this lesson to help the children continue to expand their knowledge of the use of homophones. Children should understand the principle that words can sound the same but be spelled differently. They should also know that it is important to consider the meaning when using a homophone in a sentence.

Working with English Language Learners

Use simple, meaningful sentences when working with English language learners. Unless they can read and understand the sentences, it will be difficult for them to distinguish between even the easiest homophones. It will be helpful to act out meanings whenever possible.

You Need

▶ Chart paper.

▶ Markers.

From *Teaching Resources*:

▶ Directions for Lotto.

▶ Three-by-Three Homophone Lotto Game Board made with Category Word List, Homophones (homophones printed on board before photocopying).

▶ Sentence Strips made from Homophone Lotto Sentences.

▶ Category Word List, Homophones.

Understand the Principle

Even when the children understand the concept of homophones and know a range of examples, it might still be challenging for them to select the right word for a given context. Many spelling errors are related to the misuse of homophones, and it is important for spellers to continue to develop knowledge in this area. For example, spell check software does not detect errors related to homophones. Often homophones are referred to as homonyms, though homonyms also include homographs.

Explain the Principle

❝ Some words sound the same but look different and have different meanings. ❞

CONTINUUM: WORD MEANING/VOCABULARY — RECOGNIZING AND USING HOMOPHONES (SAME SOUND, DIFFERENT SPELLING AND MEANING)

plan

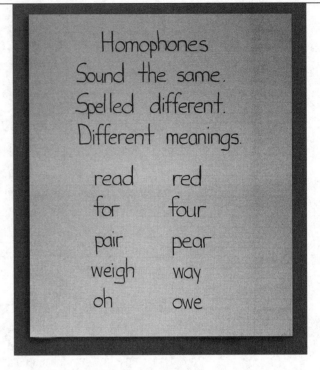

Homophones
Sound the same.
Spelled different.
Different meanings.

read	red
for	four
pair	pear
weigh	way
oh	owe

Explain the Principle

" **Some words sound the same but look different and have different meanings.** "

① Tell the children that they will work with homophones and learn more about how to decide which word to use.

② Suggested language: "You know a lot of homophone pairs such as *hair* and *hare*. Who can think of an example?"

③ Children suggest a variety of examples. Suggested language: "Homophones are words that sound the same but are spelled differently and have different meanings. It is sometimes hard to decide which word to use in a sentence. We will practice that today."

④ Have the children read a variety of homophone pairs and briefly discuss the different meanings. You may ask them to think of some creative ways to distinguish among the words. Children's ideas can be silly or far-fetched. The process of noticing something about the word is what's important. Children usually suggest some interesting ideas. For example:

▸ "*Red* is a color. *Read* is spelled the same as *read*. I *read* a book yesterday."

▸ "Walking in this *pair* of shoes is like walking on *air*."

▸ "*Four* is the number. It has *4* letters in it."

▸ "I can think about something that would *weigh eight* pounds—the *eigh* is in both."

▸ "*Oh*, no! I *owe* money!"

⑤ After discussing the words, have the children write words as you read them aloud in a sentence. Suggested language: "I am going to use a word in a sentence. It will be a word that has a homophone. Write the word as quickly as you can and put down your pencil." (Use a few of the Homophone Lotto Sentences.) Read each sentence and, after a short pause, have the children hold up their predictions of the spelling of the word. Then hold up the right word so they can check themselves.

⑥ Remind the children of the directions for Lotto and tell them that they will take turns reading sentences. They will put markers on their cards if they have the right word for the sentence. "Remember: Don't be tricked by homophones!"

take card
read sentence
match word
cover space

▸ Have small groups of children play Lotto with homophones.

▸ In this game, players take turns drawing a card and reading a sentence with a blank.

▸ To cover a square, the player must have the word (with the correct spelling) that fits into the sentence. Since there are homophone pairs across the game boards, the task is tricky.

▸ The first player to cover all the words wins. Be sure children know to read the sentence with the correct word inserted before covering the square.

Invite the children to talk about what they have noticed about the homophone pairs. They may have more creative ideas to share about how they are deciding which word to use. The more ideas they suggest to help them distinguish between pairs, the greater facility they will have when writing them.

Link

Interactive Read-Aloud: Read books that include homophones in humorous or creative ways. Have children notice how the author or illustrator uses creative ideas to help readers remember what a word means.

- ▶ *Into the A, B, Sea: An Ocean Alphabet* by Deborah Lee-Rose
- ▶ *My Little Sister Ate One Hare* by Bill Grossman

Shared Reading: Select poetic texts with a variety of homophones and have children highlight them.

Guided Reading: During word work, have children practice quickly reading pairs of homophones. Select them from the Category Word List: Homophones (see *Teaching Resources*).

Guided/Independent Writing: Have the children reread their writing to notice whether they have used the correct spelling for the particular homophone they want to use (e.g. *they're, their,* or *there*).

assess

- ▶ When the children hold up the words they have written during the lesson, you will get a good idea of those who are able to make quick and accurate decisions. You may want to play Lotto yourself with a small group to help those having difficulty.
- ▶ Conduct a quick individual check by laying out cards with homophones and having children point to the word that fits into a sentence that you read.

Expand the Learning

Repeat the lesson to expand the list of homophone pairs the children have encountered using the Category Word List: Homophones (see *Teaching Resources*). Encourage them to look closely at the words and find ways to link them to meaning.

Connect with Home

Have the children take home pages of homophone pairs to read, match, and think about. They can ask family members to help them think of ways to remember the meaning.

Invite the children to make a list of ten homophone pairs to bring to school to share.

Recognizing Homophones, Synonyms, and Antonyms
Word Grids

Consider Your Children

Use this lesson when children understand the principles of synonyms, antonyms, and homophones. In this lesson they will expand their vocabularies in these categories. With regard to homophones, children should know that words can sound the same but be spelled differently and have different meanings. They should be able to suggest a few examples of homophones and be able to distinguish between some pairs by knowing the different meanings. The principles underlying homophones, synonyms, and antonyms are all basic to making connections between and among words.

Working with English Language Learners

Homophones pose special difficulties for English language learners; it may be hard for them to switch from one way of thinking to another as they learn English words. You can adapt the application activity by focusing on only one or two kinds of words. For example, make a die with H on only half the sides, leaving the other sides blank. The child has to roll an H before looking for homophones to cross out. Work with children during the word work part of guided reading to help them recognize synonym, antonym, and homophone pairs.

You Need

▶ Synonym, antonym, and homophone charts from previous lessons.

▶ Chart paper.

▶ Markers.

▶ Die for Word Grid Game with "H" on two sides, "A" on two sides, and "S" on two sides.

From *Teaching Resources*:

▶ Directions for Word Grids.

▶ Word Grids (scatter pairs of homophones, synonyms, and antonyms in the spaces on the Word Grid Template before photocopying. Select from Word Cards made from Lessons WM/V 5 through WM/V 9 Word Cards and the Word Grid Template).

Understand the Principle

Homophones are words that sound the same, but are spelled differently. They are a form of *homonym*. Homonyms can also be *homographs*, which are words that sound the same, look the same, and can be pronounced differently—e.g. *present*. It is important for children to become flexible words solvers who see words in different ways and develop categories that help them remember these special characteristics of words. Connecting words in several different ways will build flexibility.

Explain the Principle

" Some words sound the same but look different and have different meanings. "

plan

Explain the Principle

" Some words sound the same but look different and have different meanings. "

A word chart showing:

big	question	go
chubby	sea	bee
city	blew	no
dear	ask	blue
fat	town	be
fix	read	your
glad	sun	cold
hair	red	empty
happy	eight	hot
hare	flower	full
hate	flour	eye
know	son	there
little	their	stop
love	ate	I
mend	see	you're

① Explain to the children that they will work with pairs of words. Suggested language: "You have learned about words that sound the same but are spelled differently and have different meanings. These words are called *homophones*." Write *homophones* on the chart and have children say it. You may want to point out that the parts of the word mean "same sound." (Connect the word to *telephone* if you think that will be helpful.)

② Quickly review the Homophone Pairs Chart from Lesson WM/V 3, or have children provide some examples and add some yourself to make a chart of about twelve homophone pairs.

③ Suggested language: "These pairs of words are homophones because they sound the same and mean something different. You know some other ways words are connected. What are words that mean the same or almost the same?"

④ Children may respond by saying *synonyms*. If they cannot remember the term, it may help them to think of "same or like name" (*syn=together; nym=a name*). Have them scan the synonym chart and suggest two or three examples.

⑤ Then remind the children of the concept of *antonyms*. It may help to think of "opposite name" (*anti=opposite* or *against; nym=a name*). Have them scan the antonym chart and suggest two or three examples.

⑥ Set the charts aside and present a chart with words in random order that form pairs of homophones, synonyms, and antonyms. Suggested language: "Now that you know about homophones, synonyms, and antonyms, you can find pairs of them. Who can find a pair of synonyms on this chart?"

⑦ One child finds a pair of synonyms. Suggested language: "Do you all agree that *happy* and *glad* are synonyms? Do they mean the same?" Children agree and then the child puts *S* next to *happy* and *glad*. Demonstrate with several more examples.

⑧ Suggested language: "You know about words that mean the same, words that mean the opposite, and words that sound the same but look different and have different meanings. Today you are going to work with all of these pairs of words. Instead of using a list like this one, you are going to use Word Grids."

⑨ Explain the Word Grid Game. Then show children how to roll the die with *H*, *S*, and *A* and then find pairs and cover them with stick-on notes.

apply

roll die
find pair
say word
cross out word

▸ Have groups of two, three, or four children play the Word Grid game.

▸ Players take turns rolling a die. If it says *H*, the child looks for a pair of homophones on his Word Grid and says them. If the group agrees that they are homophones, he crosses them out. (If the die says *A*, the child looks for antonyms; if it says *S*, he looks for a pair of synonyms.)

▸ Each time, the group must agree that the words fit the symbol on the die. They may keep a dictionary handy to settle disagreements if they arise. If a child cannot find a pair to fit the symbol, others in the group may help.

▸ The winner is the first player to cross out all of the words (or who has crossed out the most words when time ends).

share

Go back to the original chart. Have partners choose and read one pair of words and tell whether they are synonyms, antonyms, or homophones.

Ask the children to talk about what they have noticed about homophones. They may respond with comments like these:

"They sound the same when you say them."

"They are spelled differently."

"You have to be careful to use the right one in a sentence."

Link

Interactive Read-Aloud: As you read books aloud to children, point out interesting words that are part of homophone pairs. Ask children to think about how it would change the meaning (or not make sense) to use the wrong spelling. Examples are:

- ▶ *My Toasting Marshmallows: Camping Poems* by Kristin O'Connell-George
- ▶ *The Absolutely Awful Alphabet* by Mordecai Gerstein

Shared Reading: In poems or other texts that children know well, say a word and ask them to name a homophone, synonym, or antonym.

Guided Reading: Use the word work component of the lesson to help children to understand homophones or distinguish among the spellings. Have the children write pairs and then orally use them in sentences.

Guided/Independent Writing: When you confer with children, untangle confusions they have about particular homophones. Place these words on their Words to Learn lists for work in the Buddy Study Spelling System (see Lessons WSA 1 through WSA 5).

assess

- ▶ Observe the children as they work with the Word Grid Game. Notice how quickly they are able to find the appropriate pairs of words.

- ▶ If the children are having difficulty switching from one concept to another, it may be that they do not fully understand one kind of pair (even though they can repeat the definition). Work individually with children on a word grid. Notice which concepts are giving them most trouble and work more with them in small groups.

Expand the Learning

You may want to return to this lesson over several days, each time using different sets of words.

Have the children play Vocabulary Concentration. The deck includes a variety of homophones, synonyms, and antonyms. Players make pairs and tell the relationship between the words. (See Directions for Concentration in *Teaching Resources*.)

Connect with Home

Send home a Word Grid Game for children to play with family members.

Invite the children to create a synonym, antonym, and homonym list with family members.

12 *Recognizing Homographs*

Sentence Pictures

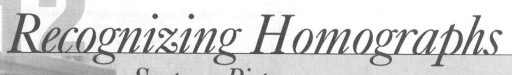

Consider Your Children

Homographs may pose comprehension difficulties for children. It may be challenging to assess whether children understand words that are spelled the same but have different meanings and pronunciations in different contexts. Using the syntax or structure of language (built through hearing it read aloud) will help children detect and understand homographs. Select words for this lesson that are in children's speaking vocabularies or in the books you have read to them often.

Working with English Language Learners

English language learners often find homographs quite difficult to understand and pronounce. They will develop understanding of the pronunciation over time. It is important that children begin to understand the principle that even though two words may look exactly the same, they are actually different. Children may find it easier to distinguish the words when listening, especially as you use them in sentences and in stories you read aloud. After the words are established in their speaking and listening vocabularies, you can share the spelling.

You Need

► Chart paper.

► Markers.

From *Teaching Resources*:

► Lesson WM/V 12 Word Cards.

► Four-Box Sheets (two per child).

Understand the Principle

Homographs are words that look the same but have different meanings (e.g., *present, read, wind)*. A homograph is a kind of homonym. The term homograph means *same letters*. Becoming aware of homographs helps children become more alert to the possibility of different pronunciations and meanings for words, while expanding their listening and reading vocabularies.

Explain the Principle

" Some words look the same, have a different meaning, and may sound different. "

CONTINUUM: WORD MEANING/VOCABULARY — RECOGNIZING AND USING HOMOGRAPHS (SAME SPELLING, DIFFERENT MEANING, AND THEY MAY HAVE DIFFERENT PRONUNCIATION)

293

plan

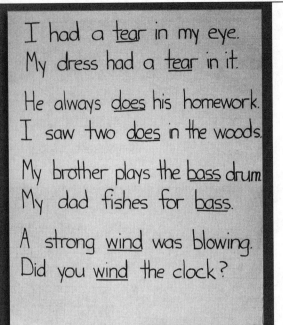

I had a tear in my eye.
My dress had a tear in it.

He always does his homework.
I saw two does in the woods.

My brother plays the bass drum.
My dad fishes for bass.

A strong wind was blowing.
Did you wind the clock?

Explain the Principle

" **Some words look the same, have a different meaning, and may sound different.** "

① Tell the children that they will learn about words that look the same but have different meanings and often are pronounced differently.

② Suggested language: "When you read the two words in a sentence, you realize that they sound different and also mean something different. I'm going to read the first two sentences."

③ Start with the easy homograph *tear*. Children probably have both words in their speaking vocabulary but some may be surprised that the words look the same. Suggested language: "What do you notice about the words that are underlined?"

④ Children may point out that you say them differently. Follow up by asking the children to state the two meanings of *tear*. Children can make new sentences with the two words.

⑤ Suggested language: "There are some words that look the same but have different meanings and usually sound different. These words are called *homographs*." Have children say *homograph*. It may help to explain that the two parts mean "*same spelling*."

⑥ Follow the same procedure with the remaining sentences on the chart. Have children read the sentences with both correct and incorrect pronunciations. If they listen carefully, they can use meaning and language structure (think whether it "sounds right" and "makes sense") to check their pronunciations.

⑦ Suggested language: "Today you will write and illustrate sentences with words that look the same but have different meanings and sound different.

write word
illustrate word
read word

▸ Have the children choose four homograph word cards.

▸ Using two Four-Box Sheets, they will write two sentences and make two illustrations for each word.

▸ Children then read their sentences to a partner and bring them to sharing.

Go around the circle, asking each child to read two of their illustrated sentences. Add selected sentences to the class chart if you need more examples.

Discuss any new words the children learned.

Link

Interactive Read-Aloud: Read aloud books that increase children's awareness of homographs and help them expand their sense of English syntax. Examples are:

- *Amelia Bedelia and the Baby* by Peggy Parish
- *The Dove Dove* by Marvin Terban

Shared Reading: Together read the chart of sentences with homographs, emphasizing pronunciation of the two words.

Guided Reading: During word work, use the whiteboard to write homographs and ask children to make oral sentences with them.

Guided/Independent Writing: During conferences, have children read their work aloud to detect any confusion they have about homographs.

assess

- When sampling oral reading, notice whether children are accurately pronouncing homographs. Corrections in pronunciation provide evidence that they are using language syntax to monitor their reading and are thinking about meaning.
- Give children several unfamiliar sentences containing homographs and ask children to read them aloud. Note their pronunciation.

Expand the Learning

Have the children collect homographs on a page in their Writing Workshop folders or in their Writer's Notebook.

Make a class book of homographs, using the illustrated sentences children have produced.

Repeat the lesson and have children select different homograph.

Connect with Home

Have the children take home Homograph Word Cards or a Word Card Template with different words and repeat the activity with family members.

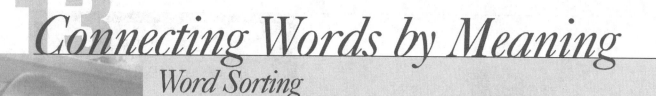

13 Connecting Words by Meaning
Word Sorting

Consider Your Children

Use this lesson when children have learned the task of sorting words by applying several different criteria. They will work with a variety of related words that can be grouped to convey more subtle shades of meaning. There may be some words in the collection that are new to children, so be sure to explain them before they begin the activity. Eliminate any words that are too difficult. Color words are used in this lesson; you will want to use other categories to expand children's vocabularies. Make note of any children who are color-blind and may have difficulty with the concepts shown here. You can substitute other words (see Expand the Learning).

Working with English Language Learners

The words in this lesson may be difficult for English language learners. You may wish to reduce the number of words and be sure that children have a color illustration as a reference. Other aids, such as acting out words or using pictures, are also helpful. Say each word several times and have children repeat them. Give children time to talk about what the words mean and why they are putting them together. Color words are a good starting point, since they are concrete and easy for children to reference and understand.

You Need

▶ Chart paper.

▶ Markers.

From *Teaching Resources*:

▶ Three-Way Sort Sheets.

▶ Lesson WM/V 13 Word Cards.

Understand the Principle

Connecting words will help children accelerate the development of their vocabularies. Understanding categories and subcategories is a foundation for understanding how information is organized and presented. In this lesson, children are required to notice the more subtle aspects of words and their connotations. Colors are used to introduce this kind of thinking.

Explain the Principle

" Some words go together because of what they mean. "

CONTINUUM: WORD MEANING/VOCABULARY — RECOGNIZING AND USING WORDS THAT ARE RELATED IN MANY WAYS

plan

Explain the Principle

" **Some words go together because of what they mean.** "

red
scarlet
brick
pink

green
lime
forest

Pink is a lighter shade of red. These things are all shades of red.

All of these are things that are green. They are different shades of green.

① Explain to the children that they will think about the ways that words are connected.

② Suggested language: "You know that you can learn new words by making connections. Today you will look at color words. You might not have seen some of them. These words are related."

③ Write *red* and *green* at the top of the chart. Suggested language: "I'm thinking of another color word. I'm thinking of *scarlet*. Where would I put *scarlet*—with *red* or with *green*?"

④ Children will probably respond by saying that *scarlet* is more like *red* than like green. If needed, find something scarlet, either in the crayon box or in something children are wearing. Have them talk about why they put *scarlet* with *red*.

⑤ Suggest several more color words. When you have several in each category, ask children if they can come up with any more color words to place under *red* or *green*. The contrast with green will help them to make decisions on words like *pink, rose,* or *plum.*

⑥ Ask the children to create statements to describe the words in each category and write them on the chart. Suggested language: "What have you noticed about some of these color words?"

⑦ Children may comment that the names of fruits and vegetables are sometimes used to describe colors. Children may also say that the colors are lighter, brighter, or darker even though they are all still green or red.

⑧ Suggested language: "Writers often use color words to help readers imagine the colors they are writing about. You may want to use some of these color words in your own writing."

⑨ Tell the children they will again sort color words for red, green, and a mystery category. Review the words on the word cards and provide examples if children do not know the color. Have them record the color words on a Three-Way Sort Sheet and then record a sentence describing each category on the back of the sheet.

write key words

sort word cards

write words on word sheet

write category names

write sentences

▸ On a Three-Way Sort Sheet, children write *red* and *green* at the top of two columns and leave the third column blank.

▸ They sort the color word cards and then write them in the three columns.

▸ Then, from the words you provide, they select some that go together. They write a name for the third column and a sentence describing each category on the back of the sheet.

▸ They bring their sheets to sharing.

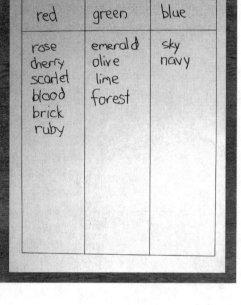

Going around the circle, have each child give the name for the third category on their Three-Way Sort Sheets. They may have different names—*blue, purple*. Have children talk about their thinking in putting these color words together. Some children may choose to put *purple* with *red*, which is acceptable as long as they can explain their thinking.

Remind children that they can use different words to describe colors when they are writing.

Link

Interactive Read-Aloud: Read aloud books such as these, which have a variety of descriptive words related to colors. Children may want to add words to the color chart or another category.

- ▶ *The Turning of the Year* by Bill Martin, Jr.
- ▶ *Donovan's Word Jar* by Monalisa Degross

Shared Reading: Have children share reading of the color poems in *Hailstones and Halibut Bones* by Mary O'Neil.

Guided Reading: Help children notice when writers use interesting color words for descriptions.

Guided/Independent Writing: Encourage children to keep a list of interesting color words and other adjectives in their Writer's Notebooks.

assess

- ▶ Notice the children's ability to articulate reasons for the categories they create.

- ▶ Notice whether the children are using a greater variety of color words in their writing or whether they comment on color words when you read aloud.

Expand the Learning

Repeat this lesson with other categories that require children to sort words according to related meanings. Each of the following sorts requires the Two-Way Sort Sheet and the Word Card Template (see *Teaching Resources*).

Sort A: *walk, clomp, plod, pace, glide, slide, run, pound, jog, dash, sprint, stroll, march, stride, toddle, stagger, hike, stomp, tiptoe, slip, slither, skate*

Sort B: *hot, cold, burning, boiling, warm, sizzling, scalding, chilly, icy, freezing, frosty, wintry, frozen, frigid, steamy*

Sort C: *mild, sunny, cold, windy, cloudy, warm, rain, hail, thunder, lightning, tornado, hurricane, hot, humid, freezing, snow, sleet, showers, sprinkling, breezy, frigid*

Connect with Home

Children can take home their lists of color words and ask family members to help them think of new ways to describe colors.

Children can work on new lists of words describing colors such as *black* or *orange*.

Learning about
Action Words (Verbs)
Verb Search

Consider Your Children

Use this lesson after children have had experience identifying action words in texts they read. Children can draw upon their implicit knowledge of the way words work within sentences. While children may not yet have explicit knowledge of parts of speech and how they work in sentences, they are beginning to focus on the function of words. Children are ready to become more aware of the action words they use in their own writing.

Working with English Language Learners

Since all languages have verbs, English language learners already have an implicit knowledge of action words in their home languages. In this lesson, use simple grammatical structures and English words whose meanings children know. Once children understand the function of verbs, they will be more aware of them when they encounter them while reading. Help children generate simple sentences through shared or partner writing, and then circle the action words. Use dramatization if necessary to help them understand the action words and their function in sentences. During word work, help children find action words in a text.

You Need

▶ Chart paper.

▶ Markers.

▶ Text for demonstration (e.g., Tomie dePaola's *Mice Squeak, We Speak: A Poem* by Arnold L. Shapiro) or any other simple book.

▶ Books to use as resources.

From *Teaching Resources:*

▶ Four-Box Sheets.

Understand the Principle

Parts of speech are the building blocks of grammar. Both implicit and explicit knowledge of how words function in sentences will help children improve their writing. As evidenced by their oral language and writing and reading behaviors, third-grade children have extensive implicit knowledge of parts of speech. Drawing their attention to action words will help them build their knowledge of this category, even before they label them as verbs. Action words (verbs) make writing more interesting and engaging.

Explain the Principle

" Some words tell what a person, object, or animal does. They are called *action words* or *verbs.* "

---

plan

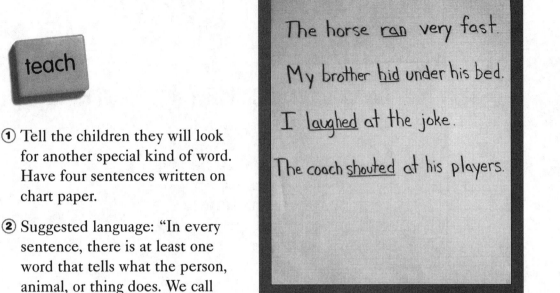

The horse ran very fast.

My brother hid under his bed.

I laughed at the joke.

The coach shouted at his players.

Explain the Principle

" Some words tell
what a person,
object or animal
does. They are
called *action words*
or *verbs*. "

① Tell the children they will look
for another special kind of word.
Have four sentences written on
chart paper.

② Suggested language: "In every
sentence, there is at least one
word that tells what the person,
animal, or thing does. We call
these words *action words* or *verbs*
to help us remember that the
word shows what someone does. Read the first sentence."

③ Give the children time to read the sentence and then ask them which word
tells what the horse did. Help them understand that *ran* describes *what* the
horse did. Help them understand that *very fast* describes *how* the horse ran.
(You are building implicit knowledge of adverbs.) Work through the next
three sentences, identifying and underlining the action words.

④ When you are sure children understand these examples, read several pages
from a book with simple examples (e.g., Tomie dePaola's *Mice Squeak, We
Speak: A Poem by Arnold L. Shapiro*). Ask students to identify the action
words that they find interesting. List the action words on chart paper and
check a few of them by rereading the sentences. Suggested language:
"Listen for the action word as I read the sentence." Students will identify
the action word (e.g., *squeak*), and then you can ask, "Who squeaks?" (e.g.,
mice).

⑤ Suggested language: "What kind of action do all of these words tell us?"
Children may say that it is the noise the animal or person makes. You can
point out that the words *say*, *speak*, and *talk* pertain to people and what they
say. Make a connection to the action word *shouted* in the last sentence on the
chart.

⑥ Make available several copies of a text or use the books children are reading for independent reading or guided reading. Have children find four action words and write them in the squares of a Four-Box Sheet. Then they write their own sentence, using the action word. If time allows, suggest that they illustrate each action word and sentence.

read word
write word
draw picture
write sentence

▸ Children search a text and select four action words and write them on a Four-Box Sheet.

▸ Then they write their own sentences, using the action word. It is all right for them to use simple examples to solidify the concept.

Many children will stretch themselves to use more colorful action words and accompany them with adverbs.

▸ Ask children to illustrate the action words and sentences.

▸ Children bring their Four-Box Sheet to sharing.

Children share one action word, sentence, and illustration.

Add a few of the action words to the chart or have children begin a list of action words in their Word Study Notebooks.

Ask children to summarize what they learned about action words.

Link

Interactive Read-Aloud: Read aloud books with interesting action words, stopping at two or three. Discuss how the action words help readers understand what is happening—how it makes the story more interesting. Here are two suggested titles:

- ▶ *To Root, to Toot, to Parachute* by Brian P. Cleary
- ▶ *The Racecar Alphabet* by Brian Floca

Shared Reading: Find action words in poems children are reading. Have them use a highlighter or highlighter tape to mark the words.

Guided Reading: During word work have children quickly locate a few action words in sentences.

Guided/Independent Writing: Have children locate action words in their own writing. Have them think about alternative words that might make their writing more interesting. By working with action words in this way, children develop the habit of noticing this category of words and improving their word choice.

assess

- ▶ Review the children's writing to determine whether they understand and are using action words within the structure of their sentences.

- ▶ Notice whether the children can locate action words when reading texts. Many sentences are more complex and include structures such as gerunds, which act as verbs. Do not get into so much detail that students become confused. They may occasionally identify phrases that

include adverbs. The important idea is that children are building their knowledge of verbs and their function in sentences.

Expand the Learning

Continue to build the class collection of action words and to call attention to them.

In another lesson, differentiate between an action word (verb) that tells *what* is being done with a describing word (adverb) that tells *how* something is done.

Connect with Home

Have children take home a reproduced version of a text and circle the action words. Then list them in their Word Study Notebooks.

As the children read independently at home, have them add action words they find to the lists in their Word Study Notebooks.

Recognizing and Using Action Words

Read Around the Room

Consider Your Children

Children may know many words, but not understand the different categories into which they fit. Use this lesson when children have had experience identifying words that represent action. The words you use for this lesson should be a part of children's oral language vocabularies. Provide charts, poems, pieces of shared writing, and other texts for children to use as resources for finding action words.

Working with English Language Learners

English language learners implicitly understand action words because they use them in their native oral languages. If you know any words in the language they speak at home, make connections between verbs they know and English words. Use words in simple sentences that children understand. Have them act out the action words to make them more accessible.

You Need

▸ Chart paper.

▸ Markers.

▸ "Autumn Leaves" poem written on chart paper.

From *Teaching Resources*:

▸ Words Around the Room Sheets.

▸ Category Word Cards, Verbs.

Understand the Principle

As children work on their writing, it will be helpful for them to think about how action words (verbs) function in sentences. Children need to learn ways to recognize them as they read and write. You can decide whether or not to introduce the term *verb*; the main purpose of this lesson is to help children begin to think about the function of words in sentences.

Explain the Principle

" Some words tell what a person, object, or animal does. They are *action words* or *verbs*. "

plan

Action Words
run   sprint   jog   scamper
walk   dance   spin   turn

<u>Autumn Leaves</u>
Autumn leaves are falling, falling.
Autumn leaves are spinning, spinning.
Autumn leaves are floating, floating.
Autumn leaves are dancing, dancing.
Autumn leaves are blowing, blowing.
Autumn leaves are falling, falling.
Autum leaves are sleeping, sleeping.

Explain the Principle

" Some words tell what a person, object, or animal does. They are *action words* or *verbs*. "

① Tell the children they will think about the different kinds of words they read and write.

② Suggested language: "There is a special kind of word called an *action word*. What do you think this kind of word is for?"

③ Children may suggest that action words tell what you do.

④ Suggested language: "Action words show what a person, object, or animal does. Look at this word." Write *run* on the chart. "This word tells what someone might do."

⑤ Point out that the word *action* means to *act* or *do something*. Explain that action words are important in sentences. Suggest a few synonyms for *run* that are also action words (*sprint, jog, scamper*).

⑥ Have children suggest and act out a few other action words. They might suggest words that are gerunds (verbal nouns), such as "*Falling down* is not fun!" or participles (verbal forms that have the characteristics of both verbs and adjectives), such as "John was running." It is not necessary to distinguish among these forms at this time. All forms refer to actions and can be considered *action words*. Add children's suggestions to the list. If they suggest words that are not action words, recognize their efforts and write the words on a list to the side.

⑦ Read aloud "Autumn Leaves." Have volunteers highlight the action words. Don't overlook the action word *are*, a "state of being" verb. *Fall* is an action word; *are falling* tells that something is engaged in falling right now.

⑧ Tell the children that they will collect action words on a Words Around the Room Sheet. They can look for words that are like each other. For example, if they find *run*, they can look for others like it. If they find *running*, they can look for other words ending with *-ing*. Even though it is difficult for some children to categorize words, trying to do so helps them notice more categories of words when they read and listen.

⑨ Suggested language: "Find at least twenty action words. Remember that some words tell what a person, object, or animal does. They are *action words*."

search for action word

read action words

write twenty action words

▸ Children find twenty action words on the materials that are displayed around the classroom.

▸ To expand the lesson, you can place additional word cards with verbs at various places in the room.

▸ They record them on a Words Around the Room Sheet.

▸ Children bring their sheets to sharing.

Go around the circle and have the children share one action word they found and recorded on their Words Around the Room Sheet.

Emphasize categories (base verb, *run;* verbs with *-ing, running;* verbs with *-ed, walked;* verbs that are past tense and change spelling, *ran).* Children can form categories in several different ways. The idea is that children will recognize a range of verbs and begin to connect them.

Link

Interactive Read-Aloud: After reading aloud a book or selection with interesting action words have children recall some of them. Here are several titles to consider.

- ▸ *Whose Garden Is It?* by Mary Ann Hoberman
- ▸ *Rimshot* by Charles R. Smith, Jr.

Shared Reading: Have children locate and highlight action words in poems or other material they are using for shared reading.

Guided Reading: After reading, have the children go back and select interesting action words in a text.

Guided/Independent Writing: Encourage the children to keep a list of interesting action words in their Writer's Notebooks or on a sheet in the Writing Workshop folder.

assess

- ▸ Examine children's Words Around the Room Sheets to be sure that they have a solid collection of action words rather than random words that have been copied.

- ▸ Work in small groups with children who are having difficulty with the concept.

Expand the Learning

You can repeat the lesson, emphasizing other action words so that children become very familiar with categories and have many examples.

Keep a class chart of interesting action words that are sorted into categories (for example, past, present, and future action). Children can add to the chart as they read and write.

Post a blank chart on the wall and challenge the class to write 100 action words.

Connect with Home

Have the children take home their Words Around the Room Sheets and collect ten more action words to share. They can look for them by noticing what people do at home or in the environment, or they can find them in bold print in magazines, newspapers, or even advertising materials.

16

Learning about Describing Words

Adjective Search

Consider Your Children

Children who have had extensive experience reading and writing text have an implicit knowledge of the way words function to create meaning in sentences. They can draw on this knowledge as they look for describing words, or *adjectives*. This is not a formal lesson on "parts of speech." It is designed to raise awareness of the function of words in sentences.

Working with English Language Learners

English syntax presents a challenge to children who speak another language in their homes and communities. In general, however, all languages have describing words. Once children understand the category, they can more readily identify words that belong. Even if they do not know a word, they will look for a descriptor as they try to solve it. During word work, help children locate describing words.

You Need

▶ Chart paper.

▶ Markers.

▶ Text for Adjective Search. (Select a text with good examples of adjectives.)

From *Teaching Resources*:

▶ Two-Column Sheets.

▶ Category Word Cards, Adjectives.

Understand the Principle

In this lesson you draw children's attention to words that describe how something looks. Being able to identify these words is an early step toward understanding parts of speech. Words and their function in sentences form the foundation of grammar; knowing them helps children revise and edit their writing and comprehend what they read.

Explain the Principle

" Some words describe a person, place, or thing. They are called *adjectives*. "

plan

Explain the Principle

" **Some words describe a person, place, or thing. They are called *adjectives*.** "

① Tell the children that they will look for a special kind of word that describes something.

② Suggested language: "When we read books, there are words that help us almost see the people, places, or animals. When you write during Writing Workshop, often you use words that describe people, places, or feelings. Today we will look for describing words.

Describing Word	What it describes
old	Triceratops
dead	animal
strong	jaws and teeth
smaller	dinosaur

③ Suggested language: "Listen carefully while I read some sentences from our new book about dinosaurs (or about the topic in the book you select). Raise your hand when you hear a describing word." Help children notice the describing words in the text. On a chart list the describing word on the left and the noun it describes on the right. Suggested language: "*Old* is a good describing word. What is old?" After children respond, write *Triceratops* in the right column. Explain that *Triceratops* is a noun because it names something and that adjectives describe nouns.

④ Discuss several other examples. It is not necessary to identify all of the adjectives. Rather, encourage children to find the most obvious examples.

⑤ Tell children they will search for ten describing words in the text you give them or a book they are reading. Before they begin, have children write *Describing Word* and *What it describes* at the top of each column on a Two-Column Sheet.

apply

find ten
describing words

write headings

write describing
words

reread sentence

write what it
describes

▸ Children find ten describing words in a text.

▸ They write the headings *Describing Word* and *What It Describes* at the top of a Two-Column Sheet.

▸ They write the describing word in the first column of a Two-Column Sheet. Then they reread the sentence and write the noun that it describes in the second column.

▸ Children choose one describing word and the noun it describes to bring to share.

Name: Evan	
Describing Word	What It Describes
brown	dress
fast	food
happy	baby
funny	clown
serious	acrobat
red	tent
beautiful	costumes
fancy	horses
big	ears
striped	zebra

share

Children share one describing word and what it describes with the group. Use a few more interesting adjectives placed on cards and have children talk about what they could describe.

Ask the children to summarize what they have learned about describing words. During Writing Workshop ask children to review one of their pieces and add a few describing words to make their writing more interesting.

Link

Interactive Read-Aloud: Read aloud books filled with interesting describing words. Discuss how they helped children understand the author's intent. Here are a few suggested titles:

- ▸ *Many Luscious Lollipops* by Ruth Heller
- ▸ *Hairy, Scary, Ordinary* by Brian P. Cleary

Shared Reading: Find describing words and the nouns they modify in pieces you have used for shared reading.

Guided Reading: During word work have children locate describing words in the text they read.

Guided/Independent Writing: Plan a word choice minilesson that helps children include more adjectives in their own writing.

assess

- ▸ Review the children's writing to determine whether they understand and use describing words.
- ▸ Notice whether children can identify describing words when they read.

Expand the Learning

Repeat this lesson with other texts, particularly informational texts. The adjectives in expository texts carry a great deal of information. You want readers to notice the fine details in adjectives that assist them in comprehending.

Start a bulletin board of interesting describing words. Invite children to write an adjective and illustrate it to resemble its meaning. For example, *spotted* might be written with spots, or *shiny* written with glitter glue.

Connect with Home

Have the children take home a reproduced version of another text. They can mark the describing words and read them to a family member.

Recognizing and Using Describing Words

Read Around the Room

Consider Your Children

Use this lesson after children have worked with action words. Children will begin to understand that words fit into different categories and function differently in sentences. The words you use for this lesson should be a part of children's oral language vocabularies. Provide charts, poems, pieces of shared writing, and other texts for children to use as resources for finding describing words.

Working with English Language Learners

Describing words are present in all languages, so English language learners will probably understand this concept in their native languages. If you know any of their languages, make connections between adjectives they know and English words. Use words in simple sentences that children understand. Use pictures to illustrate the function of words. You may wish to begin with color words, which are the simplest describing words.

You Need

► Chart paper.

► Markers.

► "Seasons" poem.

From *Teaching Resources*:

► Words Around the Room Sheets.

Understand the Principle

Describing words, or *adjectives,* are very important in writing. Adjectives help us to create visual images while reading that contribute considerably to reading enjoyment. Children have encountered many describing words in oral language as well as in the texts you read aloud. You can decide whether to introduce the term *adjective.*

Explain the Principle

" Some words describe a person, place, or thing. They are called *adjectives.* "

plan

teach

Explain the Principle

" **Some words describe a person, place, or thing. They are called *adjectives*.** "

① Tell the children they will think about the different kinds of words they read and write.

② Suggested language: "There is a special kind of word called a *describing word*. What do you think this kind of word is for?"

③ Children may suggest that describing words help you think about what someone or something might look like. Suggested language: "Describing words tell you about how a person or thing looks, feels, sounds, or tastes. They might help you imagine how scenery looks or how something feels. Describing words make writing more interesting.

④ Begin with *big*. Suggested language: "Look at this word. What could *big* describe?" Encourage children to offer examples of what *big* might describe. Have them use the word in a sentence.

⑤ Have children suggest other describing words. Even though these words are adjectives, it is not necessary for children to know the term at this time. It is more important for them to build a category of words that describe.

⑥ Read aloud "Seasons." Have volunteers highlight the describing words. They will notice that in this poem the describing words end in *y*.

⑦ Tell children that they will collect describing words on a Words Around the Room Sheet. They can look for words that are like each other. For example, if they find *thin*, they can look for others like it in some way; if they find *happy*, they can look for other words that end in *y*. Even though it is difficult for some children to categorize words, trying to do so helps them notice the variation in describing words (for example, words with *y, -er, -est)*.

⑧ Suggested language: "Find at least twenty describing words. Remember that describing words help you understand what someone or something is like."

Describing
Words

big   green
little   salty
tiny   floppy
funny

Four Seasons

Spring showery, flowery, bowery
Summer hoppy, croppy, poppy
Autumn slippy, drippy, nippy
Winter breezy, sneezy, freezy

apply

search for
describing words
read words
write words

► Children find
describing words on
materials displayed
around the
classroom and
record them on a
Words Around the
Room Sheet. To
increase the challenge, place additional describing words on word cards at
various places in the room.

► Ask them to choose one or two describing words to share with the class.

Name: Genna   Words Around the Room

thinner
stronger
faster

happy   finest
shiny   happiest
glossy   fastest
funny   scariest
tasty
smelly

Describing
Words

fast   blue
little   purple
quiet   yellow
               black

share

Go around the circle and have children share one describing word they
found and recorded on their Words Around the Room Sheets.

Highlight some words that are new for the children.

Link

Interactive Read-Aloud: After reading aloud a book with descriptive words, have children remember some of the words in the text that helped them form mental images. You can read aloud a section and have them identify the words. Here are two titles to consider.

- ▸ *Beautiful Blackbird* by Ashley Bryan
- ▸ *Ellsworth Extraordinary Electric Ears* by Valerie Fisher

Shared Reading: Have the children highlight describing words in poems or other materials they are using for shared reading.

Guided Reading: After reading, have the children go back and select words that describe how a person looks or feels.

Guided/Independent Writing: Encourage the children to keep a list of describing words in their Writer's Notebook or on a sheet in the Writer's Workshop folder.

assess

- ▸ Examine individual Words Around the Room Sheets to be sure that students have a solid collection of describing words rather than random words that have been copied.

- ▸ Work in small groups with children who are having difficulty with the concept.

- ▸ Some students may have collected a few adverbs (for example, *write quickly*) and this is good thinking. You can say that these words do describe *how* something is done.

Expand the Learning

Repeat this lesson, emphasizing other describing words so that children become familiar with a range of adjectives and have many examples.

Using a variety of adjectives is a goal of writing in third grade and throughout elementary school. Keep a class chart of describing words that are sorted into categories. Children can add to the chart as they read and write (e.g., base words, words with *-er,* words with *-est)*.

Post a blank chart on the wall and challenge the class to write 100 describing words.

Connect with Home

Have children take home their Words Around the Room Sheets and look for more examples of describing words.

Ask children to look around their homes and use a Writer's Notebook or Word Study Notebook to list any describing words they find. They can categorize their list by room. Have them share their lists in Writer's Workshop or word study. Children may wish to write descriptive pieces about their homes.

Learning about Nouns— Words for People, Places, Things

Noun Sort

Consider Your Children

Use this lesson when children have demonstrated that they are able to identify words that name people, places, or things. Be sure children have used these words in sentences so that they have an intuitive sense of how they function in sentences.

Working with English Language Learners

More than likely, children began learning English by making connections with their native language labels for people, places, and things. Many nouns can be illustrated concretely to make them more understandable. Remember to include nouns that children know when teaching this lesson.

You Need

▶ Chart paper.

▶ Markers.

From *Teaching Resources:*

▶ Three-Way Sort Sheets.

▶ Category Word Cards, Nouns.

Understand the Principle

Nouns (words that stand for a person, place, or thing) are the labels that children acquire. Nouns may be concrete (*house, dog*) or abstract (*love, anger, fear*). They already have implicit knowledge of this category of words and can usually identify them. In this lesson, they work with a collection of nouns and examine their characteristics more closely by sorting them. For purposes of this lesson, tell children to use *person* to stand for a human or animal. *Things* are inanimate objects or ideas. The name of a particular person, place, or thing is a proper noun (*Maria, Boston, Pearl Street*). A word that takes the place of a noun is a pronoun (*he, she, they, them*).

Explain the Principle

" Some words stand for a person, a place, or thing. They are called *nouns.* "

plan

teach

**Explain
the Principle**

" Some words stand
for a person, a
place, or thing. They
are called *nouns*. "

> Dolphins look like fish. They live
> their whole lives where fish
> live. But they are not fish.
> They are mammals just like
> you and me. That is why
> dolphins come to the top of
> the water so often. Like
> all mammals they must
> breathe air.

① Explain to children that they will
work with a special category of
words and learn the name for
these words.

② Suggested language: "I am going
to read part of the introduction to
a book. There is a word that tells
what the book is about—the
person (or animal, a living thing),
place, or thing. Listen for that word." Read the first four sentences.

③ Suggested language: "Which word tells what this book is about?" Children
may offer *dolphins* or *fish*. Explain that the book is about dolphins and that
two other words in the paragraph tell more about dolphins—the dolphin is
not (a *fish*) and what kind of animal the dolphin is (a *mammal*). Underline
the words on the chart.

④ Suggested language: "All three of these words stand for a thing, an animal.
They are *nouns*. A noun is a word for a person, place, or thing. It may be a
word for an animal, which is living like a person. Listen to the next
paragraph and see if you can find another noun."

⑤ Read the final two sentences and underline nouns that children find. It is
not necessary to find every noun in the passage. If children suggest *they*,
recognize their thinking because they are considering the way the word
functions in the sentence. Ask children to think about who *they* might be
(*dolphins*). Tell children that *they* is a word that stands for the noun *dolphin*.
(You do not need to teach pronouns as a category at this time, yet you can
begin building the foundation for future learning.)

⑥ After several words are identified, repeat to children that these words stand
for a person, place, or thing. The name for this kind of word is *noun*.
Explain that a noun can stand for an animal, a substance (e.g., *water*), a
place (e.g., *school, playground, top, bottom*), or even something you cannot see
(e.g., *happiness*).

⑦ Tell children they will sort nouns on word cards into three categories: person, place, or thing. Some words will fit into more than one category. They will then list their sort on a Three-Way Sort Sheet and read it to a partner.

apply

read word
sort words
write words
read list

▸ Children read and sort noun word cards into categories *person, place, thing*.

▸ Then they list their completed sorts as on a Three-Way Sort Sheet and read their lists to a partner.

▸ They bring their sheets to sharing.

Name: Jamal   Three-Way Sort

person	place	thing
policeman grandfather brother aunt florist	country church market bedroom	water sailboat turnip table lamp truck

THREE-WAY SORT SHEET • 233

share

Children read their sort to a different partner.

Review the principle and invite small groups to name two or three more nouns for each category. Ask students to describe any words that presented difficult decisions.

Link

Interactive Read-Aloud: After reading aloud a text, ask the children to write one or two sentences and identify the nouns that tell them what the text is about. Here are a few suggested titles:

▶ *A Mink, a Fink, and a Skating Rink* by Brian P. Cleary

▶ *Mice and Beans* by Pam Munuz Ryan

Shared Reading: Find nouns in selections that children have shared. Highlight them with marker or highlighter tape.

Guided Reading: Have children find four or five nouns in the books they read. Have them tell if these nouns name a person, place, or thing (including an idea).

Guided/Independent Writing: Notice the nouns children use in their own writing. Encourage them to notice that every sentence has a noun.

assess

▶ Review children's writing to determine whether they understand the use of nouns.

▶ Notice whether children can easily identify what a sentence is about.

Expand the Learning

Repeat the lesson with a different text or a different set of word cards.

Connect with Home

Have the children take home a reproduced version of another text and mark nouns, then read them to a family member.

As an alternative, children can hunt for nouns in magazines and newspapers.

Learning about Nouns, Describing Words, Action Words

Three-Way Sort

Consider Your Children

Use this lesson after children have had extensive experience identifying words according to their function. It is not necessary for children to know the technical terms for the parts of speech or be able to identify every type of word in a sentence. If they can identify easy and obvious examples of each of the different types of words, then they are well on their way to learning the parts of speech and how they function.

Working with English Language Learners

English language learners can draw on their implicit knowledge of word functions in their native language. Once they understand the principles, they can begin to categorize words. It is not necessary for them to recognize explicitly the parts of speech while reading or writing. However, when children use categories of words, they enrich their writing and make it more interesting.

You Need

- ► Chart paper.
- ► Markers in three different colors.
- ► Sample text on chart.

  From *Teaching Resources:*
- ► Three-Way Sort Sheets.
- ► Lesson WM/V 19 Word Cards.

Understand the Principle

Children probably do not have formal knowledge of the parts of speech. Nonetheless, they are building implicit knowledge that they will use as a foundation for learning conventional grammar and when selecting words to make their writing more interesting. Word functions relate to comprehension of text, so it is important that children quickly and automatically use the syntactic structure of language when they read.

Explain the Principle

" Some words stand for a person, place or thing. They are called *nouns*. "

" Some words tell what a person, object, or animal does. They are called *action words* or *verbs*. "

" Some words describe a person, place, or thing. They are called *adjectives*. "

plan

Explain the Principle

" Some words stand for person, place or thing. They are called *nouns*. "

" Some words tell what a person, object, or animal does. They are called *action words* or *verbs*. "

" Some words describe a person, place, or thing. They are called *adjectives*. "

① Tell the children they will learn more about nouns (words that stand for people, places, and things), actions words, and describing words.

② Suggested language: "You have been working with different kinds of words and the way they work in sentences." Review the function of nouns, describing words *(adjectives)*, and action words *(verbs)*.

③ Read aloud the text you have written on chart paper. Have children quickly locate and circle in different colors (or otherwise indicate) the three categories of words in the selection. On a separate sheet, list the three categories of words in three columns.

④ Tell children they will sort nouns (words that name a person, place, or thing), describing words, and action words. Have them write key words *book, smooth, jump* across the top of a Three-Way Sort Sheet. Children draw one word card at a time, read it to themselves, and write the word in the correct column until they have sorted twenty words. Then they add two words of their own to each column. Children read their sorts to a partner.

> ### The Garden on Garden St.
> Everybody on our block really cares about the neighborhood. That's why we started the garden on Garden Street. It grows where an empty lot used to be. It used to look awful here.
>
> Before the garden, people left trash in the lot. You wouldn't believe the junk that piled up there: old car tires, broken bottles, old tables, chairs. Anything that people didn't want ended up on our block.

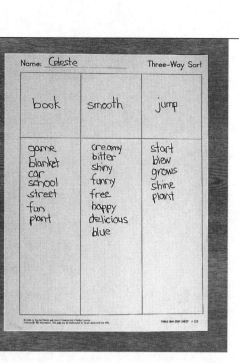

Name: Celeste — Three-Way Sort

book	smooth	jump
game	creamy	start
blanket	bitter	blew
car	shiny	grows
school	funny	shine
street	free	plant
fun	happy	
plant	delicious	
	blue	

write key word
read word
sort words
write word
add words
read list

▸ Have the children write key words
book, smooth, jump across the top of a
Three-Way Sort Sheet.

▸ They sort twenty word cards and
list each word in the correct
category. Some words may fit in
more than one category.

▸ Then they add two words of their
own to each category.

▸ Children read their sorts to a partner.

Invite the children to share some of the words they added to the three
categories. Have them name any words that fit in multiple categories. They
can use these words in sentences to show that the sentence context tells
you the function of a word. "I will plant a tomato plant!"

Link

Interactive Read-Aloud: After reading aloud a story, invite children to notice a particularly interesting or effective noun, action word, or describing word. Talk about why the author might have chosen this particular word. Here are a few suggested titles:

- ▸ *Merry-Go-Round: A Book About Nouns* by Ruth Heller
- ▸ *Delivery Van* by Betty Maestro

Shared Reading: Highlight any of the three categories of words in a piece of shared reading. Use highlighter tape or highlighter marker. On individual copies, children can mark nouns, verbs, and adjectives in different colors.

Guided Reading: Have children quickly locate any category of word in a book they are reading. Make a list on a whiteboard.

Guided/Independent Writing: Encourage the children to identify nouns, describing words, and action words in the pieces they write. Remind the children to vary these words to make their writing more interesting.

assess

- ▸ Observe the children's ability to identify how words function in sentences in books they read during guided reading.
- ▸ Observe the children's use of nouns, adjectives, and verbs in pieces they write.

Expand the Learning

Repeat this lesson with a variety of other words. Give the children Four-Box Sheets (see *Teaching Resources)* so they can draw and label four words in each category.

Create an interesting action word list that children can add to on a regular basis. Do the same for adjectives and nouns.

Connect with Home

Send home a Word Card Sheet for children to sort at home.

Have the children find five words for each category in their homes or neighborhoods and write them on a sheet of paper or in a Word Study or Writer's Notebook.

20 Exploring Words
Word Maps

Consider Your Children

Use this lesson after children have learned to make connections (see Lesson WSA 4) and can easily describe relations between words. This lesson helps children think more deeply about the relationships among words. You can use any book that you have read aloud. Repeat the lesson with a variety of words to develop vocabulary. The book *Visiting Day* by Jacqueline Woodson is used as the example in this lesson, but you should select any book with interesting language.

Working with English Language Learners

Talking about words and what they mean (with good examples) will help English language learners expand their speaking, reading, and writing vocabularies. Keep in mind that it may not be beneficial for English language learners to work with sophisticated or difficult words. Some students may need to use easier English words (*silly, crazy, glad*) in their Word Maps. Work with children in a small group after reading aloud a text several times. Have the children suggest words that are new to them that they would like to understand better.

You Need

► Chart paper.

► Markers.

► A read-aloud text or other shared reading text from which to generate words.

From *Teaching Resources*:

► Word Map Sheets.

Understand the Principle

Words are not learned as isolated items. Understanding words (and how to learn them) is enhanced as we weave meaning around individual words. Making connections quickly and automatically embeds word learning strategies into the reading children do as well as into their listening and conversing experiences. It is important that children learn to associate words and to go beyond simple definitions and synonyms to think about different ways words communicate meaning.

Explain the Principle

" You can make connections to help you to understand a word better. "

CONTINUUM: WORD MEANING/VOCABULARY — MAKING CONNECTIONS TO UNDERSTAND WORDS

plan

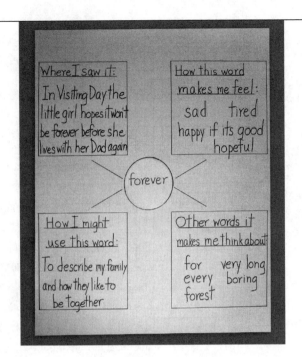

Explain the Principle

❝ You can make connections to help you to understand a word better. ❞

① Explain to children that they will learn to look at a word in different ways. Tell them that connecting words will help them use parts of words you know to read or write new words. Suggested language: "You already know how to make some connections between words. Today you will learn how to make new connections. You will make a Word Map." Write the focus word (*forever*) in the center of the chart paper. Divide the chart into four boxes. (You can vary the functions of these boxes as children become familiar with mapping words.)

② Suggested language: "I chose the word *forever* so I wrote it in the center of my chart. I liked that word because when we read *Visiting Day* I got the feeling that the little girl waited so long to see her father that it seemed like *forever*, a really long time. Her grandmother makes her feel hopeful when she says, 'It won't be *forever*.' In this box, we can write other words that we connect with *forever*. What are some other words *forever* makes you think of? You can think of several words or phrases, not just a single word." Write what children generate in the top left box.

③ Suggested language: "In this box, I'm going to write where I saw the word. I'm also going to write something about it." Demonstrate writing the book title and what the word meant in the book. Children may think of another context to add—there can be more than one.

④ Suggested language: "In this box, I'll write how the word makes me feel. It might be happy, sad, or scared." Demonstrate writing the connotations of the word; recognize that children may have very different responses to any given word.

⑤ Suggested language: "In my last box, I'm going to think of how I might use this word in my writing or when I talk. I can think of a sentence or describe how I might use it." Demonstrate, using children's suggestions.

6 "Today you will focus on another word from our book *Visiting Day*—*patiently*. Read the page from the book that has the word. Make a Word Map that looks at the word in four different ways. You can use parts of words you know to read or write new words. You can use what you know about words to read new words. Making many different connections will help you to understand a word better."

► Children use a Word Map Sheet to analyze *patiently*. They connect words in four different ways.

► Children can work alone or work with a partner to generate connections. Partners can encourage one another to look at the word in different ways.

► Finally, they read their maps to their partners.

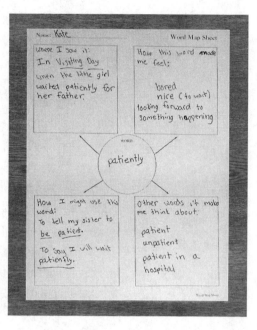

Children share their Word Map Sheets in groups of three or four. Find two or three sheets that show different perspectives. Chances are they will all mention *Visiting Day*, but will talk about it in different ways.

Share these different perspectives with the group. Emphasize that the purpose of a word map is not to get one answer but to think about the word in different ways. This will help children to be flexible in their thinking.

Link

Interactive Read-Aloud: Read books aloud that will introduce children to a rich range of vocabulary such as:

- ▶ *The Boat Alphabet Book* by Jerry Pollatta
- ▶ *Summer: An Alphabet Acrostic* by Steven Schnur

After reading, ask children if there were any words in the story they could use to make a word map.

Shared Reading: Find poems with unusual words and have children read them together. It may be interesting for them to discuss words that are used in a unique way in poetry, for example as metaphors.

Guided Reading: Help children notice new words that are interesting. You can discuss various perspectives on vocabulary.

Guided/Independent Writing: Help children remember the new words they have explored in reading and think about them. They may want to keep a page of interesting new words in their Writer's Notebooks or in their Writing Workshop folders.

assess

- ▶ Have the children turn in their Word Map Sheets. Examine them to notice the depth and breadth of their thinking.

- ▶ At the end of guided reading, ask the children to choose a word and tell you some connections either orally or in writing. This quick check will let you know whether they find it easy to think flexibly about words.

Expand the Learning

As a Writer's Notebook or Word Study Notebook exercise, children can search for and keep a list of interesting new words they want to use.

Repeat the lesson several times, allowing children to choose their own words for the Word Map. Work at this task until children quickly and automatically analyze words and make connections.

Placing a word in the center, create word maps with different categories such as
1. What is it?
2. What other words does it look like?
3. What does it remind you of?
4. When would you use it?

Connect with Home

Have the children take their Word Map Sheets home to share.

Have children take blank Word Web Sheets to use when they find interesting words in the books they take home for independent reading.

Recognizing and Using Metaphors and Similes
Making Comparisons

Consider Your Children

Use this lesson after children have had extensive experience listening to, reading, and collecting poems. Children will then have examples to bring to the lesson. In addition, they will have implicit knowledge of how comparisons are used to help readers form sensory images. The major task in this lesson is the oral discussion of poetry as a means of understanding how writers use words effectively to show comparison.

Working with English Language Learners

Figurative language (simile and metaphor) will probably challenge English language learners. The direct and implied comparisons make language interesting but also make it much more difficult to understand. Start with very simple comparisons. For example, use "like" to help them realize the comparisons. "Stars are like sparkling diamonds in the sky." Children are using comparisons and figures of speech in their native languages; these are valuable resources for you to use when helping them understand the principle. Explain and illustrate comparisons in as concrete a way as possible.

You Need

▸ Chart paper on which is copied the poem "December Leaves."

▸ Markers.

Understand the Principle

A beginning understanding of how comparison is used by writers is basic to helping children comprehend the literary language that they will meet in texts in grade three and beyond. Writers use figurative language such as similes (comparisons using *like* or *as*) or metaphors (comparisons without *like* or *as*) to help readers form sensory images.

Explain the Principle

" You can use words to compare things to make your writing more interesting. "

plan

"December Leaves"
by Kaye Starbird

The fallen leaves are cornflakes
That fill the lawn's wide dish,
And night and noon,
The wind's a spoon
That stirs them with a swish.

The sky's a silver sifter
A-sifting white and slow,
That gently shakes
On crisp brown flakes
The sugar known as snow.

Explain the Principle

" You can use words to compare things to make your writing more interesting. "

① Explain to the children that they will think about the language that makes poetry and stories interesting.

② Suggested language: "In the poems and stories we read, writers often use words that help us picture what they mean. They compare things. Sometimes they use *like* to help us see what they mean. If a writer says *the pond was like glass*, how does that help us see the pond?" You can use any comparison here that has meaning for children.

③ Have the children suggest words that describe the surface of the water, for example *like a mirror;* or *smooth as glass; glassy.*

④ Suggested language: "Writers use *like* or *as* to make comparisons—to show us how two things are alike—and they also compare things in other ways. Listen while I read this poem."

⑤ Read aloud "December Leaves." Ask children to think about the meaning of the poem. You may wish to read it two or three times while children think about it.

⑥ Suggested language: "There are some comparisons in this poem. When the poet writes 'fallen leaves are cornflakes,' she means that the leaves are *like* cornflakes. Do you think that brown leaves on the ground are a little bit like cornflakes?" Children respond. "She also writes 'the lawn is a dish.' She means that the lawn is *like* a dish or bowl that holds cornflakes. You can think about how cornflakes in a dish look and compare it to how fallen leaves look on a lawn."

⑦ Continue, helping the children compare the wind to a spoon stirring the leaves/cornflakes, the moon as a sifter, and the snow as sugar. You might need to explain the meaning of *sifter*.

⑧ Explain to the children that they will copy and illustrate the poem. There are four major comparisons in the poem. Children copy the poem on one side of the paper. They turn the paper over and choose one of the comparisons, fold a paper in half, and create the real image (fallen leaves on a lawn) on one side and the comparison image (cornflakes in a dish) on the other side.

copy poem
read poem
choose image
draw image
label image

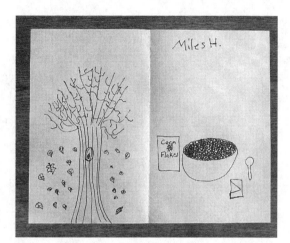

▶ Children copy the poem onto one side of a sheet of paper.

▶ They fold the paper in half.

▶ On the back, they draw two images—the realistic image and the comparison image.

▶ You may wish to have children label their drawings.

Go through the four comparisons in the poem and have children share their drawings.

Children can talk about what they were thinking as they created their drawings.

Link

Interactive Read-Aloud: Read aloud books that have good examples of figurative language. Allow time for discussion of the comparisons that children noticed. Here are two titles to consider.

- ▶ *My World of Color* by Margaret Wise Brown
- ▶ *Winter: An Alphabet Acrostic* by Steven Schnur

Shared Reading: Copy a selected page or paragraph from a book you have read to children that contains metaphor or simile. Have children read it in a shared way.

Guided Reading: In book introductions, have children locate and talk about figurative language. Prompt them to remember some language to share after reading.

Guided/Independent Writing: Encourage the children to experiment with figurative language in their own writing. At first, they can make comparisons using *like*, or *as* (simile), but guide them to make direct comparisons (metaphor), as in "December Leaves."

assess

- ▶ Examine the children's drawings to determine the extent to which they represent images.
- ▶ Do a quick check using some very simple comparisons. Read them to children and ask them to talk about what they mean. Listening to their conversation will give you a clearer understanding of how they are thinking about figurative language.

Expand the Learning

Repeat the lesson with other books that you read aloud to the children. After reading a story at least twice, have them identify the comparisons the author used to help them make mental pictures. In this way children learn how to write from analyzing the work of other writers and using them as mentors.

Begin a list of interesting figurative language on a chart.

Encourage the children to record interesting comparisons in their Writer's Notebook.

Connect with Home

Have the children take home their poems and drawings to share with family members.

Encourage the children to collect comparisons and figures of speech as they converse with their family members. This may prompt them to listen more carefully and to appreciate expressions that family members use.

Recognizing and Using Blended Words

Matching Words

Consider Your Children

Children already use many blended words in the oral vocabularies, but they probably do not realize that these words were created by combining words. Start with words they know (e.g., *brunch—breakfast* and *lunch*) so that they have a basis for understanding the principle. Some of the blended words are simple and others very sophisticated. You will want to select particular ones for the lesson.

Working with English Language Learners

English language learners have probably learned some blended words. Even if they know blended words and are using them well, it may be hard for them to understand the principle of this lesson because they may not know the component words that have been put together over time. You may not want to use this lesson if there are more important principles for your English language learners to understand. On the other hand, if you think the lesson is appropriate, discussing the idea of blended words may help them not only remember a particular word but learn the component words.

You Need

▸ Chart paper.

▸ Markers.

From *Teaching Resources*:

▸ Lesson WM/V 22 Word List.

▸ Two-Column Sheets.

Understand the Principle

Examining blended words will be interesting to children and will help them realize the constantly changing nature of language. The purpose for this lesson is not to help children learn particular words; in fact, many of these words are not frequent enough in written language to be useful. The great benefit, however, is that children will realize the creativity of English and learn to look below the surface of words they meet in reading or want to use in writing.

Explain the Principle

❝ Some words are made by blending together two words. The meaning of the blended word is related to both parts. ❞

plan

Blended Words

brunch = breakfast + lunch
clash = clap + crash
smash = smack + mash
smog = fog + smoke
splatter = splash + spatter
squiggle = squirm + wiggle
skylab = sky + laboratory

Explain the Principle

" Some words are made by blending together two words. The meaning of the blended word is related to both parts. "

① Explain to the children that they will look at some interesting words that have been made by blending or putting together two words. Children may bring up the idea of compound words. Explain that these are not compound words because they combine word parts rather than whole words.

② Suggested language: "This is one of my favorite words." Write *brunch* on the chart. "I like to eat brunch. Does anyone know what *brunch* is?" Children may respond that they have gone to brunch on a weekend morning.

③ Suggested language: "People usually eat brunch late in the morning. It is a meal that is both breakfast and lunch. Can you tell which two words were blended to make *brunch*?"

④ Children may say *breakfast* and *lunch*. Write *breakfast + lunch* on the chart and have one child highlight the parts of each word that are still in *brunch*. Ask them to talk about what they notice. They may comment that not much of each word is used but that you can still tell that the two words were blended.

⑤ Use the same approach to discuss several more words.

⑥ Tell the children that they are going to match blended words. Using a set of word cards that includes both blended words and the component words, children find the blended word and match it with two words that go together to make the blended word. Then they will write the blended word in the first column and the two words that make it in the second column. They will make ten blended words.

Name: Sasha

smog	smoke + fog
smash	smack + mash
clash	clap + crash
horrific	horrible + terrific
brunch	breakfast + lunch
splatter	splash + spatter
squiggle	squirm + wiggle
o'clock	of the clock
skylab	sky + laboratory
motel	motor + hotel

© 2002 by Gay Su Pinnell and Irene C. Fountas from Phonics Lessons.
Portsmouth, NH: Heinemann. This page may be photocopied for single classroom use only.

TWO-COLUMN SHEET • 231

apply

find words
match parts
write list

▶ Have the children read and match ten blended words to their component words.

▶ Then they record all the words on a Two-Column Sheet.

▶ They bring their sheets to sharing.

share

Children go around the circle, sharing one blended word and its two component parts.

For fun, have the children make up their own blended words.

Children can talk about how contractions and blended words are alike and different. For example, contractions are verbs and use an apostrophe to replace the letters. Blended words do not usually have an apostrophe. The full word form and the contraction are mutually interchangeable, which is not always true for blended words.

Link

Interactive Read-Aloud: Read aloud selections that illustrate blended words. Have the children generate the component words. Here are some titles to consider.

- *Jump Rope Magic* by Afi-Odelia Scruggs
- *Dig, Wait, Listen* by April Pulley-Sayre

Shared Reading: Have the children read the list of blended words and component words together. Add more words to the chart as children notice them.

Guided Reading: After the children read a text, point out any blended words. Have the children talk about how the author uses these words to make writing more interesting to readers. Add them to the collection.

Guided/Independent Writing: When the children use blended words, point them out and ask the children to share them with the class.

assess

- Look at children's blended words to check whether they have accurately listed the component words.
- Notice the children's awareness of blended words as they encounter them throughout the day.

Expand the Learning

Engage the children in a conversation about the difference between compound words and blended words. There are many more compound words, although we may not actually know some blended words because they have a long history of use.

Repeat the lesson with a different variety of blended words.

Connect with Home

Children can take home their lists of blended words to read to family members.

Many family members will not realize that blended words were originally made from combining two words. This provides children the opportunity to be word "experts" for their families.

Recognizing and Using Words That Mimic Real Sounds

Labeling

Consider Your Children

Use this lesson after children have extensive experience listening to poetry and reading it for themselves. We recommend that you teach this lesson mid-year after children have collected their own poems in poetry anthologies and have explored many poetry books. In this lesson children will learn about words that have a special effect in that they mimic actual sounds.

Working with English Language Learners

English language learners will enjoy saying English words that mimic sounds. They also have such words in their own language. Have children offer examples once they understand the principle. Children can compare (for example, the sound a kitten makes) in the two languages. They may notice some important similarities. Be sure that the sounds being mimicked are within children's ability to comprehend (for example, animals they know or sounds they have heard and can identify). Use sound effects when appropriate and help children compare the real sound with the sound of the word.

You Need

▶ Collection of poems.

▶ Chart paper.

▶ Markers.

▶ Poetry Notebooks.

From *Teaching Resources:*

▶ Category Word Cards, Onomatopoetic Words.

Understand the Principle

This lesson helps children create a category for and examples of *onomatopoetic* words that sound like what they mean. It is not necessary to teach children to say this difficult word. The purpose of this lesson is to help children become more sensitive to words by examining a very easy-to-detect use of language. This sensitivity is a step towards noticing other literary devices that make language descriptive and poetic.

Explain the Principle

" Some words mimic the sounds they represent. You often see these words in books and poetry. "

plan

Words that Mimic Real Sounds

splishes

sploshes

buzz

crash

wham

click

quack

"Slip on Your Raincoat"

Slip on your raincoat,

Pull on your galoshes;

Wading in puddles

Makes splishes and

sploshes

splosh   splish

Explain the Principle

" **Some words mimic the sounds they represent. You often see these words in books and poetry.** "

① Explain to the children that they will learn about words that mimic or "sound like" some real sounds that we hear.

② Read aloud "Slip on Your Raincoat." Ask children to identify some words in the poem that sound like real sounds. They will mention *splishes* and *sploshes*.

③ Show your drawing of the poem with the onomatopoetic words as "sound effects."

④ On another sheet of chart paper, start a list of words that mimic real sounds. Children can think of more words from poems they know or that they have experienced.

⑤ Read several more poems that you have selected from any poetry book, each time having children identify words that mimic sounds. They can decide whether to add the words to the chart.

⑥ Ask children to talk about how words like these make poetry more interesting and enjoyable. Suggested language: "Have you used words like these in your own writing?" Children can talk about words they have used to describe sounds. Stretch their thinking to include such words as *bark*, *cluck*, *quack*, *knock* that they might not think about as easily as *buzz* or *wham*.

⑦ Suggested language: "Today, you will find poems with words that mimic real sounds. Find a poem that has at least one of these words and copy it into your personal poetry notebook. Remember to copy the poem exactly the way it is in the book—with lines and spaces. After you copy the poem, illustrate it. You may want add labels with 'sound effects' like I did." If children do not have personal poetry books, they can copy it onto the bottom half of a sheet of paper.

apply

read poems
choose poem
copy poem
illustrate poem
label sound words

▸ Children look through a collection of poetry books or selected poems and find a poem with words that mimic sounds.

▸ They copy the poem into their personal poetry books or on the bottom half of a sheet of paper.

▸ They illustrate the poem, adding labels to their pictures for "sound effects."

> The Rain
>
> Splish, splash
> splish, splash
> Drip, drop
> Drip, drop
> Will the rain ever stop?

share

Have the children share their selected and illustrated poems to bring to sharing in small groups.

After sharing, have the children suggest some more words to add to the chart.

Link

Interactive Read-Aloud: Read aloud books that have words that mimic real sounds. After reading, children can identify words and add them to the chart. A few examples are:

- ▸ *Alphabeep* by Deborah Pearson
- ▸ *The River* by Nik Pollard

Shared Reading: Have the children read poems with words that mimic sounds. Instead of saying the words, have children make the actual sounds, using their voices or sound effects.

Guided Reading: Point out words that mimic sounds in the texts children are reading. Talk about how they make the writing interesting.

Guided/Independent Writing: Encourage children to use words that mimic sounds to make their own writing more interesting.

assess

- ▸ Examine the poems children have copied, as well as their illustrations and labels.

- ▸ You may want to have individual children read their poems and then highlight or frame the words that mimic sounds.

Expand the Learning

Repeat the lesson using another poem that can also be sung to the tune of "Are You Sleeping?"

"I Hear Thunder"
I hear thunder, I hear thunder,
Hark don't you? Hark don't you?
Pitter patter raindrops, pitter patter raindrops,
I'm wet through, so are you!

Keep adding to the chart of words that mimic sounds.

Encourage the children to write interesting words that mimic sounds on one page of their Writer's Notebooks.

You can use this lesson structure to help children become more aware of "describing words."

Connect with Home

Children can take home the poems they have copied and illustrated.

Encourage them to be on the lookout for more words that mimic sounds.

Word Structure

Looking at the structure of words will help students learn how words are related to each other and how they can be changed by adding letters, letter clusters, and larger word parts. Being able to recognize syllables, for example, helps readers and writers break down words into smaller units that are easier to analyze.

Words often have affixes, parts added before or after a word to change its meaning. An affix can be a prefix or a suffix. The word to which affixes are added can be a *base* word or a *root* word. A base word is a complete word; a root word is a part that may have Greek or Latin origins (such as *phon* in telephone). It will not be necessary for young children to make this distinction when they are beginning to learn simple affixes, but working with suffixes and prefixes will help children read and understand words that use them as well as use affixes accurately in writing.

Endings or word parts that are added to base words signal meaning. For example, they may signal relationships (*prettier, prettiest*) or time (*running, planted*). Principles related to word structure include understanding the meaning and structure of compound words, contractions, plurals, and possessives as well as knowing how to make and use them accurately. We have also included the simple abbreviations that students often see in the books they read and want to use in their writing.

Connect to Assessment

See related WS Assessment Tasks in the Assessment Guide in *Teaching Resources:*

▸ Recognizing Syllables in Words

▸ Writing Syllables in Words

▸ Understanding and Forming Contractions

▸ Recognizing Compound Words

▸ Forming Plurals

▸ Reading Words with Suffixes

▸ Recognizing and Using Verbs with Endings to Denote Tense

Develop Your Professional Understanding

See *Word Matters: Teaching Phonics and Spelling in the Reading/Writing Classroom* by G.S. Pinnell and I. C. Fountas. 1998 Portsmouth, NH: Heinemann.

Related pages: 80, 95–99, 120–121, 154–162

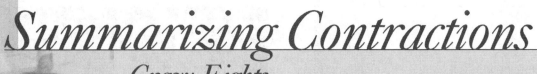

Summarizing Contractions
Crazy Eights

Consider Your Children

Be sure that children have good control of each group of contractions (those with *is, will, are, not, have, would,* and *had*) prior to this lesson. To make the experience less challenging you can eliminate the last one or two categories. (The most challenging categories are those made with *would, had,* and *have.*) If children have not learned how to play Crazy Eights, then demonstrate how the game is played. If they already know the game, only a quick review is necessary.

Working with English Language Learners

It is important for English language learners to hear contractions used in sentences so they have a meaningful context for these words. Children can gain control of the easier contractions and thereby learn to understand the concept. You may wish to be selective about the contractions used in this lesson. The summary chart will organize their knowledge and provide a useful reference.

You Need

▶ Chart paper.

▶ Markers.

From *Teaching Resources:*

▶ Pocket Chart Card Template.

▶ Directions for Crazy Eights.

▶ Crazy Eight Game Cards made from Lesson WS1 Word Cards and Deck Card Template.

▶ Four-Box Sheets.

Understand the Principle

When two words are put together in a shortened form, one or more letters is left out and an apostrophe is put in. This shortened, or contracted, form is called a *contraction.* Contractions appear frequently in oral and written language. *Is* can be used with the names of people, places, or objects (e.g., *Peter's sick today. The candle's flickering in the wind.*) An *'s* can represent *is* or *has.* An *'d* means *would* or *had,* showing a difference in meaning.

Explain the Principle

" To make a contraction, put two words together and leave out a letter or letters. "

" Write an apostrophe where the letter(s) are left out. "

WS 1
WORD STRUCTURE

plan

Explain the Principle

" To make a contraction, put two words together and leave out a letter or letters. "

" Write an apostrophe where the letter(s) are left out. "

① Tell the children that today you will review words that are put together to form contractions.

② Write *are, have, will, not, is,* and *had* and *would* at the top of six columns on chart paper. Show enlarged word cards with the two words to be joined (*they, had*) and ask children to give its contraction (*they'd*). Write the contraction in the corresponding column. Repeat with several other examples until children have had sufficient practice thinking about words that form contractions. Some of the same contractions will fit the columns for *had* or *would.*

③ Comparing the contraction to the possessive when using a name may spark quite a discussion. ("This is Tom's bike." "Tom's riding his bike.") Point out that this kind of contraction is frequently used when we talk but is not used very often in writing, except to make dialogue sound real.

④ Tell the children they will play Crazy Eights with words that are contractions. If children are new to Crazy Eights or have not played it recently, demonstrate the game with two players.

⑤ Have the children choose four contraction base words and write three to five contractions made with each word on a Four-Box Sheet.

apply

read word
match word
put card down
write contractions

▸ In pairs or small groups, the children play Crazy Eights with contraction word cards.

▸ Players discard cards from their hands that show a contraction made with the same word as the card facing up (*are*, *have*, *will*, *not*, *is*, *had* or *would*). The first player to discard all her cards wins the game.

▸ Then children write three to six contractions made with four of the words on a Four-Box Sheet.

▸ Tell the children they will only be able to write three examples with *are*, because you want them to try the harder contractions and encourage them to have a good variety.

Name: Kyle

they're we're you're	it'll we'll you'll she'll
here's there's it's he's she's	I'd he'd she'd they'd

share

Have the children read their word lists to a partner. Add new examples to the class chart as they come up, so the chart can serve as a comprehensive resource for the class.

Link

Interactive Read-Aloud: Read aloud a variety of books that include contractions. Then write two or three of the contractions on a chart. Here are a few suggested titles:

▶ *Chicken Soup by Heart* by Esther Hershenhorn

▶ *Beautiful Blackbird* by Ashley Bryan

Shared Reading: Have children locate and highlight contractions in familiar texts on a transparency.

Guided Reading: After reading and discussing a text, have the children locate several contractions and tell the two words that form it.

Guided/Independent Writing: Have the children refer to the summary chart to check the spelling of contractions in their writing.

assess

▶ Dictate two words that make a contraction using *is, will, are, not, have,* and *would,* or *had* to assess children's control.

▶ Notice how children spell contractions in their writing to determine the need to repeat the lesson or focus on a particular contraction group.

Expand the Learning

Have the children play Crazy Eights several times for additional practice. Use a different variety of contractions.

Have the children do a Three- or Four-Way Sort with word cards for four or five of the contraction groups represented (see *Teaching Resources*).

Connect with Home

Have children take home word cards and play Crazy Eights with family members. You can send the sheets of words on the Deck Card Template for children to cut and make their card decks.

Recognizing Syllables in Words with Double Consonants

Checkers

Consider Your Children

This lesson involves two-syllable words with double consonants in the middle. Children should have strong control of basic phonogram patterns so they can notice and use word parts in longer words. Children will learn where syllables divide so that they can use the knowledge as readers and writers. You can create checkerboards with a different variety of words for the pairs of players to use.

Working with English Language Learners

English language learners may still be acquiring knowledge of the patterns of English one-syllable words, but encountering multisyllable words with double consonants in texts they are expected to read. They need to learn how to take apart these longer words and to use components in solving them. Say each word clearly and have children repeat it several times while looking at its visual representation. At first, limit the examples to those words that children can say easily. Be sure they know the meaning of the words. If you know examples of multisyllable words in children's home languages, point out that this kind of word appears in many different languages. Reinforce this principle during word work.

You Need

▶ Pocket chart.

▶ Checkers or black and red discs.

From *Teaching Resources:*

▶ Pocket Chart Card Template.

▶ Checkerboard Template.

▶ Directions for Checkers.

▶ Lesson WS 2 Word List.

Understand the Principle

A *syllable* is a word part or unit of pronunciation that helps readers and writers use parts larger than individual letters. Children can use word parts to take apart or write longer words. Many two-syllable words have two consonants in the middle. In this lesson the two consonants are the same letter (e.g., *better*). When children learn that they can divide a word between its two consonants, they can solve two-syllable words more easily.

Explain the Principle

" Divide the syllables between the consonants when a word has two similar consonants in the middle (*run-ning, bet-ter*). "

plan

Explain the Principle

" Divide the syllables between the consonants when a word has two similar consonants in the middle (*run-ning, bet-ter*). "

① Explain to the children that you will help them think about parts of words.

② Display *kit-ten* on a large word card that you have cut in the middle and placed in the pocket chart. Ask children to read the word. Repeat with *pepper, sudden, suggest,* and *cottage*. Invite the children to tell what they notice about all the words.

③ Suggested language: "You noticed that each word has two syllables with the same two consonants in the middle. When a word has two of the same consonants in the middle, you can divide the syllables between the consonants." Ask children to suggest several other examples and add them to the chart.

④ Demonstrate how to play Checkers with a pair of volunteers. Remind the children that they need to say the two parts and the whole word each time.

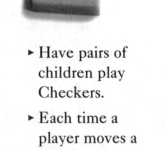

apply

move piece
read word
read word

▸ Have pairs of children play Checkers.

▸ Each time a player moves a checker into a white square, he reads the word in two parts and then reads (e.g, *beg-gar, beggar*) the whole word.

share

Invite the children to suggest more examples and add them to the chart.

Place a piece of chart paper in a convenient location and challenge students to find and list one hundred double consonant words over the next few weeks.

Link

Interactive Read-Aloud: Read aloud a variety of books that have two syllable words with double consonants. Here are a few suggested titles:

▸ *Talking Like the Rain* by X. J. Kennedy

▸ *Fables* by Arnold Lobel

Shared Reading: After several readings of a poem, have children clap the syllables of two or three words with double consonants.

Guided Reading: On a whiteboard, write four to six two-syllable words for children to read quickly.

Guided/Independent Writing: Have children notice and check the spelling of two-syllable words as they edit their writing.

assess

▸ Dictate four to six words with double consonants in the middle.

▸ Have children read a few words with double consonants in the middle and notice how easily they read them.

Expand the Learning

Have the children play Checkers several times with different checkerboards.

Small groups of children can play the game Concentration (see *Teaching Resources*) with one syllable of a word on one card and the other syllable on a second card. Players put together two syllables to make a real word.

Connect with Home

Send home a Checkerboard or Concentration game card deck for children to play with a family member.

As an alternative, children can make their own checkerboards or card decks to share with family members.

Recognizing Words with Open Syllables

Word Plot

Consider Your Children

In word structure lessons, children are beginning to systematize their knowledge of the six common syllable patterns in multisyllable words that are very useful to readers and writers. In this lesson children focus on syllables that end in a vowel. Be sure to use words the children have in their oral vocabularies and have worked with syllables so that they can quickly and automatically have the breaks in a multisyllable word.

Working with English Language Learners

Words in all languages have syllables, so English language learners will have the same implicit awareness of these word parts as native speakers. Have them practice on one-syllable words that they understand until they can hear the difference between long and short sounds of vowels. Be sure that they know the difference between consonants and vowels. For multisyllable words, use easy examples and check to see if children understand the words.

You Need

▶ Chart paper.

▶ Markers.

▶ Dice (one with A, B, C, D, E, and Free Choice; one with 1, 2, 3, 4, 5, and Free Choice)

▶ Index cards.

From *Teaching Resources:*

▶ Directions for Word Plot.

▶ Word Plot Sheets.

▶ Lesson WS 3 Word List.

Understand the Principle

A *syllable* is a word part or a unit of pronunciation. Children need to understand the concept of a syllable as a unit of pronunciation with *one* vowel sound. Children can notice and use the syllable patterns to help them read and write words. When children pronounce an open syllable, the vowel sound is long and their mouths are open at the end. When they read unfamiliar words with a single consonant in the middle, they can try to pronounce the word with the first vowel short (as a closed syllable) or with the first vowel long (as an open syllable). Each principle works about half the time.

Explain the Principle

❝ When a syllable ends with a vowel, the vowel sound is usually long (*ho-tel*). ❞

CONTINUUM: WORD STRUCTURE — RECOGNIZING AND USING SYLLABLES ENDING IN A VOWEL (OPEN SYLLABLE)

plan

**When a syllable ends with a
vowel, the vowel sound is
usually long.**

go	music
no	photo
hi	pilot
me	open
	recent

① Tell the children you will help
them notice more about word
parts.

② Write *go, no, hi* and *me* on the
chart and ask children to read
the words. Help them notice
that when they pronounce each
word their mouths are open at
the end. Ask them to describe
the vowel sound. (It is long.)

③ Write *music, photo, pilot, open, recent* on the chart. Ask children to read each
word and think about its syllables. Explain that every syllable has one vowel
sound. Children will notice that each first syllable ends with a long vowel
sound. Explain that it is called an *open syllable.* Demonstrate how your
mouth is open at the end when you pronounce it.

④ Summarize the understanding. Suggested language: "When a syllable ends
with a vowel, the vowel sound is usually long." Write this principle at the
top of the chart.

⑤ Demonstrate the Word Plot game with two players. Each player has a Word
Plot Sheet. In turn, each player tosses the dice, revealing one letter and one
number (e.g., A and 4). The player finds that row and column, (e.g., Row A,
Column 4) reads the word in the space, and then tells the two syllables
(e.g., *program, pro-gram*). If FREE appears on a roll, the player can choose
any word in that row or column. Each time a player reads the word and its
syllables correctly, he crosses out the word on his Word Plot Sheet. The first
player to cross out all the words wins the game.

⑥ Have children write two words in syllables on an index card and bring it to
group share.

apply

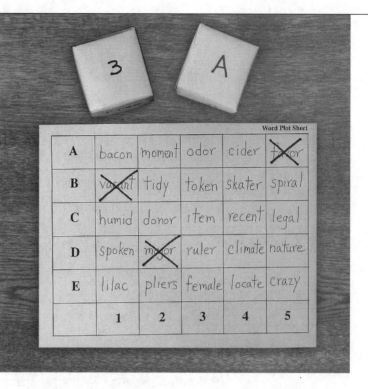

Word Plot Sheet

	1	2	3	4	5
A	bacon	moment	odor	cider	~~favor~~
B	~~vacant~~	tidy	token	skater	spiral
C	humid	donor	item	recent	legal
D	spoken	~~major~~	ruler	climate	nature
E	lilac	pliers	female	locate	crazy

roll die
find word
say word
cross out word
write words

► Have children play Word Plot in groups of two to four.

► Then they write two words in syllables on an index card.

► They bring their cards to group share.

share

Have each child read one word in parts as you list them on the chart.

Encourage the children to think about the way they usually pronounce words. Seek some clear examples that they understand. Ultimately, they will rely on this implicit knowledge when breaking down words. Today, skill at hyphenating words is not so important in writing because of word processing tools; however, students will meet hyphenated words while reading and will also need awareness of syllables to take words apart to solve them.

Link

Interactive Read-Aloud: Read aloud a variety of books that include multisyllable words. Following the reading, have children clap two or three words with open syllables. Here are a few suggested titles:

- ▸ *Take Me Out of the Bathtub* by Alan Katz
- ▸ *Sun Song* by Jean Marzallo

Shared Reading: Read poems that are on a transparency. Invite children to highlight two or three words with open syllables.

Guided Reading: When children come to an unknown word with an open syllable, teach them how to cover the last part and focus on the open syllable.

Guided/Independent Writing: As children edit for spelling, they should notice that words with an open syllable have a single consonant in the middle.

assess

- ▸ Have the children read four to six words with open and closed syllables.
- ▸ Dictate three to five words with open and closed syllables to see children's control of syllables in writing.

Expand the Learning

Construct Word Plot Sheets with a different variety of open syllable words.

Have the children play Follow the Path with words that have open syllables (see *Teaching Resources*).

Connect with Home

Send home Word Plot Sheets and a set of dice so children can play the game with family members.

Recognizing Words with Closed Syllables

Taking Words Apart

Consider Your Children

This lesson should follow Lesson WS 3, since it introduces the second common syllable pattern in multisyllable words. Children need to understand the concept of a syllable and know that every syllable contains one vowel sound. Be sure to use words that children understand. They should know how to try pronouncing the word with the first vowel short (as a closed syllable) or with the first vowel long (as an open syllable). Since each principle works about half the time, this process is helping them narrow the choices.

Working with English Language Learners

If you know something about the language a student speaks, use words in that language to illustrate the concept of syllable and be sure they understand it and can hear and clap word breaks. If needed, demonstrate closed syllables in simple words first (*black, red*). Help children be conscious of the shape of their mouths as they say the syllables. Use words they understand. Show them the spelling with syllables marked.

You Need

▶ Chart paper.

▶ Marker.

From *Teaching Resources:*

▶ List Sheets.

▶ Lesson WS 4 Word Cards.

Understand the Principle

Open syllables (those ending with a vowel) and closed syllables (those ending with a consonant) are common syllable patterns in words. When children pronounce a syllable that is open, the mouth is open at the end; when they pronounce a closed syllable the mouth is closed. A closed syllable can be a vowel followed by a single consonant (e.g., *robin*), a vowel followed by two of the same consonants (e.g., *button*), a vowel followed by two different consonants (e.g., *window*), or a vowel followed by three different consonants (e.g., *complain*) pattern. The second syllable can begin with a vowel (e.g., *lem-on*) or a consonant (e.g., *wel-come*). The final consonant sound in a closed syllable can be a cluster (e.g., *kitch-en*). By dividing multisyllable words, children learn more about word structure.

Explain the Principle

" When a syllable ends with a vowel and at least one consonant, the vowel sound is usually short (*lem-on*). "

CONTINUUM: WORD STRUCTURE — RECOGNIZING AND USING SYLLABLES ENDING IN A VOWEL AND AT LEAST ONE CONSONANT (CLOSED SYLLABLE)

plan

Explain the Principle

" When a syllable ends with a vowel and at least one consonant, the vowel sound is usually short (*lem-on*). "

When the first syllable ends with a single consonant, it usually has a short vowel sound.

robin	rob-in
panic	pan-ic
cabin	cab-in

① Tell the children they will learn more about syllables in words. Write *robin, panic, cabin* on the left side of the chart.

② Suggested language: "Read these words with me and help me think about the syllable parts you hear." Read each word and have children tell the first syllable they hear. Rewrite the word to show the syllable division (e.g., *rob-in*).

③ Suggested language: "What do you notice about the syllables?" Children will notice that there are two syllables, each has a vowel, and the first syllable ends with a consonant. Prompt them to identify the sound of the first vowel and conclude that it is short. Explain that when the first syllable ends with at least one consonant, it usually has a short vowel sound. Write the principle at the top of the chart.

④ Explain that when children try to read a new word, they should look at its syllables. If they see one consonant in the middle of a word, they can divide the word after the first consonant (creating a closed syllable) and try the short sound to see if it sounds right. (Here they will be using their own oral language knowledge of a word to check their reading.)

⑤ Tell the children they will read twenty word cards and cut apart the syllables.

cam el	at om	liz ard
pun ish	clev er	rap id
riv er	pet al	shiv er
sad den	prop er	com et
shad ow	fig ure	prod uct
en gine	mod ern	den tist
rab bit	pump kin	

Name: Jeanne

1. cam-el
2. at-om
3. liz-ard
4. pun-ish
5. clev-er
6. rap-id
7. riv-er
8. pet-al
9. shiv-er
10. sad-den
11. prop-er
12. com-et
13. shad-ow
14. fig-ure
15. prod-uct
16. eng-ine
17. mod-ern
18. dent-ist
19. rab-bit
20. pump-kin

LIST SHEET

take card
read word
cut syllables
write list

▸ Demonstrate how to cut a word card to show separate syllables.

▸ Children take a word card, read it, and cut it into two syllables.

▸ Then they write the divided word on a List Sheet or in their Word Study Notebooks.

▸ They repeat this process for twenty words.

Invite a few children to share their words and demonstrate separating a few words into syllables. Review the concept of a closed syllable.

WS 4
WORD STRUCTURE

Link

Interactive Read-Aloud: Read aloud books that have multisyllable words. After reading, have children look at two or three words with closed syllables on a whiteboard.

- ▸ *My House Is Singing* by Betsy Rosenthal
- ▸ *Where the Big Fish Are* by Jonathan London

Shared Reading: After reading a poem, point out two or three words with closed syllables.

Guided Reading: When children come upon unknown words, show them how to focus on the first syllable as closed or open.

Guided/Independent Writing: When children write new words, have them think about whether the first syllable is open or closed.

assess

- ▸ Dictate four to six words with closed first syllables (or a mix of closed and open) and have children write them.
- ▸ Observe how easily children take apart words that have closed first syllables.

Expand the Learning

Repeat this lesson with a different set of words with closed syllables.

As an alternative, create a page of words (Word Card Template) with a mix of closed and open syllables using Lesson WS3 Word List and WS4 Word Cards.

Have children play Lotto with words that have closed first syllables (see *Teaching Resources*).

Have children play Word Plot with words that have open and closed syllables (see *Teaching Resources*).

Connect with Home

Send home a set of word cards with closed syllables for children to cut apart into syllables. They can glue them on a sheet and bring them to school to share.

Recognizing Syllables in Words with a Silent e Pattern

Syllable Lotto

Consider Your Children

Children should have good control of the silent e pattern in single syllable words. This lesson should follow those on open and closed syllables (Lessons WS 3 and WS 4) since it focuses on a third basic syllable pattern (vowel, consonant silent e) that is found in multisyllable words. Teach children how to play Syllable Lotto if they have not played Lotto before. Be sure to choose words that children understand.

Working with English Language Learners

English language learners may be familiar with a language that has very few silent letters. It will be helpful for them to understand that in English, some letters in a word may not be associated with an audible sound. Seeing silent letters as part of a commonly occurring pattern will turn their attention to other aspects of words. They will be able to understand that looking for these larger patterns will help them solve words and that these patterns exist both in simple words and in multisyllable words. Use easy examples in the beginning; review all the words in the Lotto game before children play it; be sure children can say each word on the card.

You Need

► Chart paper.

► Markers.

► Die or block with sides: a-e, e-e, o-e, i-e, u-e, Free.

► Game markers.

From *Teaching Resources:*

► Directions for Lotto.

► Four-by-Four Lotto Game Boards.

► Lesson WS 5 Word List.

Understand the Principle

Many single-syllable words have a vowel-consonant-silent e pattern (e.g., *home, name*). In this lesson children learn how to notice this VC*e* pattern in words with two syllables. The pattern can form the first syllable (e.g., hope*less*) or second syllable (e.g., *com*pete). The vowel-consonant-silent e pattern is one of several common patterns that are helpful in solving multisyllable words.

Explain the Principle

❝ When a vowel and a silent e are in a word, the pattern makes one syllable with a long vowel sound (*hope-ful*). ❞

plan

Explain the Principle

" When a vowel and a silent *e* are in a word, the pattern makes one syllable with a long vowel sound (*hope-ful*). "

① Tell the children you will help them learn more about syllables in words.

② Write *name, home, line, cute, Pete* (or another name) on a chart. Invite children to read the words and tell what they notice. Guide them to conclude that each word has one syllable that consists of a long vowel sound and a silent *e* (VC*e* pattern).

③ Now write *hopeful, refuse, decide, fireman, amaze,* and *prepare* on the chart and have children read each word, listening for its parts.

④ Help children notice that each word has two syllables and that there is a vowel, consonant, and silent *e* pattern in each word. Have a child underline the pattern each time. Point out that this pattern can be in the first part of the word (e.g., hope*ful*) or the last part (e.g., *pre*pare).

⑤ Tell the children they will read words with a vowel-consonant-silent *e* pattern as they play Syllable Lotto. Demonstrate the game with two players if needed.

name   home   line
cute   Pete

hopeful   refuse   decide

fireman   amaze   prepare

roll die
find word
read word
cover word
write two words

▶ Have the children play Syllable Lotto with two-syllable words that have a VC*e* pattern.

▶ In turn, each player tosses the die. Each side of the die has a pattern, such as *a-e*. The player looks on his card for a word with that vowel pattern (e.g., *be*-have, *pa*-rade*)*, says the word aloud, and covers it with a marker. If the player rolls a "Free," he can mark any space and read the word.

▶ The first player to cover all the squares on his card wins the game.

▶ After playing Syllable Lotto, the children write two examples of words that have a syllable with a long vowel sound and a silent *e* in a Word Study Notebook or on an index card.

Invite the children to share one new word with the VC*e* pattern as you add it to the chart.

Link

Interactive Read-Aloud: Read aloud books that have two-syllable words with a VC*e* pattern. Point out two or three words after reading. Here are a few suggested titles:

- ▸ *Little Dog Poems* by Kristine O'Connell George
- ▸ *City Dog* by Karla Kuskin

Shared Reading: On the first reading of a text, cover the VC*e* pattern in a word and invite volunteers to spell it.

Guided Reading: Prompt the children to look at syllable patterns to take apart words quickly.

Guided/Independent Writing: Encourage children to check spelling by saying the word and thinking about its syllable patterns.

assess

- ▸ Dictate three to five words with a VC*e* pattern. Notice whether students quickly write word parts.
- ▸ Notice how easily children take apart multisyllable words when reading a text.

Expand the Learning

Repeat this lesson with a different variety of words.

Have children complete a Four-Way Sort with words that have four of the vowels in the VC*e* pattern (see *Teaching Resources*).

Connect with Home

Send home the Lotto game for children to play with family members. Children can make their own die to take home. As an alternative, they can write the patterns on word cards, and put them in a bag or container. They can then choose one card per turn (replacing their pattern card to the container before the next player's turn).

Send home word cards for children to sort according to the vowel they hear in the VC*e* pattern.

Recognizing Parts in Compound Words

Compound Rummy

Consider Your Children

By this time, children will have a strong understanding of compound words as a principle and will be able to quickly call up many examples. In this lesson they develop flexibility using parts of words that appear in several different compound words. They get a lot of practice with multisyllable, compound words.

Working with English Language Learners

The meaning of compound words may be confusing for English language learners, especially when the compound word does not clearly reflect the meaning of its component parts (e.g., *butterfly*). Help children understand the meaning of compound words by identifying and isolating the component parts. Have them say the words and build examples with magnetic letters or cut-up word cards. Stay with words they have some familiarity with at first.

You Need

► Chart paper.
► Markers.

From *Teaching Resources:*

► Pocket Chart Card Template.
► Directions for Rummy.
► Rummy Game Cards made from Category Word Cards, Compound Words and Deck Card Template (make 52 cards from 26 pairs of compound words with the same base word).

Understand the Principle

A compound word is made of two smaller words. Often its meaning can be derived from the meaning of the words that comprise it, though there are exceptions. When a compound word is divided, each of the two word parts represents a whole word. The ability to notice and use component parts to quickly derive the meaning of compound words increases reading efficiency.

Explain the Principle

" You see some words often in compound words. "

" You can make connections among compound words that have the same word parts. "

plan

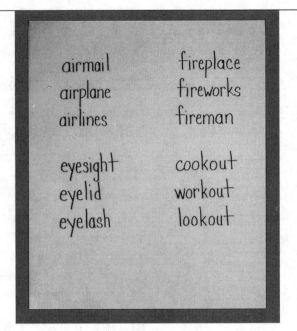

airmail   fireplace
airplane   fireworks
airlines   fireman

eyesight   cookout
eyelid   workout
eyelash   lookout

Explain the Principle

❝ You see some words often in compound words. ❞

❝ You can make connections among compound words that have the same word parts. ❞

① Tell the children they will learn more about a special type of word. Have *airmail, airplane, airlines, fireplace, fireworks, fireman* written on chart paper.

② Ask children to read the words and tell what they notice. Help them conclude that each word is a compound word made of two whole words and that some compound words have the same word parts.

③ Review other compound word families *(eye-, -out)*. Explain that some words appear often in many different compound words. You can look for the same part in some compound words and you can use it to connect words.

④ Summarize the lesson. Suggested language: "You see some words often in compound words. You can make connections among compound words that have the same word parts."

⑤ Explain that they will play Compound Rummy. Demonstrate the game with two players.

▸ The object of the game is to discard all cards and have the most pairs. Pairs are made when two compound words have the same word part.

▸ The dealer (one player) gives each player ten cards and the remaining deck is placed on the table face up. The top card in the pile is placed face up next to the deck. If any players have a pair, they read the pair and place the cards face up in front of them as a pair.

▸ The player to the left of the dealer takes a card from the deck or the one on top of the discard pile (which is face up), reads it, checks her hand for a pair, and lays it down.

▸ The player then must discard a card from her hand. If a player opts to take the top card from the discard pile, all the cards below it are also picked up and the top card must be used to make a pair.

▸ When a player is out of cards, she says "Rummy!" Each player then counts her pairs; the player with the most pairs wins the game.

apply

take card
read word
make pair
put pair down
put card down

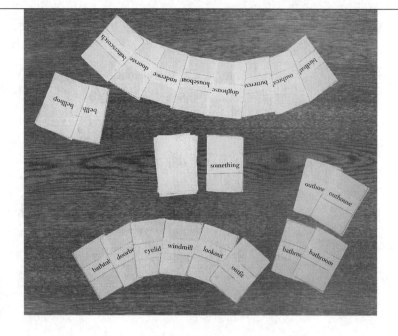

▸ Children play Compound Rummy in groups of two to four players. If three or four play, then deal seven cards to each player; otherwise deal ten cards.

▸ Players form pairs of compound words that have the same word part.

▸ The player with the most pairs at the end of the game wins.

share

Have children share some of the word pairs they made. Invite them to think of compound words that have *back*, *candle*, *hair*, *foot*, or *tooth* in them as you list them on a chart. Review the principle and talk about any new words the children learned.

Link

Interactive Read-Aloud: Read aloud a variety of books that include compound words. After reading, list a few of the words. Here are two suggested titles:

- ▸ *Fishing Day* by Andrea Davis Pinkney
- ▸ *Madison Finds a Line* by Sunny Warner

Shared Reading: After reading a poem, have children circle the compound words.

Guided Reading: After reading a text, ask children to locate one or two compound words. Encourage children to use the component words to help them solve compound words.

Guided/Independent Writing: As children write, encourage them to notice the compound words they use. Remind them that the component words can help them spell the compound words.

assess

- ▸ Notice how easily children take apart compound words as they read text.
- ▸ Give children two or three words (*tooth, snore, some)* and have them write two or three compound words with each.

Expand the Learning

Repeat this lesson with different compound words. (See Compound Word List, *Teaching Resources.)*

Have children play Rummy with a deck of 26 groups of three compound words, and have children make threes instead of pairs.

Connect with Home

Send home materials for a Compound Rummy Deck for children to play with family members. (See Word Card Template and Deck Card Template in *Teaching Resources*.)

Children and a family member can hunt for compound words in magazines and newspapers.

Forming Plurals of Words That Add *es*

Three-Way Sort

Consider Your Children

Use this lesson when children have a good understanding of the concept of plurals and can easily recognize plurals while reading and are using them in writing. Children should have an understanding of basic plurals in which *s* is added to a base word. If children understand adding *es* to words that end with the letters listed, then skip this lesson and move on to the more challenging plural lessons. This lesson includes words that add *s* and *es*.

Working with English Language Learners

Use examples that English language learners have successfully read in texts or have heard and understood when you read aloud. Work with a small group, using shared writing to create sentences that require plurals. Children can highlight the plural forms. Put a number of easy examples of plural forms on a whiteboard and ask children what they notice. They will first learn that an *s* or *es* at the end of a word may signal plurality. Then they can begin establishing categories of each plural form. Finally, they begin to distinguish the difference between a plural form and a word that simply ends in *s*.

You Need

▶ Pocket chart.

From *Teaching Resources:*

▶ Pocket Chart Card Template.

▶ Three-Way Sort Sheets.

▶ Lesson WS 7 Word Cards.

Understand the Principle

This lesson helps children refine their knowledge of how plurals are formed. Some add *s* or *es*; some change the spelling of the base word before *s* or *es* is added; and some have a completely different spelling (e.g., *man, men*). When words end with the particular consonants listed in this lesson, *es* is added and the *es* forms another syllable.

Explain the Principle

❝ Add *es* to words that end with *x, ch, sh, s, ss, tch, zz* to make them plural. ❞

❝ The *s* at the end sounds like /z/. ❞

CONTINUUM: WORD STRUCTURE — Recognizing and Using Plurals That Add *es* When Words End with *x, ch, sh, s, ss, tch, zz*

plan

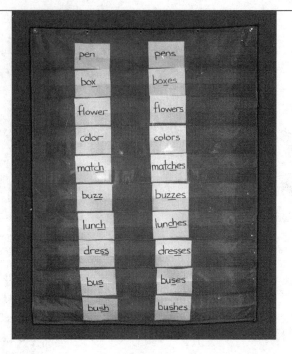

Explain the Principle

" Add *es* to words that end with *x, ch, sh, s, ss, tch, zz* to make them plural. "

" The *s* at the end sounds like /z/. "

① Explain that you will help the children learn more about words that mean more than one, or plurals.

② Place a variety of words in singular and plural form in two columns in a pocket chart. Ask children to read the words and tell what they notice about how each plural is formed. Help them conclude that in the plural that adds *es* they hear another syllable. Also help them see that the words that end in *ch, x, ss, s, tch, sh* and *zz* have *es* added. Underline the ending letters.

③ Tell the children that they will say words and form their plurals. On a Three-Way Sort Sheet, they write *pens* at the top of the first column, *boxes* at the top of the second column, and a *?* (question mark) above the third column.

④ Children take one word card (the singular form) at a time, write the plural form below *pens* if *s* is added, under *boxes* if *es* is added, and under *?* (question mark) if it does not belong in either column. Children continue until they have listed twenty words.

apply

take cards
read word
write plural form

▸ Have children take twenty word cards.

▸ They read each card and write its plural form in the appropriate column of a Three-Way Sort Sheet.

▸ Children select one example to bring to sharing.

Name: _____   Three-Way Sort

pens	boxes	?
holidays animals folders letters schools flowers coats vases shirts	peaches crutches foxes classes pitches inches itches catches brushes	men geese

share

Have the children suggest more examples to add to the class chart.

Share with students that they will be learning several more plural forms.

Link

Interactive Read-Aloud: Read aloud books that include a variety of plural forms. Here are two examples:

- ▶ *Bottle Houses: The Creative World of Grandma Prisbrey* by Melissa Eskridge Slaymaker

- ▶ *A Is for Apple and All Things That Grow* by Megan Bryant

Shared Reading: After reading a familiar poem, have children highlight the plural forms that appear within the context.

Guided Reading: During word work have children find a few singular words and change them to their plural forms.

Guided/Independent Writing: Have children check their spelling of plural forms when they reread and edit their work.

assess

- ▶ Dictate a few singular words and have children form the plurals.

- ▶ Observe how easily children recognize or take apart plural words as they read text.

Expand the Learning

Have children play Plural Concentration with pairs of singular and plural forms of words (see *Teaching Resources*). You will need to use the Word Card Template (see *Teaching Resources*) to make plural forms.

Have children find ten plural words in print around the room and make a list.

Connect with Home

Send home plural word cards for children to cut and sort at home (use Word Card Template in *Teaching Resources*).

Forming Plurals with Words Ending with y

Two-Way Sort

Consider Your Children

Children should have knowledge of basic plurals that add *s* or *es* to words. In this lesson, they focus on words that end in *y*, some of which require a change in the spelling of the base word. Be sure that children understand the terms *singular* and *plural* and that as examples you use words children understand.

Working with English Language Learners

Learning that English has many different plural forms helps children uncover the complexities of the language, but, initially, using plurals is challenging. Stay with very concrete examples, even using pictures, as long as necessary for children to understand the concept and use simple plurals (adding *s* and *es*). Use shared reading and writing to help them understand how plurals function in sentences. For example, sentences about the classroom or everyday events can be structured to include plurals. Have children highlight plurals on the chart. Use magnetic letters to show them how to take away the *y* from the singular word and add *ies*.

You Need

▶ Pocket chart.

▶ Markers.

From *Teaching Resources:*

▶ Pocket Chart Card Template.

▶ Two-Way Sort Sheets.

▶ Lesson WS 8 Word Cards.

Understand the Principle

This lesson expands children's knowledge of plural forms by helping them learn that *s* is usually added to words ending in a vowel and *y*, and the *y* is changed to an i when the word ends with a consonant and *y*, expands children's knowledge of the categories of plurals. Once they understand these categories, they will reduce their uncertainty in spelling and reading plural forms.

Explain the Principle

66 Add *s* to words that end in a vowel and *y* to make them plural. 99

66 Change the *y* to *i* and add *es* to words that end in a consonant and *y* to make them plural. 99

plan

Explain the Principle

" Add *s* to words that end in a vowel and *y* to make them plural. "

" Change the *y* to *i* and add *es* to words that end in a consonant and *y* to make them plural. "

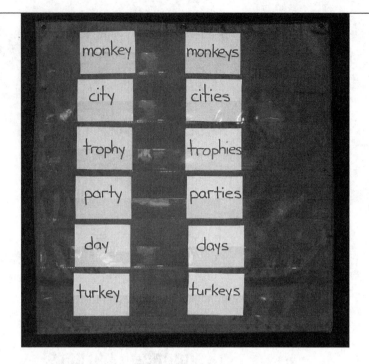

① Tell the children that you are going to help them learn more about the way plurals are spelled.

② Place *monkey-monkeys, city-cities, trophy-trophies, party-parties, day-days, turkey-turkeys* in two columns on a pocket chart. Ask children to read the words with you and then tell what they notice.

③ Help them conclude that when the singular form ends in a vowel plus *y*, the plural is made by adding *s*. When the singular form ends in a consonant plus *y*, the plural is made by changing the *y* to *i* before adding *es*.

④ Ask children to suggest a few other examples (e.g., *puppy, donkey, key, lady*).

⑤ Explain that children will use a Two-Way Sort Sheet to sort plural forms. They will write *monkeys* at the top of the first column and *parties* at the top of the second column. They take one word card at a time and write the plural form under the left column if *s* is added and under the right column if *y* is changed to *i* and *es* is added. Children continue to select cards until they have listed twenty words.

apply

- Have the children choose a word card and form the plurals for twenty words.
- They list each under the correct key word on a Two-Way Sort Sheet.
- Children read over their lists in preparation for sharing.

Name: Sadye   Two-Way Sort

monkeys	parties
days	bodies
turkeys	pennies
donkeys	supplies
	countries
	ladies
	fairies
	ponies
	counties
	puppies
	copies
	trophies
	stories
	candies
	rubies
	guppies

share

Have the children read their word sorts to a partner.

Ask the children to discuss what they have learned about plurals. They can describe the different actions in making plurals for *boy*, *day*, and *lady*.

Link

Interactive Read-Aloud: Read aloud books that feature a variety of plural forms. After reading, write a few of the plural words on a chart. Here are a few suggested titles:

- ▸ *Cherry Pies and Lullabies* by Lynn Reiser
- ▸ *Coolies* by Yin

Shared Reading: After reading a familiar poem, have the children highlight the plural forms in context using a highlighter or highlighter tape.

Guided Reading: During word work have children write three to five words in their plural forms on a whiteboard or paper. They can use the class chart as a reference.

Guided/Independent Writing: During the editing process, have the children check their spelling of plural forms. They can use the class chart as a reference.

assess

- ▸ Give the children a list of five words that end in *y* and have them write the plural form. You can increase the difficulty of this task by dictating the list of words.
- ▸ Notice how easily children read plural forms in text.

Expand the Learning

Have children play Plural Rummy with pairs made from the singular and plural forms of words (see *Teaching Resources*).

Connect with Home

Send home a sheet of word cards for children to read and then write the plural form. (Use the Word Card Template in *Teaching Resources*.)

Children can Read and Write Around their Homes (like Read and Write Around the Room, see *Teaching Resources*) to discover words ending in *y* and then write their plural forms.

Forming Plurals with Words Ending in f, fe, or lf

Making Words

Consider Your Children

Be sure that children understand the concept of plural and can form simple plurals and those for words ending in *y*. This lesson focuses on a less frequent principle. It is important that the words be familiar to children in their speaking and writing vocabularies. Children should already be very familiar with and able to recall other categories of plural forms. They should know the meaning of the words *singular* and *plural*.

Working with English Language Learners

It is important for English language learners to hear, say, and read plural forms in sentences because plurality is signalled differently across languages; for example, the article before the plural may change. Work with simple examples and use concrete graphic illustrations when possible. Develop a way to tell them when a plural is an exception (depart from the principle).

You Need

▸ Chart paper.

▸ Markers.

From *Teaching Resources:*

▸ Two-Column Sheets.

▸ Lesson WS 9 Word Cards.

Understand the Principle

This lesson will further expand children's knowledge of singluar and plural forms by focusing on a less frequently used form, the principle for changing the *f* to *v* before adding *s*. Children can usually determine the change by listening to the sound of the word in oral language (e.g., *lives*). As always, there are some exceptions to the principle (e.g., *roofs*). Taking on this more complex plural form will build another category to compare with those they already know.

Explain the Principle

“ Change *f* to *v* and add *s* or *es* to words that end with *f, fe,* or *lf* to make them plural. ”

CONTINUUM: WORD STRUCTURE — RECOGNIZING AND USING PLURALS THAT CHANGE *F* TO *V* AND ADD *ES* FOR WORDS THAT END WITH *F, FE, LF*

375

WS 9
WORD STRUCTURE

plan

teach

life
lives

calf
calves

hoof
hooves

Explain the Principle

" Change *f* to *v* and add *s* or *es* to words that end with *f, fe* or *lf* to make them plural. "

① Tell the children they will learn more about how to change words from singular to plural.

② Suggested language: "You know how to form plurals for many words. Today you will learn about forming plurals with words that end in *f, fe*, and *lf*."

③ Write *life* and *lives*, *calf* and *calves*, *hoof* and *hooves* on chart paper.

④ Ask children how the spelling of each word changes when it is made plural. They will notice that the *f* is changed to *v* and *es* is added.

⑤ Summarize the principle: "Change *f* to *v* and add *es* for words that end with *f, fe*, or *lf*."

⑥ Explain that children will take twelve word cards to make and then write. They make each word with magnetic letters and write it in the first column of a Two-Column Sheet. Then they make the plural form with magnetic letters, and write the plural form in the second column. Finally, they read their list to a partner.

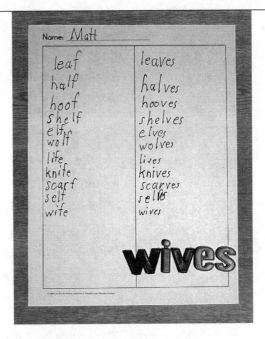

Name: Matt

leaf	leaves
half	halves
hoof	hooves
shelf	shelves
elf	elves
wolf	wolves
life	lives
knife	knives
scarf	scarves
self	selves
wife	wives

wives

apply

take card
make word
write word
change letter
add letter
write word
read list

▶ Children each take twelve word cards. They make each singular word with magnetic letters. Then they write it in the first column on a Two-Column Sheet.

▶ Next, they make the plural form with magnetic letters and write the plural form in the second column.

▶ Finally, they read their lists to a partner.

▶ Children select a word and think about it in a sentence to contribute during sharing.

share

Ask volunteers to make a sentence using one of their plural words.

Draw children's attention to the change in pronunciation when you change words that end in *f* or *fe* to plural form. It might be interesting to have them notice that their mouths have the same shape.

Link

Interactive Read-Aloud: Read aloud books that include a variety of plural forms. Point out one or two of them after reading. Here are two suggested titles:

▸ *Where Go the Boats: Play Poems of Robert Louis Stevenson*

▸ *Why Butterflies Go By on Silent Wings* by Marguerite Davol

Shared Reading: Cover the last part of a few plural words on the first reading of a poem. Ask children to predict the letters and then uncover the words to confirm their predictions.

Guided Reading: During word work, make a few singular words that end in *f, lf,* or *fe* and have children tell or quickly write and show the plural form.

Guided/Independent Writing: Have children edit their writing for correct spelling of plural forms.

assess
_____

▸ Dictate five words ending in *f, lf,* or *fe* and have children write the singular and plural forms.

▸ Observe children's reading of plural forms to see how easily and quickly they recognize them.
_____

Expand the Learning

Have the children play Concentration with twelve pairs of singular and plural forms. To make it more challenging, include words with a variety of pairs of singular and plural principles represented (see *Teaching Resources*).

Connect with Home

Have children make a Word Search with plural forms for family members to complete (see *Teaching Resources*).

Children can ask a family member to help search magazines and newspapers for words ending in *f, lf,* or *fe*. Together they can record the plural forms.

Noticing and Using Abbreviations

Abbreviation Concentration

Consider Your Children

Children see common abbreviations in texts they read and use them when there is limited space. In this lesson they focus on common abbreviations: *Mr. Mrs. Dr. Ave. Rd. Ln. St. Sun. Mon. Tues. Wed. Thurs. Fri. Sat. Jan. Feb. Mar. Apr. Jun. Jul. Aug. Sept. Oct. Nov. Dec.* Once the concept is understood they can apply it to other abbreviations. Children should be familiar with Concentration. If they are not, demonstrate how to play the game.

Working with English Language Learners

Every language uses abbreviations, so it is possible that English language learners are familiar with this concept and know some examples from their own language. Having them sort and compare abbreviations on word cards will help children think about the categories. It is also helpful to have children match the long and abbreviated forms, noticing, for example, the particular letters from state names that are used in the shortened forms.

You Need

▶ Chart paper.

▶ Markers.

From *Teaching Resources:*

▶ Directions for Concentration.

▶ Concentration Game Cards made from Lesson WS 10 Word Cards and Deck Card Template.

▶ List Sheets.

Understand the Principle

Abbreviate means shorter; *abbreviations* are shortened forms of particular words. Children see abbreviations in their environment and in texts they read. Abbreviations are usually intended for limited spaces, though some have become common in writing simply to save time. Months of the year and days of the week are generally abbreviated when there is limited space. A period is used after an abbreviation. An exception to this is state postal abbreviations which have no period and are written in capital letters (e.g., *MA, NY, AZ, OR*). Abbreviations are often used in writing, though in some more formal contexts it is preferable to write the whole word. It is preferable not to abbreviate *June* or *July*, but an option of *Je.* for *June* and *Jl.* for *July* is mainly used in indexes of periodical literature.

Explain the Principle

❝ Some words are made shorter by using some of the letters and a period. They are called *abbreviations.* ❞

plan

Explain the Principle

" **Some words are made shorter by using some of the letters and a period. They are called** *abbreviations*. "

① Tell children that they will learn about some words that can be made shorter. They see them when they read and use them when they write.

② Have a variety of whole words that are commonly abbreviated written on chart paper.

③ Write the abbreviation with the period to the right of each full word. Suggested language: "Here are some words. Help me underline the part of the word that is written when the word is used in its shortened form."

④ Have children read three or four words with you and underline the letters included in the abbreviation.

⑤ Tell the children that the shortened forms are called *abbreviations* and have them clap the word with you. Tell them a period follows each to show it is shortened.

⑥ Explain that some abbreviations are commonly used (e.g., *Mr., Dr.*) while others are used when there is limited space (e.g., *Aug., Fri.*)

⑦ Tell children they will play Abbreviation Concentration, trying to match an abbreviation with its whole word. The player with the most matched pairs wins the game. Children then make a list of twenty different abbreviations on a List Sheet.

Mister	Mr.	January	Jan.
Doctor	Dr.	February	Feb.
		March	Mar.
Street	St.		
Avenue	Ave.		
Road	Rd.	August	Aug.
		September	Sept.
Sunday	Sun.	December	Dec.
Monday	Mon		
Friday	Fri.		
Saturday	Sat.		

apply

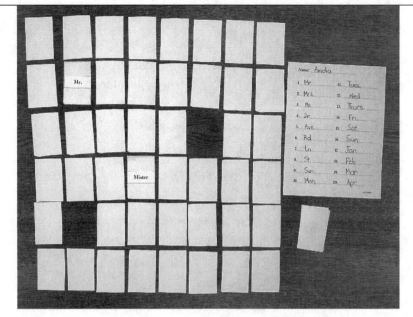

| turn card |
| read word or abbreviation |
| match word or abbreviation |
| write list |

▶ In groups of two to four, children play Abbreviation Concentration.

▶ On the word cards, you will notice the word Missus, which is an informal or colloquial version of *Mistress* (now usually *Mrs.*). If you prefer, you can substitute *Mistress* or *Missis* (also informal and colloquial).

▶ Then they make a list of twenty different abbreviations on a List Sheet.

share

Invite a few children to write an abbreviation on the board while the other children tell the complete word.

If there is time, "flash" cards with abbreviations so that the children see them briefly and say the whole word.

Link

Interactive Read-Aloud: Read aloud a variety of books with abbreviations. After reading, show two or three abbreviations on the board. Here are a few suggested titles:

- ▸ *Mrs. Mack* by Patricia Polacco
- ▸ *Thank You, Mr. Falker* by Patricia Polacco

Shared Reading: After reading a poem that has a few abbreviations, have children highlight them on a transparency. Conversely, have the children find one or two words that can be abbreviated.

Guided Reading: After reading a text, have children find one or two abbreviations or words that can be abbreviated.

Guided/Independent Writing: Have children proofread their work for correct spelling and punctuation of abbreviated words.

assess

- ▸ Dictate six to ten words for children to abbreviate.

- ▸ Notice the children's use of abbreviations in their writing to be sure they are formed correctly.

Expand the Learning

Repeat this lesson with other more challenging abbreviations, such as state names that are shortened and written in capital letters without a period.

Connect with Home

Send home the Deck Card Template (see *Teaching Resources*) with words and abbreviations for the game Abbreviation Concentration. Children can play it with family members.

Recognizing Syllables in Words with Vowel Combinations

Taking Words Apart

Consider Your Children

This lesson focuses on two-syllable words with vowel combinations. Before participating in this lesson, children should have strong control of common spelling patterns with vowel combinations in single syllable words. Be sure children understand all the words you select.

Working with English Language Learners

Vowel combinations within words, especially those with multiple syllables, often challenge spellers of any age. English language learners need to learn to recognize vowel pairs. It will be helpful if they divide words into syllables and understand that the vowel pairs usually stay together, forming a pattern. Have children work with magnetic letters during word work. They can build the words and then physically divide them, noticing the vowel pairs.

You Need

▶ Chart paper.

▶ Markers.

From *Teaching Resources:*

▶ List Sheets.

▶ Lesson WS 11 Word Cards.

Understand the Principle

Many vowel sounds are represented by vowel combinations such as *ai, ee, ow, ea, ay, oo, ou.* Sometimes *y* and *w* represent a vowel sound when paired with a vowel. The vowel combinations appear in the same syllable. Sometimes the vowel sound is the same as the name of the first vowel (e.g., *meet*) and sometimes it represents a unique sound (e.g., *house, moon*). Children need to know the patterns in one-syllable words before they can attend to them in multisyllable words.

Explain the Principle

" When vowel combinations are in words, they usually go together in the same syllable (*poi-son, cray-on*). "

plan

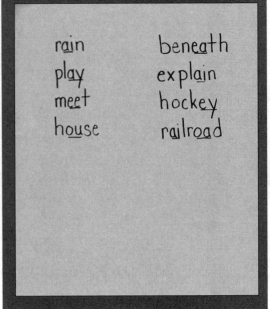

① Tell the children you will teach them more about word parts, or syllables.

Explain the Principle

" When vowel combinations are in words, they usually go together in the same syllable (*poi-son, cray-on*). "

② Write *rain, play, meet,* and *house* on a chart. Ask the children to read each word and tell how many parts they hear. Guide children to conclude that the vowel combinations *ai, ay, ee,* and *ou* represent one vowel sound in these single-syllable words.

③ Next write *beneath, explain, hockey,* and *railroad*. Have children read them and clap the syllables they hear. In each syllable they hear, help them notice and underline the vowel sound.

④ Point out that when the word is broken into parts, the vowel combination stays together in the syllable. Suggested language: "When vowel combinations are in words, they usually go together in the same syllable."

⑤ Review several more words, using the same process (e.g., *crayon, peanut, yellow*).

⑥ Tell the children they will select one word card at a time, read it, and write it in parts on a List Sheet. Demonstrate with two words. They will select twenty different words.

apply

take card
read word
divide word
write word

▸ Children work with twenty words.

▸ They take one word card and read it and think about how to divide it.

▸ Then they write the word on the List Sheet, divided by a space at the appropriate place.

Name: Tiffany

1. hock ey
2. sail boat
3. hol i day
4. en joy
5. see saw
6. poi son
7. fel low
8. car toon
9. un read
10. train er
11. ap pear
12. cof fee
13. rail road
14. mush room
15. bal loon
16. al low
17. mon key
18. re veal
19. pil low
20. re main

LIST SHEET

share

Invite the children to share a few words that are not yet on the chart and tell or demonstrate how to divide them. Explain to the children that when they are writing, sometimes they will not be able to fit the whole word at the end of a line. Show them how they can write one or two syllables, a hyphen, and the final syllable or syllables on the next line.

Link

Interactive Read-Aloud: Read aloud a variety of books that have vowel combinations in two-syllable words. After reading, write two or three words on a whiteboard and divide them. Here are two suggested titles:

- ▶ *Scien-Trickery: Riddles in Science* by J. Patrick Lewis
- ▶ *Raccoon Moon* by Nancy Carol Willis

Shared Reading: Have children locate several two-syllable words with vowel combinations in familiar poems and mark them with highlighter tape.

Guided Reading: Prompt children to notice and use syllables to take apart words. During word work, children can focus on families of words with the same vowel combination.

Guided/Independent Writing: As children write new words, have them think of each syllable and the vowel sound they hear.

assess

- ▶ Give children a list of five words with vowel combinations and ask them to divide them.
- ▶ Notice how easily children use word parts to solve new words they encounter in text.

Expand the Learning

Repeat this lesson with a different variety of words.

Have the children play Follow the Path with two-syllable words with vowel combinations. When they land on a space, they say the word in parts (see *Teaching Resources*). To increase the challenge, try a few three-syllable words.

Connect with Home

Send home a sheet of two-syllable words for children to take home, cut into syllables and glue on a sheet of paper. (Use Word Card Template in *Teaching Resources*.)

Noticing and Using the Past Tense with ed

Trumps

Consider Your Children

Use this lesson when children have had experience with each of the principles for adding *ed* to words, and understand how to change the spellings. In this summary lesson, they will review the sound of each. Be sure to use words the children understand. If the children are not comfortable with the principles, you may want to select one or two instead of working with all of them at once.

Working with English Language Learners

All languages have the concept of past tense, but verbs are inflected in many different ways. Encourage English language learners to make links to their own language to help them understand the concept. Be sure they know the meaning of the words you are using. Model using the words in sentences and at the same time provide the visual example. Children will need many opportunities to say the different verb forms slowly and think about how the word endings *sound* and *look*.

You Need

▶ Pocket chart.

▶ Markers.

From *Teaching Resources:*

▶ Pocket Chart Card Template.

▶ Directions for Trumps.

▶ Trumps Game Cards made from Lesson WS 13 Word Cards and Deck Card Template.

Understand the Principle

The suffix *ed* can represent three different sounds (/d/, /ed/, /t/). Verbs that end in *y* require changing of the *y* to *i* before adding *ed*. Some verbs—usually those with a short vowel sound—require a doubling of the consonant before adding *ed*, which makes the ending sound like /d/ or /t/ (e.g., *planned, shopped*).

Explain the Principle

❝ When you add *ed* to a word, sometimes it sounds like /d/. ❞

❝ When you add *ed* to a word, sometimes it sounds like /ed/. ❞

❝ When you add *ed* to a word it may sound like /t/. ❞

❝ Sometimes you change the *y* to *i* and add *ed* and the ending sounds like /d/. ❞

❝ Double the consonant before adding *ed* to words ending in a short vowel and one consonant. ❞

CONTINUUM: WORD STRUCTURE — Recognizing That *ed* Added to a Word to Make It Past Tense Can Sound Several Different Ways

387

WS 12
WORD STRUCTURE

plan

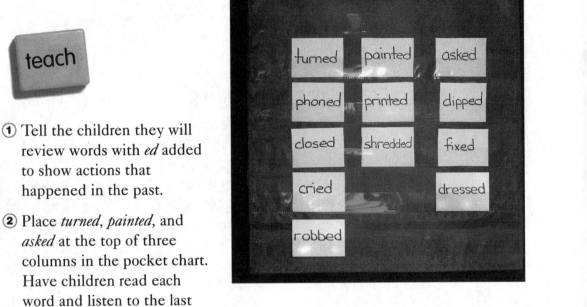

Explain the Principle

" **When you add *ed* to a word, sometimes it sounds like /d/.** "

" **When you add *ed* to a word, sometimes it sounds like /ed/.** "

" **When you add *ed* to a word it may sound like /t/.** "

" **Sometimes you change the *y* to *i* and add *ed* and the ending sounds like /d/.** "

" **Double the consonant before adding *ed* to words ending in a short vowel and one consonant.** "

① Tell the children they will review words with *ed* added to show actions that happened in the past.

② Place *turned, painted,* and *asked* at the top of three columns in the pocket chart. Have children read each word and listen to the last part of each.

③ Then show *phoned, printed, dipped, closed, shredded, fixed, cried* and as you show each, have children read the word and place it in the column with other words that have the same ending sound. These verbs have a short vowel sound.

④ When you finish the columns, invite children to share what they notice. They will see that some words have a doubled consonant. They will also see that some words had a *y* that changed to *i* before *ed* was added. You may need to quickly write the base word and word with ending on a whiteboard to make the change explicit. Help students think about the ending sound in each column and label them /d/, /ed/, and /t/. Suggested language: "When you add *ed* to a word, sometimes it sounds like a /d/, sometimes it sounds like a /t/, and sometimes it sounds like /ed/. Children may notice that when you make a word like *phone* past tense, the *e* is already there, so you just add *d*.

⑤ Tell children that in groups of three, they will play Trumps. Demonstrate the game with two children. The object of the game is to collect all of the cards or to have the most cards at the end of the game. Trump cards show words ending with *ed* and a drawing of the sun. The dealer deals sixteen cards to each player. The first player places a card face-up on the table. Each player around the table puts down a card that ends in *ed* and has the same ending sound (/d/, /t/ or /ed/). If a player has no card to match, he passes and the next player takes a turn. The first player who played the card with the feature takes the cards unless someone plays a trump card. If more than one trump card is played, the first player to play it takes the cards. The player with the most cards at the end wins the game.

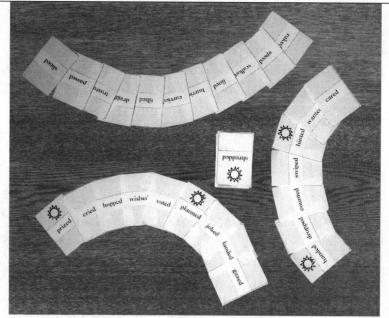

put card down
match sound
take cards

▶ Children play
Trumps with
verbs that have
ed added. They
take turns
matching the
sounds made by
the *ed* ending.
The player with
the most cards
at the end of the game wins.

▶ After playing, children can think of additional words to add to the
class chart.

Have the children suggest an additional word for each category on the class
chart. Discuss with the children any new words they learned.

Link

Interactive Read-Aloud: Read aloud a variety of books with *ed* added. Point out two or three words that have *ed* added. Here are a few suggested titles:

- ▶ *Storm Is Coming* by Heather Tekavec
- ▶ *If You Hopped Like a Frog* by David M. Schwartz

Shared Reading: After reading a poem, have children find several words with *ed* added and ask them to identify the ending sounds.

Guided Reading: When the children come to unfamiliar words with *ed*, encourage them to use what they know about the ending sound and be sure the word sounds right in the sentence.

Guided/Independent Writing: When the children proofread their writing, remind them to check the spelling of verbs in the past tense to make sure they are correct.

assess

- ▶ Dictate three to five words with *ed* added.
- ▶ Give children a list of three to five words with *ed* added to read aloud while you observe their speed and accuracy in recognition.

Expand the Learning

Have the children play Crazy Eights with words that have *ed* added (see *Teaching Resources*).

Create Word Grids (see *Teaching Resources*) for children to play the game.

Connect with Home

Use the Deck Card Template (see *Teaching Resources*) to send home a duplicated set of word cards for a Three-Way Sort. Have the key words *turned*, *painted*, and *asked* underlined.

Forming New Words by Adding -er

Two-Way Sort

Consider Your Children

Before using this lesson, be sure that the children are familiar with the concept that words have endings such as *ing*. Also, be sure children have experience adding *ed* and *d* to base words that do not require a spelling change (Lesson WS 12). They should have a good understanding of the CVC structure of words, not using technical language necessarily, but being able to pronounce and spell them. Children should have a repertoire of words with endings and understand that sometimes there are spelling changes in the base word, such as doubling the final consonant. They also should have worked with vowels and vowel digraphs before they attempt the tasks in this lesson.

Working with English Language Learners

Sorting and comparing the visual features of words with suffixes will help English language learners sort out complex features of the language. It helps to put an article (e.g., *the* or *a*) in front of the word with *-er* to signal that it is a noun, or to use the word in a sentence to clarify its meaning. Have children add the ending with magnetic letters or highlight it to draw their attention to the added letters.

You Need

▶ Chart paper.

▶ Markers.

From *Teaching Resources:*

▶ Two-Way Sort Sheets.

▶ Lesson WS 12 Word Cards.

Understand the Principle

An *affix* is any word part that is added to a base word. A *suffix* is an affix added to the end of a word. When you add the suffix *-er* to a verb, it becomes a noun that names a person who does something. This lesson does not include words in which adding *-er* requires a spelling change such as doubling the consonant or changing the *y* to *i*. Some words add *-or* instead of *-er* (e.g., *actor, survivor*). Making connections among these words will help children remember the particular vowel involved. When the words have silent *e,* then thinking of the base word helps.

Explain the Principle

❝ Add *-er* to a word to tell about a person who can do something. *John can read. John is a reader.* ❞

❝ Add *-r* to words that end in silent *e* to make the *er* ending. ❞

plan

> Add -er to a word to talk about a person who can do something.
> Add -r to words that end in silent e to make the -er ending.
>
> read   reader
> play   player
> hike   hiker
> drive   driver

Explain the Principle

" Add -er to a word to tell about a person who can do something. *John can read. John is a reader.* "

" Add -r to words that end in silent e to make the er ending. "

① Tell the children they will learn about adding the *-er* suffix.

② Have these four pairs of words written on the chart: *read-reader, play-player, hike-hiker, drive-driver.*

③ Suggested language: "John likes to read. John is a reader. Gabriella likes to play. She is a player. Darnell likes to hike. He is a hiker. Uncle Pete likes to drive. He is a driver." Point to each word on the chart as you say it.

④ Ask what children notice about the spelling of the second set of words. Children will say that two of the base words have *-er* added to them, and the two words that end in *e* and have just an *r* added because the *e* is already there. Write these principles at the top of the chart.

⑤ Invite children to give two or three more examples and add them to the chart.

⑥ Have children write the key words *read* and *reader* at the top of a Two-Way Sort Sheet. Ask them to take ten word cards and list them in the first column. Then they write each word in the second column with the *-er* ending added.

⑦ Finally, they choose five pairs of words to use in five sentences that they write on the back of the Sort Sheet.

apply

read	reader
paint	painter
write	writer
climb	climber
work	worker
dream	dreamer
teach	teacher
clean	cleaner
jump	jumper
pack	packer
speak	speaker

Name: Alex   Two-Way Sort

write key words
take card
write word
write new word
write sentence

▸ Have the children write key words *read* and *reader* at the top of a Two-Way Sort Sheet.

▸ Ask them to select ten word cards and write the words in the first column.

▸ Then children write each word with the *-r* or *-er* ending in the second column.

▸ Then have them select five of the pairs of words to use in sentences. They write the sentences on the back of their sheets, using both words in the same sentence and underline both words. (Since I was the *speaker*, I had to speak clearly.)

share

With the children, add to the chart two more examples of words to which *-r* is added and two more with *-er* added. If any of the word meanings are new to the children, discuss their meanings. You may want the children to read a few sentences they constructed.

Link

Interactive Read-Aloud: Read aloud books that contain words with *-er* endings. Here are a few suggested titles:

▸ ***Milton the Early Riser*** by Robert Kraus

▸ ***Leo the Late Bloomer*** by Robert Kraus

Shared Reading: After you have read and enjoyed a poem together, have children find one or two words that have the *-r* or *-er* suffix and highlight them.

Guided Reading: During word work, write five or six verbs. Add *-r* or *-er* and have the children read the new words.

Guided/Independent Writing: When children proofread their stories, have them check the spelling of base words with *-er* endings.

assess

▸ Dictate four or five words to which *-r* or *-er* is added.

▸ Observe the children's ability to read and write words with *-er* endings.

Expand the Learning

Repeat this lesson with base words that have more than one syllable (e.g., *performer, complainer, recorder*). Make word cards for multisyllable words using the Word Card Template (see *Teaching Resources*).

Connect with Home

Send home a selection of verbs to which you can add *-er*. Have children write them each in a sentence and add *-r* or *-er*, and then read them to family members.

Using Compound Word Parts to Understand Meaning

Battle

Consider Your Children

By now children have a great deal of experience with easy compound words and are ready to solve more complex examples. They can also think more analytically about how each word contributes to the meaning. If children have already played Battle, then briefly review how the game is played.

Working with English Language Learners

It is challenging for English language learners to recognize compound words, notice their components, and think about the meaning of the components and the larger word. Gaps in any of this knowledge cause difficulty. Once children understand the principle, however, they will have acquired a powerful tool for acquiring new English vocabulary. It is especially helpful for them to work with compound words that are connected (e.g., *anywhere, anytime, anyway; inside, outside*).

You Need

► Chart paper.

► Markers.

► Index cards.

From *Teaching Resources:*

► Directions for Battle.

► Battle Game Cards made from Lesson WS 14 Word Cards and Deck Card Template. (Select thirty compound words and sixteen that are not compound.)

Understand the Principle

A *compound word* is two words put together. Each of the component words usually contributes to the meaning of the compound word, though there are exceptions. Some words form part of several compound words (e.g., *outside, outhouse, outfield, hideout, lookout*). In this lesson children learn how word parts contribute to the meaning of a compound word.

Explain the Principle

❝ The word parts in compound words often help you think about the meaning. ❞

CONTINUUM: WORD STRUCTURE — Recognizing and Understanding More Complex Compound Words (*AIRPLANE, AIRPORT, ANOTHER, ANYONE, HOMESICK, INDOOR, JELLYFISH, SKYSCRAPER, TOOTHBRUSH*)

(395)

plan

Explain the Principle

" The word parts in compound words often help you think about the meaning. "

① Tell the children that you will help them think about word parts.

② Have *starfish, barnyard, doorbell,* and *wheelchair* written in parts on the left side of the chart and as whole words on the right.

③ Help the children think about how the meanings of *star* and *fish* contribute to the meaning of the whole word.

> The word parts in compound words often help you think about the meaning.
>
> star + fish   starfish
>
> barn + yard   barnyard
>
> door + bell   doorbell
>
> wheel + chair   wheelchair

④ Repeat this process with each word. Ask children to suggest other compound words and discuss them (e.g., *motorboat, headphone, motorcycle, candlestick, grapevine, houseboat, clothespin, blackbird, headache*).

⑤ Tell the children they will play compound-word Battle in pairs, and demonstrate the game. The goal of the game is to take all the cards or get the most cards in the allotted time. The deck should consist of thirty compound words and sixteen words that are not compound.

- ▶ Deal the entire deck face down so that each player has a face-down deck of cards.

- ▶ Each player turns over one card from his deck.

- ▶ If one player has a compound word he says Battle, reads the word, tells its meaning, and takes both cards.

- ▶ If both players have a compound word, they both tell the meanings but neither gets the cards and they turn another card.

- ▶ They continue to turn over cards until one player gets a compound word but the other does not.

- ▶ When all the cards have been played, players turn over the piles of cards, shuffle them, and begin play again.

- ▶ The game ends when one player has taken all the cards or when time is up. The player with the most cards wins.

turn
define
take

▶ Have the children play Battle with compound words in pairs.

▶ They both turn over one card from their individual piles. The goal is to get all the opponent's cards.

▶ After playing Battle, they select one compound word and write it on a card to bring to sharing.

Have each child read the compound word he brought to share and use it in a sentence. Discuss any new word meanings that may have come up.

Link

Interactive Read-Aloud: Read aloud a variety of books that include compound words. After discussing the text, point out a few compound words. Here are a few suggested titles:

- ▸ *Earth Songs* by Myra Cohn Livingston
- ▸ *No Star Nights* by Anna Egan Smucker

Shared Reading: After performing a familiar poem, have children highlight two or three compound words.

Guided Reading: In the introduction of a text or after reading, have children locate one or two compound words.

Guided/Independent Writing: As children reread their writing, ask them to notice any compound words. You may find children have joined some words as if they are compounds. Take the opportunity to clear up confusions and confirm their thinking about words that would be likely compounds. Also, show them how to check with the dictionary.

assess

- ▸ Observe children's use of compound words in their speaking and writing.
- ▸ Have a five-minute writing spree in which children write as many compound words as they can. Study their responses to note whether they are connecting component words to generate more compound words.

Expand the Learning

Repeat this lesson with a different variety of compound words. (See Compound Word Lists in *Teaching Resources*.)

Ask children to select eight compound words and illustrate their meanings on a Four-Box Sheet (see *Teaching Resources*).

Connect with Home

Send home a deck of Battle cards (see Deck Card Template) so children can play the game with family members.

As an alternative, have children take home two or three compound words to illustrate in a humorous way (for example, *butterfly* or *houseboat*). These illustrations can be compiled into a class book.

Reading Two-Syllable Words with a Vowel and r

Checkers

Consider Your Children

Children should have experience with single-syllable words that have a vowel influenced by the letter *r* (e.g., *fern, shirt, park, form, turn*). In this lesson children learn to notice and use two-syllable words that have the five vowels influenced by *r*. Be sure to select words children understand. If students are less experienced, then select only words with one or two of the vowels at first.

Working with English Language Learners

In English, when a vowel is followed by *r*, the pronunciation is different from that same vowel sound in other words. Many English language learners may find words with *r* difficult to pronounce, so figuring out the vowel sound represents a challenge. Be sure children know simple one-syllable words before working with multisyllable words. Work with a small group to explore examples on a whiteboard, or make a chart that provides them with one or two very clear examples of each kind of *r*-controlled vowel.

You Need

▶ Chart paper.

▶ Markers.

▶ Checkers or black and red discs.

From *Teaching Resources:*

▶ Directions for Checkers.

▶ Checkerboard Template (with words written in the white squares).

▶ List Sheets.

▶ Lesson WS 15 Word List.

Understand the Principle

The letter *r* is often part of a syllable and influences the sound of the vowel in that syllable. The vowel sound is usually neither long nor short, but unique. The syllable with *r* can comprise the first or second syllable of two-syllable words. Giving specific attention to syllables with *r* will help children understand the changes in vowel sounds and move to conventional spelling.

Explain the Principle

❝ When a vowel is followed by an *r*, the *r* and the vowel form a syllable (*cor-ner, cir-cus*). ❞

plan

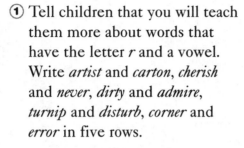

Explain the Principle

" **When a vowel is followed by an *r*, the *r* and the vowel form a syllable (cor-ner, cir-cus).** "

① Tell children that you will teach them more about words that have the letter *r* and a vowel. Write *artist* and *carton*, *cherish* and *never*, *dirty* and *admire*, *turnip* and *disturb*, *corner* and *error* in five rows.

② Have children read the word pairs and help them listen for and notice the two syllables. Underline the syllable with the vowel and *r*. Help them notice the similarities and differences in pronunciation. (For example, the *ir* in *dirty* sounds like the *er* in *never*, but sounds different from the *ir* in *admire*, which is more like a long *i*.) Have them notice the silent *e* in *admire*, which signals a long vowel sound.

③ Add a few more words to each column with examples from the children or the word list. Each time have children listen for syllables and underline the one with a vowel and *r*.

④ Suggested language: "When a vowel is followed by an *r*, the vowel and the *r* go together in a syllable. The syllable will often include additional letters as well *(cher-ish, car-ton)*."

⑤ Review how to play Checkers. Explain that when a player moves a checker into a box, she reads the word and tells the syllables. Upon completion of the game, children write twenty words on a List Sheet.

apply

move piece
read word
tell syllables
write

▶ Pairs of children play Checkers with words that have a vowel followed by *r*.

▶ When they move a checker on to a new space, they read the word, tell the number of syllables, and specify the particular vowel + *r* combinations.

▶ After playing, they select twenty of the words and write them in syllables on a List Sheet.

Name: Aaron   List Sheet

1. er ror   11. bit ter
2. ger bil   12. air plane
3. win ter   13. birth day
4. hair brush   14. din ner
5. cir cus   15. ter ri ble
6. gui tar   16. dif fer
7. re turn   17. dair y
8. cel lar   18. let ter
9. dol lar   19. ham mer
10. bliz zard   20. gar den

                              LIST SHEET

share

Ask children for a few more examples of two-syllable words with a vowel and *r* and add them to the chart.

Keep a running list, in vowel-alike categories. Over a period of time, encourage children to read down a category, noting words that go together and also noticing where pronunciation can be helpful in deciding on the right vowel.

Link

Interactive Read-Aloud: Read aloud a variety of books with two-syllable words that have a vowel and *r* in them. After reading, write one or two of the words on a whiteboard. Here are a two suggested titles:

- ▶ *Epposumondas* by Colleen Salley
- ▶ *Beto and the Bone Dance* by Gina Freschet

Shared Reading: After reading a poem, underline two or three words with a vowel and *r*.

Guided Reading: When children come to unfamiliar multisyllable words with a vowel and *r*, encourage them to notice and use the syllable to take it apart.

Guided/Independent Writing: As children write unfamiliar multisyllable words, help them notice and use syllable parts to help them spell the words correctly.

assess

- ▶ Notice children's use of multisyllable words with a vowel and *r* in them.
- ▶ Dictate three to five two-syllable words with a vowel and *r* in them.

Expand the Learning

Repeat this lesson with a different variety of multisyllable words with *r*-influenced vowels.

Have the children play Concentration with pairs of similar words that have two syllables and *r*-influenced vowels (see *Teaching Resources*).

Connect with Home

Send home checkers and a checkerboard for children to play at home with family members. (See *Teaching Resources*.)

Alternatively, children can use coins as markers at home.

Forming Plurals for Words Ending in o

Four-Way Sort

Consider Your Children

Teach this lesson after children have had extensive experience with more common plural forms and can write them correctly. This lesson includes words that end in *o* and are formed with *es*. Other plural forms are also included for review. You may wish to review the easier principles on the continuum or write them with one or two examples prior to teaching the lesson. Be sure to select words that children understand.

Working with English Language Learners

Consider working with small groups to help children understand the many different ways that plurals are formed in English. Seeing and connecting several examples helps them establish categories of plural formations. Begin by sorting simple examples and then gradually introduce more words, helping children connect them to a category. This process also helps children to connect the singular and plural forms.

You Need

▶ Chart paper.

▶ Markers.

From *Teaching Resources:*

▶ Four-Way Sort Sheets.

▶ Four-Way Sort Cards.

▶ Lesson WS 16 Word Cards.

Understand the Principle

Children need to understand a wide variety of plural forms. Words in their plural forms are constructed in a variety of ways, depending on their final letters. This lesson teaches how to form plurals with words that end with *o*. If the word ends with a consonant followed by *o*, then an *es* is added. If the word ends in *o* and is preceded by a vowel, than an *s* is added. This principle applies to a relatively small number of words.

Explain the Principle

" Add *s* to words that end in a vowel and *o* to make them plural. "

" Add *es* to words that end in a consonant and *o* to make them plural. "

CONTINUUM: WORD STRUCTURE — RECOGNIZING AND USING PLURALS FOR WORDS THAT END IN A CONSONANT AND *O* BY ADDING *ES*, AND FOR WORDS THAT END IN A VOWEL AND *O* BY ADDING *S*

plan

teach

Explain the Principle

“ Add *s* to words that end in a vowel and *o* to make them plural. ”

“ Add *es* to words that end in a consonant and *o* to make them plural. ”

Add <u>s</u> to words that end in a vowel and <u>o</u> to make them plural.

Add <u>es</u> to words that end in a consonant and <u>o</u> to make them plural.

<u>tomato</u>es <u>radio</u>s
<u>potato</u>es <u>rodeo</u>s
<u>hero</u>es <u>zoo</u>s

cities peaches
ponies glasses

① Tell the children they will learn about how to form the plural of words that end with *o*. Have *tomatoes, potatoes, heroes, radios, rodeos, zoos* written in two columns on a chart.

② Read the words with children. Suggested language: "What do you notice about these words?" Children will notice that they are all plurals (showing more than one) and end with *s*. Underline the base word in each.

③ Guide them to notice that some end in *es* and to discover that those have a consonant and *o* at the end of the base word.

④ Summarize the principle and write it at the top of the chart. Suggested language: "Add *s* to words that end in a vowel and *o* to make them plural. Add *es* to words that end in a consonant and *o* to make them plural."

⑤ Review a few examples of words that form a plural by changing *i* to *y* (e.g., *cities, ponies*) and those that added *es* because they end in *tch, sh, zz, ch, ss, x, s* (e.g., *peaches, glasses*).

⑥ Tell the children they are going to work with partners to make four different kinds of plurals. Demonstrate the process. Children write *tomatoes, radios, ponies,* and *peaches* at the top of a Four-Way Sort Card. Partners take turns drawing a word card, reading it, deciding how to form the plural, and writing the plural in the correct column on a Four-Way Sort Sheet. Each pair of children should work with twenty word cards. Finally, each child should read the whole list to a partner.

Name: Vanessa C.

tomatoes	radios	ponies	peaches
potatoes heroes zeroes tornadoes volcanoes	kangaroos zoos	countries ladies berries pennies bodies copies	lunches matches inches guesses dishes foxes

apply

take
read
sort
write
read

▸ Partners complete a Four-Way Sort with word cards as you demonstrated.

▸ Each partner chooses twenty word cards to sort and then records the plurals on a Four-Way Sort Sheet. Finally, each child reads a list to a partner.

share

Invite the children to read their lists to a different partner. Add a few more examples to the chart.

Invite the children to summarize what they know about plural forms.

Link

Interactive Read-Aloud: Read aloud a variety of books that feature many words in their plural form. Here are a few examples:

- *Brave Potatoes* by Toby Speed
- *Blue Potatoes, Orange Tomatoes* by Ruth Heller

Shared Reading: In familiar poems, have children find a few words that end in *o* in their plural form. Use a highlighter or highlighter tape to mark them.

Guided Reading: During word work write four to six words and have children explain how to form the plurals.

Guided/Independent Writing: During the editing process, remind children to notice and correct the spelling of plural words.

assess

- ▶ To assess children's control of spelling principles, dictate a sampling of words in their singular form and ask them to form the plurals.
- ▶ Observe how children write plural words to assess their control of the principles.

Expand the Learning

Have children play Plural Lotto. Include words to which only *s* is added and those that end in *f, fe,* or *lf* (see *Teaching Resources*).

Connect with Home

Send home a sheet of word cards with words in their plual form (Word Card Template; see *Teaching Resources*) for children to sort at home.

Send home a Two-Column Sheet. Ask children to list twenty objects from their home or neighborhood and to write the plural form.

Forming Plurals: Summary

Plural Lotto

Consider Your Children

Teach this lesson after children have experienced a range of common and less common principles for forming plurals. In this lesson they continue to consolidate their understandings and apply their skills. Included here are words that require a spelling change to make them plural (e.g., *children, men, feet*). Two new categories are introduced in this lesson: (1) words that change spelling in the plural; and (2) words that remain the same in the plural form.

Working with English Language Learners

In this lesson children expand their knowledge of plurals to include a more challenging form. To create some plural forms, not only does spelling change, but so does pronunciation. Have children say each word slowly to distinguish its ending sound and any other helpful sound to letter relationships. They can also look for useful patterns. Provide four or five clear, easy examples that children can use as references when considering the plural form (e.g., *It's like* knife.). During word work have children use magnetic letters to build singular words and change them to plural forms.

You Need

▶ Chart paper.

▶ Markers.

▶ Index cards.

From *Teaching Resources:*

▶ Pocket Chart Card Template.

▶ Directions for Lotto.

▶ Four-by-Four Lotto Game Boards.

▶ Lesson WS 17 Word Cards.

Understand the Principle

It is helpful for children to consolidate their understandings of how to form plurals so that they have categories of knowledge to draw on as they solve words.

Explain the Principle

❝ Add *s* to some words to make them plural. ❞

❝ Add *es* to words that end with *x, ch, sh, s, ss, tch*, or *zz*. ❞

❝ Add *s* to words that end in a vowel and *y*, but change the *y* to *i* and add *es* to words that end in consonant and *y*. ❞

❝ Change *f* to *v* and add *es* to words that end in *f, fe*, or *lf*. ❞

❝ Add *es* to words that end in a consonant and *o*, but add *s* to words that end in a vowel and *o*. ❞

❝ Add *s* to words that end in a vowel and *o*. ❞

❝ Some words change spelling and some remain the same. ❞

plan

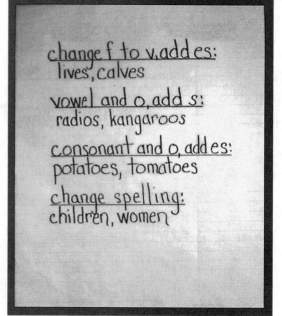

change f to v, add es:
lives, calves

vowel and o, add s:
radios, kangaroos

consonant and o, add es:
potatoes, tomatoes

change spelling:
children, women

Explain the Principle

" Add *s* to some words to make them plural, . "

" Add *es* to words that end with *x, ch, sh, s, ss, tch,* or *zz*. "

" Add *s* to words that end in a vowel and *y,* but change the *y* to *i* and add *es* to words that end in consonant and *y*. "

" Change *f* to *v* and add *es* to words that end in *f, fe,* or *lf*. "

" Add *es* to words that end in a consonant and *o,* but add *s* to words that end in a vowel and *o*. "

" Add *s* to words that end in a vowel and *o*. "

" Some words change spelling and some remain the same. "

① Tell children they will practice what they know about changing words from singular to plural forms.

② Have ready a list of the ways to make plurals as well as some large word cards showing the singular form of a variety of words.

③ Show a singular word (e.g., *beach*) and ask children how to form the plural. Then write the word under the correct principle (add *es*).

④ Repeat with several examples of each principle and add a few examples that children suggest.

⑤ Tell children they will play Plural Lotto. Demonstrate the process using all kinds of plurals. They should make note of two to three plurals that are new or interesting to bring back to group share.

take
read
tell
match
cover
write

- ▸ Children play Plural Lotto in small groups.
- ▸ Players take turns drawing a word card. They read the word and tell the principle that applies.
- ▸ Then they look for the word in its plural form on their Lotto Board.
- ▸ The first player to cover all of the words on his card wins the game.
- ▸ Children make note of two to three new or interesting plurals on an index card to bring to share.

LOTTO

berries	lunches	clocks	men
boxes	patches	families	wheels
studios	peaches	fairies	guesses
flashes	women	wishes	trays

patches

Using their notes as resources, ask children to suggest one more word for each principle, which you add to the chart.

Remind children they can use the chart as a reference when they write.

Link

Interactive Read-Aloud: Read aloud books that include a variety of plural forms. Write two or three of the words on a whiteboard after reading. Here are a few suggested titles:

- ▸ *Feathers: Poems about Birds* by Eileen Spinelli
- ▸ *Cornflakes: Poems* by James Stevenson

Shared Reading: On the first reading of a poem, cover the plural ending with a stick-on note. Ask children to spell the word before you uncover it.

Guided Reading: During word work have children make several singular words with magnetic letters and then change them to their plural form.

Guided/Independent Writing: Encourage children to use the summary chart when checking their spelling of plural forms.

assess

- ▸ Dictate a few words in plural form and have children write the singular form, and *vice versa*, to evaluate their flexibility with the principles.

Expand the Learning

Repeat this lesson with a variety of other words.

Have children play Go Fish with singular and plural forms (see *Teaching Resources*).

Have children complete a Read Around the Room Sheet (see *Teaching Resources*). In each category they write the shortened form of the principle. In the appropriate category, they write the plural forms of the words they find.

Connect with Home

Send home cards and game boards for Plural Lotto (see *Teaching Resources*) for children to play with family members.

Noticing Syllables in Multisyllable Words
Connect

Consider Your Children

Be sure children can hear and identify syllables in words and apply basic syllabication principles. In this lesson, they will listen for the consonant clusters in the middle of words. It is important for children to understand the structural elements of words. If children have not played Connect, then demonstrate how it is played with two players.

Working with English Language Learners

Longer words challenge English language learners, especially if they lack full control of the words in their speaking vocabularies. Being able to break words into syllables will help. Nonetheless, children might have difficulty pronouncing the words, which makes it more difficult to make connections. Say words and syllables clearly and have children repeat them several times. Consider having children cut apart and reassemble words written on word cards.

You Need

▶ Chart paper.

▶ Markers.

From *Teaching Resources:*

▶ Directions for Connect.

▶ Connect Game Cards made from Lesson WS 18 Word Cards and Deck Card Template.

Understand the Principle

Syllable juncture refers to the joining together of syllables. In this lesson children learn more about syllable units. Words can have the same letters at the juncture (e.g., *kitten*) or they can have different letters (e.g., *winter*). In either case, syllables are formed by dividing the two consonants. When there is a consonant digraph (consonants representing one sound) at the juncture, then the word is divided after the digraph.

Explain the Principle

" Divide the word after the first consonant in a consonant blend that joins two syllables in a word (*plas-tic*). "

" Divide the word after the consonant digraph that joins two syllables in a word (*wish-ful*). "

CONTINUUM: WORD STRUCTURE — RECOGNIZING AND USING SYLLABLES IN WORDS WITH THE VCC PATTERN (SYLLABLE JUNCTURE)

plan

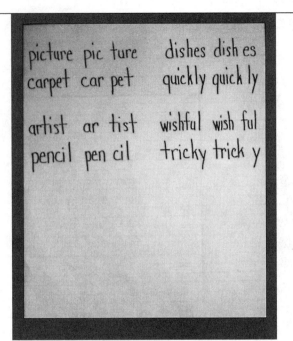

Explain the Principle

" Divide the word
after the first
consonant in a
consonant blend
that joins two
syllables in a word
(*plas-tic*). "

" Divide the word
after the consonant
digraph that joins
two syllables in a
word (*wish-ful*). "

① Tell children they will learn
more about syllables in words.

② Have *picture*, *carpet*, *dishes*, *quickly*
written in two columns on chart
paper with space to create a
second column next to each. Ask
children to read each word with
you and listen for the parts. Next
to each word write its parts.

③ Help children notice the final
letters in the first syllable and distinguish the syllables that have a consonant
digraph (*dishes*, *quickly*). Show them how the syllable ends after the digraph.
In contrast, point out where the syllables join in the words that have two
consonants in the middle that represent different sounds (*picture*, *carpet*).

④ Add *tricky*, *artist*, *pencil*, *wishful*, each time talking about where the two
syllables join. Summarize the principle. Suggested language: "Divide the
word after the first consonant in a consonant blend that joins two syllables
in a word (*plas-tic*). Divide the word after the consonant digraph that joins
two syllables in a word (*wish-ful*)."

⑤ Tell children they will play Connect with words that have two syllables
joined by a consonant blend (you can hear each consonant) or consonant
digraph (you hear one sound).

⑥ Demonstrate the game with two students. Each player is dealt eight cards.
The first player lays down a card, reads it aloud, and tells where to divide
the syllables. The second player follows suit by playing another word with
the same type of syllable juncture. After each player puts down a matching
card, the pile is moved to the side and not played again. If a player cannot
play a matching card, he is skipped and the next player goes. Wild cards
have a smiley face or some other symbol on them. They can be discarded at
any time. The first player to run out of cards wins the game.

place
read
tell
match

▸ Groups of two to four players play Connect. Players follow suit by matching words that have syllables that join in the same way. The goal is to run out of cards.

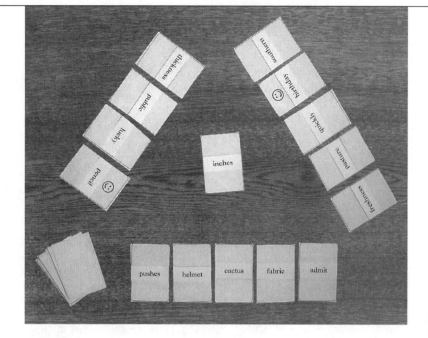

▸ Children bring one or two words to group share.

Ask the children for examples of other words with both types of syllable joining. Write them on the chart and review the principle.

Link

Interactive Read-Aloud: Read aloud a variety of books with words that have two syllable words. Choose two or three words that exemplify a syllable juncture with a consonant blend or a consonant digraph and write them on a chart. Here are a few suggested titles:

- ▸ *One of Each* by Mary Ann Hoberman
- ▸ *Bein' with You This Way* by W. Nikola-Lisa

Shared Reading: After enjoying a poem, point out two or three words that exemplify the two patterns of syllable juncture. Have children mark the syllables.

Guided Reading: When children come upon tricky words with two syllables, prompt them to look at the first part and the last part.

Guided/Independent Writing: When children write new words, remind them to think about syllable parts in order to figure out the spelling.

assess

- ▸ Dictate three to six words and have children write them in their syllable parts.

- ▸ Notice how children write two-syllable words and how easily they take them apart when they read.

Expand the Learning

Repeat this lesson with a different variety of two-syllable words.

Have children complete a Two-Way Sort, saying and sorting the words according to their type of syllable juncture (see *Teaching Resources*).

Connect with Home

Send home Deck Card Template sheets (see *Teaching Resources*) with two-syllable words for children to make a set of Connect cards to play with family members.

Identifying Syllables in Multisyllable Words

Trumps

Consider Your Children

Teach this lesson once children have strong control of syllable juncture in two-syllable words. In this lesson they develop flexibility in noticing parts in three- and four-syllable words so that they can solve multisyllable words easily and quickly. Be sure to use words children understand. The ability to notice word parts will help them write words. If children do not know how to play Trumps, then demonstrate the game.

Working with English Language Learners

As children work more with syllables, they find it easier to solve multisyllable words. You may wish to have English language learners keep a collection of multisyllable words on cards that they can cut apart and reassemble. During word work have them take apart several words from the text they are reading. Magnetic letters will also be helpful to them because they will need to physically move and group letters, providing a very concrete example.

You Need

▶ Chart paper.

▶ Markers.

From *Teaching Resources:*

▶ Directions for Trumps.

▶ Trump Game Cards made from selected Lesson WS 19 Word Cards and Deck Card Template (to make 52 cards, 26 with three-syllable words, 26 with four-syllable words, and four in each category with a sun on them).

Understand the Principle

Each syllable, or part, in a word contains a vowel sound. Children can listen for the parts in a word to help them write it. When they look at word parts, they solve words more easily, and know where to divide words in their writing when there is not enough room to write the whole word at the end of a line. Children will be able to notice the places syllables begin and end by listening for the syllables. If they have skill in using a dictionary, they can check the syllable parts, which are shown with black dots in entries.

Explain the Principle

" You can look at the syllables in a word to read it (*bi-cy-cle, to-geth-er, ev-er-y, won-der-ful, li-brar-y, com-pu-ter, au-to-mo-bile, a-quar-i-um, un-der-wat-er*). "

plan

Three Syllables | Four Syllables
icicle | unusual
forever | alligator
invention | adorable
cucumber | mysterious
tornado | watermelon

cam/er/a   mag/nif/i/cent

cu/ri/ous   spec/tac/u/lar

un/der/neath   en/ter/tain/ment

bi/cy/cle   a/dor/a/ble

① Tell the children they will learn more about parts in longer words.

② Have the children say *icicle, forever, invention, unusual, alligator, cucumber, adorable, mysterious, tornado, watermelon* and then clap each word. Write the words in two columns (three-syllable and four-syllable-words) on chart paper.

Explain the Principle

" You can look at the syllables in a word to read it (*bi-cy-cle, to-geth-er, ev-er-y, won-der-ful, li-brar-y, com-pu-ter, au-to-mo-bile, a-quar-i-um, un-der-wat-er*). "

③ Next write the following words and ask children to look for the parts as you place a slash mark to divide them: *cam/er/a, mag/nif/i/cent, cu/ri/ous, spec/tac/u/lar, un/der/neath, en/ter/tain/ment, bi/cy/cle, a/dor/a/ble.*

④ Summarize the principle. Suggested language: "You can look at the syllables in a word to read it."

⑤ Tell children they will play Trumps. Demonstrate the game with two players.

▶ The first player deals thirteen cards to each player and places the deck face down.

▶ The player to the right of the dealer places a card face up on the table and reads the word.

▶ The second player discards a card with the same number of syllables and reads it.

▶ The first player takes both cards.

▶ If a player does not have a card to follow suit, he takes a card from the deck.

▶ A trump card takes all the cards.

▶ The game ends when one player has all the cards or the most cards at the end of the time period.

apply

| place card |
| read word |
| match syllables |
| take card |

▸ Have the children play Trumps in groups of two to four players. The goal of the game is to follow suit and get as many cards as possible until one player has all the cards.

▸ Have children save words to share and add to class lists.

share

Ask the children to suggest three new words to add to the chart. Summarize the principle and remind children to notice the syllables when they read longer words. Invite children to share any words they found difficult to read or to break into syllables.

Link

Interactive Read-Aloud: Read aloud books that have many multisyllable words. After reading, write several of the words on the syllable chart and have children mark the parts. Here are a few suggested titles:

- ▸ *I Stink* by Kate and Jim McMillan
- ▸ *Uptown* by Byron Collier

Shared Reading: As children read new poems, prompt them to notice the syllables in longer words.

Guided Reading: As children read the text, use prompts such as these to help them solve unfamiliar words. *Do you see any parts that can help you? Look at the first part, the next part.*

Guided/Independent Writing: As children try to write longer words, encourage them to think of the syllable parts and write each one.

assess

- ▸ Give children a list of six to ten words and have them draw lines to show the syllable parts.
- ▸ Dictate four to six words to assess whether children write syllables to construct longer words.

Expand the Learning

Repeat this lesson with a variety of other three- or four-syllable words.

Have children play Word Plot with three- and four-syllable words (see *Teaching Resources*).

Have children complete a Four-Way Sort with one-, two-, three-, and four-syllable words or a Two-Way Sort with three- and four-syllable words (see *Teaching Resources*).

Connect with Home

Send home a Word Grid (see *Teaching Resources*) with three- and four-syllable words for children to read to family members.

Alternatively, send home two word grids and word cards (Word Card Template, *Teaching Resources*) for families to play the Word Grid Game.

Forming Comparisons with -er, -est

Making Words

Consider Your Children

If children have good control of all four principles, then combine them in this lesson. Otherwise, work with one or two principles at a time and limit the examples accordingly.

Working with English Language Learners

Use pictures or live props to ensure that English language learners understand the base word and that they are making comparisons. Have them label pictures with word cards. Give children simple examples and let them highlight the *-er* and *-est* endings; have them use whiteboards to show the base word and the suffix.

You Need

► Chart paper.

► Markers.

From *Teaching Resources:*

► Two-Column Sheets.

► Lesson WS 20 Word Cards.

Understand the Principle

An adjective can be changed by adding letters to show comparisons. Sometimes the letters *-r, -er,* or *-st* or *-est* are merely added. Other times the spelling changes before the *-er* or *-est* is added. The new words show the characteristic to a greater degree (*-er*) or to the furthest degree *-est*). Understanding how to form and recognize comparatives will help children expand their vocabulary.

Explain the Principle

" Add *-er* or *-est* to show how one thing compares with another. "

" Add *-r* or *-st* to words that end in silent *e* to make the *-er* or *-est* ending. "

" Double the consonant and add *-er* or *-est* to words that end in a short vowel and one consonant. "

" Change the *y* to *i* and add *-er* or *-est* to words that end in *y.* "

CONTINUUM: WORD STRUCTURE — RECOGNIZING AND USING ENDINGS THAT SHOW COMPARISON

plan

teach

① Tell children they will learn more about describing words, or adjectives.

② On chart paper, write *blue, bluer, bluest* at the top of three columns. Then write each word in a sentence. *The shirt is* blue. *The vase is* blue*r. The cup is the* blue*st.* Underline the base word *blue* in each.

③ Repeat the process with several other adjectives.

④ Ask children to notice the spelling of the words with *-er* and *-est*. They will notice that

  ▸ *-r* or *-st* is added to words with *e* on the end (e.g, *blue, brave*);

  ▸ *-er* or *-est* is added to words with a long vowel and one or two consonants at the end (e.g., *clean, bold*);

  ▸ the consonant is doubled when words end in a short vowel and one consonant (e.g., *hot, thin*); and

  ▸ the *y* is changed to *i* when words end in one or more consonants and *y* (e.g., *frosty, curly*).

⑤ Tell the children they will make words that show comparison by adding *-er* and *-est* to twenty describing words and write them on a Two-Column Sheet. Demonstrate with two or three principles. Each child takes a word card and says the word. Then the child writes it with *-er* in the first column and *-est* in the second column. Finally, children read their lists to a partner.

Explain the Principle

❝ Add *er* or *est* to show how one thing compares with another. ❞

❝ Add *r* or *st* to words that end in silent *e* to make the *er* or *est* ending. ❞

❝ Double the consonant and add *-er* or *-est* to words that end in a short vowel and one consonant. ❞

❝ Change the *y* to *i* and add *er* or *est* to words that end in *y*. ❞

apply

take card
write word
write word
read list

▶ Children take twenty word cards one at a time. They write the comparative forms on a Two-Column Sheet.

▶ They write the word with *-er* and then *-est.* Then they read their lists to a partner.

▶ Children come to sharing prepared to add some words to the chart.

Name: Cam

harder	hardest
slimmer	slimmest
lovelier	loveliest
tanner	tannest
wetter	wettest
nearer	nearest
darker	darkest
warmer	warmest
luckier	luckiest
madder	maddest
juicier	juiciest
flatter	flattest
smaller	smallest
odder	oddest
newer	newest
thinner	thinnest

share

Have the children suggest a few more words to add to the chart.

Create a four-column chart to group together words that follow the same principle.

Link

Interactive Read-Aloud: Read aloud books that show words in their comparative forms. Here are a few suggested titles:

- ▸ *Alphabeasts* by Wallace Edwards
- ▸ *Much Bigger Than Martin* by Steven Kellogg

Shared Reading: Present poems on a transparency and then have students read together. Then have children mark one or two words that show comparison.

Guided Reading: During word work write a few words on a whiteboard and have children tell how to change them when adding *-er* or *-est*.

Guided/Independent Writing: Remind children to check their spelling of words showing comparisons and using *-er* or *-est*.

assess

- ▸ Give children a list of four to six words and have them add *-er* or *-est* to evaluate their control of the principles.
- ▸ Observe how easily children solve words with *-er* or *-est* when reading text.

Expand the Learning

Repeat this lesson with a different variety of adjectives (see Category Word List, Describing Words in *Teaching Resources*).

Have children complete a Four-Way Sort, dividing words according to each of the four principles in the lesson (see *Teaching Resources*).

Connect with Home

Send home a Word Grid with adjectives that have *-er* or *-est* for children to read with family members.

Recognizing Words with a Prefix (un-)

Making Words

Consider Your Children

Children should have good control of base words and common suffixes *-s, -ed, -ing*. Use this lesson late in grade three. Once children understand that a prefix adds meaning and can easily identify base words, it will be easy to add to the list of prefixes they know.

Working with English Language Learners

To work successfully with prefixes, English language learners should know the base words well and be familiar with some common words with prefixes. Begin with simple examples that children will easily understand; help them use the words in sentences or act them out. Contrast the word with the prefix to the word without it (e.g., *happy* and *unhappy*). Creating pictures contrasting base words and words preceded by *un-* will help them think specifically about the meaning of the words.

You Need

▶ Magnetic letters.

▶ Cookie sheet or magnetic whiteboard.

From *Teaching Resources:*

▶ List Sheets.

▶ Lesson WS 21 Word Cards.

Understand the Principle

A prefix is a group of letters, or word part, placed at the beginning of a base word. A prefix can have more than one meaning. When you remove it from a word, the word that remains has its own meaning. When the prefix *un-* is added to a word, it makes the word take the opposite meaning, or it means *not.* A word like *uncle* also has *un-*, but it is not a prefix because it is not added to a base word. Understanding prefixes helps readers efficiently decode multisyllable words.

Explain the Principle

" Add a word part or prefix to the beginning of a word to change its meaning. "

" Add *un-* to the beginning of a word to mean *not* or the *opposite of.* "

CONTINUUM: WORD STRUCTURE — RECOGNIZING AND USING COMMON PREFIXES (*UN–* MEANING *NOT* OR *THE OPPOSITE OF*)

plan

① Tell children they will learn more about parts, or prefixes, that can be put at the beginning of words.

② Build *unreal* and *unlucky* with magnetic letters. Cover *un-* and ask children to read each word. Uncover *un-* and read the whole word. Suggested language: "*Unreal, unlucky.* What do they mean?" Children will conclude that they mean *not real* and *not lucky.* Point out that *real* and *lucky* are words by themselves and that the *un-*, a prefix or a word part, is added to the beginning to mean *not.*

③ Ask children to suggest several other words that begin with *un-* and build them with magnetic letters. If they suggest words that do not use *un-* as a prefix (e.g., *under*), build the words and demonstrate that when you remove *un-* the remaining letters do not make a word.

④ Tell children that they will make words with the prefix *un-* and a base word. Show a base word (e.g., *pack*) and put the word part *un* in front of it to make *unpack.* Remind children that when they put together the parts, they must form a real word. If they are unsure if a word is real, they can look it up in a dictionary or bring it to sharing for others to consider. Each time children make a word, they write it on a List Sheet or in their Word Study Notebook. Then they write three sentences that each use a *un-* word on a sheet of paper or in their notebook.

My horse tried to unseat me.

Haley learned to tie and untie her shoes.

After our trip I had to unpack.

Name: Greg   List Sheet

1. unlucky
2. unjust
3. unlikely
4. unlimited
5. unload
6. unmotivated
7. unoccupied
8. unpack
9. unreal
10. unoriginal
11. unreliable
12. unreachable
13. undone
14. unskilled
15. unsafe
16. unseat
17. unstoppable
18. unsteady
19. unzip
20. untie

LIST SHEET

make word

write list

write three sentences

▸ Have children use word cards and *un-* word part cards to make twenty words that they write on a List Sheet or in the Word Study Notebooks.

▸ Then they write three sentences, each using a word with the *un-* prefix on the back of the List Sheet or in their notebooks.

Add a few more examples of *un-* words to the chart and put a word with *un-* on the word wall as an example.

Invite each child to read one sentence she wrote. Have children share any words they created where they are unsure if the word is real. Invite the group to consider the word.

.

Link

Interactive Read-Aloud: Read aloud books that include words with *un-* prefixes. Here are a few suggested titles:

▸ ***Billy's Unusual Adventure*** by Robert Pfeiffer

▸ ***Annabelle's Un-Birthday*** by Steven Kroll

Shared Reading: After you have read and enjoyed a poem together, have children find words that have *un-* prefixes. Have them tell the base word and highlight the prefix.

Guided Reading: When children encounter new *un-* words, show them how to look at the base word and then the prefix. During word work, make three or four base words and add *un-*.

Guided/Independent Writing: When conferring with writers, point out a word with an *un-* prefix.

assess

▸ Observe children's ability to decode words with the *un-* prefix.

▸ Ask children to write three words with the prefix *un-*.

Expand the Learning

Repeat this lesson with other prefixes (*in-, im-, mis-, il-, dis-, non-, uni-, bi-, tri-, pre-*).

Connect with Home

Send home four or five word cards that show words with the prefix *un-*. Have children and their family members write three more sentences containing the *un-* words.

Recognizing Words with a Prefix (re-)

Follow the Path

Consider Your Children

Use this lesson late in the school year, after children have good control of base words and inflected endings. Understanding prefixes supports the children's ability to take apart words, learn their meaning, and spell them correctly. To add more challenge to this lesson, consider adding more prefixes, such as *pre-* or *non-*. This lesson is also helpful for expanding vocabulary.

Working with English Language Learners

Learning some simple prefixes helps English language learners rapidly expand their knowledge of English. Begin with simple examples; be sure children know the base words you use. Demonstrate adding and removing prefixes by using magnetic letters or cut-up words. Have children say the base word and the word with the prefix.

You Need

- ▸ Magnetic letters.
- ▸ Cookie sheet or magnetic whiteboard.
- ▸ Die.

From *Teaching Resources:*

- ▸ Directions for Follow the Path.
- ▸ Follow the Path game boards made from Lesson WS 22 Word List.

Understand the Principle

A prefix is a group of letters placed at the beginning of a base word. There can be more than one meaning for a prefix. When you remove a prefix from a word, a meaningful word remains. The prefix *re-* means *again (rewrite)*. It can also mean *back* (e.g., *recall*). *In-, im-, mis-, pre-, il-, dis-, non-, uni-, bi-,* and *tri-* are common prefixes. The ability to identify common word parts helps children take apart a word, spell it, and think about its meaning.

Explain the Principle

" Add a word part or prefix to the beginning of a word to change its meaning. "

" Add *re-* to the beginning of a word to mean *do again.* "

plan

Explain the Principle

" Add a word part or prefix to the beginning of a word to change its meaning. "

" Add *re-* to the beginning of a word to mean *do again.* "

① Tell the children they will learn more about word parts.

② Make *refill* and *remake* with magnetic letters.

③ Read the words and ask children what they mean. They will likely tell you that *refill* means *to fill again* and *remake* means *to make again.* Show children that when you take away *re-*, a base word remains.

④ Ask them to suggest other words that begin with *re* (meaning *again*). If children offer a word like *reason*, make it and then explain that if you take away *re-* you do not have a base word.

⑤ Tell children they will play Follow the Path with words that have the prefix *re-*.

apply

roll dice
move piece
read word
use in sentence

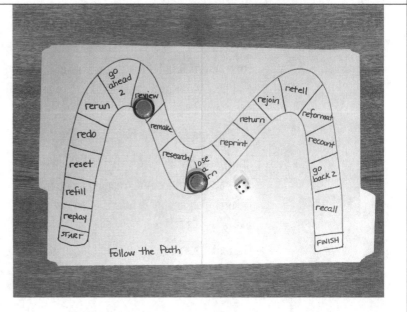

Follow the Path

▶ Have the children play Follow the Path with words that have the *re-* prefix.

▶ On each space of the game board is a word that begins with *re-*.

▶ Children roll a die, move that number of spaces, read the word, and use it in a sentence. (An alternative is to leave the spaces on the path blank, and write the words on word cards that the children choose.)

share

Ask children to give a few more examples of *re-* words for the class chart.

Put an example of a *re-* word on the word wall as an example.

Link

Interactive Read-Aloud: Read aloud books that have words with *re-* prefixes. Here are a few suggested titles:

- ▶ *The Spotted Little Fish* by Jane Yolen

- ▶ *Family Reunion* by Mary Quattlebaum

Shared Reading: After reading a poem, have children find and mark two or three words with the *re-* prefix.

Guided Reading: Show children how to look for the base word and the prefix when they attempt to read unknown *re-* words.

Guided/Independent Writing: As you help children use more interesting words in their writing, point out words with the *re-* prefix.

assess

- ▶ Observe children's ability to take apart words with *re-* prefixes.

- ▶ Dictate four or five words that have *re-* prefixes and have children write them in a sentence.

Expand the Learning

Repeat this lesson or make Lesson WS 21 more challenging by adding more words that have *re-* prefixes meaning *back* (e.g., *replace, return, rebound*).

Repeat this lesson and make it more challenging by focusing on more prefixes (*dis* meaning opposite of, *non* meaning not, *mis* meaning wrong, *pre* meaning before, *uni* meaning one, *bi* meaning two, *tri* meaning three, *in* meaning not). Choose prefixes and base words that children understand and will use.

For more sophisticated learners, research a word's history and explain it in an interesting way to children.

Connect with Home

Send home a Follow the Path game board and word cards so that children can play the game with family members.

Word-Solving Actions

Word-solving actions are the strategic moves readers and writers make when they use their knowledge of the language system to solve words. These strategies are "in-the-head" actions that are invisible, although we can infer them from some overt behavior. The principles listed in this section represent children's ability to use the principles in the previous sections of the Continuum.

All lessons related to the Continuum provide opportunities for children to apply principles in active ways; for example, through sorting, building, locating, reading, or writing. Lessons related to word-solving actions demonstrate to children how they can problem-solve by working on words in isolation or while reading or writing continuous text. The more children can integrate these strategies into their reading and writing systems, the more flexible they will become in solving words. The reader/writer may use knowledge of letter/sound relationships, for example, either to solve an unfamiliar word or to check that the reading is accurate. Rapid, automatic word solving is a basic component of fluency and important for comprehension because it frees children's attention to focus on the meaning and language of the text.

Connect to Assessment

See related WSA Assessment Tasks in the Assessment Guide in *Teaching Resources:*

▶ Sorting Words

▶ Using Known Words to Read or Spell New Words

▶ Using Letter, Sound, and Word Knowledge to Solve Words and Monitor Reading

▶ Making New Words by Using What You Know

Develop Your Professional Understanding

See *Word Matters: Teaching Phonics and Spelling in the Reading/Writing Classroom* by G.S. Pinnell and I. C. Fountas. 1998 Portsmouth, NH: Heinemann.

Related pages: 62–63, 100–101, 104–105, 123–124, 128–130, 149–167, 168–188, 233–248

Learning How to Learn Words: Buddy Study 1

Choose, Write, Build, Mix, Fix, Mix

Consider Your Children

The five-day Buddy Study system provides a systematic way for children to learn spelling principles. In third grade, use the five lessons in the Buddy Study system early in the year to get children started in the differentiated spelling system. If they have used the system previously, then this lesson serves as a review to ensure effective learning routines. Prior to this lesson, give High Frequency Word tests to assess children's needs and to create a list of words they need to learn. Highlight the known words on the list and then children can choose from among those that are not known. In addition, have children list on a Words-to-Learn List the words that they misspell in their own writing. The number of words children choose for the five-day cycle will vary; from five to ten is sufficient. You can select any principle to illustrate the routines of the five-day sequence, but for the first lesson in a series, it is best to feature a spelling principle that is easy for children to grasp and apply.

Working with English Language Learners

Your class will be studying these words for five days, so it is important that the words your English language learners choose are meaningful to them. Avoid confusing words that they find difficult to pronounce. Easy high frequency words they do not know (or they nearly know) are always appropriate.

You Need

► Chart paper.

► Markers.

► Cookie sheet or magnetic whiteboard.

► Blank index cards.

► Magnetic letters.

► Buddy Study Pocket Chart (library pocket cards in which students place cards with lists of words for the week. *Word Matters*, 1998).

► Word Study Folder (includes High Frequency Word Test and Words-to-Learn List).

From *Teaching Resources:*

► Words-to-Learn Sheet.

► High Frequency Words List. (Select appropriate list.)

Understand the Principle

This lesson helps children notice visual features of words and encourages them to take charge of their own learning. Using magnetic letters helps them to attend to and remember visual details. Consider beginning the five-day Buddy Study sequence on Tuesday so that students can continue to make connections over the weekend (see WSA 4).

Explain the Principle

" You can make a word several times to learn the sequence of letters. "

plan

Explain the Principle

" You can make a word several times to learn the sequence of letters. "

① Present a lesson on a principle that children easily understand such as adding *ed* to words. Suggested language: "Sometimes you add *ed* to words to show that something happened in the past. This ending sounds different in some words." Show a list of words that illustrate the principle. Have children suggest several words that illustrate the principle.

② Suggested language: "Today you will choose five words from our lesson. These will be your *core words*. You will also look at your Words-to-Learn List in your Word Study Folder and choose *five personal words*. Then you will have ten words to work with. Write each word on your card and then I'll check them." Have children choose words from the lesson (at least one word from each category you have introduced).

③ Check each word for accuracy and place your initials on the card.

④ Suggested language: "Next, you will make each word with magnetic letters and check it letter by letter." Demonstrate making a word with magnetic letters and checking it with the word on the card, saying the names of letters aloud. "Then mix the letters and quickly build and check the word two more times." Explain that children will build, mix, and make each of their ten words three times.

⑤ Show children how to put the index cards back in the Buddy Study Library Pocket Chart so they will be available next time they are needed.

choose word
write word
build word
mix word
fix word (3x)

▸ Have the children choose ten words: five words from the minilesson list and five from their Individual Words-to-Learn List.

▸ They write each word on an index card.

▸ Confirm that each word on the card is spelled correctly and initial children's cards.

▸ Children build each word three times with magnetic letters, each time checking the spelling letter-by-letter with their card.

▸ Children place their cards in the Buddy Study Library Pocket Chart so that they are available for the cycle of learning activities.

Have children share one of the words they are trying to learn.

Ask children to talk about what they notice about the words they are learning.

Discuss how building the words with magnetic letters helps them notice the letter sequences.

Link

Interactive Read-Aloud: Read aloud books that invite children to inquire about words. Here are a few suggested titles:

- ▶ *It's about Time* by Heide/Gilliard/Pierce
- ▶ *A Gaggle of Geese* by Philippa-Alys Browne

Shared Reading: Have the children examine a poem or other text that has been used for shared reading and locate words that illustrate specific principles about how words work.

Guided Reading: During word work, have children work more with magnetic letters. For children having difficulty learning how words work, magnetic letters provide an important support.

Guided/Independent Writing: Remind children to be sure that they accurately spell the words that they are studying in the Buddy Study system.

assess

- ▶ Notice whether children build words accurately and quickly.
- ▶ Look at children's independent writing over several weeks to determine whether they are using the lesson principle and accurately spelling the words they have studied.

Expand the Learning

Repeat this lesson if needed to be sure that children have learned the routine of choosing and building words.

Connect with Home

Have the children make a second copy of their index cards to take home so they can practice making their words at home with magnetic letters or letter cards.

Have children share their Words-to-Learn with a family member who can help them study the words.

Learning How to Learn Words: Buddy Study 2

Look, Say, Cover, Write, Check

Consider Your Children

In the previous lesson, children learned a principle and selected core words as well as some personal words for their individual spelling lists. They learned how to select their own words to learn and keep track of their learning.

They are now ready to use the study method Look, Say, Cover, Write, Check. Each student needs a spelling buddy; be sure that pairs of children are able to read one another's words. Have children self-evaluate how well they use the routine.

Working with English Language Learners

Help English language learners by working with them in a small group and providing explicit demonstration of the routine. This set of routines will support their independent study of word patterns. It is important that children work with words that are meaningful to them.

You Need

► Index cards with Buddy Study words.

► Highlighters.

► File folders with one side cut in three or four strips (see illustration).

► Large version of Look, Say, Cover, Write, Check Sheet (for your demonstration).

From *Teaching Resources*:

► Look, Say, Cover, Write, Check Sheets (select from two different forms).

Understand the Principle

This routine helps children learn a way of studying words by looking closely at them and noticing the details that distinguish them. Children need to learn how to look at words, say them, remove them from sight (cover them), and then check them with the initial word. The deliberate moves in Look, Say, Cover, Write, Check will help children build strategies for remembering and checking words. This slow-paced method of considering a word will eventually become automatic.

Explain the Principle

" You can look at a word, say it, cover it, write it, and check it to help you learn to spell it correctly. "

teach

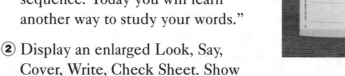

Explain the Principle

❝ You can look at a word, say it, cover it, write it, and check it to help you learn to spell it correctly. ❞

① Review the principle taught on Day 1 of the Buddy Study cycle. Then explain this routine for Day 2. Suggested language: "Yesterday you chose words you need to learn and made them with magnetic letters so that you could practice the sequence. Today you will learn another way to study your words."

② Display an enlarged Look, Say, Cover, Write, Check Sheet. Show children a standard Look, Say, Cover, Write, Check Sheet, and then place it in a precut file folder with all the flaps open. Explain that you will demonstrate how to use Look, Say, Cover, Write, Check to study words.

③ Suggested language: "You will write one of your words in the first column and say it. Then you check it with the same word on your index card letter-by-letter or part-by-part to be sure you wrote it correctly." Demonstrate this procedure and then ask a volunteer to repeat the demonstration.

④ Suggested language: "Then you will look carefully at the word, say it, and cover the word in the first column with the flap. Lift up the next flap and write the word in the second column. Then check it letter-by-letter or part-by-part with the word that you know is correct." Demonstrate this process.

⑤ Show children how to look, cover, and say the word in the first column again and write it in the third column (and fourth if you are using the Four-Column folder). Children check the word each time and notice any mistakes.

⑥ If a word is still misspelled in the last column, show children how to highlight the part to remember (e.g., an omitted letter, a substituted letter, or a reversed letter). Then demonstrate how to make the misspelled word three times with magnetic letters and check it with the word on the card.

apply

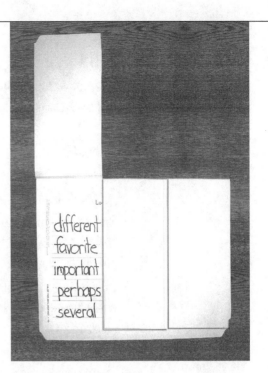

look at word
say word
cover word
write word
check word

▸ Have children use the Look, Say, Cover, Write, Check procedure with their ten spelling words.

▸ They work on one word at a time, writing and checking it in all the columns.

▸ If they misspell the word in the last column, they highlight the part to remember and make (and check) it three times with magnetic letters.

share

Ask children to talk about the principle that is highlighted in this Buddy Study cycle.

Ask them to talk about what they learned from doing Look, Say, Cover, Write, Check.

Explain to children that they will be using the Buddy Study system each week to help them learn to spell words.

Link

Interactive Read-Aloud: Read aloud books that invite children to inquire about words. Here are a few suggested titles:

- ▶ *Weather Words and What They Mean* by Gail Gibbons
- ▶ *The Distant Talking Drum* by Isaac Olaeye

Shared Reading: Using a familiar text, ask children to find words that illustrate the principles children are studying.

Guided Reading: Help children notice when words they are learning to spell occur in their reading.

Guided/Independent Writing: Instead of copying words, encourage children to use a quick version of Look, Say, Cover, Write, Check as they use words on the word wall or on charts in the classroom. They can look at the word, try to write it, and then check it.

assess

- ▶ Notice whether children apply the principle taught in this lesson in their daily writing.
- ▶ Observe and document those children who are using Look, Say, Cover, Write, Check routines easily and those who need more practice.

Expand the Learning

Repeat the routines as needed to be sure that children understand how to use Look, Say, Cover, Write, Check.

Connect with Home

Have children take their Buddy Study cards home so that they can practice spelling and writing the words, or making them with letter cards or magnetic letters with family members.

For children who need more practice you may want to send home a Look, Say, Cover, Write, Check Sheet for extra practice.

Learning How to Learn Words: Buddy Study 3

Buddy Check

Consider Your Children

Provide adequate demonstration and guidance so that children can use this helpful routine. They will need to have spelling partners. Be sure that partners have about the same spelling ability; they should be able to read one another's words and use them in sentences.

In this lesson, children use a new strategy for learning words. They learn to write a word; and, if it does not "look right," they write it again and check its accuracy.

Working with English Language Learners

Buddy Check offers English language learners a systematic way of checking and tracking their own learning of words. Be sure that partners know how to pronounce the words and use them in sentences. Also be sure that students understand how to carefully check the words and show their partners the correct spelling when needed. Work with a small group if necessary to facilitate saying the words and using them in sentences.

You Need

▶ Highlighters.

▶ Markers.

▶ Magnetic letters.

▶ Cookie sheet or magnetic whiteboard.

▶ Index cards with Buddy Study words.

▶ Large version of Buddy Check Sheet for your demonstration.

From *Teaching Resources:*

▶ Buddy Check Sheets.

Understand the Principle

It is important for children to learn how to notice and correct spelling errors so that they can arrive at the conventional spelling of a word. The first step in achieving standard spelling is to know when a word does not "look right." This step in the Buddy Study system will help children detect errors and try letter sequences until the word looks right and is spelled correctly.

Explain the Principle

❝ You can write a word, look at it, and try again to make it 'look right.' ❞

❝ You can notice and think about the parts of words that are tricky for you. ❞

❝ You can write words to see if you know them. ❞

(BUDDY STUDY) WSA 3 WORD-SOLVING ACTIONS

plan

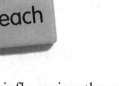

Explain the Principle

❝ You can write a word, look at it, and try again to make it 'look right.' ❞

❝ You can notice and think about the parts of words that are tricky for you. ❞

❝ You can write words to see if you know them. ❞

① Briefly review the principles from Days 1 and 2. Tell children they will use the words they are studying in a new way.

② Suggested language: "Yesterday you used Look, Say, Cover, Write, Check to study words. Today you will use Buddy Check to see which words you already know. This will help you learn how to fix your own spelling errors."

③ Display an enlarged version of the Buddy Check Sheet. Have a volunteer demonstrate by writing his words (which you say one at a time and use in a sentence) in the first column of the sheet. Arrange with the demonstrator for at least one error so that you can show the other children what to do.

④ When the child has finished writing the words in the first column, check them one at a time and make a check mark by each word that is written correctly. Make an X next to any incorrect words and ask the child to try them again as you say each word. If there are any words still wrong after the second try, the child writes these words correctly in the last column. You can guide the correct writing of the words.

⑤ Ask the child to look at the correct spelling of the words in the last column and tell specifically what he wants to remember about spelling each word correctly. Have him write the words in the bottom section of the sheet and highlight the tricky parts.

⑥ The child then makes each word three times with magnetic letters and writes what he wants to remember.

⑦ Tell children that they will do Buddy Check with their spelling partners.

apply

write word
try again
write word
try again
mark tricky parts

▸ Have partners complete the Buddy Check with a partner.

▸ Buddies should take care to say words clearly and use them in sentences. They wait for their partners to say "ready" before giving the next word.

▸ On words they missed, children highlight the part to remember, make the word three times with magnetic letters, and write something about the word to help them remember (e.g., "double *t* in the middle").

share

Have children share some of the statements they made on their sheets about the tricky words.

Link

Interactive Read-Aloud: Read aloud books that invite children to inquire about words. Here are a few suggested titles:

- ▶ *If You Were a Writer* by Joan Nixon
- ▶ *When I First Came to This Land* by Harriet Ziefert

Shared Reading: Demonstrate how to check a word in text by thinking about how it looks and then examining it to see if it "looks right."

Guided Reading: During word work help children learn how to check their word knowledge. They can quickly write two or three words you dictate; then partners can check one another's work. Children can highlight word parts they want to remember. If there is time, have children turn over their papers and dictate the words again.

Guided/Independent Writing: Hold children accountable for accurately spelling words they have studied when using them in their writing.

assess

- ▶ Observe children's self-correction strategies when they write independently. You should be able to see that they stop and look at difficult words.

- ▶ Remind children to proofread their writing. It is important that they notice and try to correct words that do not "look right."

Expand the Learning

Repeat this lesson, featuring a different principle in order to establish the routine of writing and thinking about the features of words.

Connect with Home

Have children take home their Buddy Check Sheets so that family members can dictate and check the words for extra practice.

Learning How to Learn Words: Buddy Study 4

Making Connections

Consider Your Children

For the first three days of the Buddy Study system, children have studied their words in a variety of ways. By this time, you should be able to observe that they know how to spell most of them. Be sure to limit the number of words. The purpose of the system is to help children learn principles as well as some individual words. They need only a few words for each principle. Too many words may lead to confusion and interfere with clear thinking about categories. You can choose one of three versions of the Making Connections Sheets; adjust the lesson accordingly. This lesson includes several ways to make connections. Show only one or two methods during any lesson; repeat it over several weeks to show many new ways. You will want to make a chart of ways to make connections that students can use as a reference.

Working with English Language Learners

Making connections requires English language learners to notice features of the words they are studying. It will be very helpful for them to make connections between and among English words as they learn more about the language. At first, making connections may be a challenge for some children because their repertoire of English words is small. Work with a small group to demonstrate the process and suggest words. Children might make connections to words in their own languages, which is a helpful and creative process.

You Need

▶ Magnetic letters.

▶ Cookie sheet or magnetic whiteboard.

▶ Index cards with Buddy Study words.

▶ Large version of Making Connections Sheet for your demonstration.

From *Teaching Resources:*

▶ Making Connections Sheets version 1, 2, or 3. (Each child may need more than one depending on the number of Buddy Study words.)

Understand the Principle

In this lesson, children go beyond the particular words they are studying. They connect them to other words by how they sound or look, or what they mean. Children need to develop networks of meaning around words so that they think about common patterns, underlying rules or principles, and larger categories. Establishing the habit of looking for patterns and making connections will help children internalize word solving strategies. Help them discover many new ways of making connections.

Explain the Principle

" You can use parts of words you know to read or write new words. "

" You can use what you know about words to read new words. "

plan

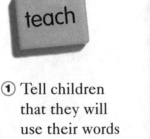

Explain the Principle

" You can use parts of words you know to read or write new words. "

" You can use what you know about words to read new words. "

① Tell children that they will use their words in a new way. Suggested language: "You know how to spell most of your words. Today you will use what you know about words to make connections to other words."

② Show children a word made with magnetic letters (e.g., *chased*). Ask if they know another word that begins like *chased*. They may suggest words like *choose* or *chair*. Then ask for words that end like *chased*; they may suggest *walked* or *hopped*. Ask children if they know any words that rhyme with *chased*. They may suggest words like *haste* or *paste*. Prompt children to think about words that mean the same as *chased* or mean the opposite. Children may suggest *ran*.

③ Suggested language: "Today you will think of three words that begin, end, rhyme, or have the same or opposite meanings as your Buddy Study words. You can use our charts, your word lists, or dictionaries as resources. I'll show you how to record your connections."

④ Display the enlarged Making Connections Sheet (any version) and demonstrate how to complete it. Show children how to underline the parts that are the same. Have them write three words that *start like, end like, rhyme with, mean the same as,* or *mean the opposite of* each Buddy Study word. Adjust the conversation to fit different versions.

⑤ Explain that during the year children will make many different kinds of connections with the words that they choose for the Buddy Study system and you will add to the list of possibilities.

► Have children use their Buddy Study words and a Making Connections Sheet to connect their words in several ways.

► They write each word on their lists.

► Then they write three words that start like, end like, rhyme with, mean the same, and mean the opposite of the Buddy Study word. Children might make some new connections of their own.

Have children share one of the connections that they have made for each word. Have them use precise language, for example:

  "*Chased* starts like *choose.*"

  "*Chased* sounds like *jumped* at the end."

  "*Chased* rhymes with *paste.*"

Post a chart that lists the kinds of connections children make.

Link

Interactive Read-Aloud: Read aloud books that invite children to make connections among words. Here are a few suggested titles:

- ▸ *Dear Mrs. LaRue* by Mark Teague
- ▸ *The Company of Crows* by Marilyn Singer

Shared Reading: When looking at a shared text, invite children to make a connection between words. As they become accustomed to looking for patterns, they will start to look at words in flexible ways, quickly making several kinds of connections.

Guided Reading: Help children solve new words by connecting them to words that they already know.

Guided/Independent Writing: Prompt children to think of words they know when they are spelling new words.

assess

- ▸ Dictate a few easy words to children. Ask them to write each word and then make two connections. Observe how quickly and easily they are able to perform the task.

Expand the Learning

Repeat this lesson to reinforce the routine. Teach children how to make other kinds of connections:

- ▸ words with the same middle sound
- ▸ words with the same vowels or vowel combination
- ▸ words that start or end the same
- ▸ words that rhyme
- ▸ words that mean about the same (synonyms)
- ▸ words that mean the opposite (antonyms)
- ▸ words that have the same ending parts
- ▸ words that are about the same topic
- ▸ words with the same number of syllables

Connect with Home

Have children take home their Making Connections Sheets and share them with family members. Consider beginning the five-day Buddy Study sequence on Tuesday or Wednesday so that they can continue to make connections over the weekend.

Encourage students to bring to class more connections after talking with friends and families.

Learning How to Learn Words: Buddy Study 5

Buddy Study Test

Consider Your Children

If children have understood the tasks and fully participated in the previous four days of the Buddy Study system, they have not only learned to spell the selected words but have made important connections to other words. Because children chose words from a list of examples of the minilesson principle, they will be able to apply their knowledge to solving new words. If children still have difficulty spelling, then examine closely the level of difficulty of the words they are choosing and note how well they understand the routines. Reteach as needed. You will collect the students' notebooks and check the tests for each student.

Working with English Language Learners

The previous four days of study have prepared English language learners to be successful in the Buddy Study Test. It is important that children learn to perform independently in a testing situation and build confidence through success. If children are having difficulty with their words, they may not understand the principle, or the words might be too difficult. Adjust the task so that children can be successful. Increased use of magnetic letters helps draw their attention to the visual features of words. Also help them use their words in meaningful sentences.

You Need

▶ Chart paper.

▶ Markers.

▶ Index cards with Buddy Study words.

▶ Word Study Notebooks.

From *Teaching Resources:*

▶ Words-to-Learn Sheets.

Understand the Principle

The ultimate goals of the Buddy Study system is to enable children to learn how to learn words and to spell many words quickly and automatically—without even thinking about them. Fluent spellers do not need models for most words and don't consciously make connections. They do so unconsciously, accessing implicit knowledge. They also know how to check their spelling, often writing a word to see if it "looks right." This test enables them to confirm their knowledge and then be held accountable for correctly spelling their words in all written products.

Explain the Principle

" You can write words to see if you know them. "

CONTINUUM: WORD-SOLVING ACTIONS — NOTICING AND CORRECTING SPELLING ERRORS

plan

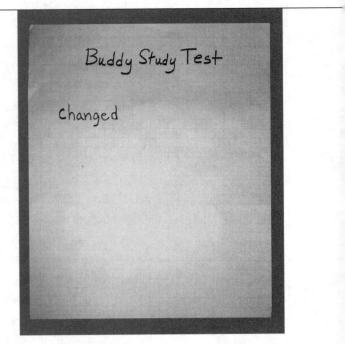

Buddy Study Test

changed

Explain the Principle

" You can write words to see if you know them. "

1. Suggested language: "You have studied your words and made connections with them. Today you will work with your buddy to test your knowledge. Your buddy will read each of your words to you and use it in a sentence, just like on the Buddy Check. You will write your words in your Word Study Notebook and put the notebook in the basket for me to check."

2. Show children the place where they turn in their notebooks.

3. Make it clear that the buddy only dictates the words and uses them in sentences. The buddy does not check the test.

4. Ask a volunteer to demonstrate saying a word and using it in a sentence (e.g., *changed*. I *changed* my mind about having dessert). Have another child write the word on the chart paper.

5. Partners who are taking the test say "ready" when they are ready to hear the next word and sentence. Remind partners who are giving the test to let the writers take the time they need to think about and write the word.

6. Suggested language: "After you give your buddy a test, then your buddy gives you the test. This will not take a lot of time. Remember to place your Word Study Notebooks in the basket and I will check them. After I return them to you, place a check mark next to the correctly spelled words on your Words-to-Learn List."

apply

Serena

appeared   because
chased   stair
wanted
stayed
hopped
favorite
friend
their

say word
say word in sentence
write word

- Have partners administer the Buddy Study Test.
- Children write in their Word Study Notebooks or on a specially designated sheet of paper.
- They place their notebooks or papers in the teacher's basket.
- Check children's work to determine how effective the week of study has been.
- When you return the Word Study Notebooks, have children make any misspelled words with magnetic letters. Have children check off correctly spelled words on their Words-to-Learn List to show that they have learned them.

share

You may want to organize your sharing to review on the principle you used on Day 1. Have children talk about what they have learned about words over the five-day period.

As an alternative, children can share word features that they found tricky and want to remember after the Buddy Study Test.

Link

Interactive Read-Aloud: Read aloud books that invite children's curiosity and expand their listening vocabularies. Here are a few suggested titles:

- ▸ *Dogs Rule!* by Daniel Kirk
- ▸ *Clara Caterpillar* by Pamela Edwards

Shared Reading: Invite children to notice aspects of words in a text they are sharing. Model some ways of noticing connections.

Guided Reading: During word work help children look more closely at features of words they find difficult. Children can work with magnetic letters, small whiteboards, or steno pads to write words quickly and then circle features that are important to notice.

Guided/Independent Writing: Be sure children know that when they have spelled words accurately on the Buddy Study Test, they will be expected to spell those words accurately in all of their writing—even on first drafts.

assess

- ▸ Observe children's accurate spelling in their independent writing.

- ▸ Keep records of the words children have spelled successfully on the weekly test.

- ▸ If children still spell words inaccurately after working with them for five days, examine the kinds of features that are giving them difficulty. Reteach small groups of children.

Expand the Learning

Repeat the Buddy Study cycles to be sure that children have learned the routines.

You will not need to spend too much time demonstrating the routines, but you may need to remind children of the specific procedures.

Connect with Home

Invite children to take home copies of their Buddy Study Tests and show family members the words they have learned to spell accurately.

Using Alphabetical Order

List Sheet

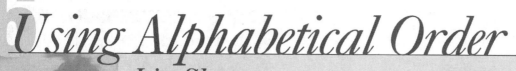

Consider Your Children

By third grade, children know the alphabet and have worked with alphabetical order in a variety of ways (e.g., putting names in order) but may not be fluent using letter order in more sophisticated ways. Use this lesson to help children understand the fundamental process of putting words in alphabetical order as well as the use of the alphabet as an organizing tool. You can use the words provided in this lesson or create your own words. Consider having children use a beginner's dictionary to check their alphabetizing work.

Working with English Language Learners

Children's familiarity with alphabetical order will depend on their previous experiences, not only with written English but also with print in their own languages. Remember that children's home languages may not be represented in writing with the Western alphabet. Give them plenty of opportunities to put simple words in order before moving to secondary levels of organization (using second or third letters). As always, it is best to create lists of words that children can read and understand.

You Need

▶ Pocket chart.

From *Teaching Resources:*

▶ List Sheets.

▶ Pocket Chart Card Template.

▶ Lesson WSA 6 Word Cards.

Understand the Principle

The alphabet is a powerful tool for organizing and accessing information. Most reference tools use alphabetical order as the organizing structure. Becoming familiar with and fluent in using alphabetical order will help children find information more quickly and free their attention for learning. Sometimes alphabetical order is referred to as ABC order.

Explain the Principle

" You can use alphabetical order to find or organize information. "

plan

Explain the Principle

" You can use alphabetical order to find or organize information. "

① Tell children that today they will work with alphabetical order. Briefly review some of the uses of alphabetical order with which children are already familiar (e.g., class name list).

② Suggested language: "You know that putting words in alphabetical order means organizing them in the same order as the alphabet. Look at the alphabet at the top of this chart. Answer these questions quickly!"

③ Raise several questions and prompt children to answer them quickly (e.g., *What letter comes before* g? *What letter comes after* f? *Does* l *come before or after* k?). This serves as a warm-up and helps children become more flexible in their thinking.

④ Suggested language: "Now let's put some words in alphabetical order. We know that the first thing we do is look at the first letter of the word." Place *add, be, car, for, hold, if, leave, now, play, rest, very,* and *you* on the chart in alphabetical order. "Looking at the first letters of these words, which is closest to the beginning of the alphabet?" Children will respond that *add* should be first. Be sure to emphasize that *add* comes first because it begins with *a*. Work through the rest of the words, placing or writing them in order.

⑤ Suggested language: "Now I have some additional words to put into our list of words in alphabetical order." Place *cloud, yellow, ask, bring, from, house, ride, home, were, into, like,* and *new* on the chart in random order.

⑥ Suggested language: "Suppose we wanted to put the word *cloud* on our list. Where does it belong?" Let the children decide where to put *cloud* and discuss using the second letter of a word. Suggested language: "*Car* and *cloud* both begin with the letter *c*, so we have to look at the second letter of the word. We know that *cloud* comes after *car* because *l* comes after *a* in the alphabet." Continue to add new words to the list, helping children learn how to use the first letters and then the second letter when the words begin with the same letters.

⑦ Tell children that they will put words in alphabetical order, or ABC order. Explain that they will have twenty word cards to put in order and then write them on a List Sheet.

read words
place in order
write list

▸ Give children twenty words on cards to put into alphabetical order.

▸ If they are new to this process, it is especially helpful for students to move the cards around as they compare words.

▸ After the words are in order, a partner checks the work or the child uses a beginner's dictionary to check the order.

again	ghost
away	ground
didn't	hallway
dollar	heap
dream	money
each	spring
every	supper
fame	sweet
flower	which
fresh	winter

Name: _____

1. again		11. ghost	
2. away		12. ground	
3. didn't		13. hallway	
4. dollar		14. heap	
5. dream		15. money	
6. each		16. spring	
7. every		17. supper	
8. fame		18. sweet	
9. flower		19. which	
10. fresh		20. winter	

LIST SHEET

▸ Then each child writes the twenty words in alphabetical order on a List Sheet.

Children bring their lists of words to sharing and read them to a new partner.

Link

Interactive Read-Aloud: Many books are organized using the alphabet (e.g., sophisticated ABC books and informational books). Select several and invite children to notice how the alphabet is used as an organizing tool. Here are a few suggested titles:

▸ *Alison's Zinnia* by Anita Lobel

▸ *The Absolutely Awful Alphabet* by Mordicai Gerstein

Shared Reading: Have children prepare and perform a sophisticated alphabet poem, such as "A Was Once an Apple Pie."

Guided Reading: When children are reading books with indexes or glossaries, point out how they are organized in alphabetical order. Have children practice using them.

Guided/Independent Writing: Help children use alphabetized word lists or simple dictionaries as tools for locating words.

assess

▸ Use one of the sets of words in Expand the Learning and make a timed assessment by having children put words in order and then write the words in alphabetical order. This assessment will help you identify children who need more work in a small group.

Expand the Learning

This lesson can be expanded many ways to increase children's agility in using alphabetization.

Show children that "no letter" comes before a letter when words start the same but one has more letters (*man, mane, manes*). Add words like these to the ABC task: *you, your, yours, yourself, in, into, inside, with, without, read, reader, reading.*

Give children lists of words that start with the same letter and require noticing the second, third, or even fourth letters of words. You can easily construct these lists by using the school dictionary and focusing on one letter (e.g., *machine, mad, made, magic, magical, magnet, make, mammal, man, mane, mango, many, map, mark, market, mask, math, maze, meal, mean, meat, medicine, meeting, men, meow, messy, met, might, mine, mist, mistake, model, moist, monkey, more, mud, musk, my, mystery*). If children can easily alphabetize a list such as this one, they will not need much more practice.

Let children choose sets of words (number words, color words, animal words, etc.) and see how quickly they can alphabetize them. Use a timer to add interest.

Connect with Home

Have children construct lists of "home words" (family and pet names, rooms, toys and other possessions), alphabetize them, and then bring their alphabetized lists to share.

7 *Using Word Parts to Solve Words*

Word Grid Game

Consider Your Children

Even though children can identify various words parts (letter clusters at the beginning or end, prefixes or suffixes, word endings, parts of compound words), they still need continued practice using these elements in flexible ways to solve words. For the Apply activity, consider choosing particular word parts, depending upon children's experiences.

Working with English Language Learners

English language learners need many experiences with words before they become comfortable looking for parts and connecting them to words they know. Begin with simple examples that they know. Play the Word Grid game with them and observe their skill in using word parts to solve words.

You Need

▶ Chart paper.

▶ Markers.

▶ Dice (with these word parts: Die 1: *thr, str, sh, ing, ant, er;* Die 2: *wh, amp, each, spr, fr, tr*).

From *Teaching Resources:*

▶ Directions for Word Grids.

▶ Word Grid Template.

▶ Lesson WSA 7 Word List.

Understand the Principle

Working with word parts in a flexible way helps children build the automatic word-solving skills that they need to use when reading. Children need to keep in mind the different kinds of word parts and apply their understanding of them.

Explain the Principle

❝ You can use word parts to solve a word. ❞

CONTINUUM: WORD-SOLVING ACTIONS — NOTICING AND USING WORD PARTS TO READ A WORD

plan

① Tell children they will use word parts to figure out words.

Explain the Principle

❝ You can use word parts to solve a word. ❞

② Write *throw, working, plant, slang, string,* and *lemon* on chart paper.

③ Hold up a whiteboard or card with -*ant* written on it. Suggested language: "Does anyone see a word on the chart that has this word part?"

④ Children identify *plant.* Have a volunteer underline the part. Discuss the first part of the word, *pl-.*

⑤ Hold up a word part and ask children to think of another word with the same part. Have children share their words with the class.

⑥ Suggested language: "You can use the parts of a word to help you read or write it."

⑦ Repeat with parts *ing, sl, str, ow* and *on.* Each time have children underline the part and then read the whole word.

⑧ Tell children they will play the Word Grid game, looking for different kinds of word parts shown on the die. They will look for beginning or ending letter clusters, word endings, and spelling patterns. The word part will always have more than one letter.

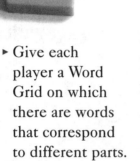

toss dice
find word
read word
cross out

▸ Give each player a Word Grid on which there are words that correspond to different parts.

▸ Each group has a pair of dice, which players use one at a time. Taking turns, each player tosses a die, looks for a word on the grid that has the same letter cluster or part, says the word, and crosses it out.

▸ After each player has tossed the first die, players switch to the second die and toss again. Players continue to switch the die back and forth. The first player to cross out all words wins the game.

Ask children to read their Word Grids to a partner.

Have children record some interesting words in their Word Study Notebooks or on a sheet of paper and underline the parts that help them.

Link

Interactive Read-Aloud: After reading aloud books, select some multisyllable words that children probably would not have read themselves. Write the words on a whiteboard and ask children to notice the parts. Here are a few suggested titles:

▸ *If You Made a Million* by David M. Schwartz

▸ *Barrio* by George Ancona

Shared Reading: Use poems that include multisyllable words. Have children notice and highlight word parts.

Guided Reading: During word work, have children put together words from cards with word parts.

Guided/Independent Writing: Prompt children to break words into parts so that they can spell them.

assess

▸ Notice children's ability to use word parts to decode words while they are reading continuous text.

▸ Dictate a list of four or five new words and ask children to spell them. Do not grade for accuracy, but notice the extent to which they can represent the word parts of interest.

Expand the Learning

Repeat this lesson, using a different set of dice to focus on other word parts (for example, -*and*, -*end*, *ser*-, -*eam*, *cr*-, etc.).

Connect with Home

Send home Word Grids and word cards. Have children set a timer for five minutes and go through the cards, crossing out matches on the Word Grid.

8 Recognizing and Using Syllables

Syllable Race

Consider Your Children

Most children are now familiar with word components and can easily divide words into the syllables they hear. However, they may not understand the rules for hyphenating words in written language. They may not automatically see the parts of words in order to take apart multisyllable words when reading or construct them in spelling. This lesson builds this skill.

Working with English Language Learners

English language learners need to hear clearly articulated pronunciations of multisyllable words so that they can begin to break them down by syllables. Accept their approximated pronunciations and also help them attend to the visual aspects of the word. Remind them that every syllable has a vowel. Consider working with small groups, having them break apart words made with magnetic letters.

You Need

▶ Chart paper.

▶ Markers.

▶ Whiteboard or magnetic letters.

From *Teaching Resources:*

▶ Directions for Follow the Path and Follow the Path Game Board adapted for Syllable Race.

▶ Syllable Race Game Cards made from Lesson WSA 8 Word Cards and Deck Card Template.

Understand the Principle

One determinant of text difficulty is the number of multisyllable words that readers are required to process. The texts that third-grade children read have many more two-, three-, and four-syllable words than at lower levels. Reading unfamiliar multisyllable words requires children to break words down into their component parts. If this analysis is performed with efficiency, then less attention is needed for word solving. Children need to know that when encountering an unfamiliar word, they should automatically break it into syllables. Besides syllable breaks, there are some rules for hyphenating (for example, not before an ending like *le* or *y*), but it would be confusing to bring these ideas in here.

Explain the Principle

❝ You can divide a word into syllables to read it. ❞

plan

Explain the Principle

" You can divide a word into syllables to read it. "

	easy
	easier
	listen
	listening

cantaloupe	can ta loupe
crocodile	croc o dile
balloon	bal loon
terrible	ter ri ble
motorcycle	mo tor cy cle
watermelon	wa ter mel on
rainbow	rain bow
catastrophe	ca tas tro phe

① Tell children they will learn more about reading longer words.

② Write *easy* and *easier* on the chart and ask children to read them. After they have read the words, ask them to clap and tell how many syllables are in each. Repeat with *listen* and *listening*.

③ Suggested language: "You know that some words have one syllable and some have more syllables. Dividing a word into syllables helps you take it apart to read it. When you read a long word, it helps to say the syllables, then look at them and connect them with other words or parts of words you know. Let's try to say and take apart these longer words."

④ Have children say the words you have written on the chart and clap a few of them. Then ask children to divide each word without clapping. Call on children to say the syllables with a break between each.

⑤ On a whiteboard (or with magnetic letters) visually make space between the parts of a word. Suggested language: "Look at the parts of *can ta loupe*. Do you see any parts that you know?" Children may respond by noticing the word *can*, pronouncing *ta*, or even noticing that the ending syllable looks a little like the word *loop*. You do not need to make these connections directly. Let children use their own thinking to figure out the parts of words.

⑥ Repeat with several more words. Explain that when a child can't fit a whole word at the end of a line he can write one or more syllables, a hyphen and the rest of the word at the beginning of the next line.

⑦ Tell children that today they will play Syllable Race. Demonstrate the game. They will take a card, read it, tell the number of syllables, and say the word in syllable parts. They will move their marker the same number of spaces as syllables in the word.

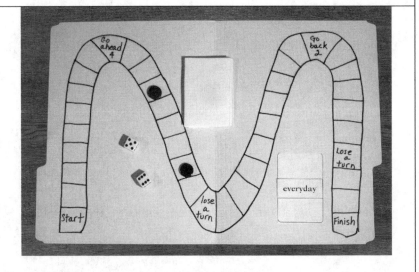

apply

take card
read word
tell syllables
move marker

▸ Have children
play Syllable
Race.

▸ The spaces on
the path are
blank except for
a few spaces that read *Go ahead 4*, *Go back 2*, *Lose a turn*.

▸ Each player places her marker at Start, takes a word card, reads the word, tells the number of syllables, and pronounces the word again slowly so that each syllable can be heard (for example, "*happening*, three, *hap-pen-ing*").

▸ The player then moves her piece the number of syllables that are in the word. The first player to reach the end wins the game.

share

Have children name a few objects in the classroom that have several syllables while you add the words to the chart. Then ask them to tell where they hear the break in these words.

Link

Interactive Read-Aloud: Read aloud books with multisyllable words. After reading, select several words that children are not likely to have in their reading vocabularies. Say and divide them into syllables and then look at the parts to solve them. Here are a few suggested titles:

- ▶ *The Awful Aardvaarks Go to School* by Reeve Lindberg
- ▶ *The Bear and the Bed* by Ruth Miller

Shared Reading: After reading a poem, help children locate three or four multisyllable words. Have them say each word in parts and then circle the parts.

Guided Reading: Encourage children to take apart multisyllable words with prompts such as these: *Look at the first part of the word. What do you know that can help? Do you see a part that you know? Is part of the word like a word you know?*

Guided/Independent Writing: As children write new words, have them say the parts. They can also say the parts to check their spelling.

assess

- ▶ Observe children's ability to take apart longer words as they read texts.
- ▶ Have children read four or five multisyllable words and notice how efficiently they approach them and whether they use parts appropriately.

Expand the Learning

Repeat this lesson with different words and provide a different set of word cards for the Syllable Race game. Increase the challenge by including more three- and four-syllable words.

Have the children play the Word Grid game with multisyllable words (see *Teaching Resources*).

Connect with Home

Send home the Syllable Race game and a sheet of word cards (see *Teaching Resources*) so children can play the game with family members.

Children can work with a family member to search newspapers and magazines for words with more than four syllables.

Making Connections between Words

Word Ladders

Consider Your Children

Throughout word study lessons and applications, as well as across reading and writing activities, children have learned to make connections between words. Use this lesson when they have had extensive practice connecting words that start the same, end the same and have common spelling patterns. In this lesson, they will make all of these connections. You can adjust the difficulty by limiting the kinds of connections.

Working with English Language Learners

English language learners will benefit from learning to connect words. These actions help them build categories for word patterns and letter clusters rather than trying to learn words in isolation. Use words that children understand and, for the most part, can read. The important learning here is to make the connections quickly, not necessarily to learn new words.

You Need

▸ Chart paper.

▸ Markers.

▸ Magnetic letters.

From *Teaching Resources:*

▸ Word Ladder Sheets.

▸ Lesson WSA 9 Word Cards.

Understand the Principle

Making connections between words is one of the most powerful tools children can use to solve unfamiliar words. As adults, we make these connections rapidly, automatically, and usually unconsciously. It is helpful when children make connections quickly and exercise flexibility when making different kinds of connections. Connecting letter sequences or patterns they know with new words they are trying to solve will make word solving more efficient.

Explain the Principle

❝ You can connect the beginning of a word with a word you know. ❞

❝ You can connect the ending of a word with a word you know. ❞

❝ You can connect words that have the same letter patterns. ❞

plan

Explain the Principle

❝ **You can connect the beginning of a word with a word you know.** ❞

❝ **You can connect the ending of a word with a word you know.** ❞

❝ **You can connect words that have the same letter patterns.** ❞

b<u>lack</u>	<u>br</u>other	s<u>ince</u>
b<u>last</u>	<u>m</u>other	pr<u>ince</u>
g<u>rass</u>	wr<u>ist</u>	<u>hand</u>
g<u>rav</u>el	dent<u>ist</u>	b<u>rand</u>
ca<u>tch</u>		
pi<u>tch</u>		

① Tell children they will look for several different ways that words can be connected.

② Suggested language: "You know that you can connect words in many different ways. Today you will connect words by the patterns you see. Some words might connect because they start the same. Look at these two words."

③ Write *black* and *blast* on the chart and have children underline the parts that are alike. Repeat with several other pairs that are connected in the same way.

④ Suggested language: "Here are two words that are connected in a different way." Invite children to underline the parts of *catch* and *pitch* that are alike. Repeat with several other pairs that are connected in the same way.

⑤ Suggested language: "Sometimes you see patterns that are alike in words." Write *since* and *prince* on the chart and have children highlight the patterns. Select as many other examples as needed to make the point that children should search for connections between words.

⑥ Demonstrate how to make Word Ladders. Write one word and change, add, or remove two to three letters to make a new word, make another new word by changing, adding, or removing one to three letters, and so on, for as many words as you can. The letters added, removed, or changed must be consecutive in the words (e.g., a beginning or ending letter or cluster or a phonogram pattern).

apply

make word
write word
change letters
write new word
highlight similar parts

▸ Children make Word Ladders on a Word Ladder Sheet.

▸ Ask them to choose a word card, make the word with magnetic letters, and write it in one of the boxes on the sheet.

▸ Then they change, add, or remove one to three letters and write the new word under the first word.

▸ The letters they add, remove, or change must be consecutive within the words (e.g., beginning, ending, or phonogram pattern). When children finish a ladder, have them underline the word parts in each word that they used from the word above on the ladder to make the new word.

Name: Randy
Date:

black	grass
blast	great
fast	meat
faster	beat
master	seat
mast	repeat
last	recall
ladder	call

wrist	
dentist	
dent	
vent	
sent	
sender	
fender	
lender	

share

Have the children read one Word Ladder to a partner. Show two or three ladders so that children can see a variety of connections.

Challenge the group as a whole to construct the longest Word Ladder you can. You can use one of the children's ladders as a starting point.

Link

Interactive Read-Aloud: Read aloud books that feature word changes. Here are two suggested titles:

- ▸ *Earth and Me: Our Family Tree* by J. Patrick Lewis
- ▸ *The Pig in the Spigot* by Richard Wilbur

Shared Reading: After reading a poem, have children quickly find a word connected to one that you say. They can also challenge each other to make connections (e.g., *I'm thinking of a word that is connected to* planter *because it is the same at the beginning*).

Guided Reading: When children encounter an unfamiliar word, remind them to make connections with known word using prompts such as: *Do you see a part you know? Do you know a word like that? The last part of the word is like _____.*

Guided/Independent Writing: Have children use known words as resources for writing new words. Encourage them to use word study charts as a resource.

assess

- ▸ Notice the kinds of connections children make. Is there a variety or do they focus on only one?
- ▸ When you prompt children to use word parts, notice their speed and success.

Expand the Learning

Repeat this lesson with different words. You can adjust the difficulty of this lesson with the words you select. If children are inexperienced, be sure that the words you use are simple. Increase the difficulty of the lesson by introducing the idea of connecting words with the same middle letter clusters.

Connect with Home

Send home a Word Ladder Sheet (see *Teaching Resources*) and have children make Word Ladders with family members using each member's name as the starting word on a ladder.

Using Guide Words in a Dictionary

Guide Word Sort

Consider Your Children

Earlier in elementary school children have used simple dictionaries and glossaries. Use this lesson when they are ready to begin using longer dictionaries and need to become efficient with finding the section of a book where a word or term appears.

Working with English Language Learners

The dictionary is an important tool for English language learners as they acquire new words and need to check their meaning. However, more understanding is needed to make dictionary work valuable. For guide words and the words children are locating, be sure to use words that children know how to spell (at least the first three or four letters) so that they can focus their attention on how a dictionary works. You may wish to start with a very simple dictionary.

You Need

▶ Chart paper.

▶ Markers.

▶ Beginning dictionaries that have guide words.

From *Teaching Resources:*

▶ Dictionary Page with Guide Words

▶ Lesson WSA 10 Word Cards and Guide Words (with dark edges).

Understand the Principle

Children may understand alphabetical order and be able to find words in lists and simple dictionaries, but efficiently working with a comprehensive dictionary requires using tools such as guide words. This lesson helps children increase their efficiency and understanding of how a dictionary works. The middle of the dictionary is approximately at the letter *M*; children can use this letter as a reference point when deciding where to open the dictionary.

Explain the Principle

" You can use guide words to help you find words quickly in a dictionary. "

plan

teach

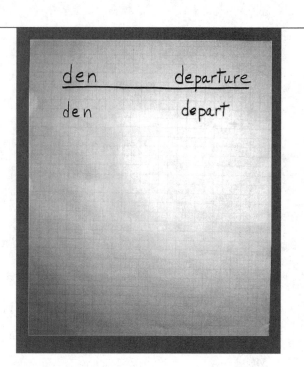

den   departure

den   depart

Explain the Principle

" You can use guide words to help you find words quickly in a dictionary. "

① Tell children that a dictionary is a reference book in which they can find information about words. Explain that all the words that begin with the letter _a_ are in a section and are in alphabetical order. The same is true for all the other letters.

② Suggested language: "Look at a page of your dictionary and point to the words on the upper corners of the left page. These are called guide words because they guide you to a word. Guide words tell you the first and last word on a page. The first guide word on this page is _den_." Identify the first word on the page. "The second word is _departure_. Is departure the last word on the page?" Explain that all words that come in alphabetical order between den and departure can be found on this page.

③ Ask: "If you are looking for _den_, or _depart_, will you find it on this page?" Repeat with _dent_ and _decay_. Children will conclude that decay does not come between the two guide words.

④ Show the children several more words such as _doctor, dentist, deny, deposit_. Give the children one word at a time and have them tell if it comes on the page. If it does, write it on the page, leaving room to place other words before it or after it in ABC order. Tell children that different dictionaries have different guide words but they all work the same way.

⑤ Tell children they will have two sample Dictionary Pages and they will place two guide words that start with the same letter on the two upper corners of each dictionary page: one on the left and one on the right. The guide words will have the dark edges. They will take a word card, look at the guide words, and place the cards that start with the same first letter in alphabetical order on the two sheets. Some words may not belong on either page. Finally, they will glue their word cards in alphabetical order on the sheets of paper.

apply

take word
look at guide words
place word
put words in order
glue words

► Have the children use the word cards and guide words to place words in alphabetical order. Some words will not belong with either set of guide words.

share

Have the children share their alphabetical lists and guide words with a partner. Invite the children to share any difficulties they had placing or alphabetizing words on the dictionary pages.

Link

Interactive Read-Aloud: Read aloud selections that may have words that are challenging in terms of meaning. Have children look up one of these words and examine its definition. Here are a few suggested titles:

- ► *How to Cross a Pond* by Marilyn Singer
- ► *Dinosaurs Forever* by William Wise

Shared Reading: Have children perform poems like "Poems for Two Voices" that have sophisticated vocabulary. Groups working on their parts may want to examine dictionary definitions of some of the words.

Guided Reading: When using informational texts, call children's attention to glossaries and indexes. Have children say what the guide words would be for any given page.

Guided/Independent Writing: Help children use guide words to look up spelling and definitions of words that they need to write or check on.

assess

- ► Observe how quickly and easily children can locate words in dictionaries.

- ► Give children a list of five words to look up in the dictionary. For each word, have them list the guide words on the page.

Expand the Learning

Expand this lesson by using a collection of challenging words and asking children to play Twenty Questions. One child says, *I am thinking of a word.* Children ask questions such as: *Is it in the first part of the dictionary? Is it in the middle of the dictionary? Is it in the last part of the dictionary?* Then they ask whether the word starts with a certain letter, and so on. Children finally ask whether the word is between certain guide words and then guess the word. The challenge is for the child to keep their word secret for all twenty questions. The person who guesses the word then thinks of a word and play resumes.

You can also expand children's ability to use guide words by having small groups work with several different kinds of dictionaries. They will notice that different dictionaries have different guide words simply because of the words on the page.

Connect with Home

Send home dictionaries for children to practice looking up words.

Ask children to play Twenty Questions with family members.

Using What Is Known to Solve Words

Word Race

Consider Your Children

Before using this lesson, be sure that children have had experience connecting words and noticing patterns and parts. They should have knowledge of many phonogram patterns and be able to connect words by their beginning and ending parts.

If the words provided for Lesson WSA 11 are not appropriate (too easy or too challenging), use any list of words that is suitable.

Working with English Language Learners

Being able to use known words to solve new words helps English language learners develop systems for reading and writing words in their new language. Once children understand the principle of using what they know about words, then it is important for them to use this strategy automatically when they read text. For this lesson, work with words that children already know so that it is easier for them to perform the operations quickly.

You Need

▸ Chart paper.

▸ Markers.

▸ Die.

From *Teaching Resources:*

▸ Directions for Follow the Path and Follow the Path Game Board (adapted for Word Race Game).

▸ Lesson WSA 11 Word List.

Understand the Principle

In this lesson children apply what they have learned about letter clusters, word patterns, and word structure to solve new words. Children need flexible ways of looking at words so that they rapidly and efficiently make connections while reading or writing. They need to be able to look quickly at the first and last part of words to take them apart.

Explain the Principle

❝ You can use word parts to solve a word. ❞

CONTINUUM: WORD-SOLVING ACTIONS — Noticing and Using Word Parts (Onsets and Rimes) to Read a Word

plan

Explain the Principle

" **You can use word parts to solve a word.** "

① Tell the children they will learn how to use word parts to read and write words quickly.

② Suggested language: "You have been noticing words and their parts. Today you will see how quickly you can use parts of words to make a word."

③ Write *fr* on the chart and tell children it is the first part of a word. Then add *ame* and tell children it is the last part of the word. Suggested language: "What is the whole word?" Children will respond.

④ Repeat the process with *friend, bird, house, sheep, which,* and any other words that you wish to use.

⑤ After working with five or six words, have children look at five more words. Have volunteers take turns underlining the parts of a word that they know. Remind them that a word part has more than one letter. Ask children to avoid saying the word until after they have underlined the part. Then other children can be invited to say the word.

⑥ Tell children that they will play Word Race. Players will think about the parts of words. Parts may be letter clusters at the beginning or end of the word, a part of a compound word, a syllable, a word ending (e.g., *-er*), or a prefix or suffix.

> fr ame = frame
> sh eep = sheep
> wh ich = which
> fr iend = friend
> b ird = bird
> h ouse = house
>
> press
> chick
> paper
> forest
> sandwich

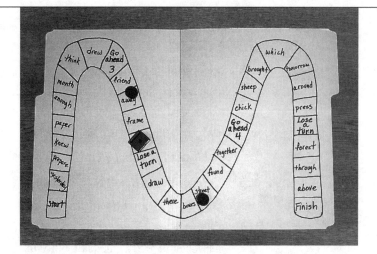

throw dice
move marker
read word
tell part

► Groups of two to four children play Word Race.

► Players take turns tossing a die and moving the number of spaces shown.

► The player reads the word in the space and identifies two parts that help him read it. If no one in the group can read and/or divide the word, one student writes it on a card and brings it to group share to ask for help from the whole group.

► If a player cannot read the word or identify two parts, he passes, and another player gives the answer.

► The first player to reach the end wins the game.

Point to a few words from the game and have the children read them and tell the parts.

Ask the children to discuss what they have learned about words. Guide children to discuss word parts that are seen in many words and how knowing word parts helps them read words. They can bring the group's attention to any words they found tricky.

Link

Interactive Read-Aloud: Read aloud some rhyming texts so that children can hear and then check the spelling of the parts that are alike. Here are a few suggested titles:

- ▸ *What a Truly Cool World* by Julius Lester
- ▸ *Town Mouse House* by Nigel Brooks

Shared Reading: After reading a text, have children use a masking card, flag, or highlighter tape to locate parts of words.

Guided Reading: During word work, use a whiteboard show parts of words.

Guided/Independent Writing: Prompt children to write word parts to help them spell new words.

assess

- ▸ Ask children to read four or five words that you know will be new for them. After reading, have them highlight a part that was helpful. Notice whether they are attempting to use word parts even if they do not read the word accurately.

Expand the Learning

Repeat this lesson with other words on the game board.

Have children play Word Race a different way. When they land on a space, they read the word and then tell another word with one part that is the same.

Connect with Home

Send home a Word Race Game Board and number cube so that children can play Word Race with family members (see *Teaching Resources*).

Children can use words off the game board as the first words in Word Ladders (see *Teaching Resources*).

Using a Dictionary to Learn Word Meaning

Word Entry Search

Consider Your Children

Use this lesson once children are quick and flexible at putting words in alphabetical order as well as finding words that are in order. They should also have previous experience using guide words to locate words in a dictionary (WSA 10). You may want to create a large reference chart for the classroom that shows a dictionary page with an entry and arrows to labels that explain the kinds of information you can get from a page.

Working with English Language Learners

Dictionary skills are an important tool for refining knowledge for English language learners. In the beginning, work with simple dictionary entries and known words. Be sure that children understand (with your help) not only the specific word you are locating, but also the words in the definition. Since entries are a new kind of text, read them aloud to children as many times as needed. You may want to "unpack" an entry by making the format easier (e.g., creating a list out of the alternative definitions).

You Need

► Chart paper on which is written one sample dictionary entry.

► Markers.

► Dictionaries (one for each child or pair of children).

► Index cards (five per child).

Understand the Principle

Children who have the ability to notice visual features of words and understand the concept of alphabetical order can use these tools effectively to locate words that they want to explore. They are probably familiar with the concept of alphabetizing from their usual classroom work. In this lesson, they will systematize their skill in using a dictionary which will be a powerful tool throughout their lives.

Explain the Principle

" Dictionary entries have many different kinds of information about a word. "

plan

draft 1. A current of air
in an enclosed space. I could feel
a cold <u>draft</u> from the open window.
2. A device that controls the flow
of air in something. Furnaces, fire-
places, and some stoves have drafts.
3. A sketch, plan or rough copy of
something written. The author wrote
three <u>drafts</u> of the novel. 4. The
selecting of persons for military
service or some other special duty.
During World War II most young men
in the United States were subject to
the <u>draft</u>.   <u>Noun</u>.

teach

Explain the Principle

" Dictionary entries
have many different
kinds of information
about a word. "

① Tell the children that they will look closely at dictionary entries. Prepare a simplified dictionary entry on chart paper, as shown. If your students are already familiar with dictionary entries, you may want to include more features (such as pronunciation guides).

② Read the entry to the children and ask them what they notice. They may comment that the definitions are not always sentences, that examples are provided by using words in sentences, and that *draft* seems to have more than one meaning.

③ Explain that *draft* has one syllable so the entry word is all one syllable. If a word has more than one syllable, a raised dot divides the syllables (de • cide).

④ Suggested language: "If a word has more than one meaning, the dictionary entry will show and number them." Underline the numbers showing the different definitions or underline each definition (exclusive of the example). Use *draft* in new sentences and have children identify the correct definition for each use. Have children take turns using *draft* in a sentence while other children find the definition that is exemplified.

⑤ Give children some simple words (e.g., *match, lean, figure*) to look up in a dictionary. Have one child read a word and its first definition, and others read any other definitions. Have children notice how many syllables are in each word.

⑥ Tell the children they will look up in a dictionary the other ten words that are listed on the chart (*net, pet, ram, groom, screen, tough, column, tables, tablet, spot*). They choose five of the words and write each of them in a sentence on one side of an index card with the appropriate definition on the other side.

find word
read definition
choose definition
write sentence
write definition

► Children use a dictionary and look up ten words.

► Children choose five of the ten words and for each word they write a sentence using the word on one side of the card and underline the word. On the other side they write the appropriate definition.

► Children bring their cards to sharing.

net
pet
ram
groom
screen
tough
column
tables
tablet
spot

The screen on my window keeps bugs out of my room.

Children bring their cards to sharing and take turns reading the word and its sentence.

Each student has a dictionary. One reads the sentence from her card. The other children find the definition that the first student used. When ready, students signal with a thumbs up. If the first person to signal answers correctly, then she reads the sentence or phrase again, and the activity continues.

Link

Interactive Read-Aloud: Read aloud books that have words with multiple meanings. Occasionally, select a word and look it up, examining several definitions. Here are a few suggested titles:

▸ *My Name Is Andrew* by Mary McManus Burke

▸ *Miss Alaineus: A Vocabulary Disaster* by Debra Frasier

Shared Reading: Select one word with several definitions and do a quick shared reading, with one group reading each definition.

Guided Reading: Discuss the meaning for new words and occasionally have children check the dictionary when the meaning is unclear. During word work practice use a dictionary with a small group of children who need more practice.

Guided/Independent Writing: Help children check on the meaning of words they use.

assess

▸ Notice the speed with which children can access dictionary entries.

▸ Give children a list of three words and have them find the definitions.

▸ Ask each child to show you an entry and talk about its meaning(s).

Expand the Learning

Repeat the lesson with other entry words.

Expand the lesson by presenting more of an entry that defines the word as another part of speech, for example:

draft—1. To make a sketch, plan, or rough copy of something. I *drafted* the letter in pencil and then typed it. 2. To select a person or persons for some special duty. Many people were *drafted* to serve in that war. *Verb*

Have the children compare the uses of the word. They can construct sentences with the word and have other students locate the precise definition they referenced.

Connect with Home

Send dictionaries and a word list home with children so that they can practice looking up words.

Have children scan newspaper and magazine articles for new words that they can look up and define. They can bring words they find to class to share.

Expanding Vocabulary through Reading Texts

Learning New Words from Reading

Consider Your Children

The most effective way to help children expand their listening, speaking, reading, and writing vocabularies is to read aloud to them. They will experience a variety of new words within rich, meaningful contexts. It is especially important to discuss the meaning of texts during and after you read them aloud, using some of the new vocabulary. Children also benefit from explicit instruction that helps them know how to think about the meaning of words in texts and also how to acquire new words that they can use when speaking and writing. In this lesson they find ways to learn word meanings and check them with a dictionary.

Working with English Language Learners

It is especially important for English language learners to hear texts read aloud. Find interesting books that children like and read them several times. Books like *Going Home* by Eve Bunting (1996) are worth reading several times because children can connect them with other texts and discuss them from several different points of view. With subsequent rereadings, children will grasp more of the meaning of the story and their discussions will be richer. Experiencing words in the text several times helps children acquire new vocabulary and at the same time learn more about English syntax. You may want to put certain books on tape so that children can listen to them several more times, while enjoying the illustrations.

You Need

▸ Chart paper (with two or three passages written on it).

▸ Markers.

▸ Children's literature book (to read aloud).

▸ Basket of children's literature (or audiobooks).

From *Teaching Resources:*

▸ Learning New Words from Reading Sheets.

Understand the Principle

Realizing that you can learn new words by reading is a valuable concept for children to understand. It is important for children to constantly acquire new words from reading because it is impossible to learn enough words as isolated items of information. Reading aloud is an extremely valuable activity for building vocabulary. In this lesson students see some explicit demonstrations of how to learn new words by thinking about the word in the sentence, paragraph, or whole text.

Explain the Principle

❝ When you read a word but don't know what it means, you can think about the meaning of the sentence to figure it out. ❞

CONTINUUM: WORD-SOLVING ACTIONS — UNDERSTANDING THAT THE CONTEXT OF THE SENTENCE HELPS DETERMINE THE MEANING OF A WORD

plan

> Papa piles our boxes and suitcases into the back of our old station wagon. He slides in our battered cooler, which is filled with food and cold drinks for the journey.
>
> "Of course. Do not worry. We are legal farm workers. We have our papeles." "Papers, Papa," I say quickly.
>
> We see how tired Mama and Papa are at night. How Papa rubs Mama's shoulders. How stiffly he moves. "Why did you ever leave?" we ask. "There is no work in La Perla. We are here for the opportunities."

Explain the Principle

❝ When you read a word but don't know what it means, you can think about the meaning of the sentence to figure it out. ❞

① The text used in this lesson is *Going Home* by Eve Bunting (NY: HarperCollins, 1996). You can use any book you have read aloud and discussed with children. Before using a book for a Word Study lesson, reread it at least once with the group for pure enjoyment and as the basis for a rich discussion. Choose a few passages to write on the chart.

② Tell children that they will find out how to learn new words from reading. Suggested language: "We have read *Going Home* by Eve Bunting and talked about it. Let's look at some of the words in this book and think about how you can learn new words when you read. You can use your new words when speaking and writing."

③ Suggested language: "When I was reading page 2, I noticed this word." Highlight the word *battered*. "What does *battered* make you think about?"

④ Children may notice *bat* in the word or mention a *batter* or even *butter*. Suggested language: "It does help to think about how the word looks and you can also learn about the word from the sentences. You can learn more about what a word means by looking at the words around them and thinking about the meaning of the sentences, paragraphs, or whole story."

⑤ Read the text to the students or have them read it in a shared way. Suggested language: "When I read, I noticed that the station wagon was old, and I thought that the cooler might be old, too, and have some dents. It might look like it has been around a long time because they use it on many trips." Highlight *old*. After this modeling, read more of the text and ask children to talk about what is helping them learn more about the meaning of *battered*. They may mention that the people might have to save their money and would use the cooler a long time. Explain that the other sentences help them think about the word's meaning.

⑥ Suggested language: "I now have a *working* definition of the word. Let's look it up and see how close my definition is." Look up the word in a dictionary and read it.

⑦ Suggested language: "This book is interesting because it has some Spanish words." Repeat the process with *papeles* and ask children to find other parts of the sentence that helped them know the meaning of this Spanish word.

⑧ Have children read the final paragraph on the chart with the key word *opportunities* and talk about how several different places in the book helped them understand the meaning. End by repeating the principle and summarizing ways they have learned to figure out the meaning of a new word.

read text
choose word
write word
find key words
or sentences
write definition
look up
use in sentence

▶ Gather books that children can read successfully and that have some interesting new vocabulary words. As an alternative, let them listen to a particular book on tape. Have children select a new word from a book and write it on a Learning New Words from Reading Sheet. They also write any key words or sentences in the text that helped them understand the word.

Name: Will	Date:
A new and interesting word:	Word in the book that helped me understand the new word:
tattered	special blanket

A place in the book that helped me understand the new word: (page or pages and tell why)

page 17   His little brother carried the blanket.

page 18   Sam never let his mother wash it.

What I think the new word means:

old and dirty

Dictionary Definition:

worn, as if used for a long time

My sentence with the new word:

The pages of my science notebook are tattered.

▶ Remind them to show the page number they referred to. Children then write a working definition of the word, and use the word in a sentence of their own. Finally, they look up the word and write a dictionary definition.

Children share their new words with a partner, along with their definitions.

Have a few individuals share their new words with the group. Revisit the text at the place they have noted and have the group think about the word and how the sentence or paragraph is helpful. If they are all using the same book, several children will come up with the same words.

Link

Interactive Read-Aloud: Repeat the process of talking about new words after reading a text aloud and discussing it. Here are a few suggested titles:

- ▸ *I, Crocodile* by Fred Marcellino
- ▸ *A Bird about to Sing* by Laura Nyman Montenegro

Shared Reading: Type and reproduce some especially interesting dialogue or an exciting paragraph from a book you have read aloud. Have children read the material in parts, thinking about the meaning and using pause and expression. Through the process, they will be using new and interesting words.

Guided Reading: Help children derive the meaning of new words by reading the sentences before and after words, looking for definitions within the text, and thinking about the whole text.

Guided/Independent Writing: Encourage children to use the new and interesting words they are reading as they compose texts in writing.

assess

- ▸ Examine children's Learning New Words from Reading Sheets. Notice the variety and types of the words children choose and their ability to derive meaning. They may not be producing precise definitions of new words. The important thing is that they learn a process for word solving that supports comprehension.

Expand the Learning

Begin an Interesting Words Chart that you post near the area where you read aloud. As children discover new words, let them decide whether to add them to the Interesting Words Chart.

Repeat this lesson over the next several weeks until children become accustomed to deriving the meaning of new words.

Expand children's ability to learn new words by repeating the lesson and the application activity. When children have completed their Learning New Words from Reading Sheets, have them also check the dictionary definitions.

Connect with Home

Have children take home their Learning New Words from Reading Sheets and share them with family members.

Encourage children to notice words in the books they are reading at home.

Remind children to use new words they learn when they write in their Reader's Notebooks.

Glossary

Affix A part added to the beginning or ending of a base or root word to change its meaning or function (a *prefix* or *suffix*).

Alphabet book A book for helping children develop the concept and sequence of the alphabet by showing the letters and people, animals, or objects that have labels related to the letters (usually the labels begin with the letters).

Alphabetic principle The concept that there is a relationship between the spoken sounds in oral language and the graphic forms in written language.

Analogy The resemblance of a known word to an unknown word that helps you solve the unknown word.

Antonym A word that has a different sound and opposite meaning from another word (*cold* vs. *hot*).

Assessment A means for gathering information or data that reveals what learners control, partially control, or do not yet control consistently.

Automaticity Rapid, accurate, fluent word decoding without conscious effort or attention.

Base word A whole word to which you can add affixes, creating new word forms (*washing*).

Blend To combine sounds or word parts.

Buddy Study A five-day word study system for learning conventional spelling strategies.

Closed syllable A syllable that ends in one or more consonants (*lem-on*).

Comparative form A word that describes a person or thing in relation to another person or thing (for example, *more, less; taller, shorter*).

Compound word A word made up of two or more other words or morphemes (*play ground*). The meaning of a compound word can be a combination of the meanings of the words it is made of or can be unrelated to the meanings of the combined units.

Concept book A book organized to develop an understanding of an abstract or generic idea or categorization.

Connecting strategies Ways of solving words that use connections or *analogies* with similar known words (knowing *she* and *out* helps with *shout*).

Consonant A speech sound made by partial or complete closure of the airflow that causes friction at one or more points in the breath channel. The consonant sounds are represented by the letters *b, c, d, f, g, h, j, k, l, m, n, p, q, r, s, t, v, w* (in most of its uses), *x, y* (in most of its uses), and *z*.

Consonant blend Two or more consonant letters that often appear together in words and represent sounds that are smoothly joined, although each of the sounds can be heard in the word (*trim*).

Consonant cluster A sequence of two or three consonant letters that appear together in words (*trim, chair*).

Consonant digraph Two consonant letters that appear together and represent a single sound that is different from the sound of either letter (*shell*).

Consonant-vowel-consonant A common sequence of sounds in a single syllable (*hat*, for example).

Contraction A shortening of a syllable, word, or word groups usually by the omission of a sound or letters (*didn't*).

Cursive A form of handwriting in which letters are connected.

Decoding Using letter/sound relationships to translate a word from a series of symbols to a unit of meaning.

Dialect A regional variety of a language. In most languages, including English and Spanish, dialects are mutually intelligible; the differences are actually minor.

Directionality The orientation of print (in the English language, from left to right).

Distinctive letter features Visual features that make every letter of the alphabet different from every other letter.

Early literacy concepts Very early understandings related to how written language or print is organized and used—how it "works."

English language learners People whose native language is not English and who are acquiring English as an additional language.

Fluency in reading Reading continuous text with good momentum, phrasing, appropriate pausing, intonation, and stress.

Fluency word solving Speed, accuracy, and flexibility in solving words.

Grammar Complex rules by which people can generate an unlimited number of phrases, sentences, and longer texts in that language. *Conventional grammar* refers to the accepted conventions in a society.

Grapheme A letter or cluster of letters representing a single sound, or phoneme *(a, eigh, ay)*.

Graphophonic relationship The relationship between the oral sounds of the language and the written letters or clusters of letters.

Guide words The words at the top of a dictionary page to indicate the first and last word on the page.

Have a try To write a word, notice that it doesn't look quite right, try it two or three other ways, and decide which construction looks right; to make an attempt and check oneself.

High frequency words Words that occur often in the spoken and written language *(the)*.

Homograph One of two or more words spelled alike but different in meaning, derivation, or pronunciation (the *bat* flew away, he swung the *bat*; take a *bow, bow* and arrow).

Homonym (a type of *homograph*) One of two or more words spelled *and* pronounced alike but different in meaning (we had *quail* for dinner; I would *quail* in fear).

Homophone One of two or more words pronounced alike but different in spelling and meaning *(meat* vs. *meet, bear* vs. *bare)*.

Idiom A phrase with meaning that cannot be derived from the conjoined meanings of its elements *(raining cats and dogs)*.

Inflectional ending A suffix added to a base word to show tense, plurality, possession, or comparison *(darker)*.

Letter knowledge The ability to recognize and label the graphic symbols of language.

Letters Graphic symbols representing the sounds in a language. Each letter has particular distinctive features and may be identified by letter name or sound.

Lexicon Words that make up language.

Long vowel The elongated vowel sound that is the same as the name of the vowel. It is sometimes represented by two or more letters *(cake, eight, mail)*.

Lowercase letter A small letter form that is usually different from its corresponding capital or uppercase form.

Morpheme The smallest unit of meaning in a language. Morphemes may be *free* or *bound*. For example, *run* is a unit of meaning that can stand alone. It is a *free morpheme*. In *runs*

and *running*, the added *s* and *ing* are also units of meaning. They cannot stand alone but add meaning to the free morpheme. The *s* and *ing* are examples of *bound morphemes*.

Morphemic strategies Ways of solving words by discovering *meaning* through the combination of significant word parts or morphemes *(happy, happiest; run, runner, running)*.

Morphological system Rules by which morphemes (building blocks of vocabulary) fit together into meaningful words, phrases, and sentences.

Morphology The combination of morphemes (building blocks of meaning) to form words; the rules by which words are formed from free and bound morphemes—for example, root words, prefixes, and suffixes.

Multiple-meaning words Words that mean something different depending on the way they are used *(run*—home run, run in your stocking, run down the street, a run of bad luck).

Onset In a syllable, the part (consonant, consonant cluster, or consonant digraph) that comes before the vowel *(cr-eam)*.

Onset-rime segmentation The identification and separation of onsets (first part) and rimes (last part, containing the vowel) in words *(dr-ip)*.

Open syllable A syllable that ends in a vowel sound *(ho-tel)*.

Orthographic awareness The knowledge of the visual features of written language, including distinctive features of letters as well as spelling patterns in words.

Orthography The representation of the sounds of a language with the proper letters according to standard usage (spelling).

Phoneme The smallest unit of sound in spoken language. There are approximately forty-four units of speech sounds in English.

Phoneme addition Adding a beginning or ending sound to a word *(h + and, an + t)*.

Phoneme blending Identifying individual sounds and then putting them together smoothly to make a word *(c-a-t = cat)*.

Phoneme deletion Omitting a beginning, middle, or ending sound of a word *(cart − c = art)*.

Phoneme-grapheme correspondence The relationship between the sounds (phonemes) and letters (graphemes) of a language.

Phoneme isolation The identification of an individual sound—beginning, middle, or end—in a word.

Phoneme manipulation The movement of sounds from one place to another.

Phoneme reversal The exchange of the first and last sounds of a word to make a different word.

Phoneme substitution The replacement of the beginning, middle, or ending sound of a word with a new sound.

Phonemic (or *phoneme*) awareness The ability to hear individual sounds in words and to identify particular sounds.

Phonemic strategies Ways of solving words that use how words *sound* and relationships between letters and letter clusters and phonemes in those words *(cat, make)*.

Phonetics The scientific study of speech sounds—how the sounds are made vocally and the relation of speech sounds to the total language process.

Phonics The knowledge of letter/sound relationships and how they are used in reading and writing. Teaching phonics refers to helping children acquire this body of knowledge about the oral and written language systems; additionally, teaching phonics helps children use phonics knowledge as part of a reading and writing process. Phonics instruction uses a small portion of the body of knowledge that makes up *phonetics*.

Phonogram A phonetic element represented by graphic characters or symbols. In word recognition, a graphic sequence composed of a vowel grapheme and an ending consonant grapheme (such as *an* or *it*) is sometimes called a *word family*.

Phonological awareness The awareness of words, rhyming words, onsets and rimes, syllables, and individual sounds (phonemes).

Phonological system The sounds of the language and how they work together in ways that are meaningful to the speakers of the language.

Plural Of, relating to, or constituting more than one.

Prefix A group of letters that can be placed in front of a base word to change its meaning *(preplan)*.

Principle In phonics, a generalization or a sound/spelling relationship that is predictable.

R-controlled vowel sound The modified or *r*-influenced sound of a vowel when it is followed by *r* in a syllable *(hurt)*.

Rhyme The ending part (rime) of a word that sounds like the ending part (rime) of another word *(mail, tale)*.

Rime The ending part of a word containing the vowel; the letters that represent the vowel sound and the consonant letters that follow it in a syllable *(dr-eam)*.

Root The part of a word that contains the main meaning component.

Schwa The sound of the middle vowel in an unstressed syllable (for example, the *o* in *done* and the sound between the *k* and *l* in *freckle*).

Segment To divide into parts *(to-ma-to)*.

Semantic system The system by which speakers of a language communicate meaning through language.

Short vowel A brief-duration sound represented by a vowel letter *(cat)*.

Silent *e* The final *e* in a spelling pattern that usually signals a long vowel sound in the word and does not represent a sound itself *(make*, for example).

Suffix An affix or group of letters added at the end of a base or root word to change its function or meaning *(handful, running)*.

Syllabication The division of words into syllables *(pen-cil)*.

Syllable A minimal unit of sequential speech sounds composed of a vowel sound or a consonant-vowel combination. A syllable always contains a vowel or vowel-like speech sound *(to-ma-to)*.

Synonym One of two or more words that have different sounds but the same meaning *(chair, seat)*.

Syntactic awareness The knowledge of grammatical patterns or structures.

Syntactic system Rules that govern the ways in which morphemes and words work together in sentence patterns. Not the same as *proper grammar*, which refers to the accepted grammatical conventions.

Syntax The study of how sentences are formed and of the grammatical rules that govern their formation.

Visual strategies Ways of solving words that use knowledge of how words *look*, including the clusters and patterns of the letters in words *(bear, light)*.

Vowel A speech sound or phoneme made without stoppage of or friction in the airflow. The vowel sounds are represented by *a, e, i, o, u*, and sometimes *y* and *w*.

Vowel combinations Two vowels that appear together in words *(meat)*.

Vowel digraph Two successive vowel letters that represent a single vowel sound *(boat)*, a vowel combination.

Word A unit of meaning in language.

Word analysis The breaking apart of words into parts or individual sounds in order to parse them.

Word family A term often used to designate words that are connected by phonograms or rimes (for example, *hot, not, pot, shot*). A *word family* can also be a series of words connected by meaning (affixes added to a base word; for example: *base, baseball, basement, baseman, basal, basis, baseless, baseline, baseboard, abase, abasement, off base, home base; precise, précis, precisely, precision*).

References

Adams, J.J. (1990). *Beginning to Read: Thinking and Learning about Print*. Cambridge, MA: MIT Press.

Allington, R. (1991). Children who find learning to read difficult: School responses to diversity. In E.H. Hiebert (ed.). *Literacy for a Diverse Society*. New York: Teachers College Press.

Armbruster, B.B., Lehr, F., and Osborn, J. (2001). *Put Reading First: The Research Building Blocks for Teaching Children to Read: Kindergarten through Grade 1*. Jessup, MD: National Institute for Literacy.

Biemiller, A. (1970). The development of the use of graphic and contextual information as children learn to read. *Reading Research Quarterly* 6: 75-96.

Blachman, B. (1984). The relationships of rapid naming ability and language analysis skills to kindergarten and first grade reading achievement. *Journal of Educational Psychology* 76: 614-622.

Blanchard, J.S. (1980). Preliminary investigation of transfer between single-word decoding ability and contextual reading comprehension of poor readers in grade six. *Perceptual and Motor Skills* 51: 1271-1281.

Bradley, L., and Bryant, P.E. (1983). Categorizing sounds and learning to read—a causal connection. *Nature* 301: 419-421.

Bryant, P.E., Bradley, L., Camlean, M., and Crossland, J. (1989). Nursery rhymes, phonological skills and reading. *Journal of Child Language* 16: 407-428.

Ceprano, M.A. (1980). A review of selected research on methods of teaching sight words. *The Reading Teacher* 35: 314-322.

Chall, J.S. (1989). Learning to read: The great debate. 20 years later. *Phi Delta Kappan* 70: 521-538.

Clay, M.M. (1991). *Becoming Literate: The Construction of Inner Control*. Portsmouth, NH: Heinemann.

Clay, M.M. (1998). *By Different Paths to Common Outcomes*. York, ME: Stenhouse Publishers.

Clay, M.M. (2001). *Change over Time in Children's Literacy Development*. Portsmouth, NH: Heinemann.

Daneman, M. (1991). Individual difference in reading skills. In R. Barr, M.L. Kamil, P. Mosenthal, and P.D. Pearson (eds.). *Handbook of Reading Research* (Vol. II, pp. 512-538). New York: Longman.

Ehri, L.C. (1991). Development of the ability to read words. In R. Barr, M.L. Kamil, P. Mosenthal, and P.D. Pearson (eds.). *Handbook of Reading Research* (Vol. II, pp. 383-417). New York: Longman.

Ehri, L.C., and McCormick, S. (1998). Phases of word learning: Implications for instruction with delayed and disabled readers. *Reading and Writing Quarterly* 20: 163-179.

Fountas, I.C., and Pinnell, G.S. (1996). *Guided Reading: Good First Teaching for All Children*. Portsmouth, NH: Heinemann.

Fountas, I.C., and Pinnell, G.S. (eds.) (1999). *Voices on Word Matters: Learning about Phonics and Spelling in the Literacy Classroom*. Portsmouth, NH: Heinemann.

Fountas, I.C., and Pinnell, G.S. (2000). *Guiding Readers and Writers: Grades 3–6*. Portsmouth, NH: Heinemann.

Holdaway, D. (1987). *The Foundations of Literacy*. Portsmouth, NH: Heinemann.

Hundley, S., and Powell, D. (1999). In I.C. Fountas and G.S. Pinnell (eds.). *Voices on Word Matters* (pp. 159-164). Portsmouth, NH: Heinemann.

Juel, C. (1988). Learning to read and write: A longitudinal study of 54 children from first through fourth grades. *Journal of Educational Psychology* 80: 437-447.

Juel, C., Griffith, P.L., and Gough, P.B. (1986). Acquisition of literacy: A longitudinal study of children in first and second grade. *Journal of Educational Psychology* 78: 243-255.

Lesgold, A.M., Resnick, L.B., and Hammond, K. (1985). Learning to read: A longitudinal study of word skill development in two curricula. In G.E. MacKinnon and T.G. Walker (eds.). *Reading Research: Advances in Theory and Practice* (Vol. 4, pp. 107-138). New York: Academic Press.

Liberman, I., Shankweiler, D., and Liberman, A. (1985). The Alphabetic Principle and Learning to Read. U.S. Department of Health and Human Services. Reprinted with permission from The University of Michigan Press by the National Institute of Child Health and Human Development. Adapted from Phonology and the problems of learning to read and write. *Remedial and Special Education* 6: 8-17.

McCarrier, A.M., Pinnell, G.S., and Fountas, I.C. (2000). *Interactive Writing: How Language and Literacy Come Together*. Portsmouth, NH: Heinemann.

Moats, L.C. (2000). *Speech to Print: Language Essentials for Teachers*. Baltimore: Paul H. Brookes.

Nagy, W.E., Anderson, R.C., Schommer, M., Scott, J., and Stallman, A. (1989). Morphological families in the internal lexicon. *Reading Research Quarterly* 24: 262-282.

National Institute of Child Health and Human Development (2001). *Report of the National Reading Panel: Teaching Children to Read: An Evidence-Based Assessment of the Scientific Research Literature on Reading and Its Implications for Reading Instruction. Reports of the Subgroups*. Washington, DC: National Institutes of Health.

New Standards Primary Literacy Committee (1999). *Reading and Writing: Grade by Grade*. Washington, DC: National Center on Education and the Economy and the University of Pittsburgh.

Pinnell, G.S., and Fountas, I.C. (2003). *Phonics Lessons: Letters, Words, and How They Work, Grade K*. Portsmouth, NH: Heinemann.

Pinnell, G.S., and Fountas, I.C. (2003). *Phonics Lessons: Letters, Words, and How They Work, Grade 1*. Portsmouth, NH: Heinemann.

Pinnell, G.S., and Fountas, I.C. (2003). *Phonics Lessons: Letters, Words, and How They Work, Grade 2*. Portsmouth, NH: Heinemann.

Pinnell, G.S., and Fountas, I.C. (2003). *Sing a Song of Poetry, Grade K*. Portsmouth, NH: Heinemann.

Pinnell, G.S., and Fountas, I.C. (2003). *Sing a Song of Poetry, Grade 1*. Portsmouth, NH: Heinemann.

Pinnell, G.S., and Fountas, I.C. (2003). *Sing a Song of Poetry, Grade 2*. Portsmouth, NH: Heinemann.

Pinnell, G.S., and Fountas, I.C. (1998). *Word Matters: Teaching Phonics and Spelling in the Reading/Writing Classroom*. Portsmouth, NH: Heinemann.

Pinnell, G.S., Pikulski, J., Wixson, K.K., et al. (1995). *Listening to Children Read Aloud: Data from NAEP's Integrated Reading Performance Record (IRPR) at Grade 4*. Report No. 23-FR-04, prepared by the Educational Testing Service. Washington, DC: Office of Educational Research and Improvement, U.S. Department of Education.

Pressley, M. (1998). *Reading Instruction That Works: The Case for Balanced Teaching*. New York: The Guilford Press.

Read, C. (1971). Pre-school children's knowledge of English phonology. *Harvard Educational Review* 41: 1-34.

Snow, C.E., Burns, M.S., and Griffin, G. (eds.) (1989). *Preventing Reading Difficulties in Young Children*. Washington, DC: Committee on the Prevention of Reading Difficulties in Young Children, Commission on Behavioral and Social Sciences and Education, National Research Council.

Treiman, R. (1985). Onsets and rimes as units of spoken syllables: Evidence from children. *Journal of Experimental Child Psychology* 39: 161-181.

Vellutino, F.R., and Denckla, M.B. (1991). Cognitive and neuropsychological foundations of word identification in poor and normally developing readers. In R. Barr, M.L. Kamil, P. Mosenthal, and P.D. Pearson (eds.). *Handbook of Reading Research* (Vol. II, pp. 571-608). New York: Longman.

Vellutino, F.R., Scanlon, D.M., Sipay, E.R., et al. (1996). Cognitive profiles of difficult-to-remediate and readily remediated poor readers: Early intervention as a vehicle for distinguishing between cognitive and experiential deficits as basic causes of specific reading disability. *Journal of Educational Psychology* 88: 601-638.